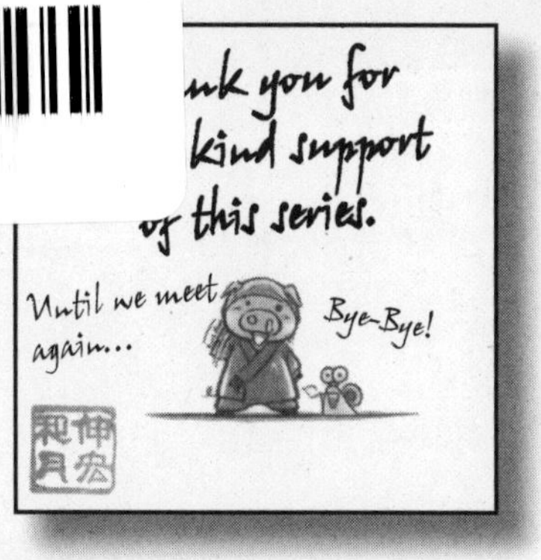

you for
kind support
this series.
Until we meet again...
Bye-Bye!

Buso Renkin

This series consists of 79 chapters and three specials, adding up to ten volumes–about a year and a half from start to finish. *Buso Renkin* ends with this volume. Truthfully, I wish I could've spent more time with Kazuki and Tokiko, but because of all the love everyone has shown me throughout this series, I think I can bid them farewell with a smile. Again, I would like to thank all you readers for your support! Thank you very much!

—Nobuhiro Watsuki

Nobuhiro Watsuki earned international accolades for his first major manga series, **Rurouni Kenshin**, about a wandering swordsman in Meiji Era Japan. Serialized in Japan's *Weekly Shonen Jump* from 1994 to 1999, **Rurouni Kenshin**, available in North America from VIZ Media, quickly became a worldwide sensation, inspiring a spin-off short story ("Yahiko no Sakabatô"), an animated TV show and a series of novels. Watsuki's latest hit, **Buso Renkin**, began publication in *Weekly Shonen Jump* in 2003 and was adapted into an animated TV series in 2006.

BUSO RENKIN
VOL. 10
The SHONEN JUMP ADVANCED
Manga Edition

STORY AND ART BY
NOBUHIRO WATSUKI

English Adaptation/Lance Caselman
Translation/Toshifumi Yoshida
Touch-up Art & Lettering/James Gaubatz
Design/Yukiko Whitley
Editor/Amy Yu

Editor in Chief, Books/Alvin Lu
Editor in Chief, Magazines/Marc Weidenbaum
VP of Publishing Licensing/Rika Inouye
VP of Sales/Gonzalo Ferreyra
Sr. VP of Marketing/Liza Coppola
Publisher/Hyoe Narita

Printed in the U.S.A.

Published by VIZ Media, LLC
P.O. Box 77010
San Francisco, CA 94107

SHONEN JUMP ADVANCED Manga Edition
10 9 8 7 6 5 4 3 2 1
First printing, February 2008

www.viz.com

SHONEN JUMP ADVANCED MANGA EDITION

Vol. 10
Period

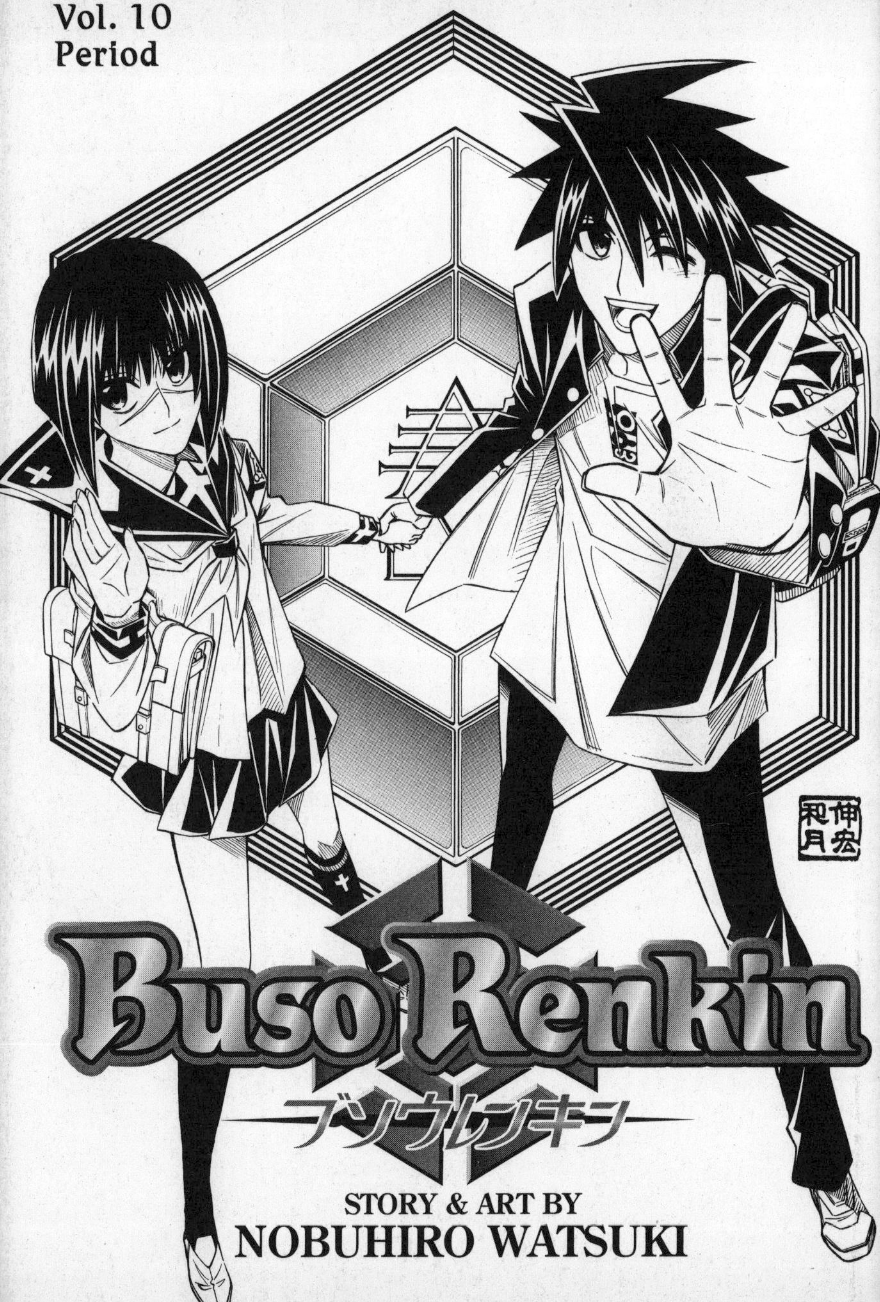

伸宏
和月

Buso Renkin

ブソウレンキン

STORY & ART BY
NOBUHIRO WATSUKI

Kakugane
Kakugane are forged from a magical alchemic alloy. They are activated by the deepest parts of the human psyche, the basic instincts. Each kakugane can materialize a unique weapon called a Buso Renkin.

Homunculus
An artificial being created by alchemy. The form and powers of the homunculus differ depending on the organism it was based on. Homunculi feed on human flesh and can only be destroyed by the power of alchemy.

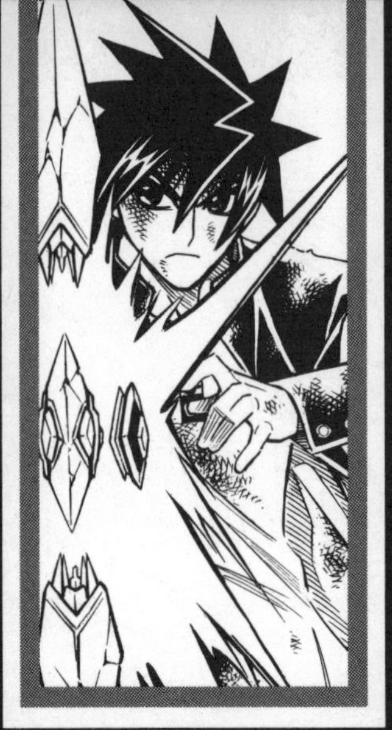

Kazuki Muto

When Kazuki is mortally wounded by a homunculus, Alchemist Warrior Tokiko saves his life by replacing his heart with a kakugane. But when it is discovered that it is a black kakugane, the Alchemist Army issues a re-extermination order for Kazuki.

武装錬金 CHARACTERS

Alchemist Army
A secret organization started by a guild of alchemists in medieval England. It regulates all things related to alchemy.

Black Kakugane
To facilitate the creation of the Philosopher's Stone, these special kakugane were created a century ago from kakugane with serial numbers I, II, and III. One of the black kakugane was used to revive the injured Great Warrior Victor, transforming him into a monster more terrible than any homunculus; he nearly destroys the Alchemist Army. During this period, the other two black kakugane go missing.

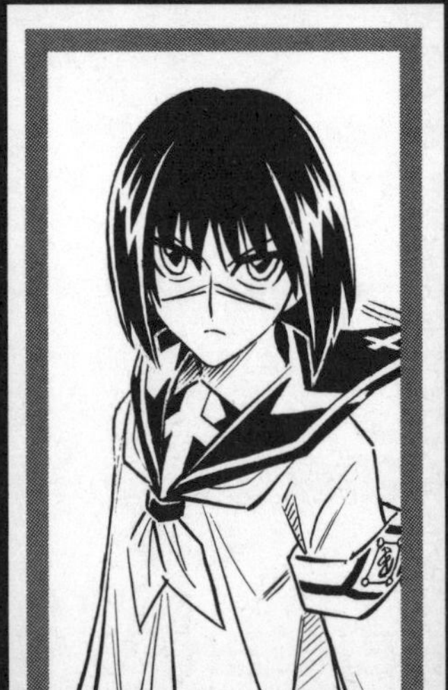

Tokiko Tsumura

A Buso Renkin expert and Alchemist Warrior. She and Kazuki fall in love, and she swears to die if he does. But during the final battle with Victor, Kazuki leaves her behind on Earth.

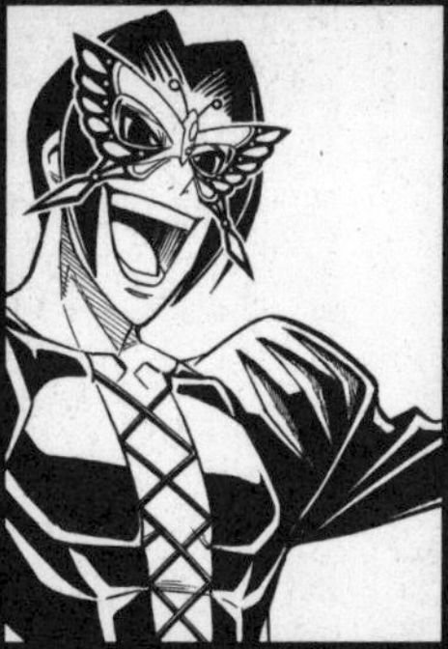

Papillon
(Koushaku Chouno)

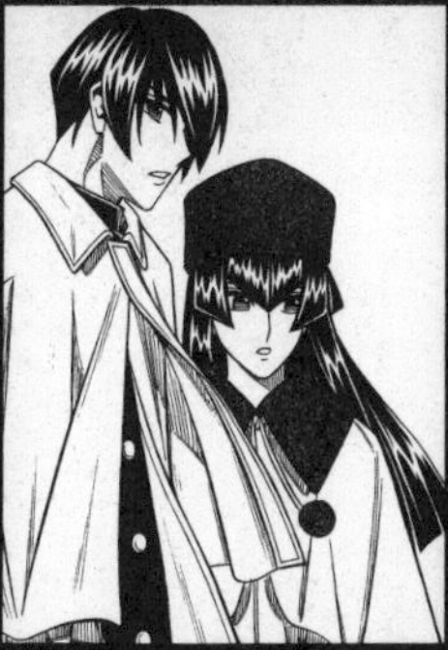

Shusui Hayasaka
Ouka Hayasaka

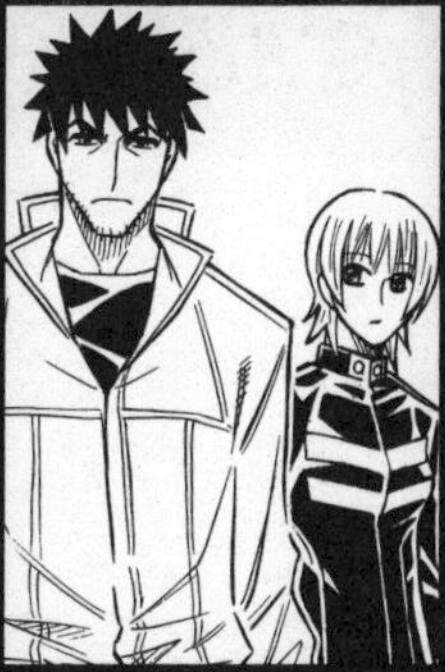

Captain Bravo
(Mamoru Sakimori)
Chitose

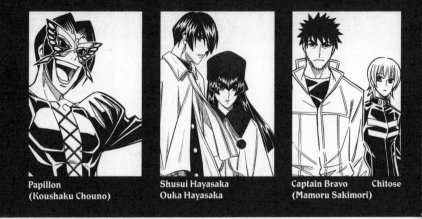

S T O R Y

Following the destruction of Dr. Butterfly, Kazuki learns that he is doomed to become a life-draining creature like Victor because of the black kakugane that serves as his heart. The leaders of the Alchemist Army, fearing that they will soon have two invincible monsters to deal with, order Kazuki's immediate termination. Hunted by friend and foe alike, Kazuki, Tokiko, and Gouta Nakamura make their way toward Newton Apple Academy for Girls, where they hope to find a way to reverse Kazuki's condition. After several battles, the Alchemist Army gives Kazuki a reprieve so that all efforts may be focused on defeating Victor. In the meantime, Kazuki's group finds Victor's daughter Victoria (now a humanoid homunculus) and wife Alexandria. Alexandria is now an array of cloned brains, but she was once a scientist for the Alchemist Army whose experiments with the black kakugane turned Victor into a monster. Just as Victor seems certain to defeat the Alchemist Army, Kazuki and Tokiko manage to drive a white kakugane into him. Unfortunately, the white kakugane's power is no match for Victor in his current state. In a last-ditch effort to save the world, Kazuki uses his remaining strength to propel himself and Victor to the moon. On the lifeless lunar surface, the two invincible warriors face each other...

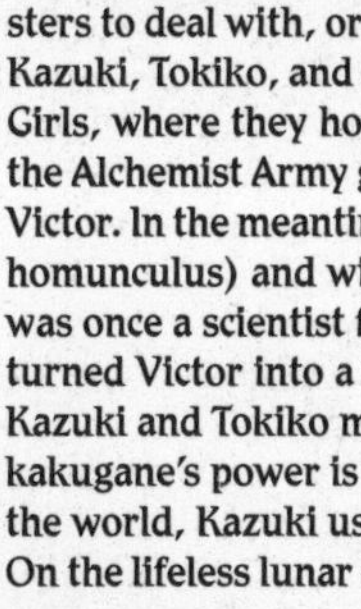

Gouta Nakamura

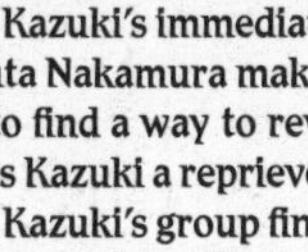

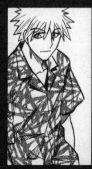

Hiwatari

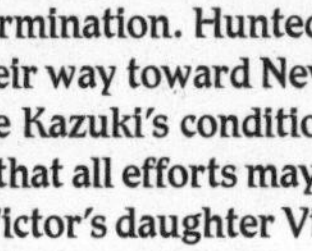

Shosei Sakaguchi
(Great Warrior Chief)

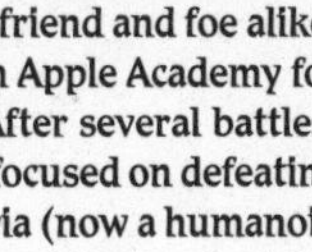

Victor

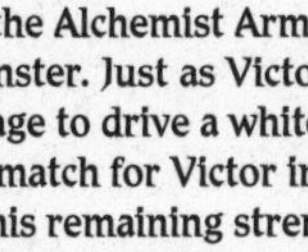

Busujima

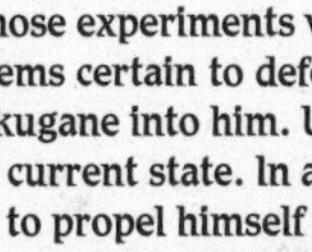

Angel Gozen

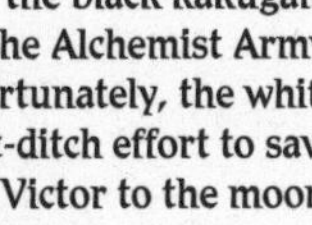

Victoria

BUSO RENKIN
Volume 10: Period

CONTENTS

BUSO RENKIN: PERIOD

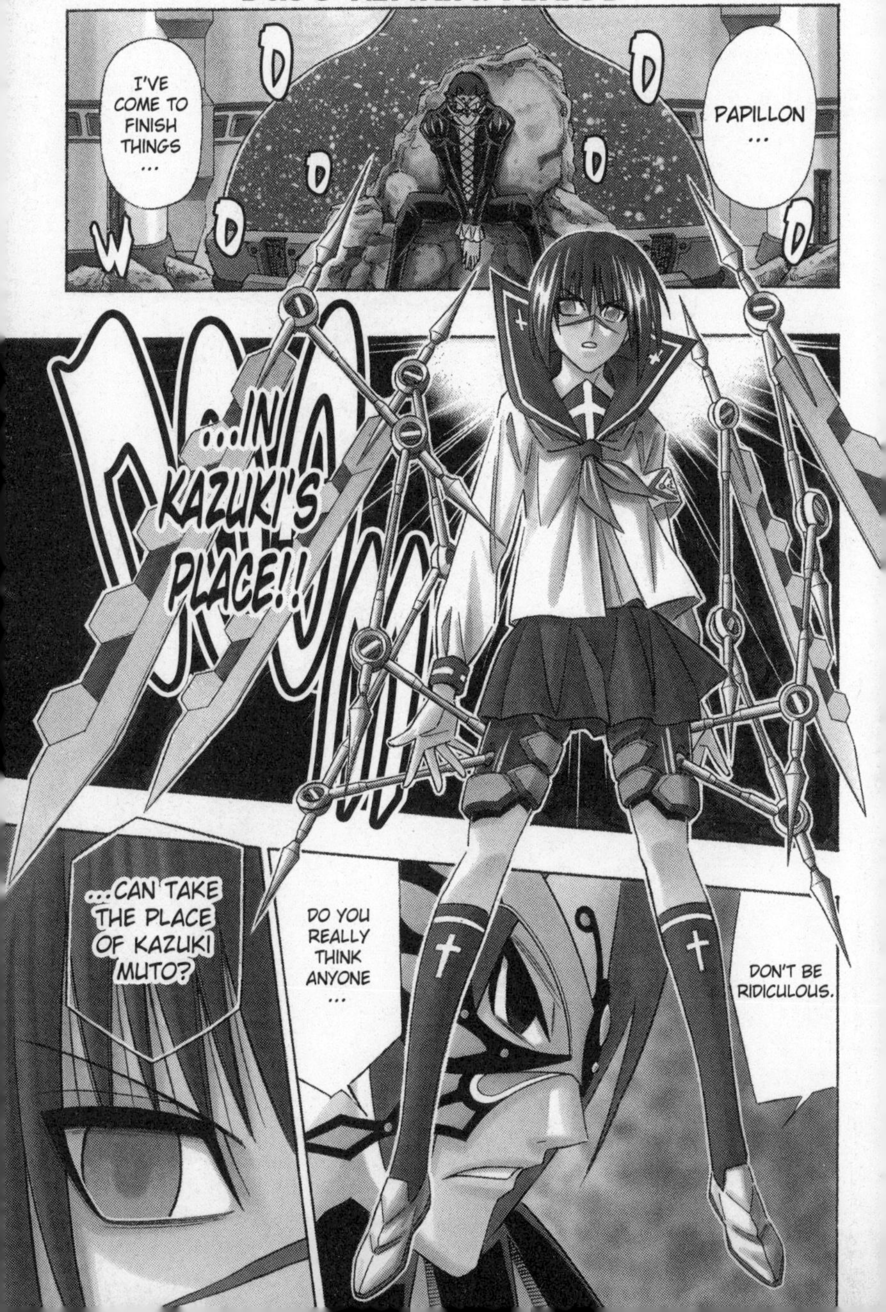

PAPILLON ...
I'VE COME TO FINISH THINGS ...
...IN KAZUKI'S PLACE!!
DON'T BE RIDICULOUS.
DO YOU REALLY THINK ANYONE ...
...CAN TAKE THE PLACE OF KAZUKI MUTO?

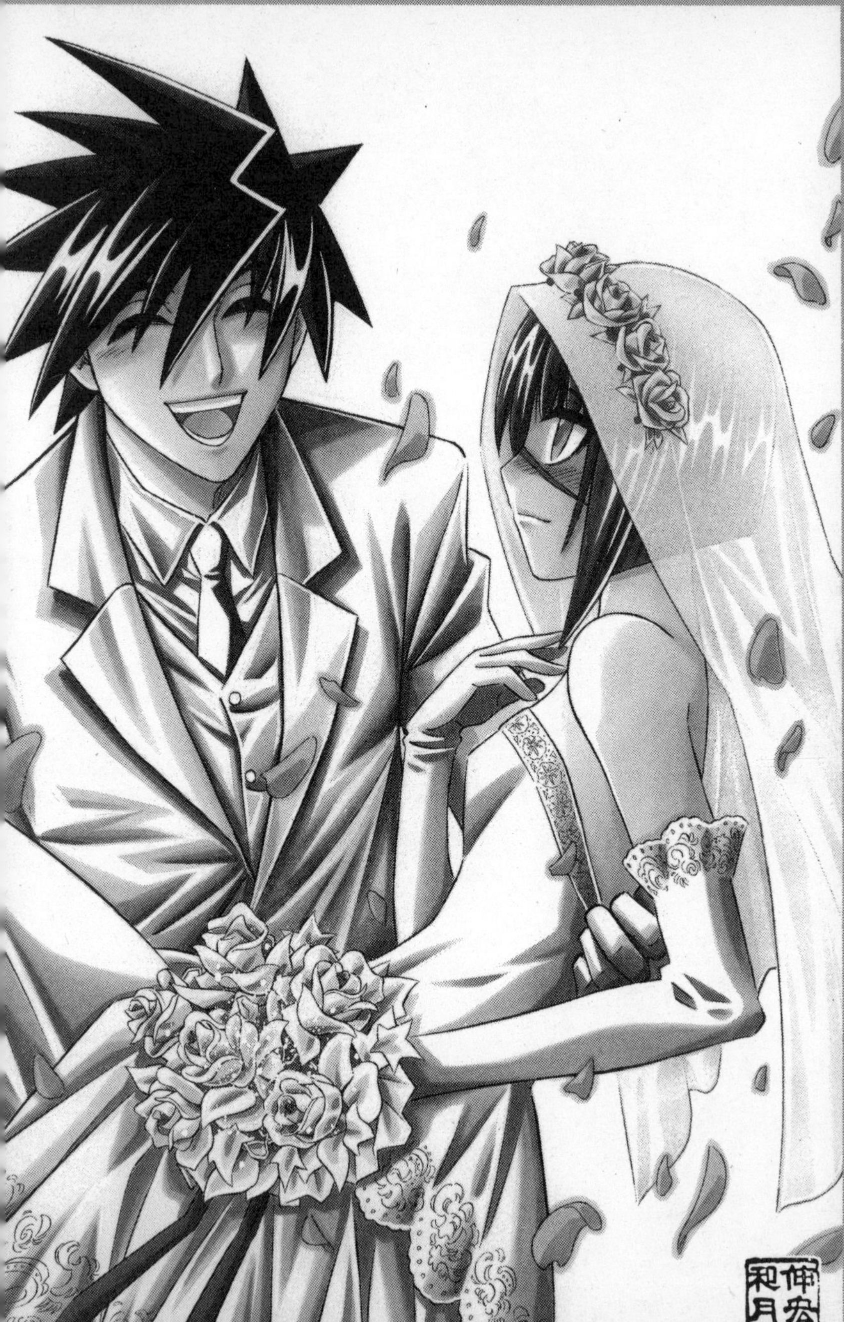
伸宏和月

武装錬金 BUSO RENKIN: PERIOD ピリオド

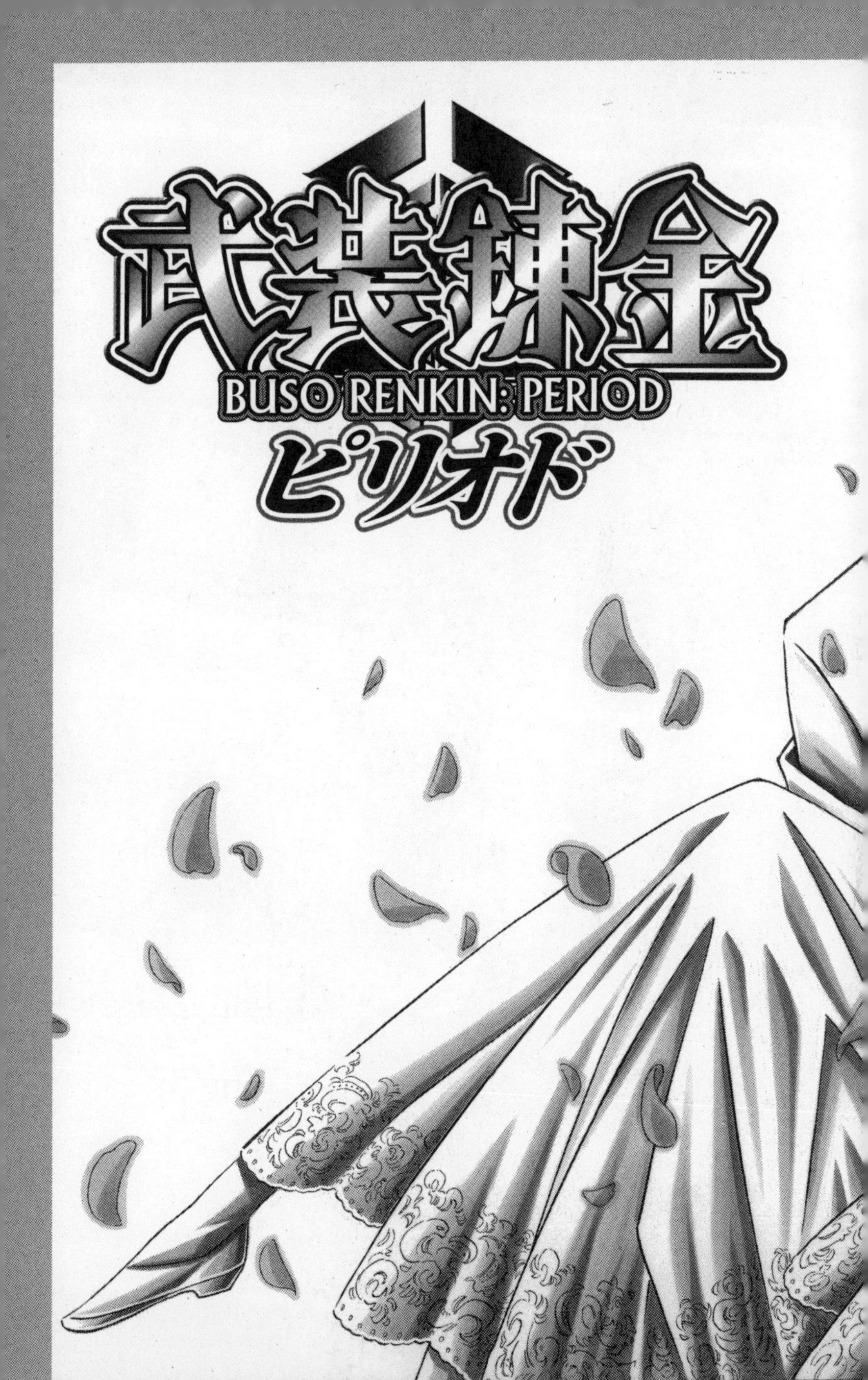

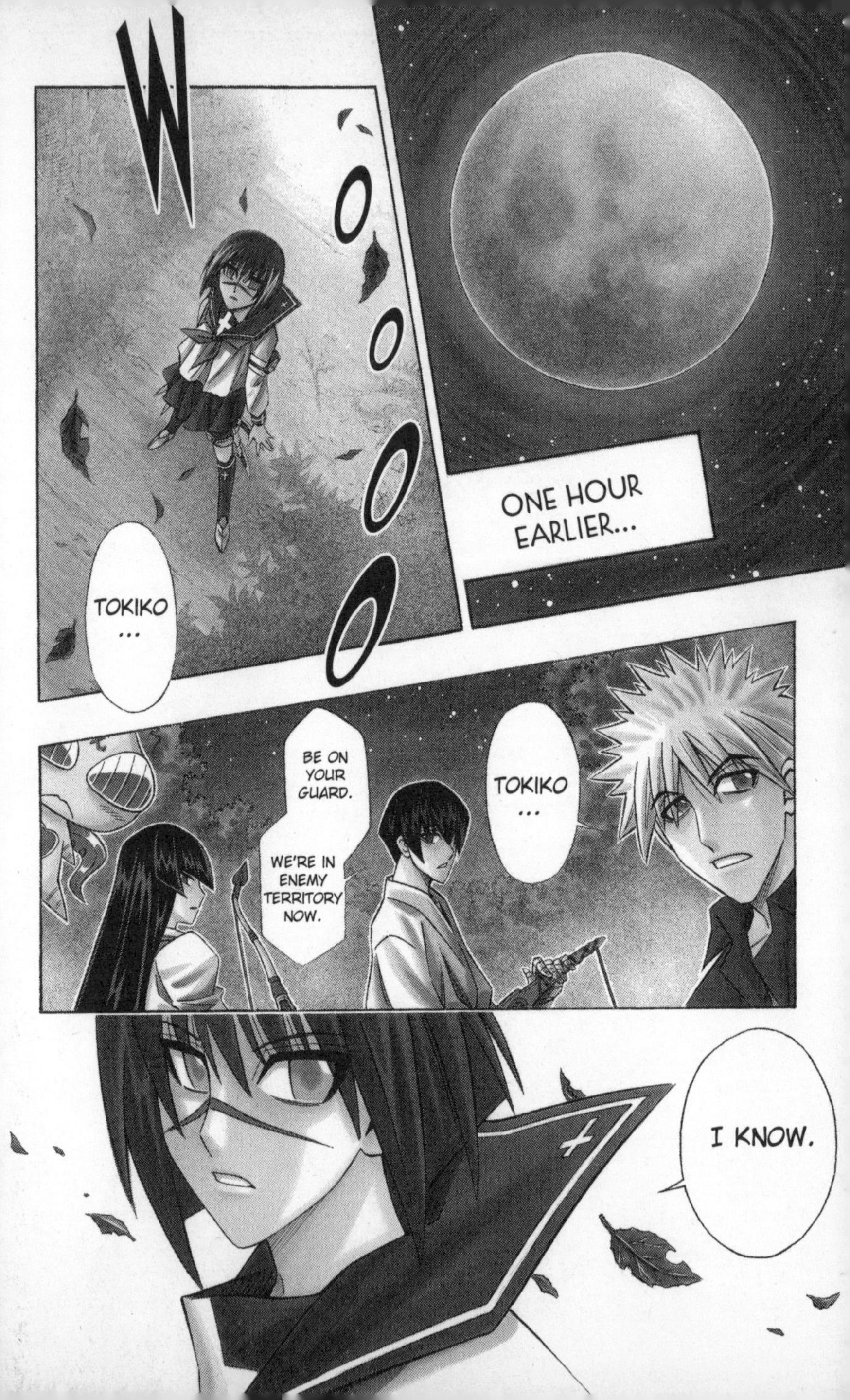
ONE HOUR EARLIER...
WOOOOO
TOKIKO...
TOKIKO...
BE ON YOUR GUARD.
WE'RE IN ENEMY TERRITORY NOW.
I KNOW.

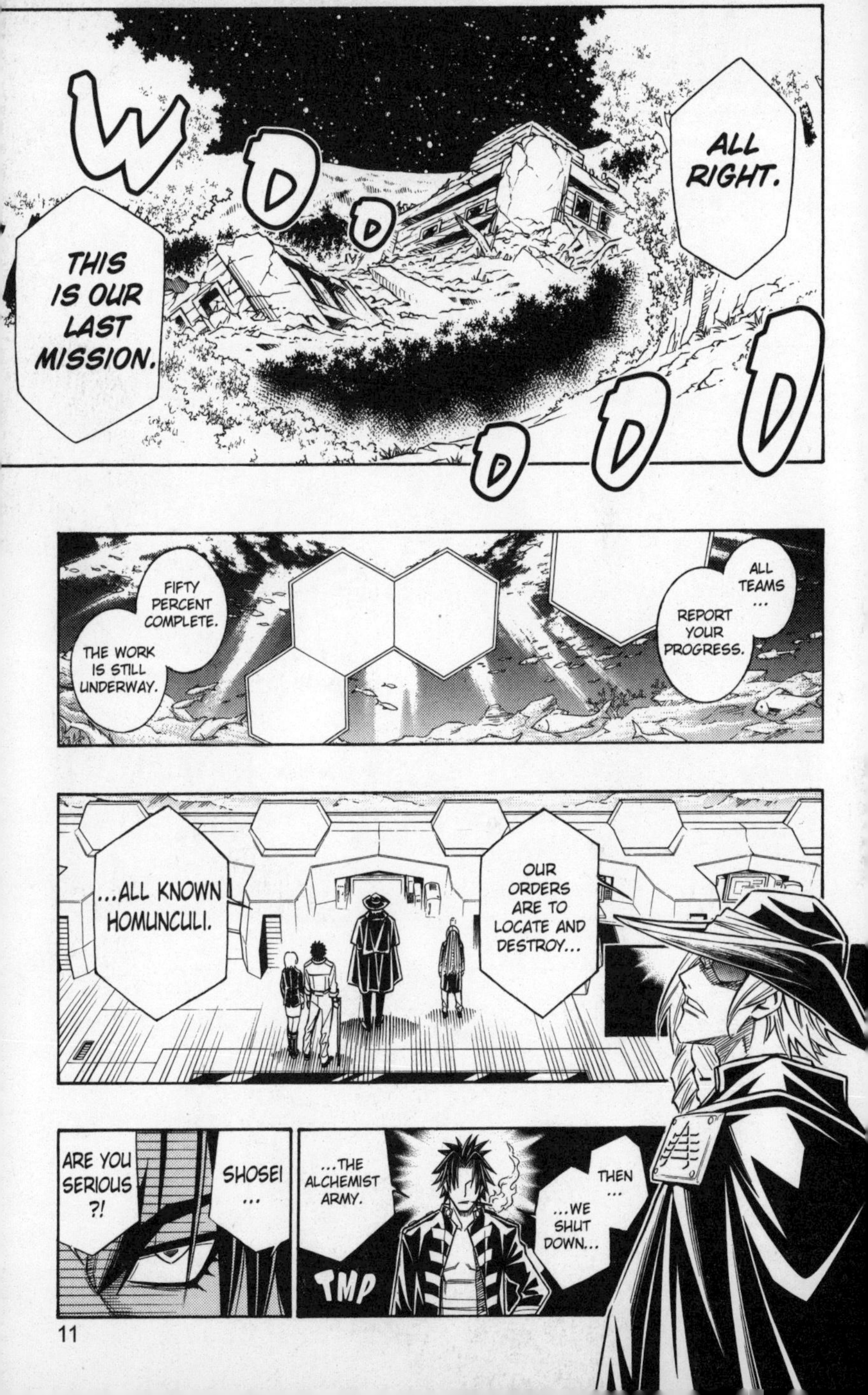
ALL RIGHT.
THIS IS OUR LAST MISSION.
WDDDDDD
ALL TEAMS...
REPORT YOUR PROGRESS.
FIFTY PERCENT COMPLETE.
THE WORK IS STILL UNDERWAY.
OUR ORDERS ARE TO LOCATE AND DESTROY...
...ALL KNOWN HOMUNCULI.
THEN...
...WE SHUT DOWN...
...THE ALCHEMIST ARMY.
TMP
SHOSEI...
ARE YOU SERIOUS?!

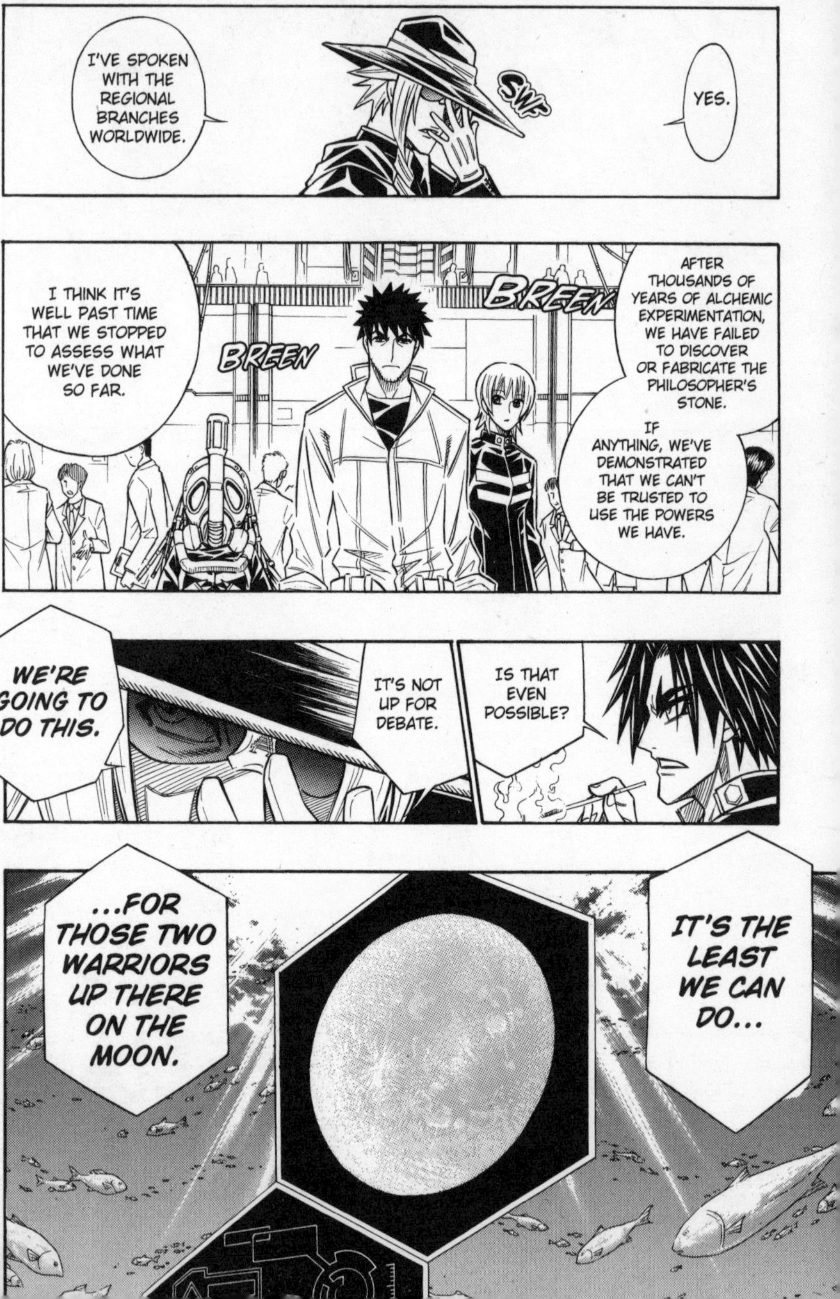
YES.
SWF
I'VE SPOKEN WITH THE REGIONAL BRANCHES WORLDWIDE.
AFTER THOUSANDS OF YEARS OF ALCHEMIC EXPERIMENTATION, WE HAVE FAILED TO DISCOVER OR FABRICATE THE PHILOSOPHER'S STONE.
BREEN
IF ANYTHING, WE'VE DEMONSTRATED THAT WE CAN'T BE TRUSTED TO USE THE POWERS WE HAVE.
I THINK IT'S WELL PAST TIME THAT WE STOPPED TO ASSESS WHAT WE'VE DONE SO FAR.
BREEN
IS THAT EVEN POSSIBLE?
IT'S NOT UP FOR DEBATE.
WE'RE GOING TO DO THIS.
IT'S THE LEAST WE CAN DO...
...FOR THOSE TWO WARRIORS UP THERE ON THE MOON.

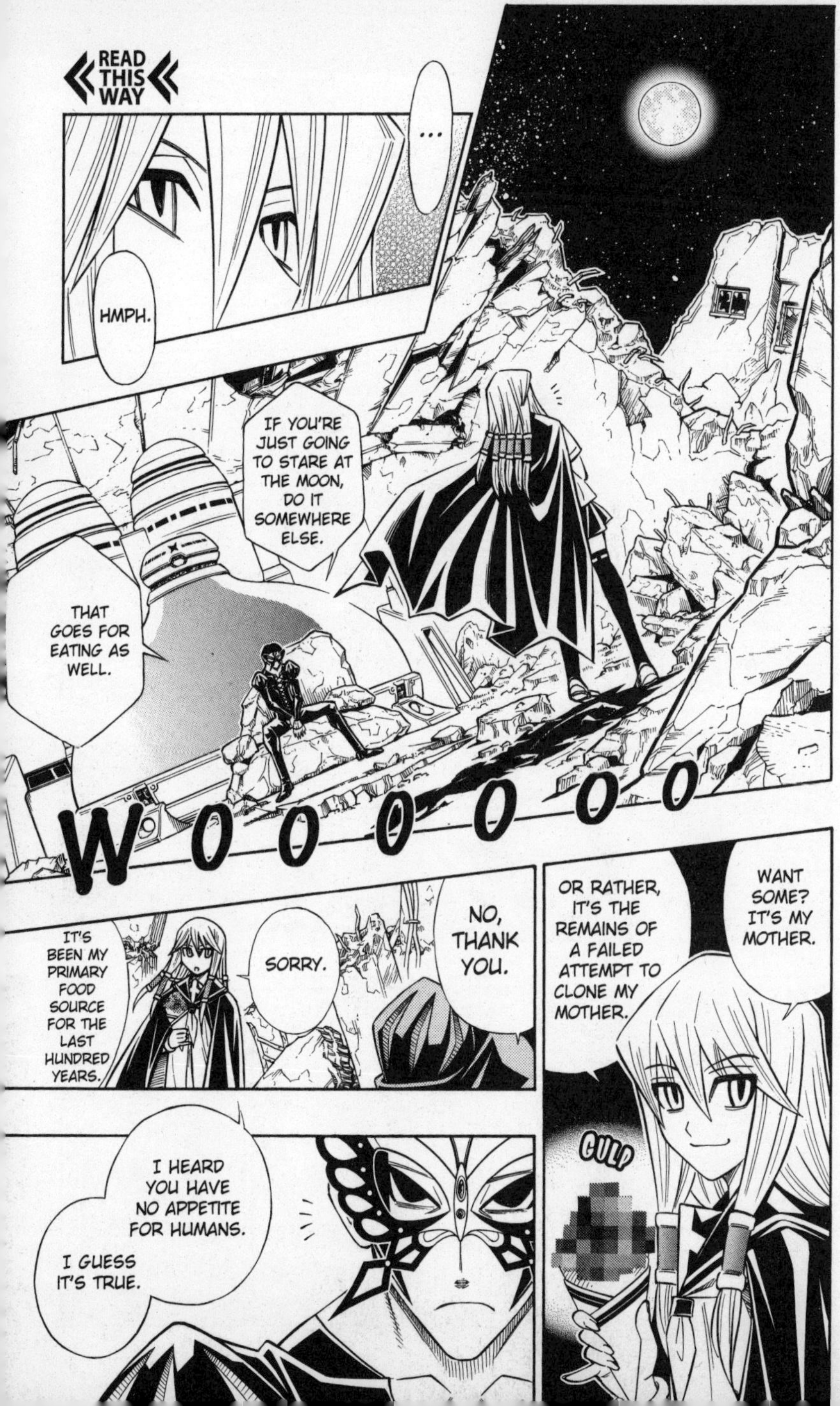
READ THIS WAY
...
HMPH.
IF YOU'RE JUST GOING TO STARE AT THE MOON, DO IT SOMEWHERE ELSE.
THAT GOES FOR EATING AS WELL.
WOOOOOOO
WANT SOME? IT'S MY MOTHER.
OR RATHER, IT'S THE REMAINS OF A FAILED ATTEMPT TO CLONE MY MOTHER.
GULP
NO, THANK YOU.
SORRY.
IT'S BEEN MY PRIMARY FOOD SOURCE FOR THE LAST HUNDRED YEARS.
I HEARD YOU HAVE NO APPETITE FOR HUMANS.
I GUESS IT'S TRUE.

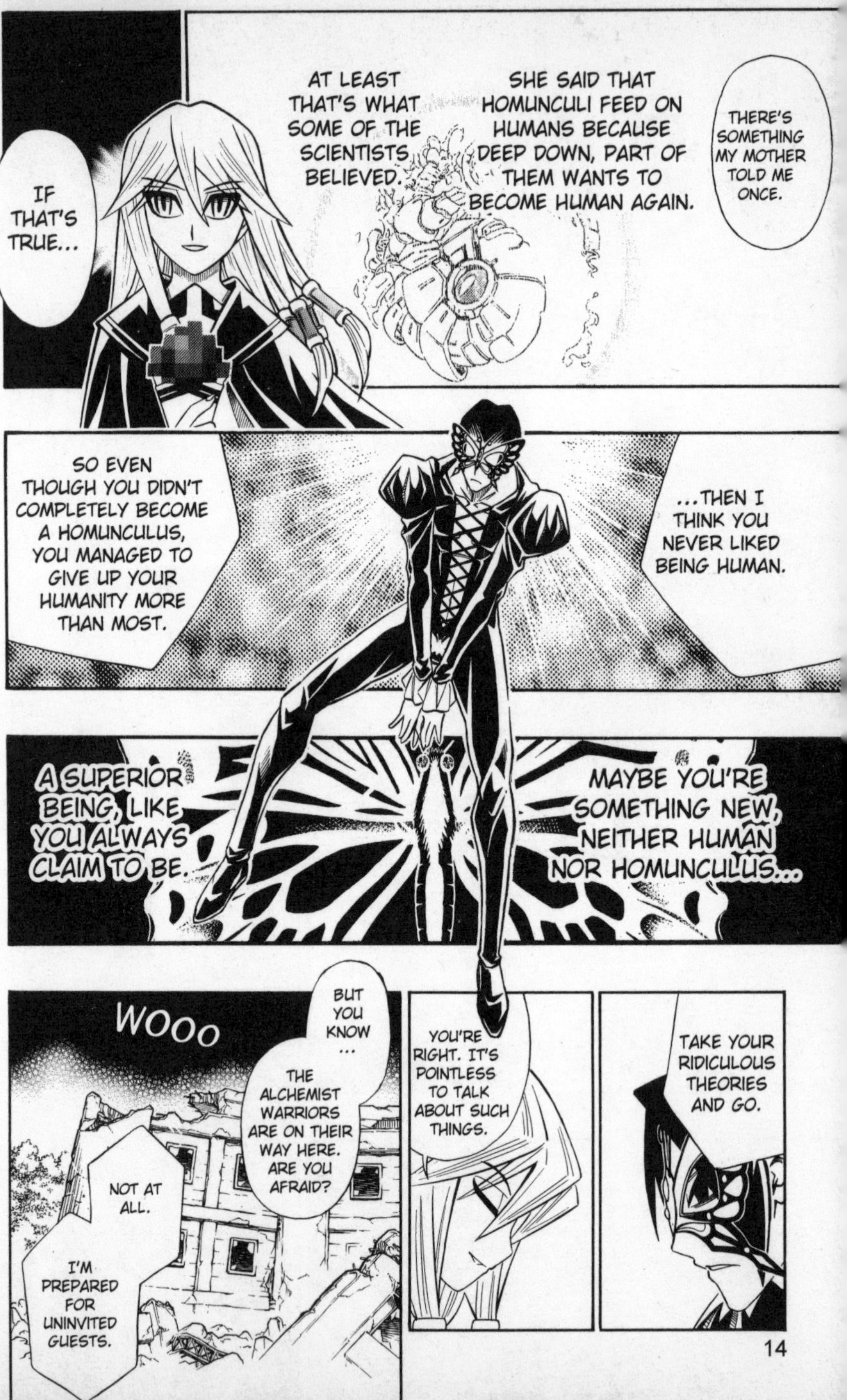

THERE'S SOMETHING MY MOTHER TOLD ME ONCE.
SHE SAID THAT HOMUNCULI FEED ON HUMANS BECAUSE DEEP DOWN, PART OF THEM WANTS TO BECOME HUMAN AGAIN.
AT LEAST THAT'S WHAT SOME OF THE SCIENTISTS BELIEVED.
IF THAT'S TRUE...
...THEN I THINK YOU NEVER LIKED BEING HUMAN.
SO EVEN THOUGH YOU DIDN'T COMPLETELY BECOME A HOMUNCULUS, YOU MANAGED TO GIVE UP YOUR HUMANITY MORE THAN MOST.
MAYBE YOU'RE SOMETHING NEW, NEITHER HUMAN NOR HOMUNCULUS...
A SUPERIOR BEING, LIKE YOU ALWAYS CLAIM TO BE.
TAKE YOUR RIDICULOUS THEORIES AND GO.
YOU'RE RIGHT. IT'S POINTLESS TO TALK ABOUT SUCH THINGS.
BUT YOU KNOW ...
THE ALCHEMIST WARRIORS ARE ON THEIR WAY HERE. ARE YOU AFRAID?
WOOO
NOT AT ALL.
I'M PREPARED FOR UNINVITED GUESTS.

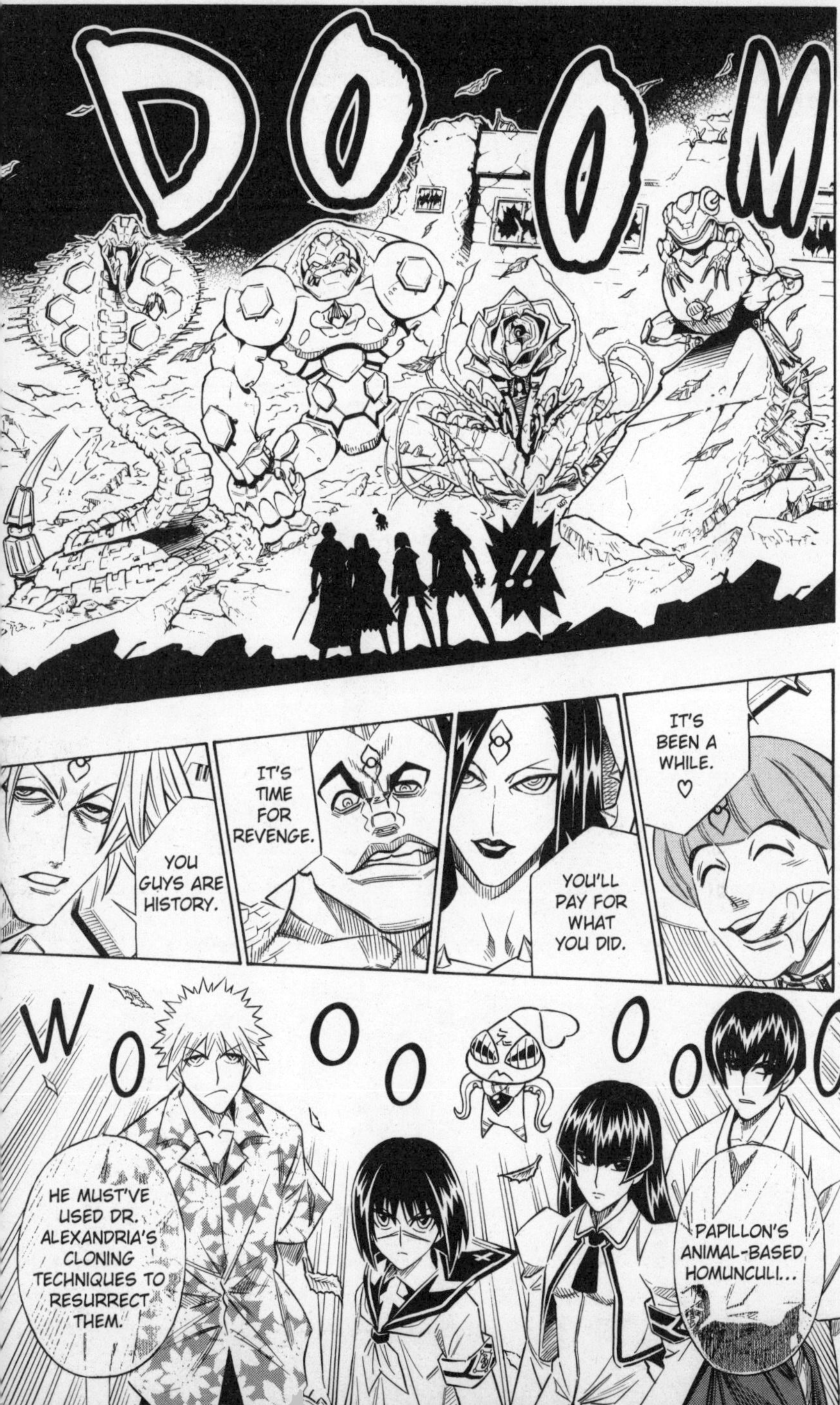
DOOM
!!
IT'S BEEN A WHILE. ♡
YOU'LL PAY FOR WHAT YOU DID.
IT'S TIME FOR REVENGE.
YOU GUYS ARE HISTORY.
WOOOOOO
PAPILLON'S ANIMAL-BASED HOMUNCULI...
HE MUST'VE USED DR. ALEXANDRIA'S CLONING TECHNIQUES TO RESURRECT THEM.

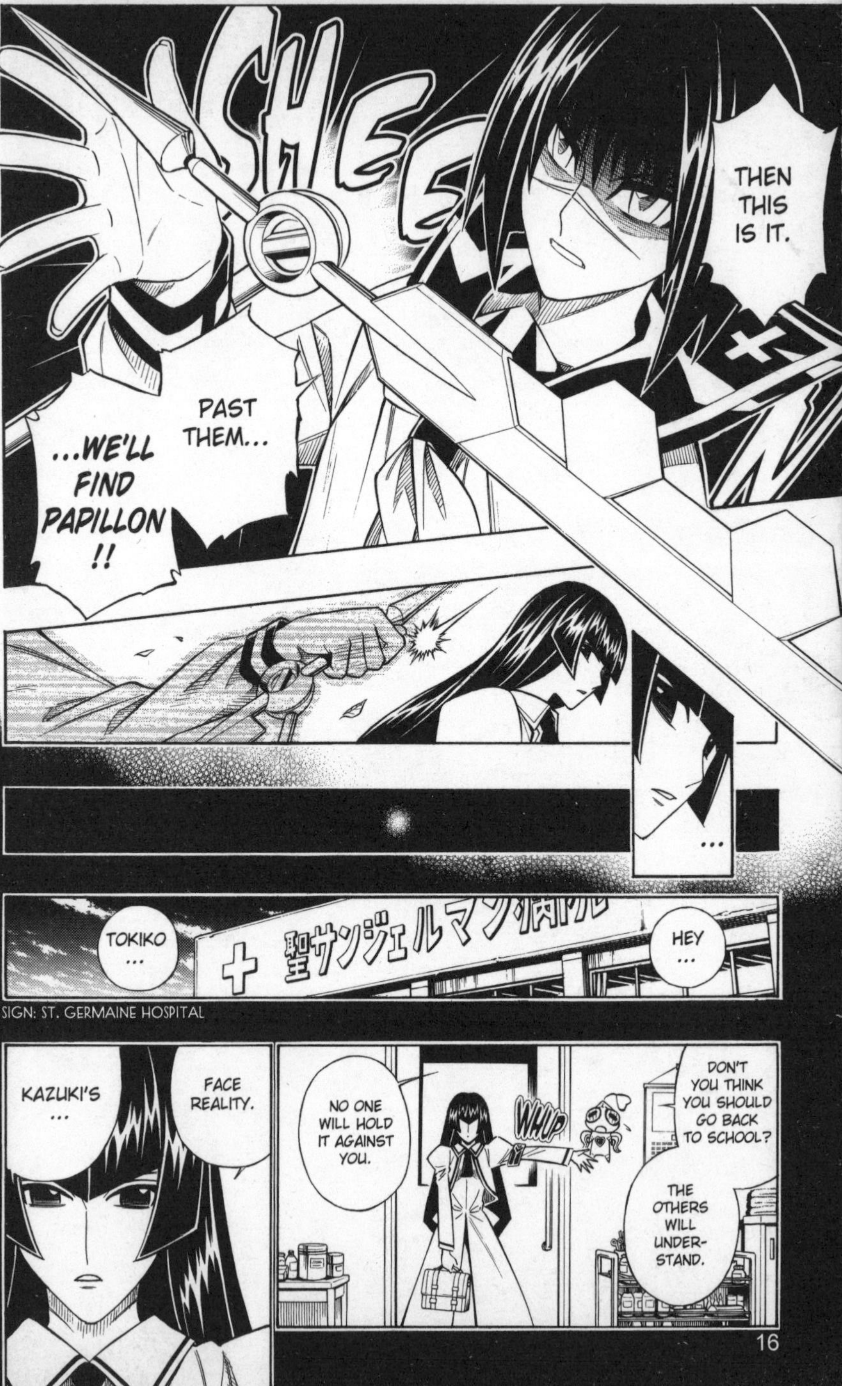
SHEE
THEN THIS IS IT.
PAST THEM...
...WE'LL FIND PAPILLON !!
...
HEY ...
聖サンジェルマン
TOKIKO ...
SIGN: ST. GERMAINE HOSPITAL
DON'T YOU THINK YOU SHOULD GO BACK TO SCHOOL?
THE OTHERS WILL UNDER-STAND.
WHUP
NO ONE WILL HOLD IT AGAINST YOU.
FACE REALITY.
KAZUKI'S ...

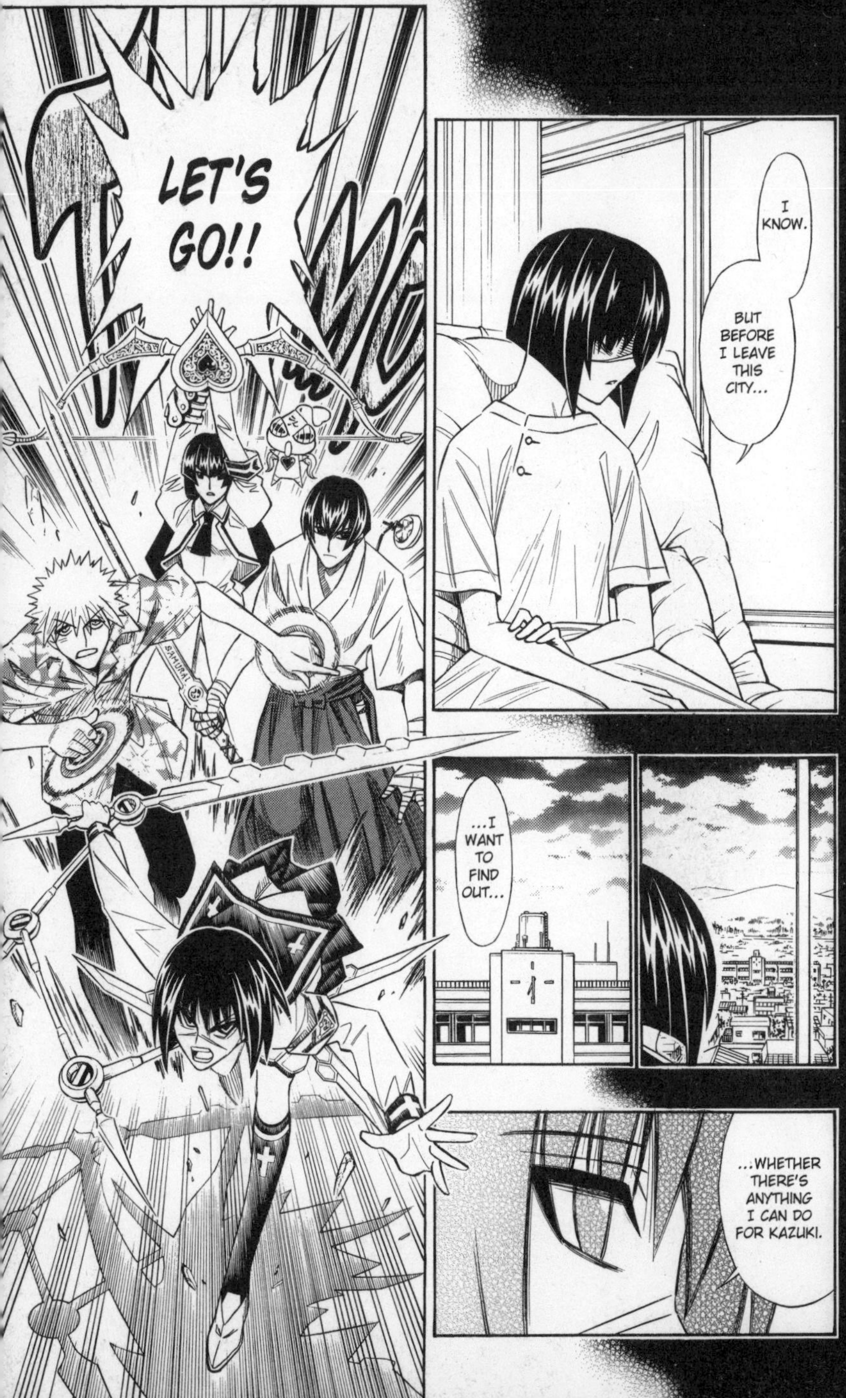
I KNOW.
BUT BEFORE I LEAVE THIS CITY...
...I WANT TO FIND OUT...
...WHETHER THERE'S ANYTHING I CAN DO FOR KAZUKI.
LET'S GO!!

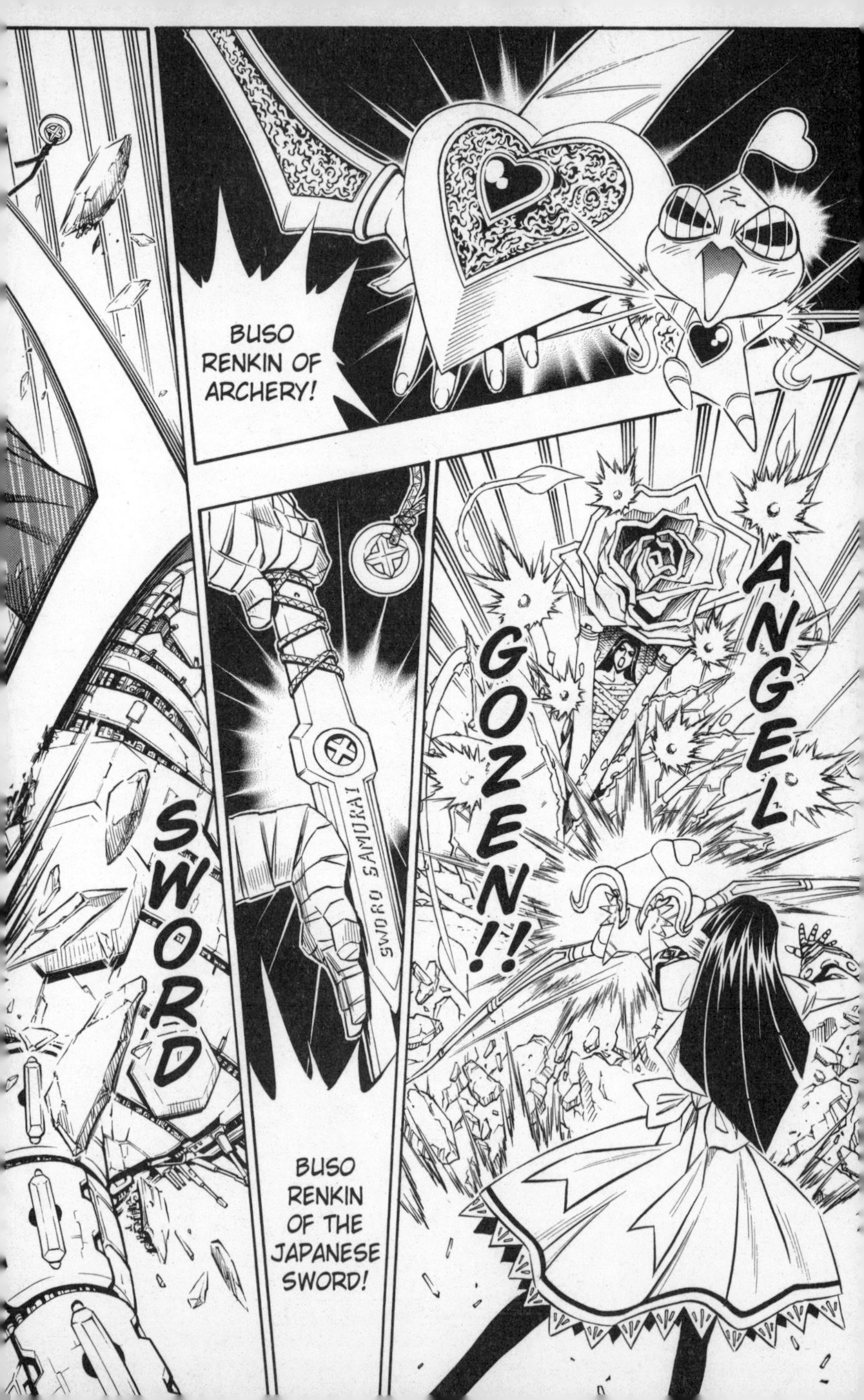

BUSO RENKIN OF ARCHERY!
ANGEL GOZEN!!
SWORD SAMURAI
BUSO RENKIN OF THE JAPANESE SWORD!
SWORD

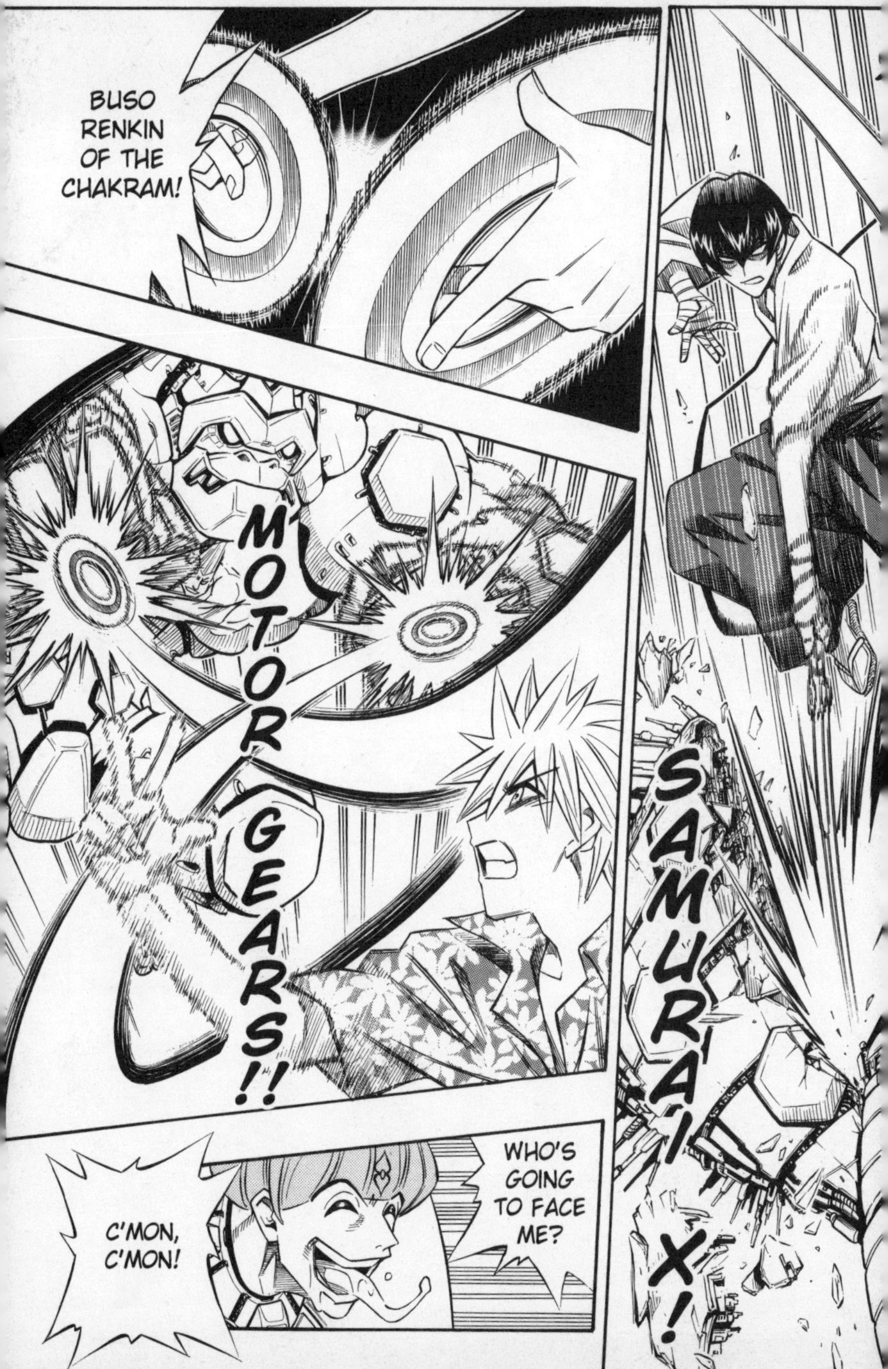
SAMURAI X!
BUSO RENKIN OF THE CHAKRAM!
MOTOR GEARS!!
WHO'S GOING TO FACE ME?
C'MON, C'MON!

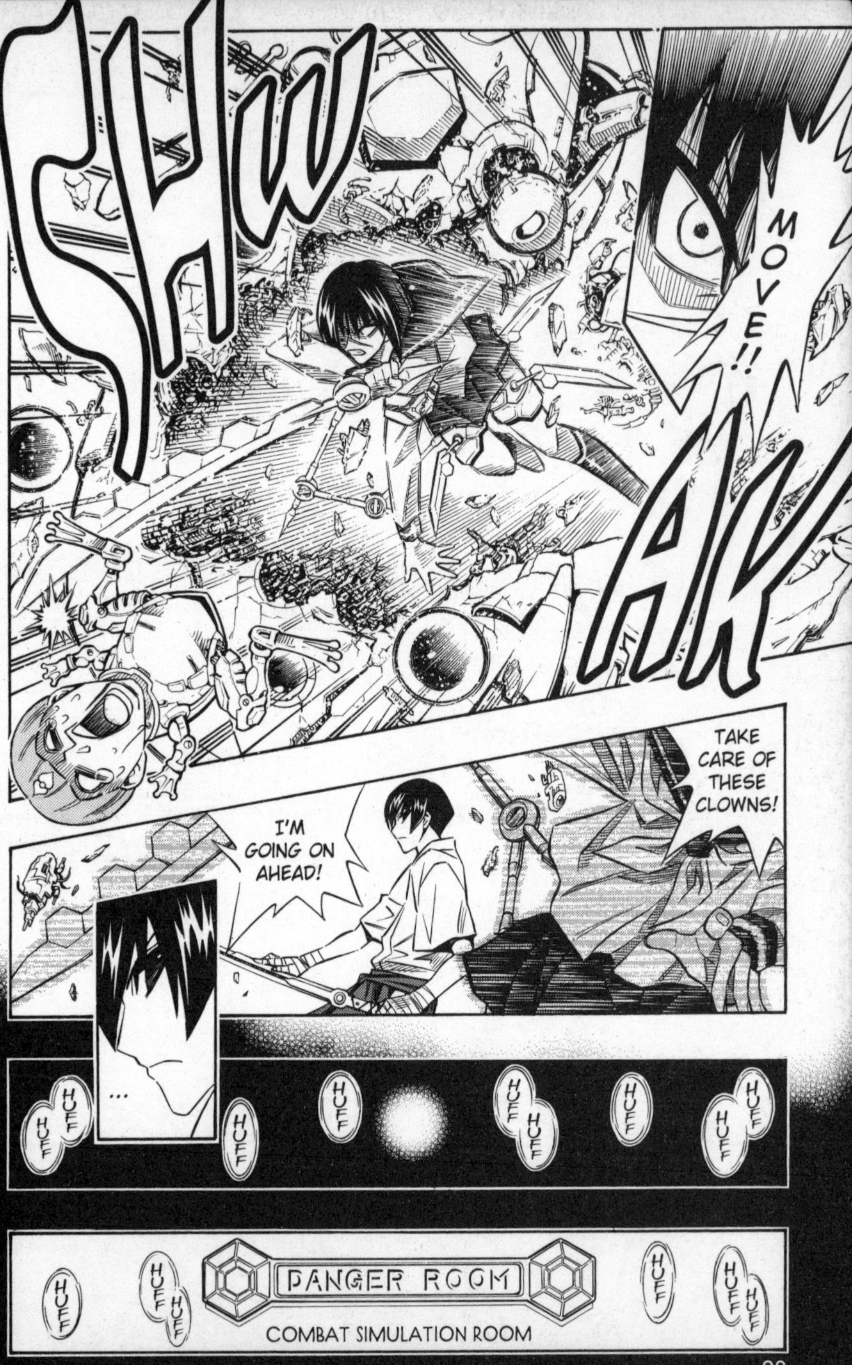
MOVE!!
SHW
AK
TAKE CARE OF THESE CLOWNS!
I'M GOING ON AHEAD!
...
HUFF HUFF
HUFF
HUFF HUFF
HUFF
HUFF
HUFF HUFF
HUFF HUFF HUFF
HUFF
DANGER ROOM
COMBAT SIMULATION ROOM
HUFF HUFF
HUFF

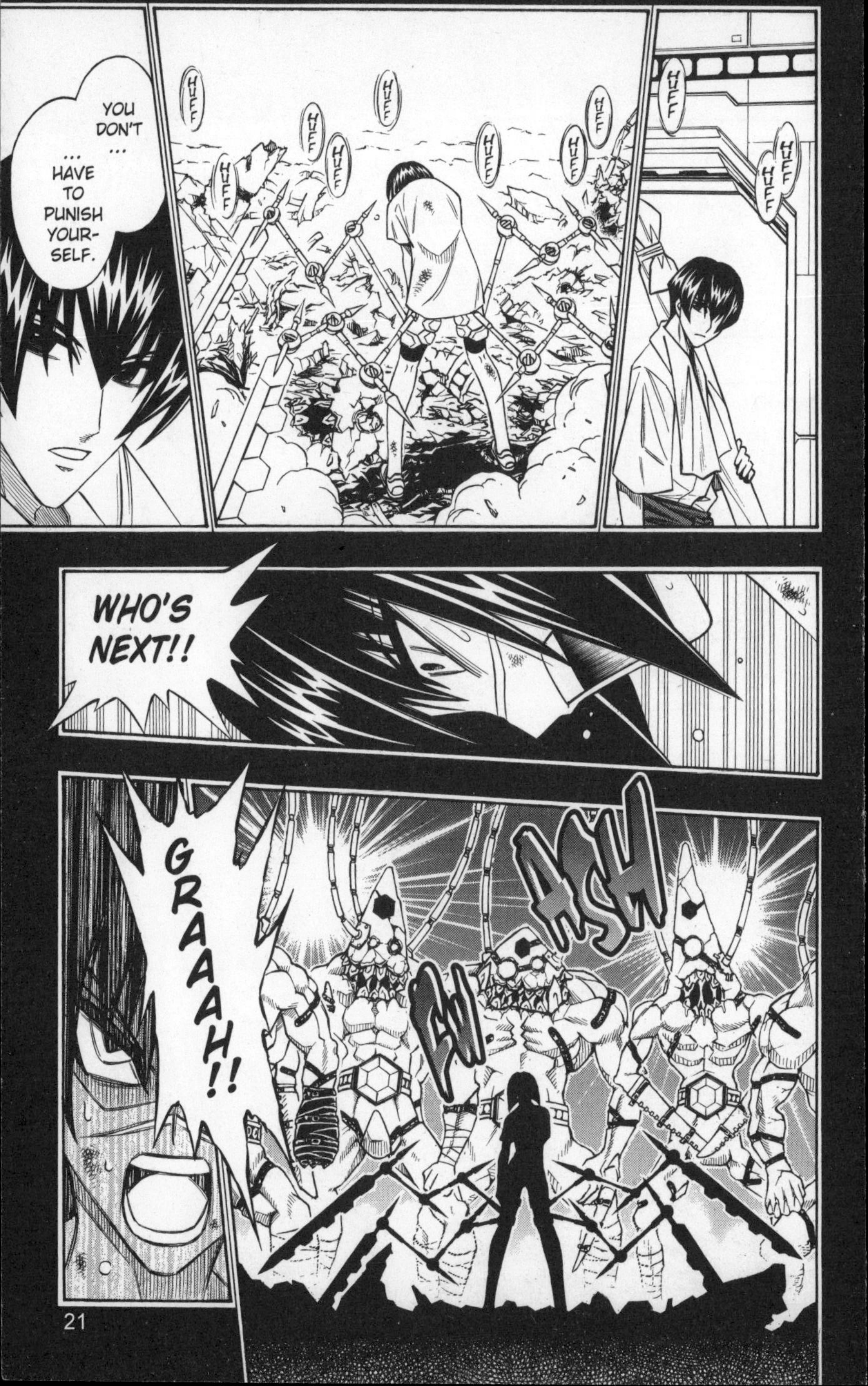
HUFF
HUFF
HUFF
HUFF
HUFF
HUFF
HUFF
HUFF
HUFF
HUFF
YOU DON'T ... ... HAVE TO PUNISH YOURSELF.
WHO'S NEXT!!
GRAAAAH!!

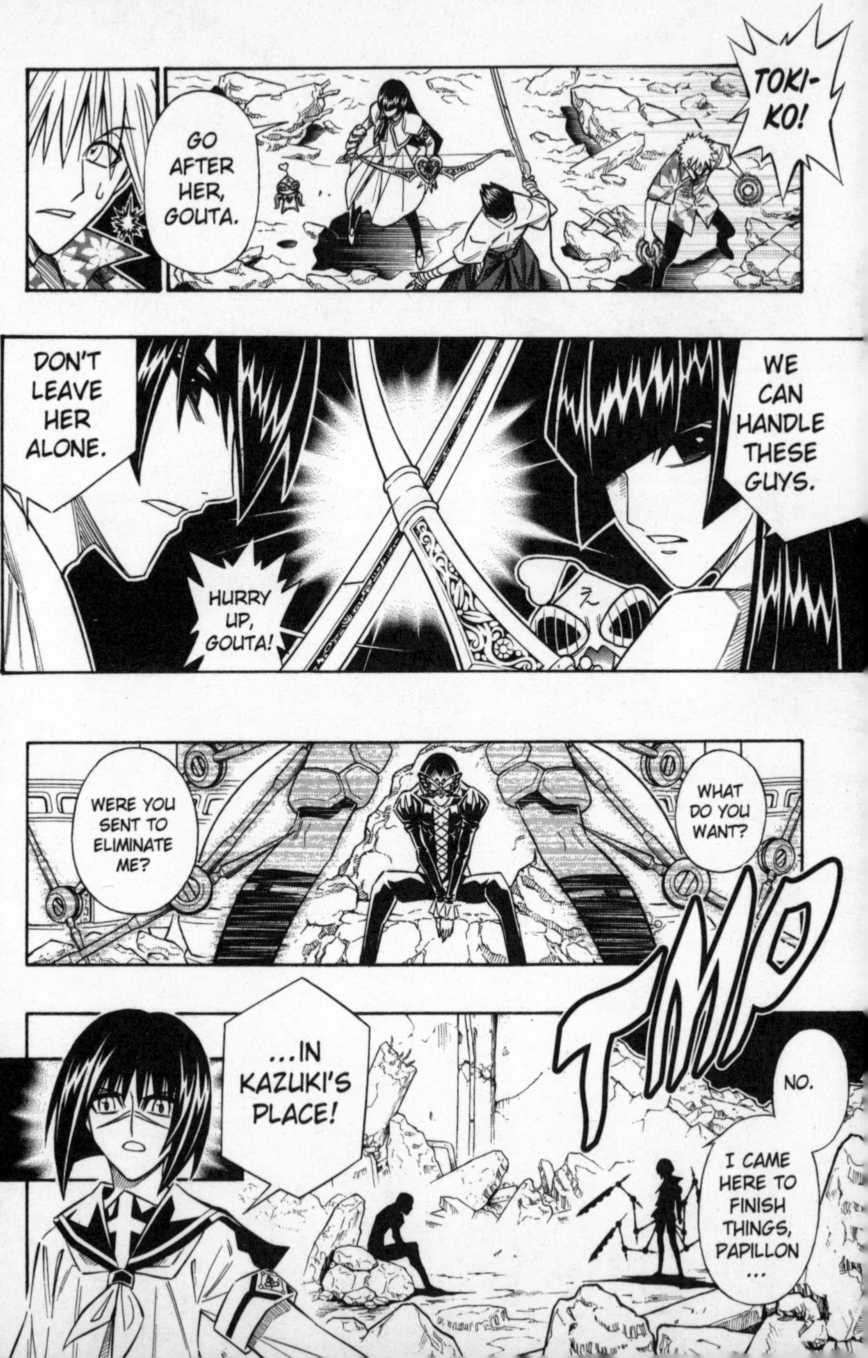
TOKI-KO!
GO AFTER HER, GOUTA.
WE CAN HANDLE THESE GUYS.
DON'T LEAVE HER ALONE.
HURRY UP, GOUTA!
WHAT DO YOU WANT?
WERE YOU SENT TO ELIMINATE ME?
TMP
NO.
I CAME HERE TO FINISH THINGS, PAPILLON...
...IN KAZUKI'S PLACE!

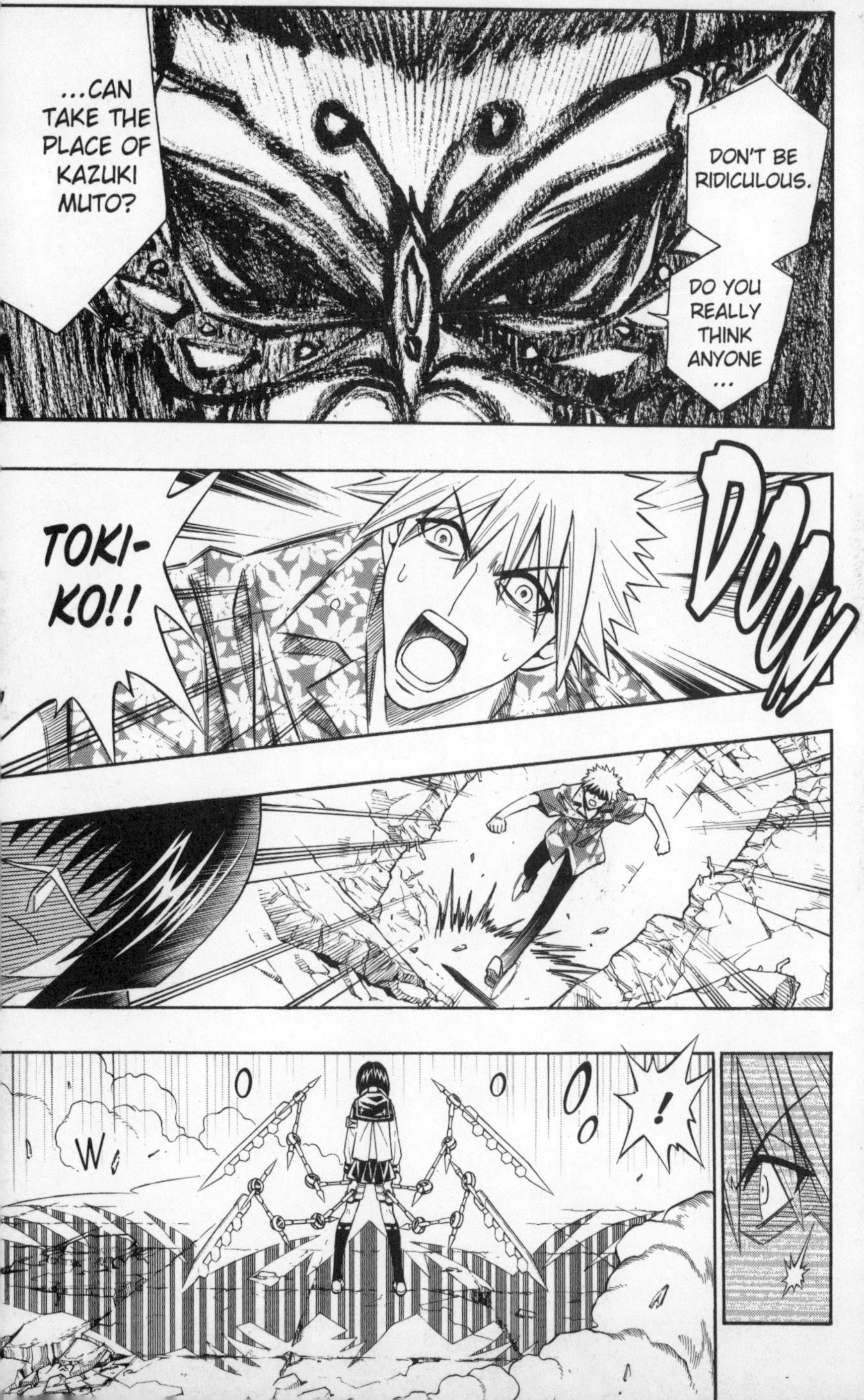
DON'T BE RIDICULOUS.
DO YOU REALLY THINK ANYONE ...
...CAN TAKE THE PLACE OF KAZUKI MUTO?
DOOM
TOKI-KO!!
!
W

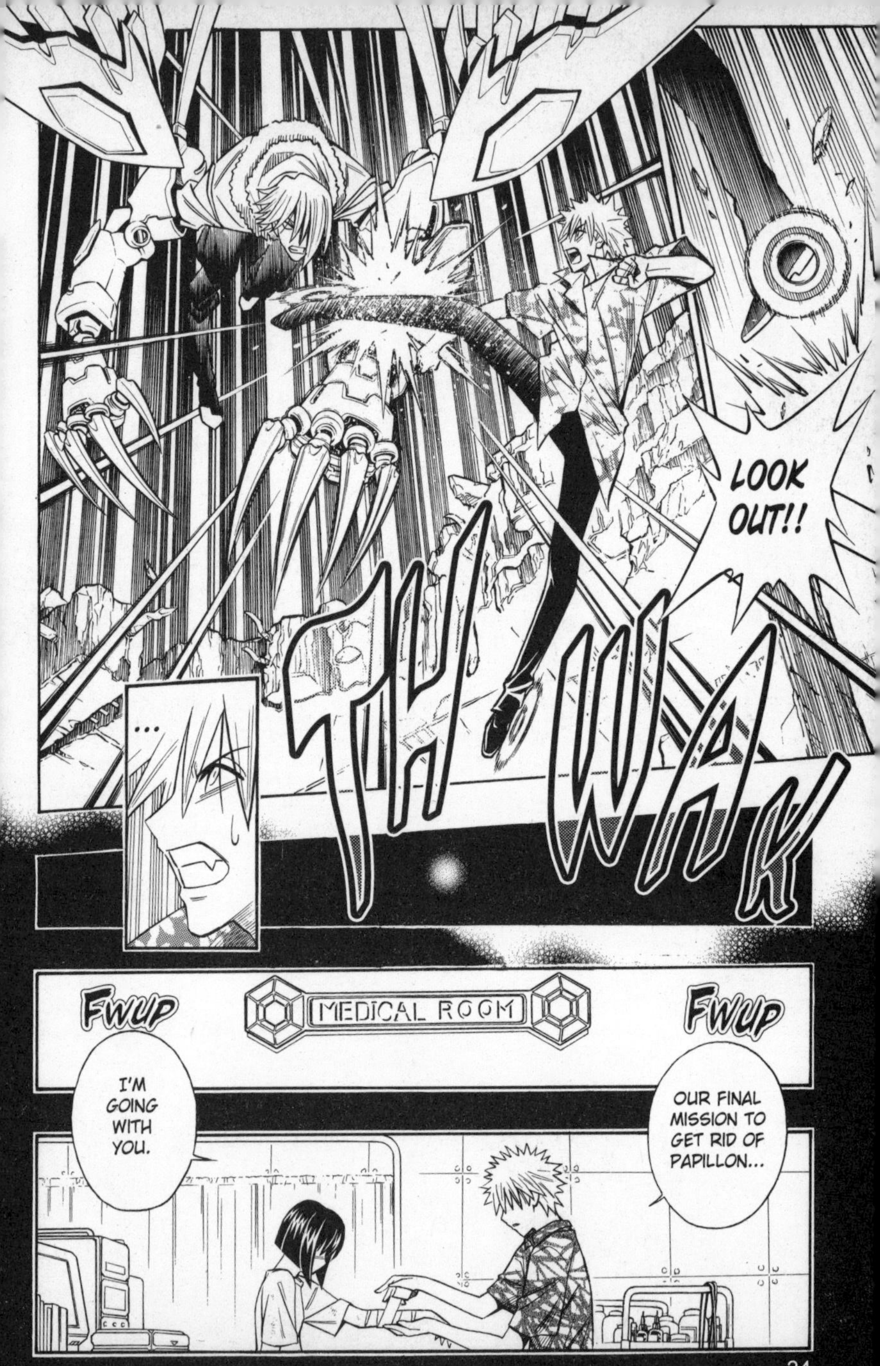
LOOK OUT!!
THWAK
...
Fwup
MEDICAL ROOM
Fwup
OUR FINAL MISSION TO GET RID OF PAPILLON...
I'M GOING WITH YOU.

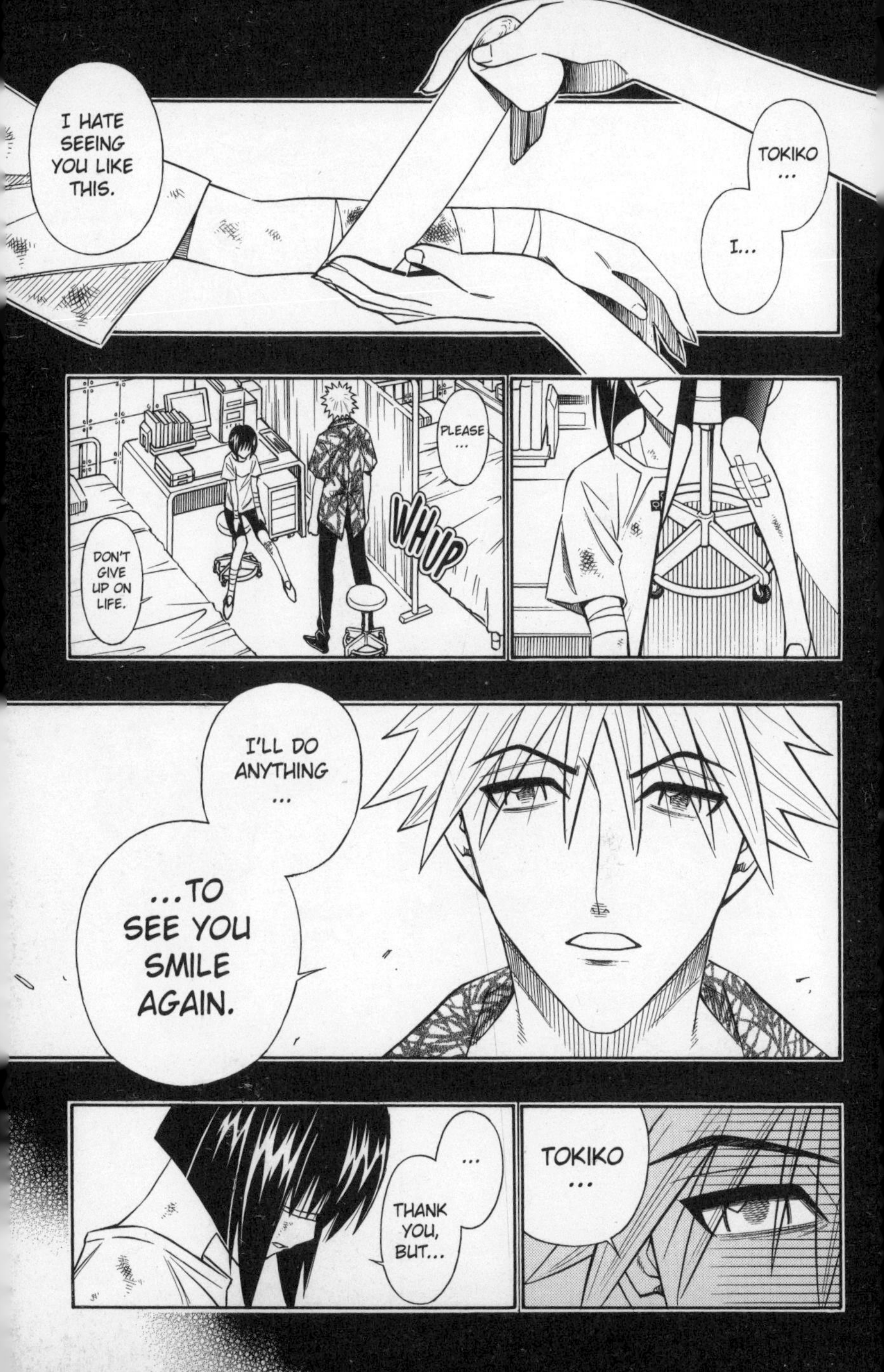
TOKIKO ... I...
I HATE SEEING YOU LIKE THIS.
PLEASE ...
WHUP
DON'T GIVE UP ON LIFE.
I'LL DO ANYTHING ...
...TO SEE YOU SMILE AGAIN.
TOKIKO ...
... THANK YOU, BUT...

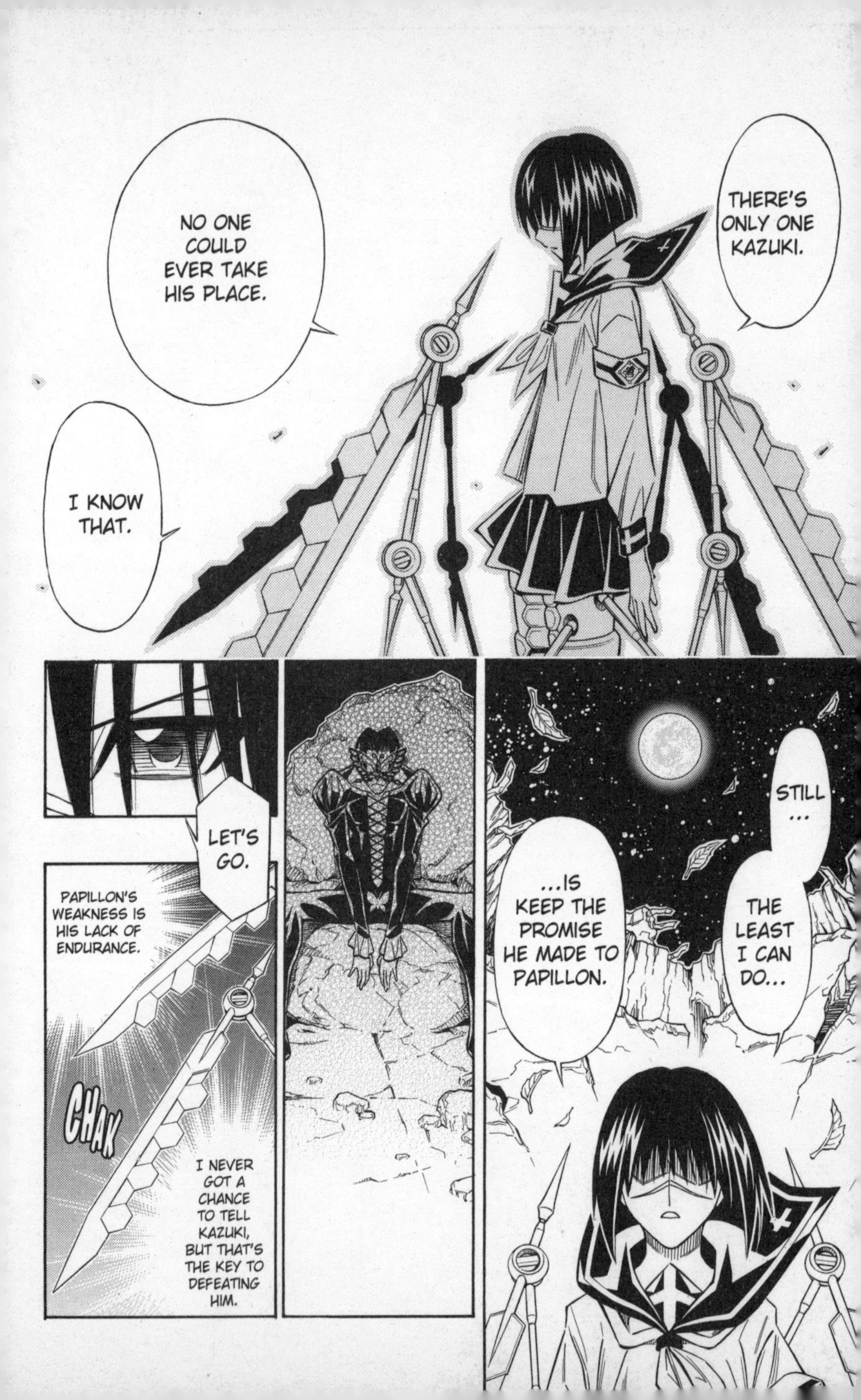
THERE'S ONLY ONE KAZUKI.
NO ONE COULD EVER TAKE HIS PLACE.
I KNOW THAT.
STILL...
THE LEAST I CAN DO...
...IS KEEP THE PROMISE HE MADE TO PAPILLON.
LET'S GO.
PAPILLON'S WEAKNESS IS HIS LACK OF ENDURANCE.
CHAK
I NEVER GOT A CHANCE TO TELL KAZUKI, BUT THAT'S THE KEY TO DEFEATING HIM.

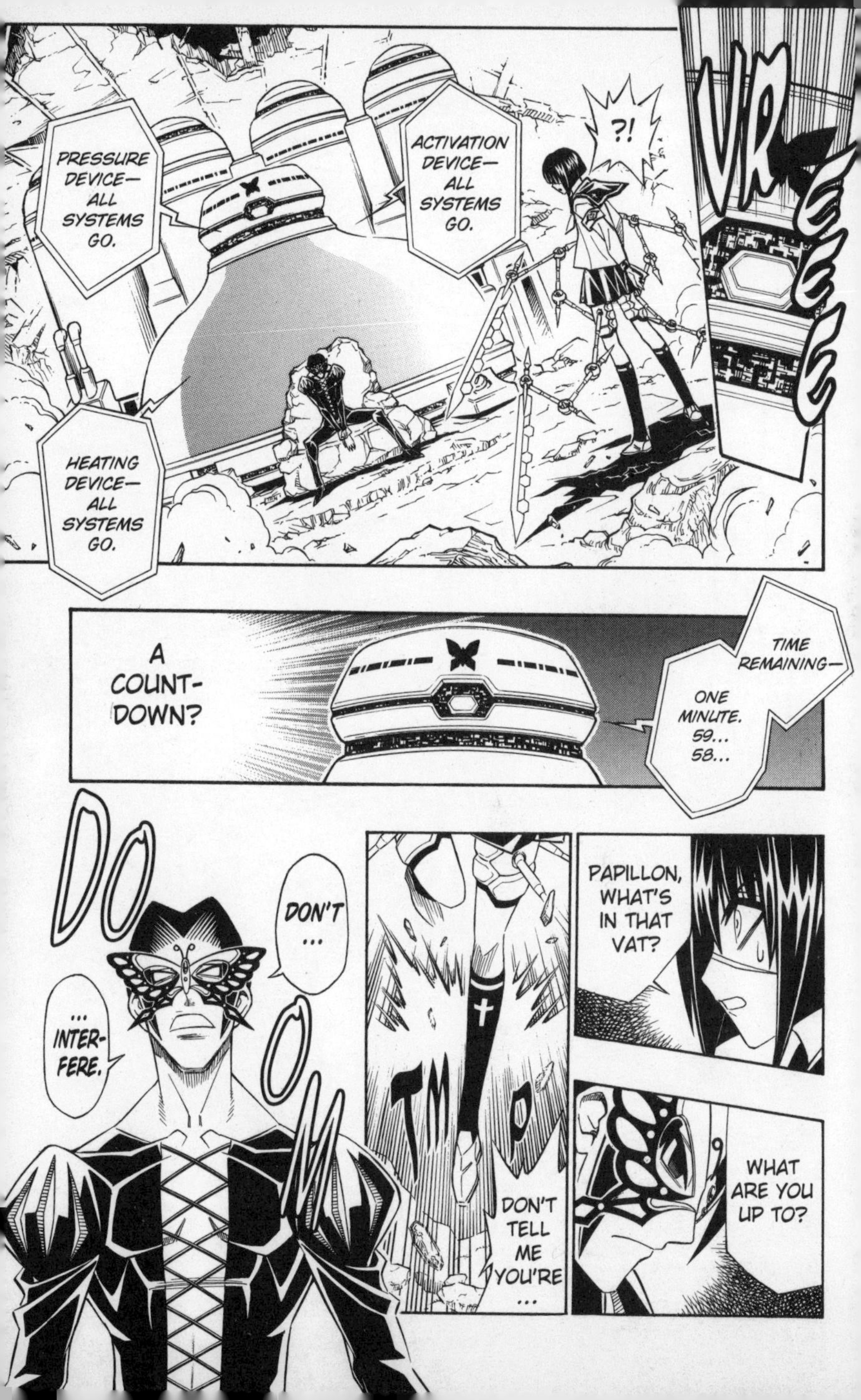
VREEEE
?!
ACTIVATION DEVICE—ALL SYSTEMS GO.
PRESSURE DEVICE—ALL SYSTEMS GO.
HEATING DEVICE—ALL SYSTEMS GO.
TIME REMAINING—
ONE MINUTE. 59... 58...
A COUNT-DOWN?
PAPILLON, WHAT'S IN THAT VAT?
WHAT ARE YOU UP TO?
TMP
DON'T TELL ME YOU'RE ...
DOOM
DON'T ...
... INTER-FERE.

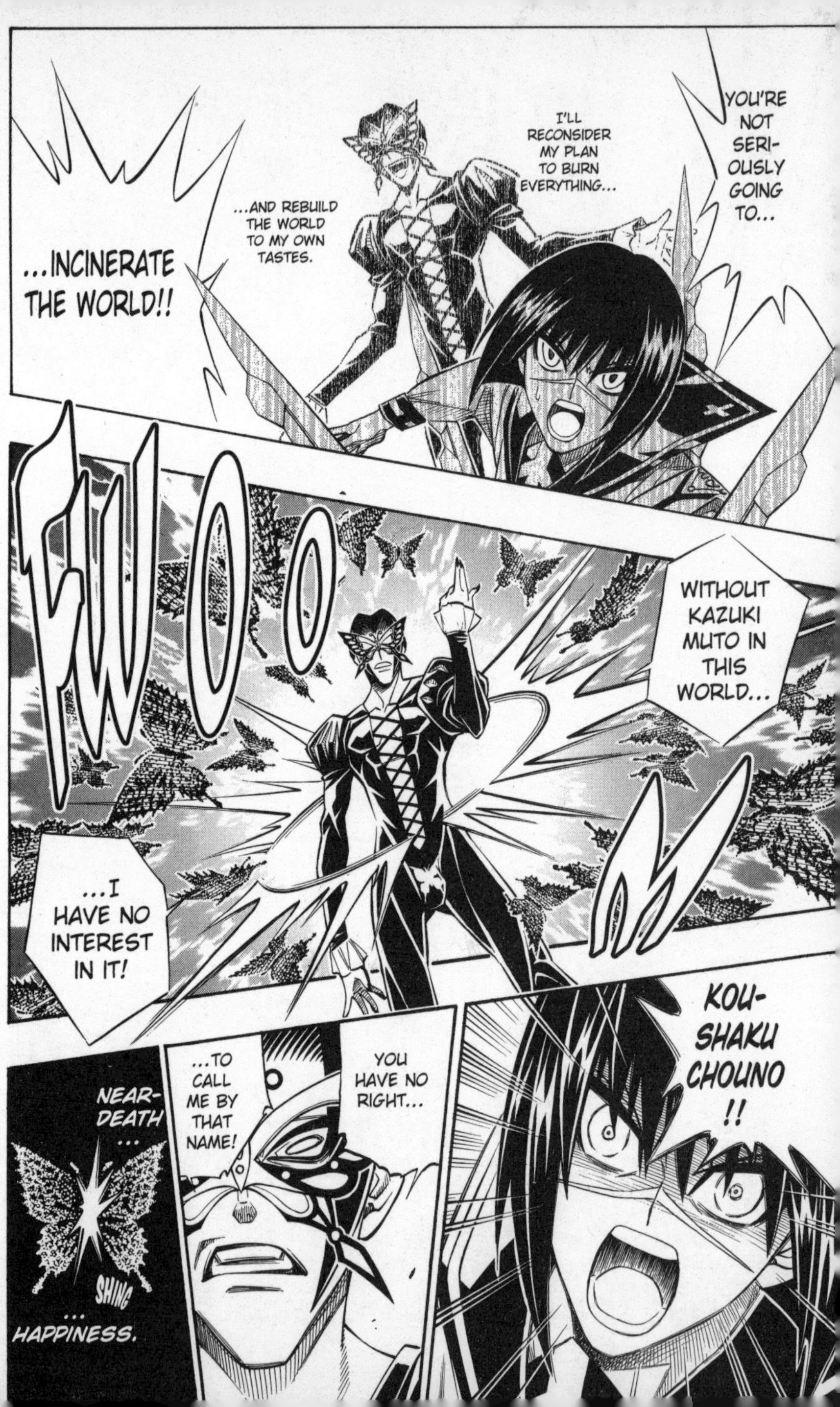
YOU'RE NOT SERI-OUSLY GOING TO...
I'LL RECONSIDER MY PLAN TO BURN EVERYTHING...
...AND REBUILD THE WORLD TO MY OWN TASTES.
...INCINERATE THE WORLD!!
WITHOUT KAZUKI MUTO IN THIS WORLD...
FWOOO
...I HAVE NO INTEREST IN IT!
KOU-SHAKU CHOUNO !!
YOU HAVE NO RIGHT...
...TO CALL ME BY THAT NAME!
NEAR-DEATH...
SHING
...HAPPINESS.

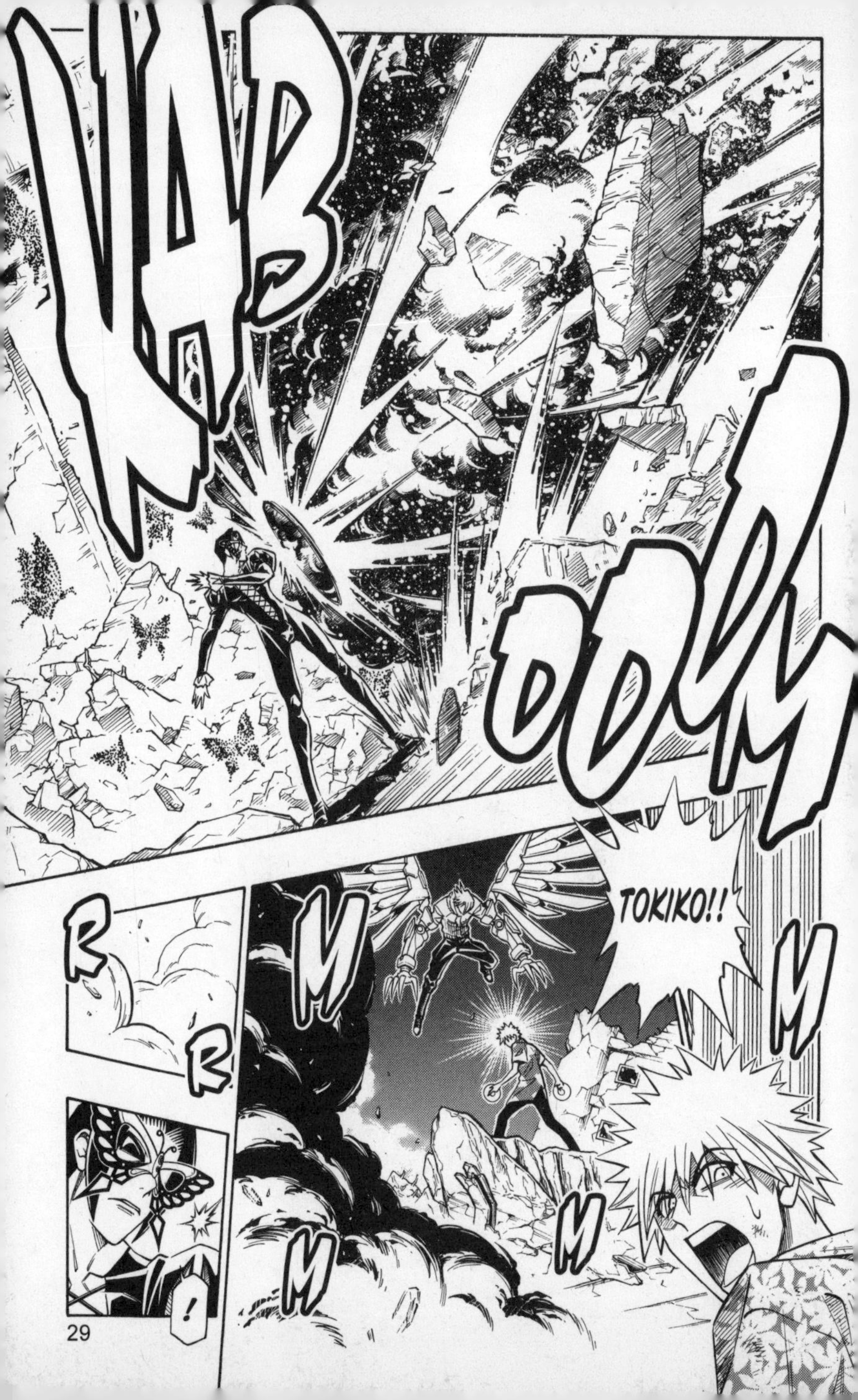
VABOOM
TOKIKO!!
MMMM
RR
!

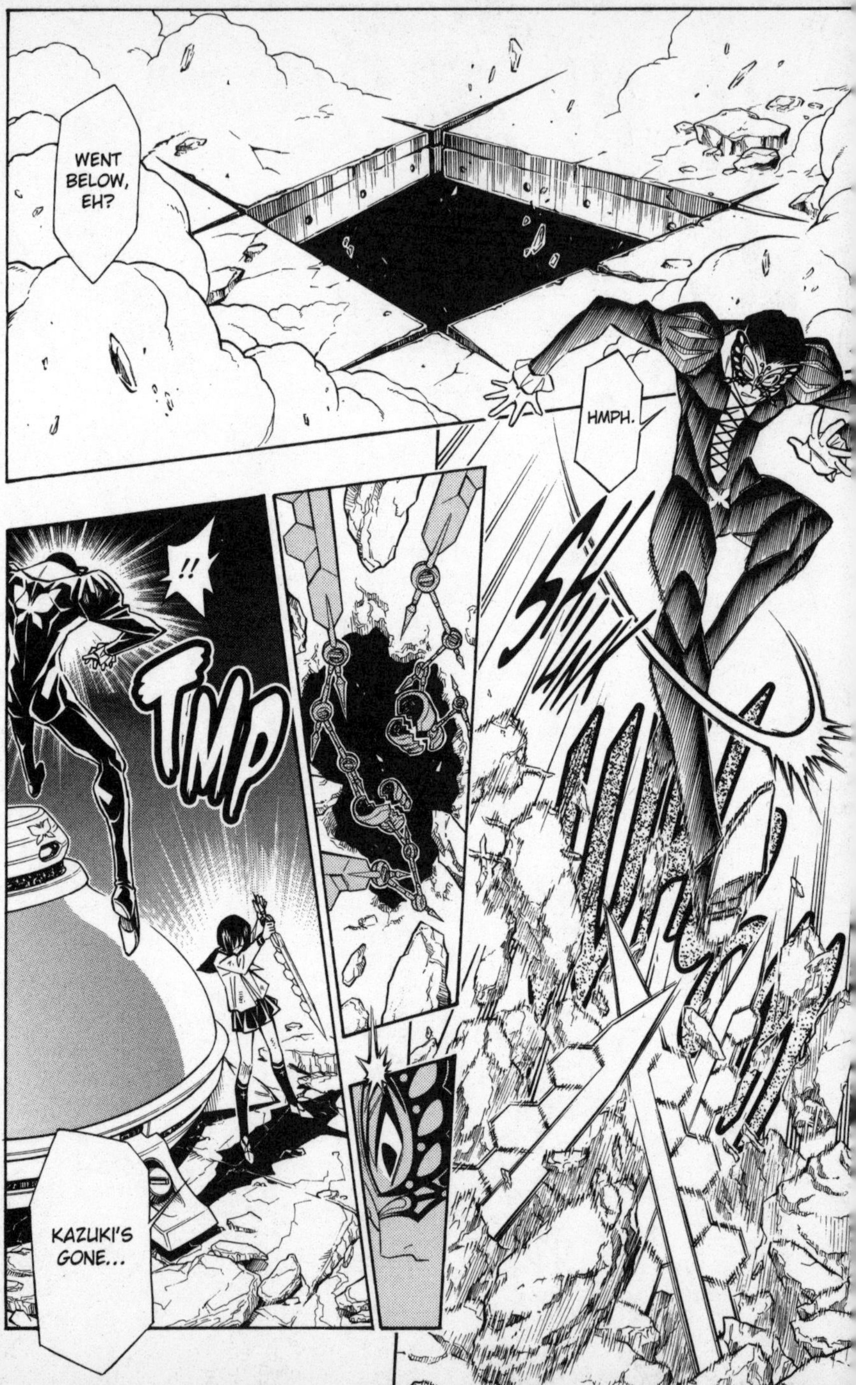
WENT BELOW, EH?
HMPH.
SHUNK
!!
TMP
KAZUKI'S GONE...

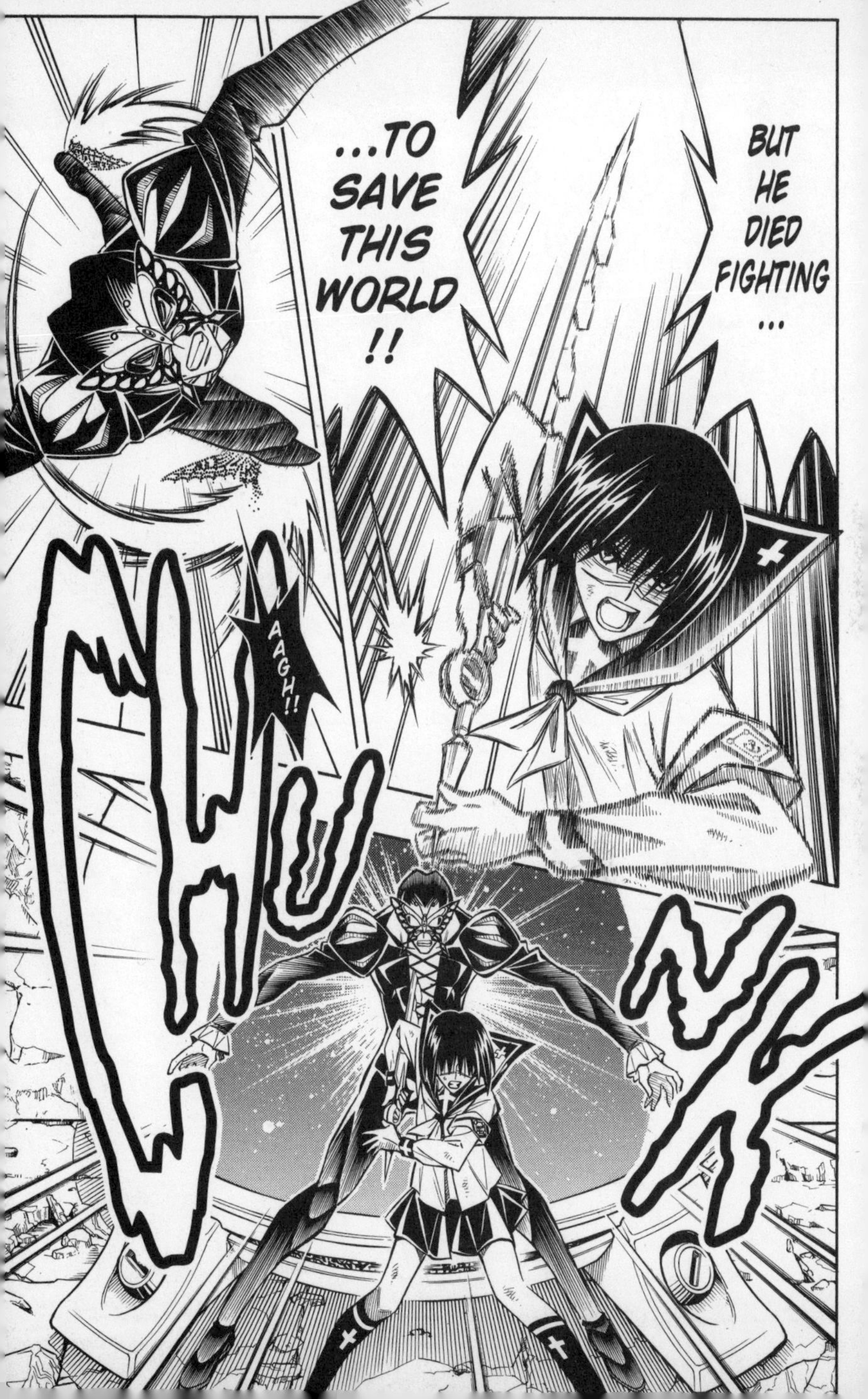
BUT HE DIED FIGHTING...
...TO SAVE THIS WORLD!!
AAGH!!
CHUNK

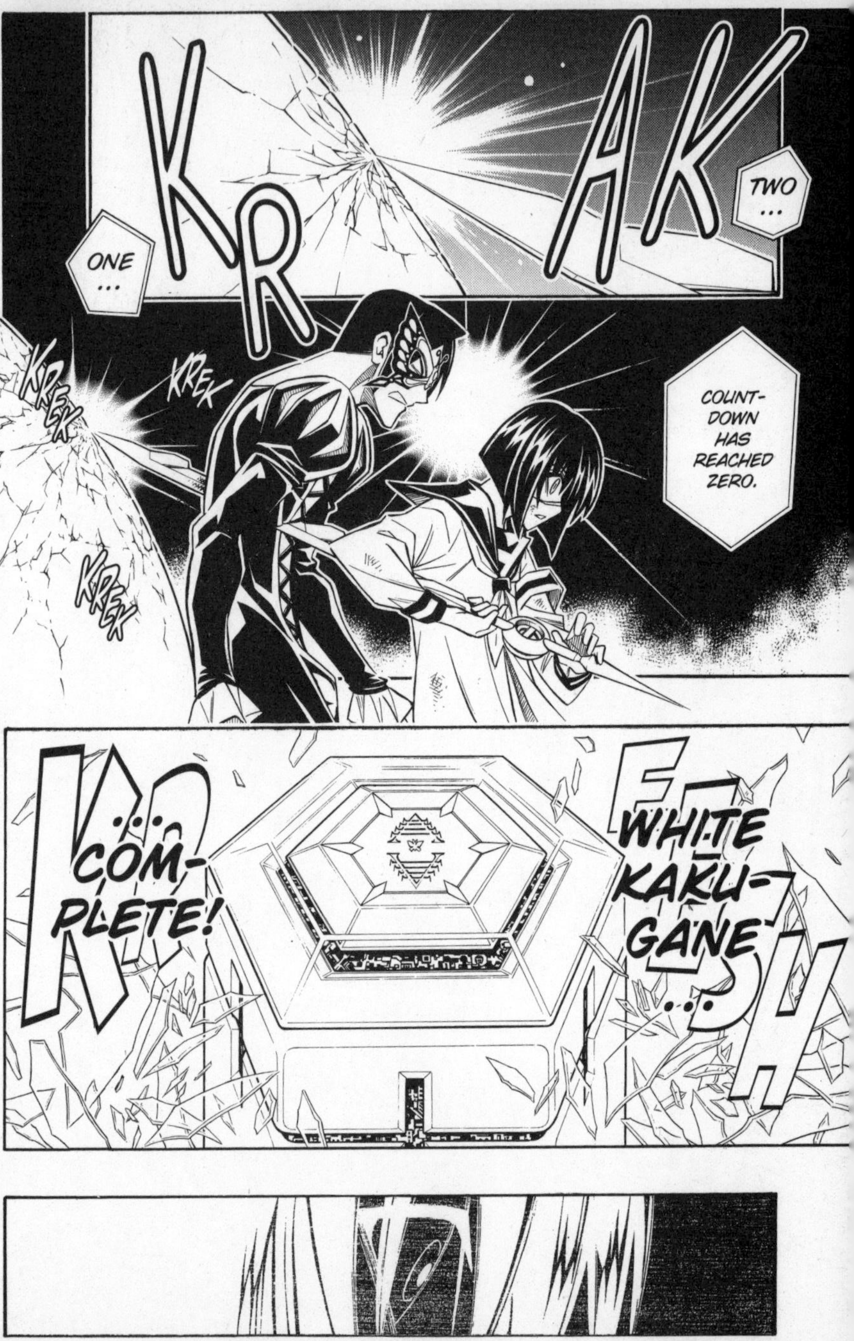
TWO ...
KRAK
ONE ...
COUNT-DOWN HAS REACHED ZERO.
KREK
KREK
KREK
WHITE KAKU-GANE ...
... COM-PLETE!

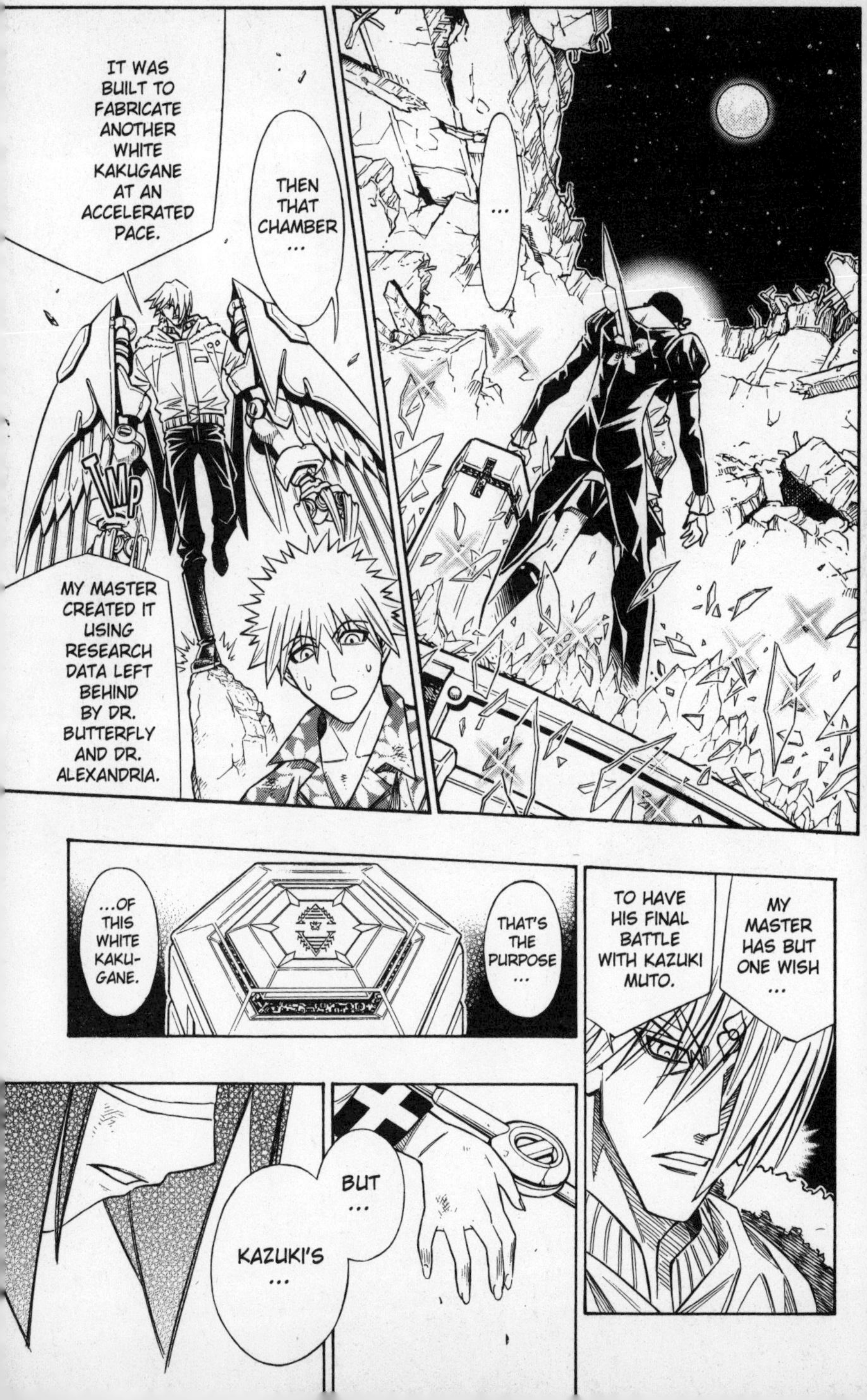
...
THEN THAT CHAMBER ...
IT WAS BUILT TO FABRICATE ANOTHER WHITE KAKUGANE AT AN ACCELERATED PACE.
MY MASTER CREATED IT USING RESEARCH DATA LEFT BEHIND BY DR. BUTTERFLY AND DR. ALEXANDRIA.
MY MASTER HAS BUT ONE WISH ...
TO HAVE HIS FINAL BATTLE WITH KAZUKI MUTO.
THAT'S THE PURPOSE ...
...OF THIS WHITE KAKU-GANE.
BUT ...
KAZUKI'S ...

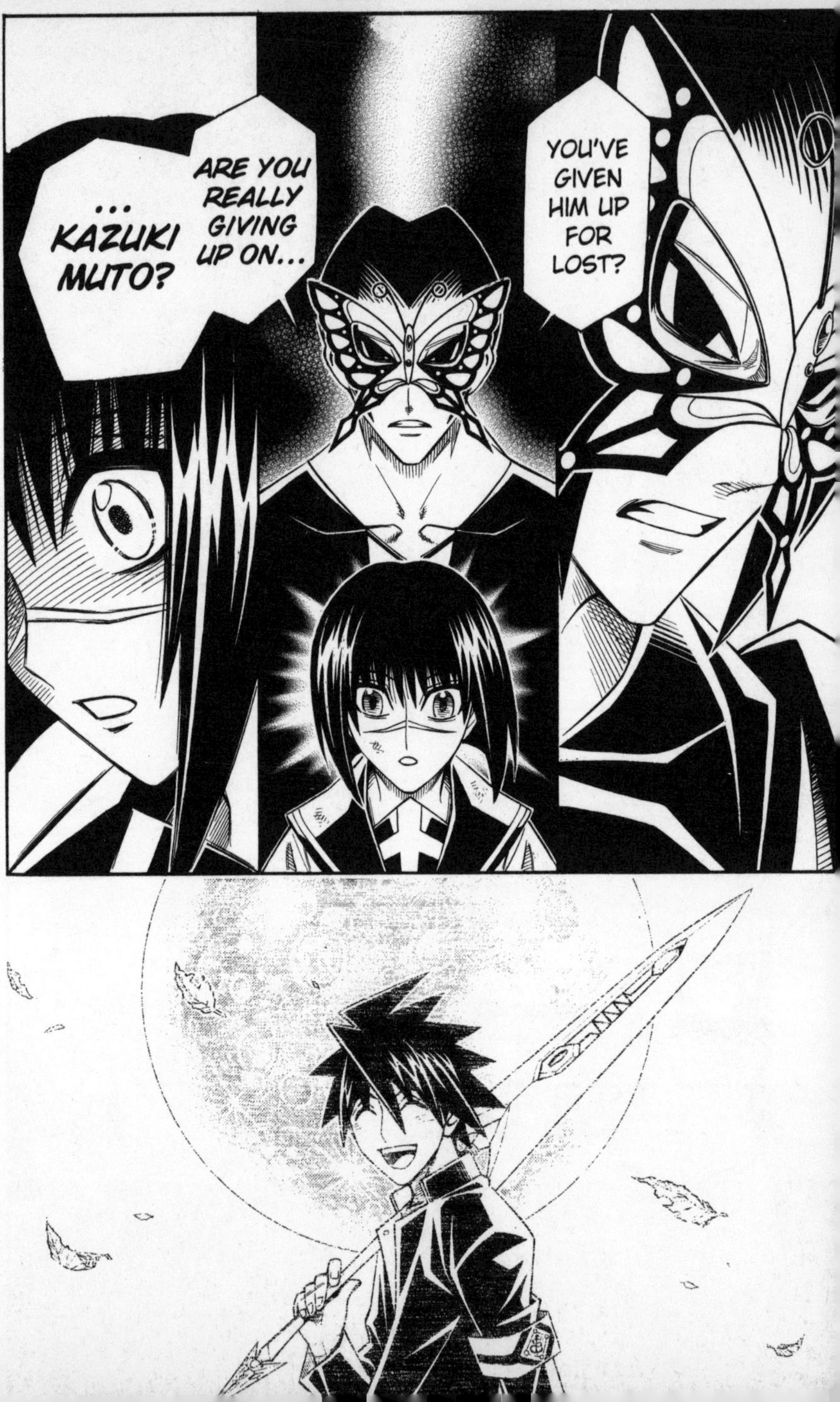
YOU'VE GIVEN HIM UP FOR LOST?
ARE YOU REALLY GIVING UP ON...
... KAZUKI MUTO?

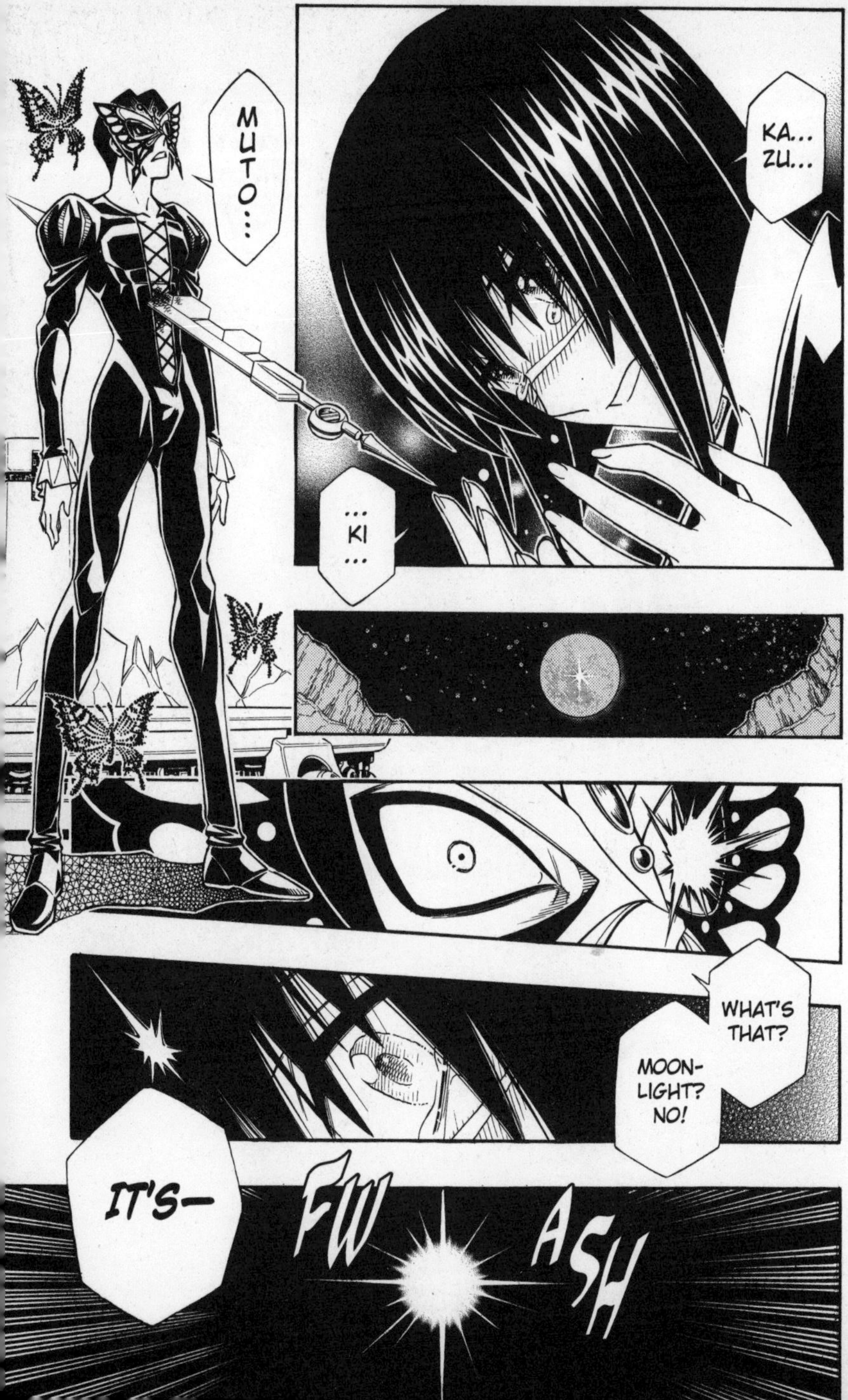
KA... ZU...
...KI...
MUTO...
WHAT'S THAT?
MOON-LIGHT? NO!
IT'S—
FWASH

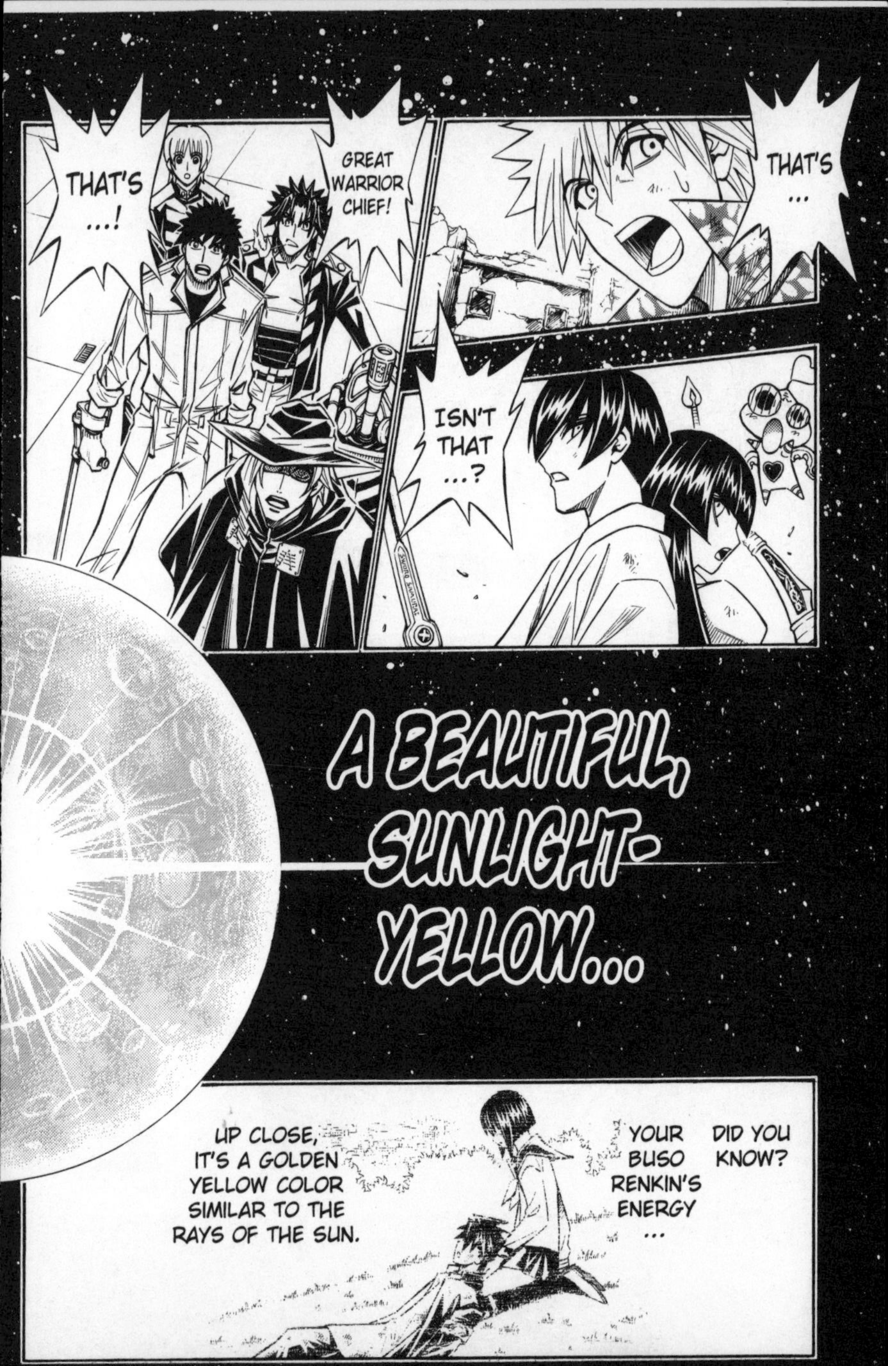
THAT'S ...
ISN'T THAT ...?
GREAT WARRIOR CHIEF!
THAT'S ...!
A BEAUTIFUL, SUNLIGHT-YELLOW...
DID YOU KNOW?
YOUR BUSO RENKIN'S ENERGY ...
UP CLOSE, IT'S A GOLDEN YELLOW COLOR SIMILAR TO THE RAYS OF THE SUN.

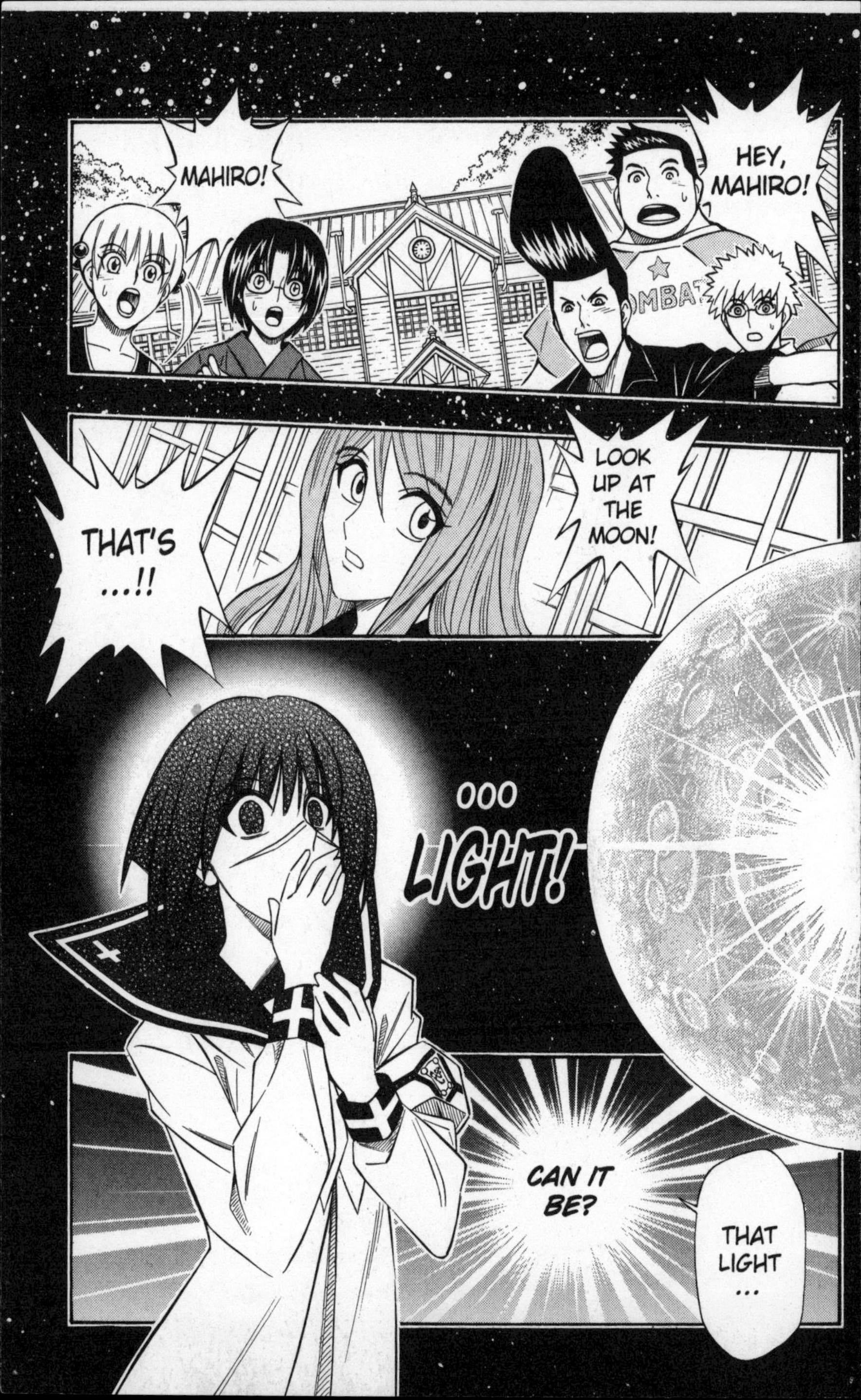
HEY, MAHIRO!
MAHIRO!
LOOK UP AT THE MOON!
THAT'S ...!!
OOO
LIGHT!
THAT LIGHT ...
CAN IT BE?

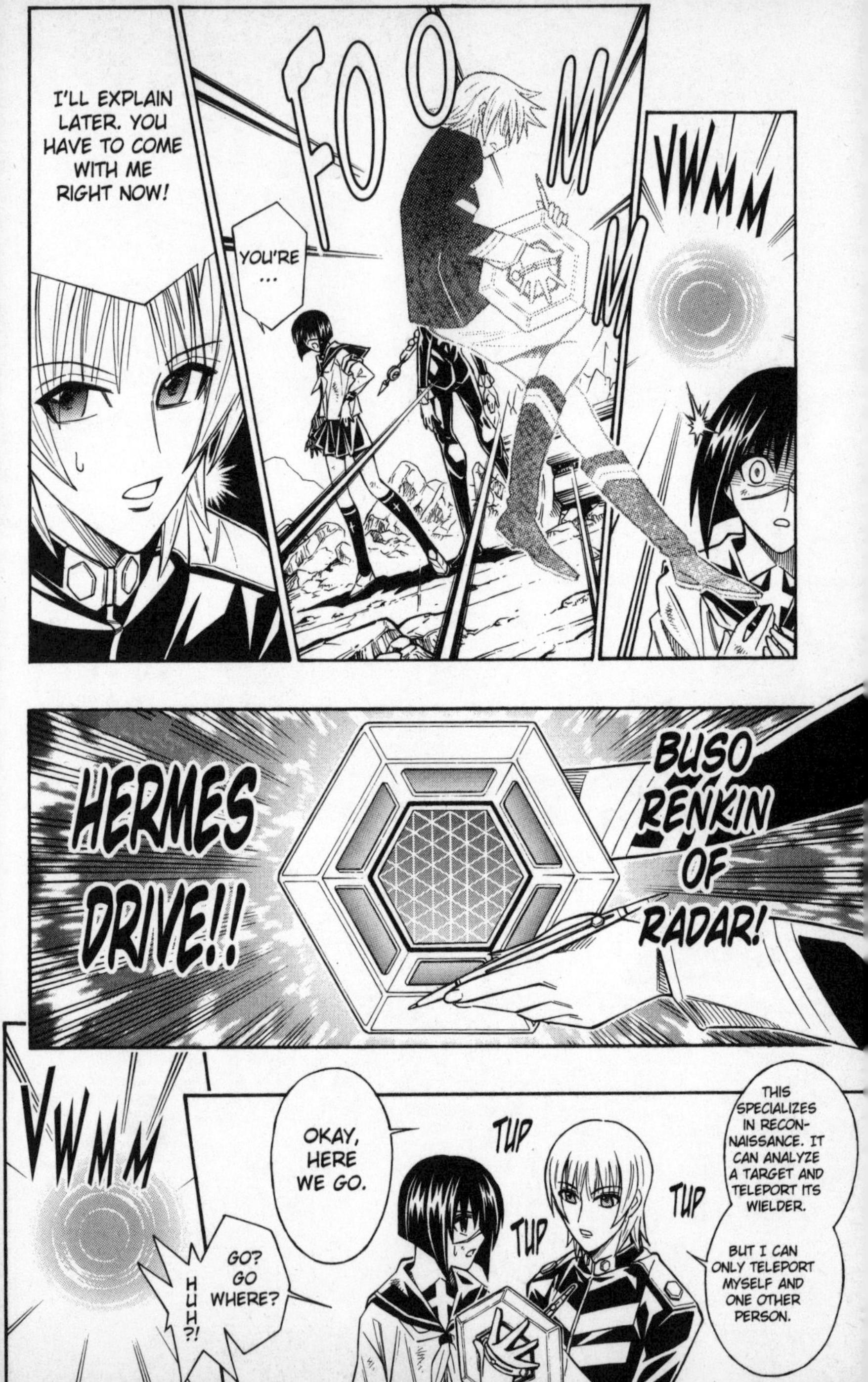
VWMM
FOOMMM
YOU'RE ...
I'LL EXPLAIN LATER. YOU HAVE TO COME WITH ME RIGHT NOW!
BUSO RENKIN OF RADAR!
HERMES DRIVE!!
THIS SPECIALIZES IN RECON-NAISSANCE. IT CAN ANALYZE A TARGET AND TELEPORT ITS WIELDER.
BUT I CAN ONLY TELEPORT MYSELF AND ONE OTHER PERSON.
TUP
TUP
TUP
OKAY, HERE WE GO.
GO? GO WHERE?
HUH?!
VWMM

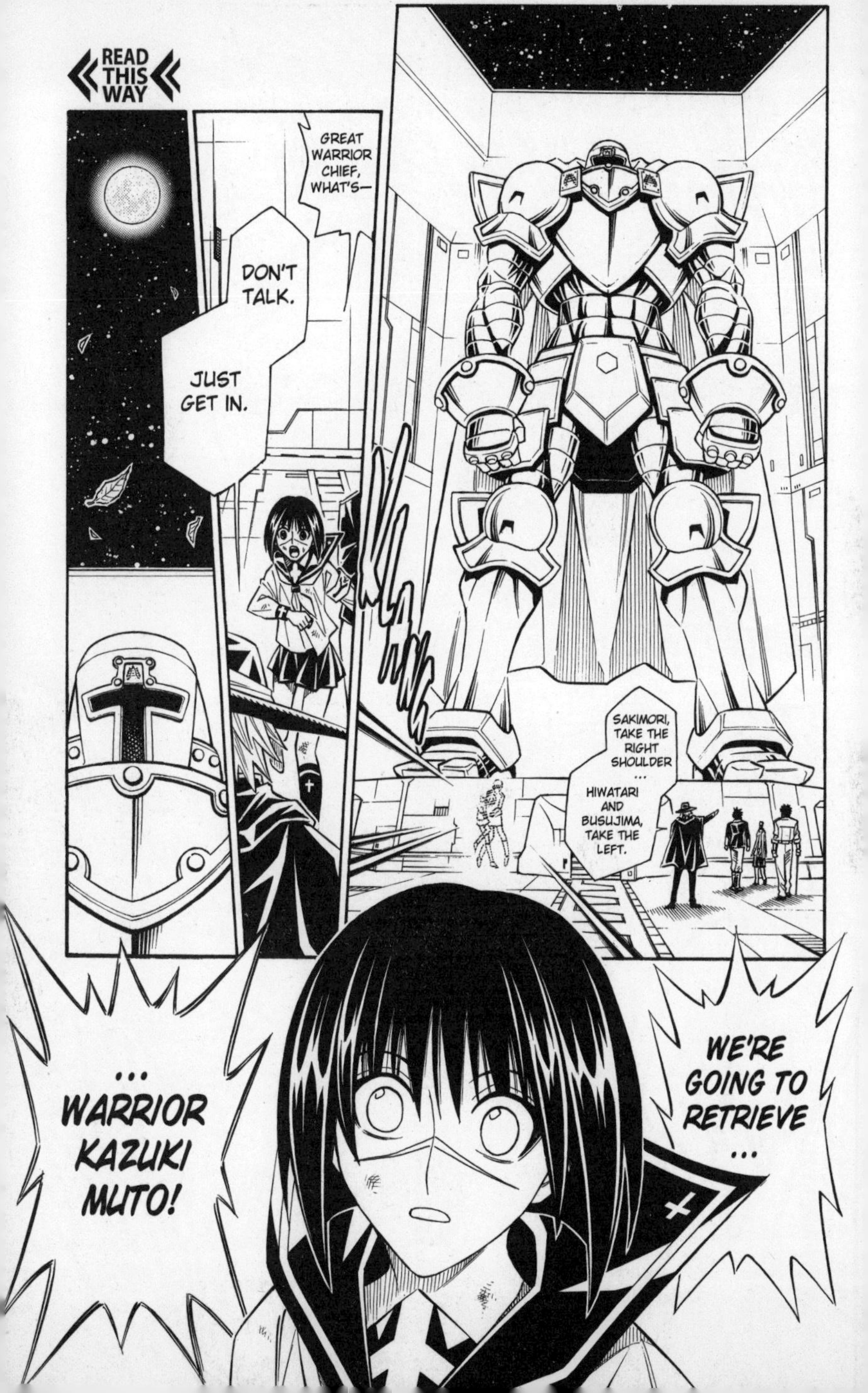
READ THIS WAY
SAKIMORI, TAKE THE RIGHT SHOULDER ...
HIWATARI AND BUSUJIMA, TAKE THE LEFT.
GREAT WARRIOR CHIEF, WHAT'S—
DON'T TALK.
JUST GET IN.
WE'RE GOING TO RETRIEVE ...
... WARRIOR KAZUKI MUTO!

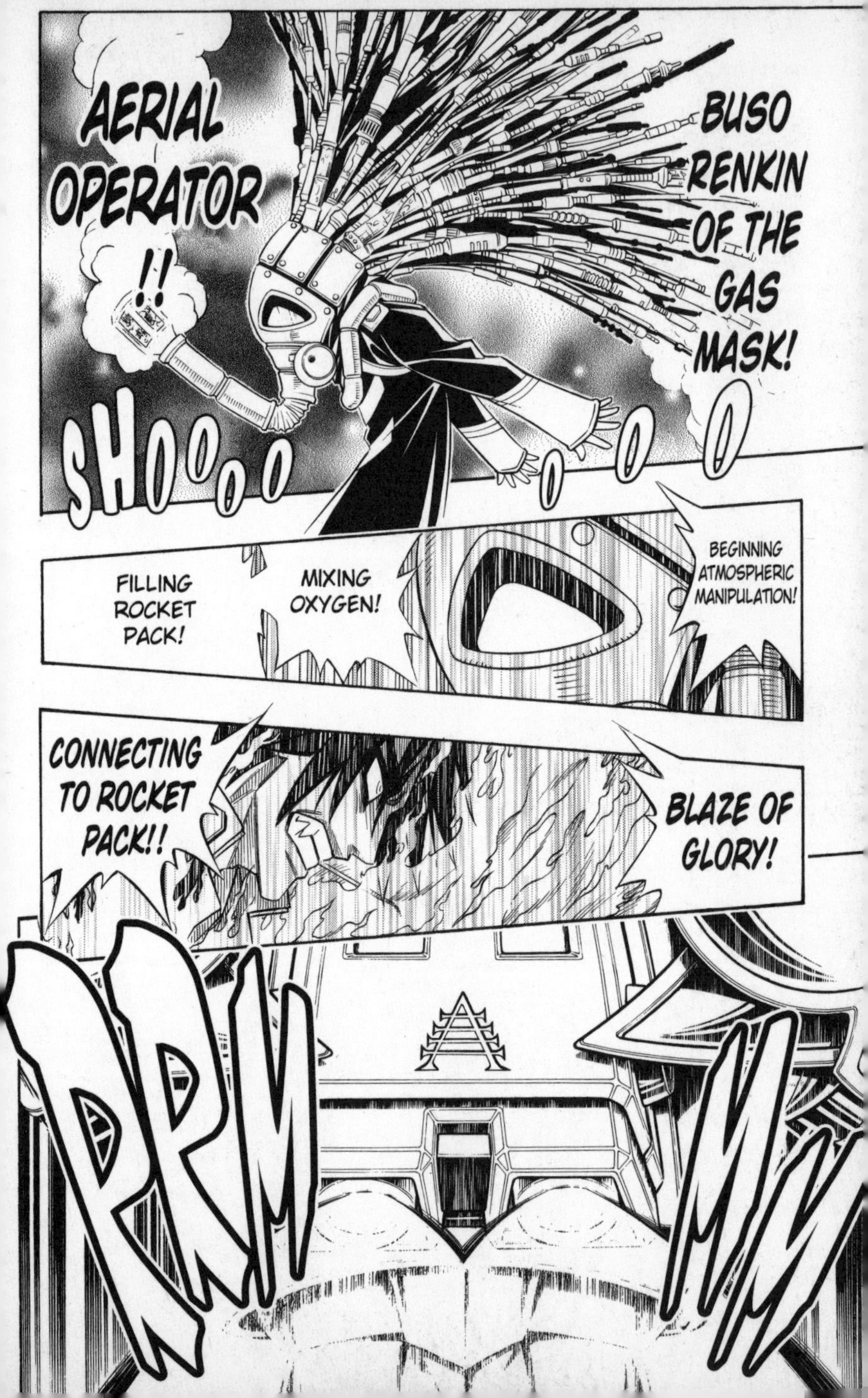
BUSO RENKIN OF THE GAS MASK!
AERIAL OPERATOR !!
SHOOOOOOOO
BEGINNING ATMOSPHERIC MANIPULATION!
MIXING OXYGEN!
FILLING ROCKET PACK!
BLAZE OF GLORY!
CONNECTING TO ROCKET PACK!!
BRMMMM

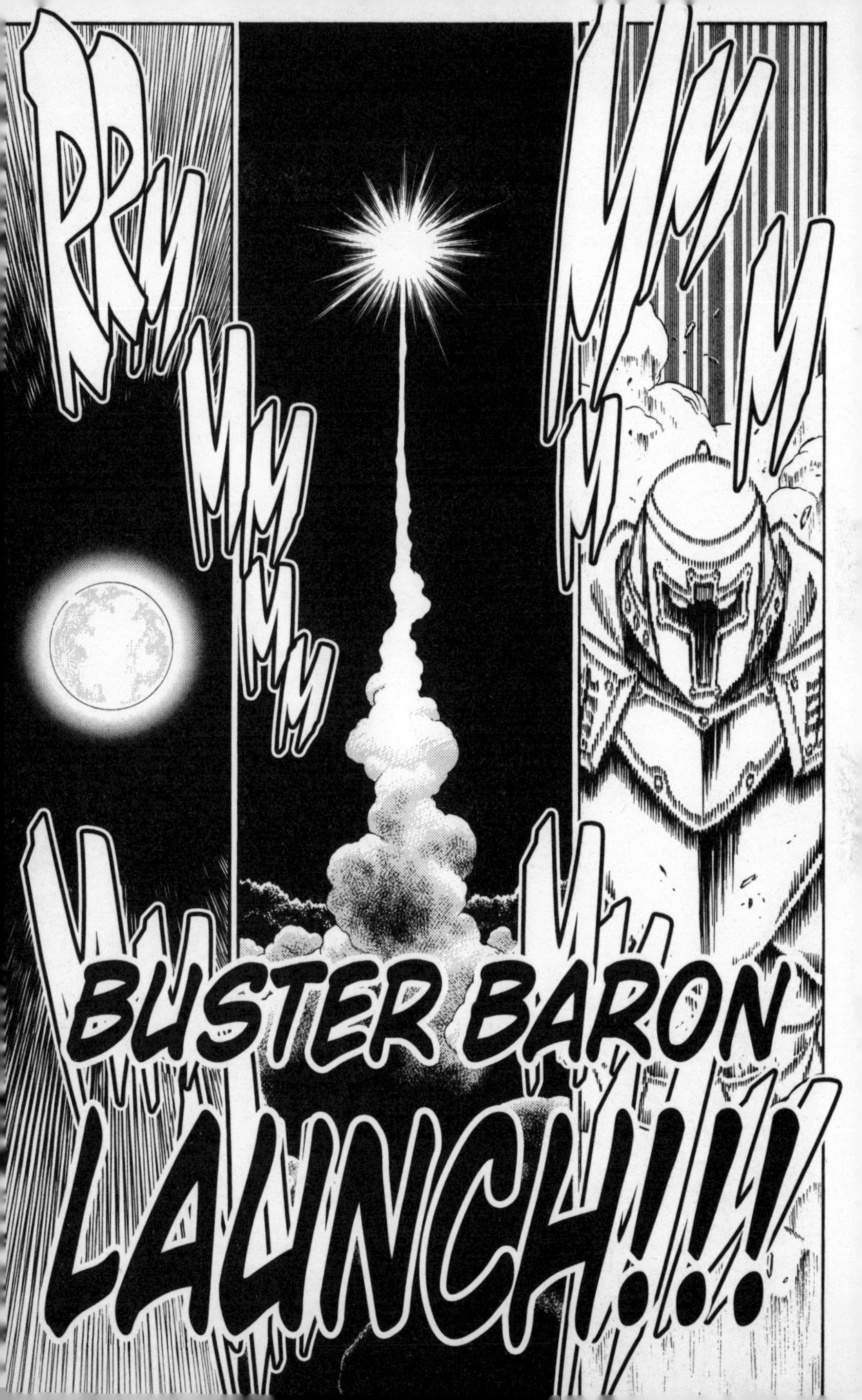
BUSTER BARON
LAUNCH!!!

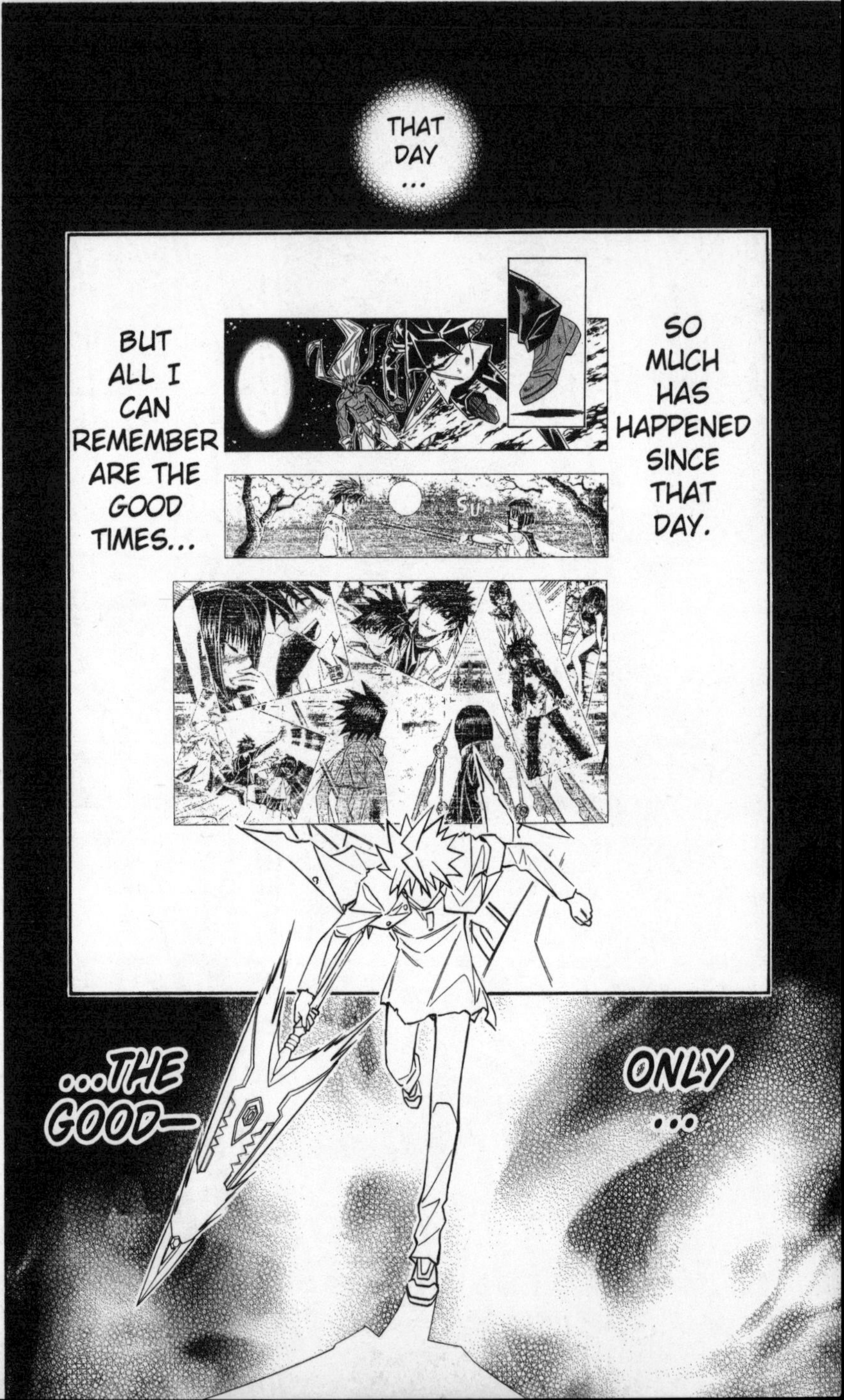
THAT DAY ...
SO MUCH HAS HAPPENED SINCE THAT DAY.
BUT ALL I CAN REMEMBER ARE THE GOOD TIMES...
SU
ONLY ...
...THE GOOD—

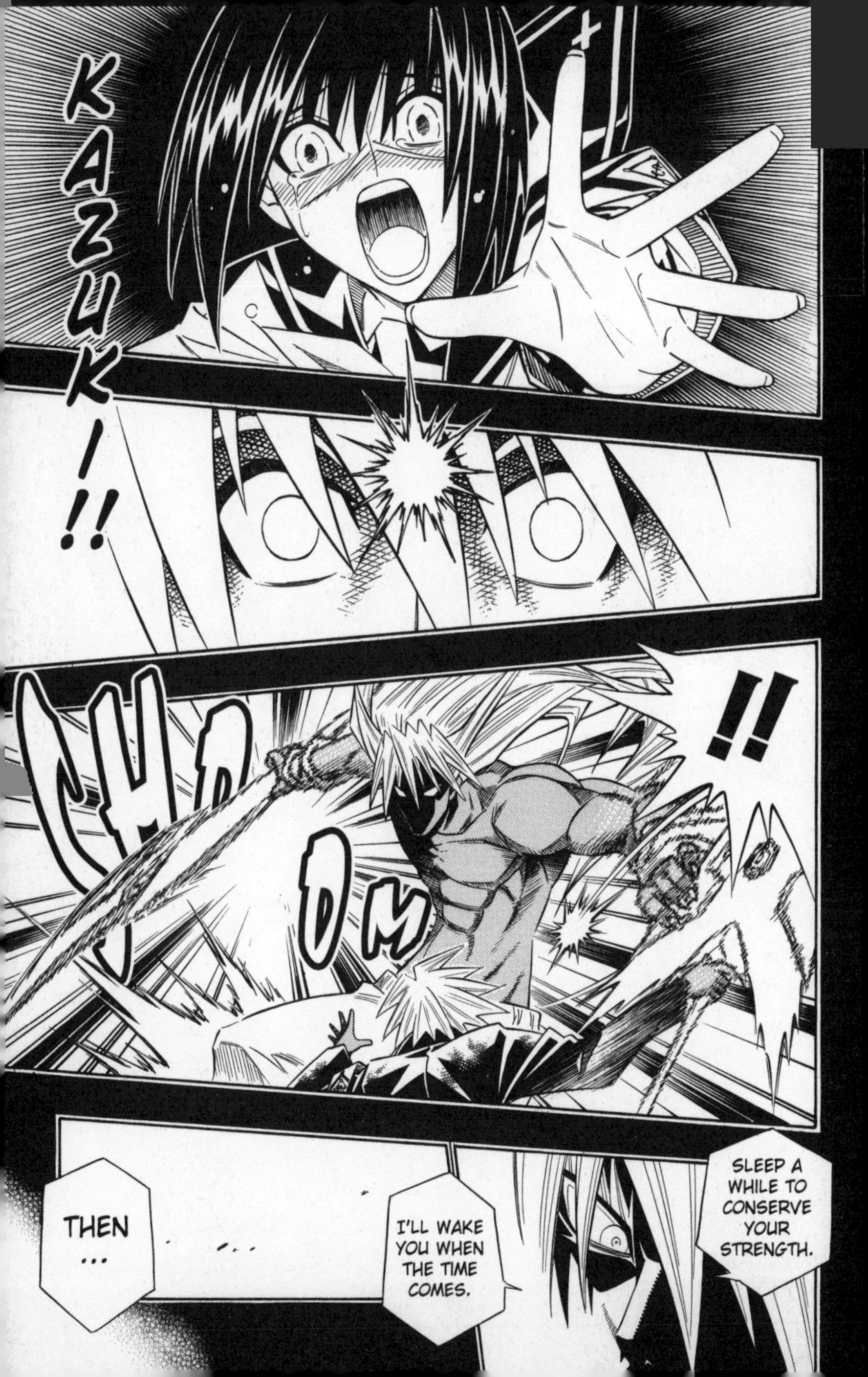
KAZUKI!!
CHOOM
!!
SLEEP A WHILE TO CONSERVE YOUR STRENGTH.
I'LL WAKE YOU WHEN THE TIME COMES.
THEN ...
...

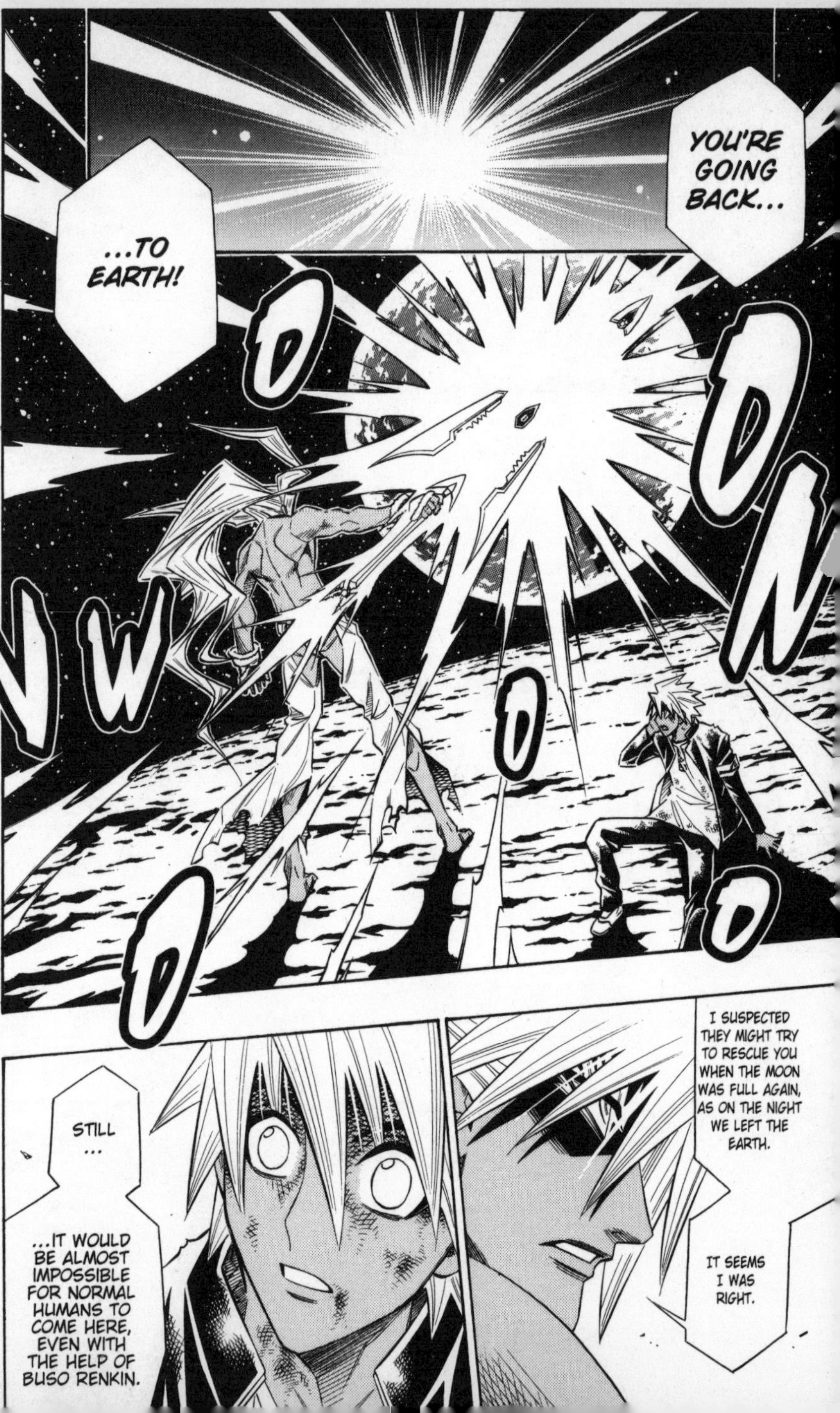
YOU'RE GOING BACK...
...TO EARTH!
I SUSPECTED THEY MIGHT TRY TO RESCUE YOU WHEN THE MOON WAS FULL AGAIN, AS ON THE NIGHT WE LEFT THE EARTH.
IT SEEMS I WAS RIGHT.
STILL...
...IT WOULD BE ALMOST IMPOSSIBLE FOR NORMAL HUMANS TO COME HERE, EVEN WITH THE HELP OF BUSO RENKIN.

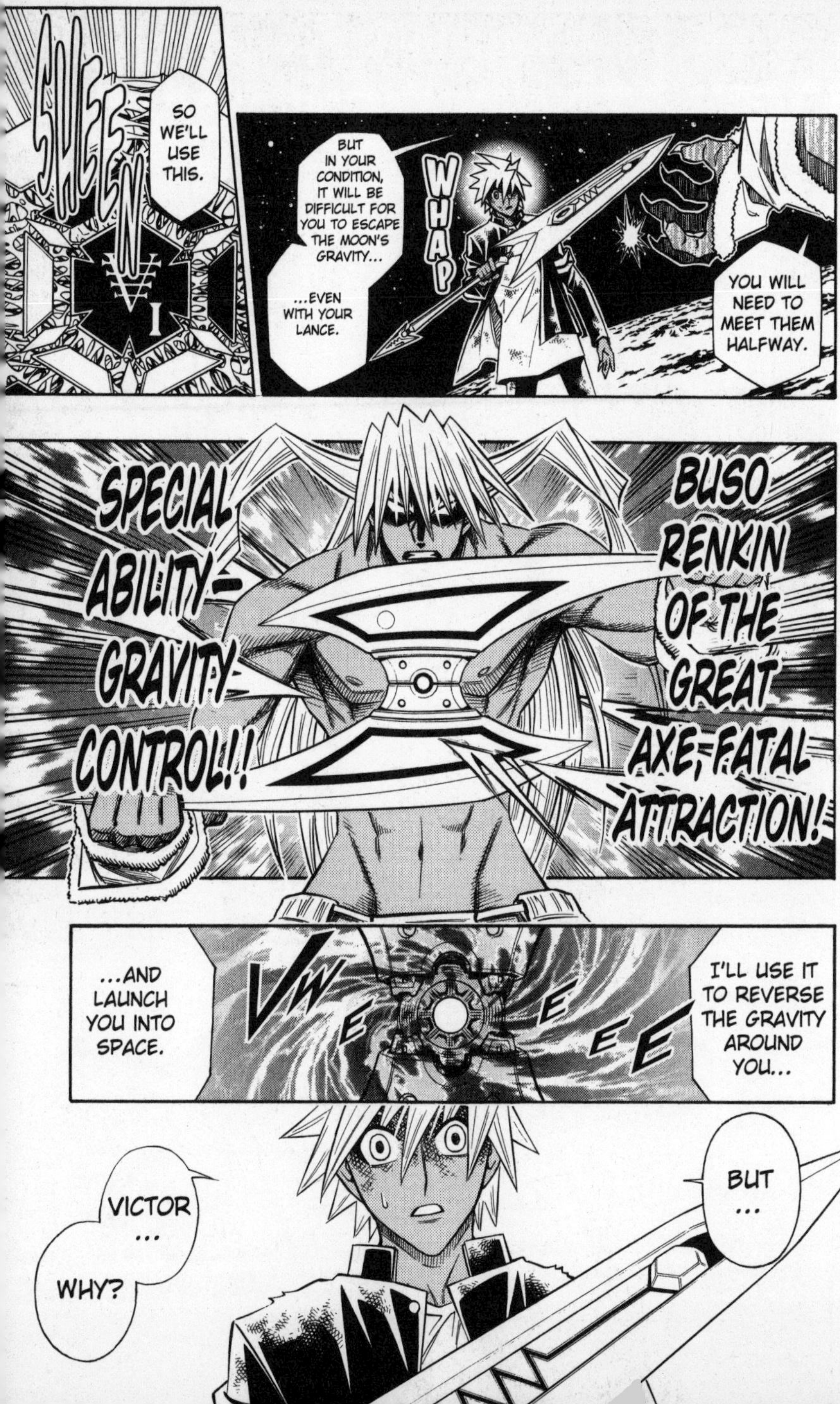

BUT IN YOUR CONDITION, IT WILL BE DIFFICULT FOR YOU TO ESCAPE THE MOON'S GRAVITY...
WHAP
...EVEN WITH YOUR LANCE.
YOU WILL NEED TO MEET THEM HALFWAY.
SHEEN
SO WE'LL USE THIS.
BUSO RENKIN OF THE GREAT AXE, FATAL ATTRACTION!
SPECIAL ABILITY- GRAVITY CONTROL!!
I'LL USE IT TO REVERSE THE GRAVITY AROUND YOU...
VWEEEEE
...AND LAUNCH YOU INTO SPACE.
BUT ...
VICTOR ...
WHY?

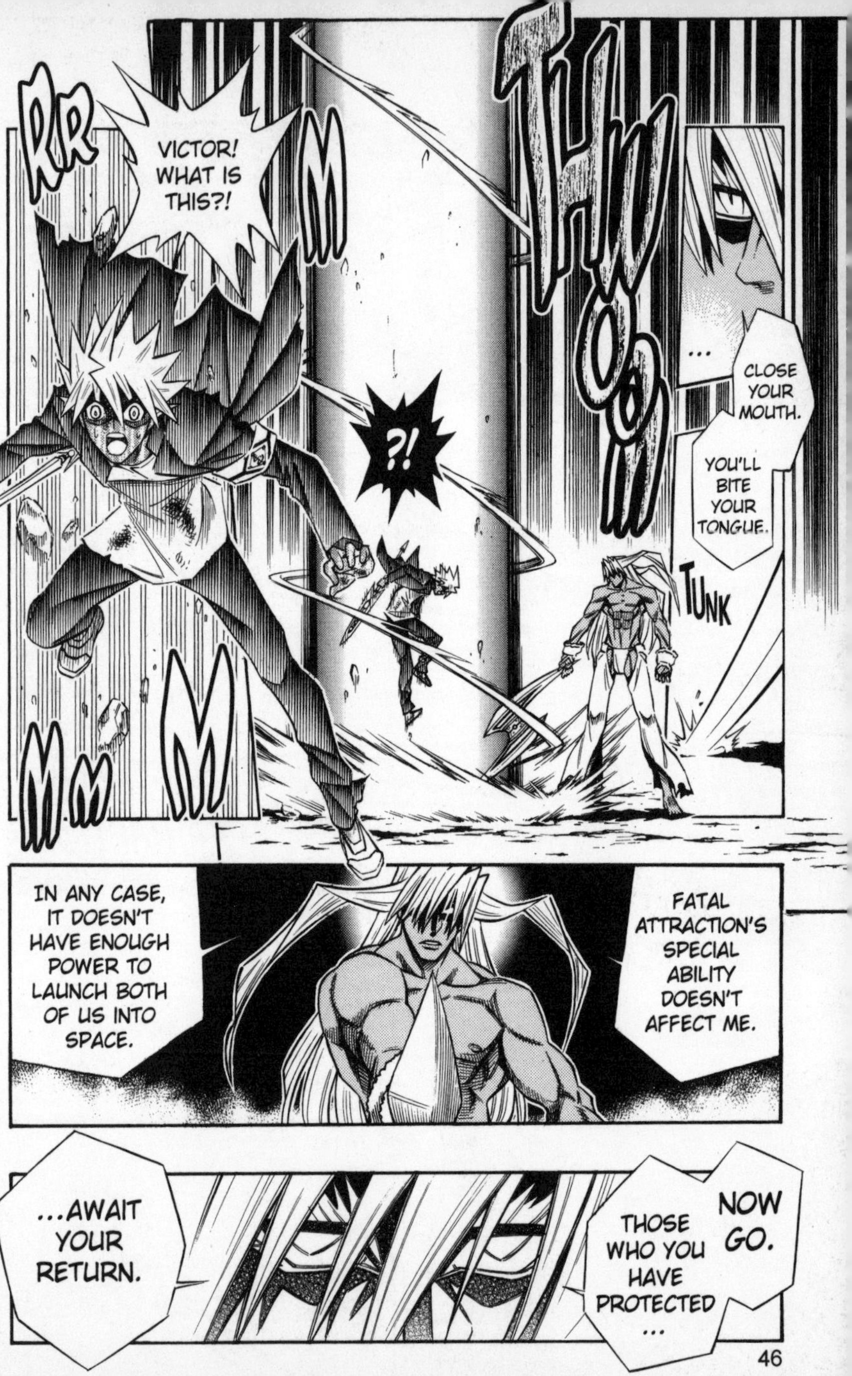
...
CLOSE YOUR MOUTH.
YOU'LL BITE YOUR TONGUE.
TUNK
?!
VICTOR! WHAT IS THIS?!
RRMMMMM
FATAL ATTRACTION'S SPECIAL ABILITY DOESN'T AFFECT ME.
IN ANY CASE, IT DOESN'T HAVE ENOUGH POWER TO LAUNCH BOTH OF US INTO SPACE.
NOW GO.
THOSE WHO YOU HAVE PROTECTED ...
...AWAIT YOUR RETURN.

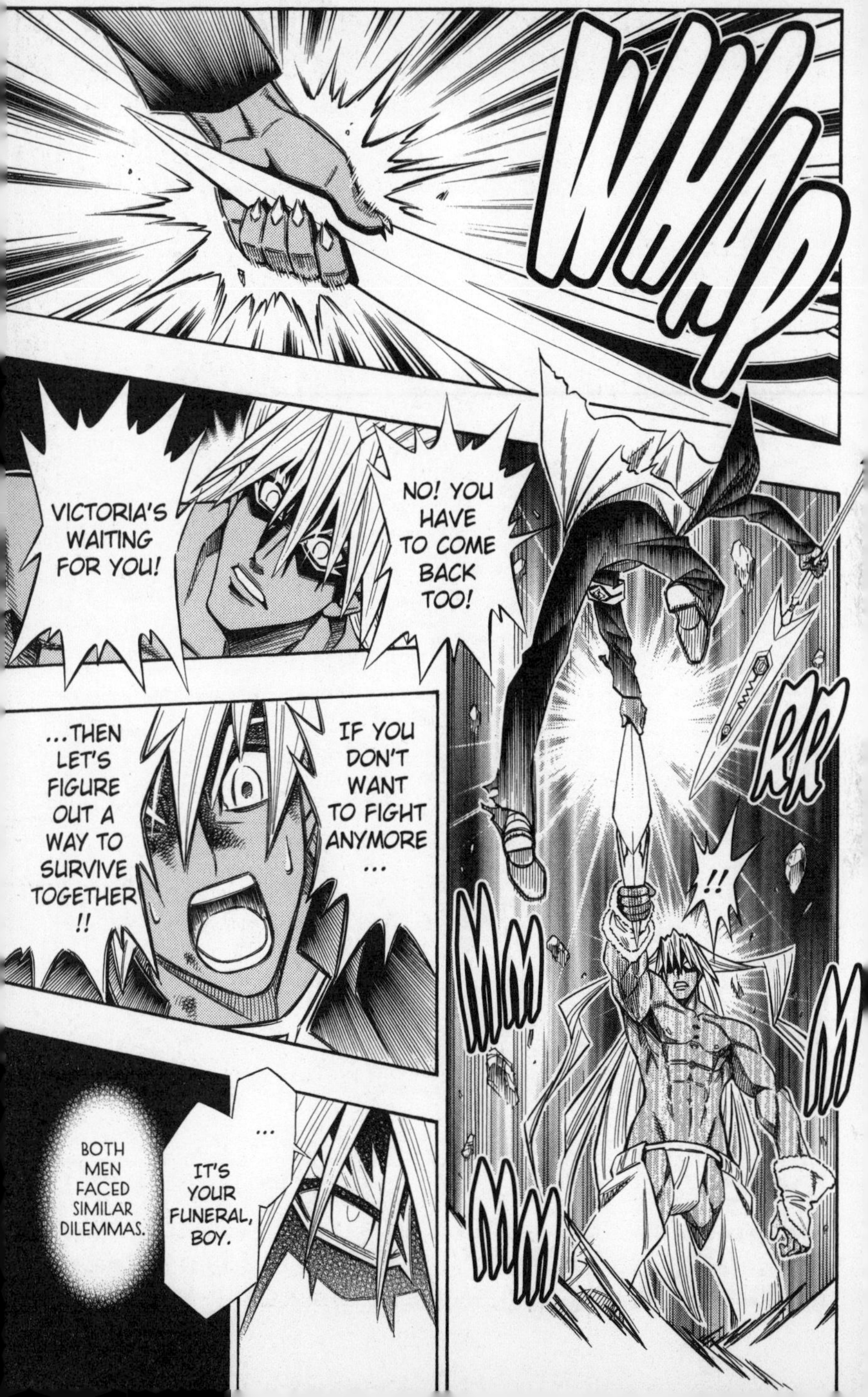
WHAP
!!
NO! YOU HAVE TO COME BACK TOO!
VICTORIA'S WAITING FOR YOU!
IF YOU DON'T WANT TO FIGHT ANYMORE...
...THEN LET'S FIGURE OUT A WAY TO SURVIVE TOGETHER!!
...
IT'S YOUR FUNERAL, BOY.
BOTH MEN FACED SIMILAR DILEMMAS.

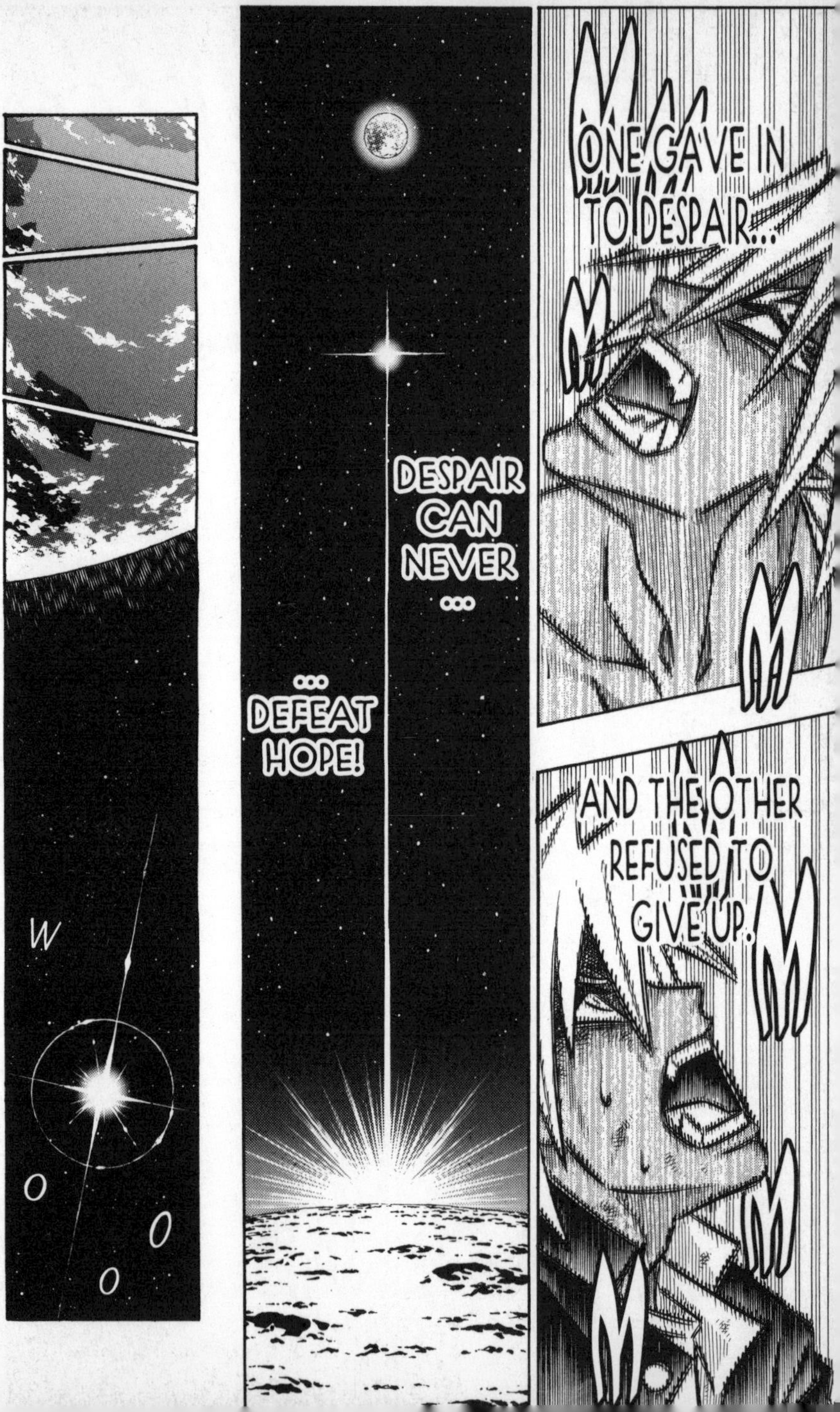

ONE GAVE IN TO DESPAIR...
AND THE OTHER REFUSED TO GIVE UP.
DESPAIR CAN NEVER ...
... DEFEAT HOPE!
W O O O

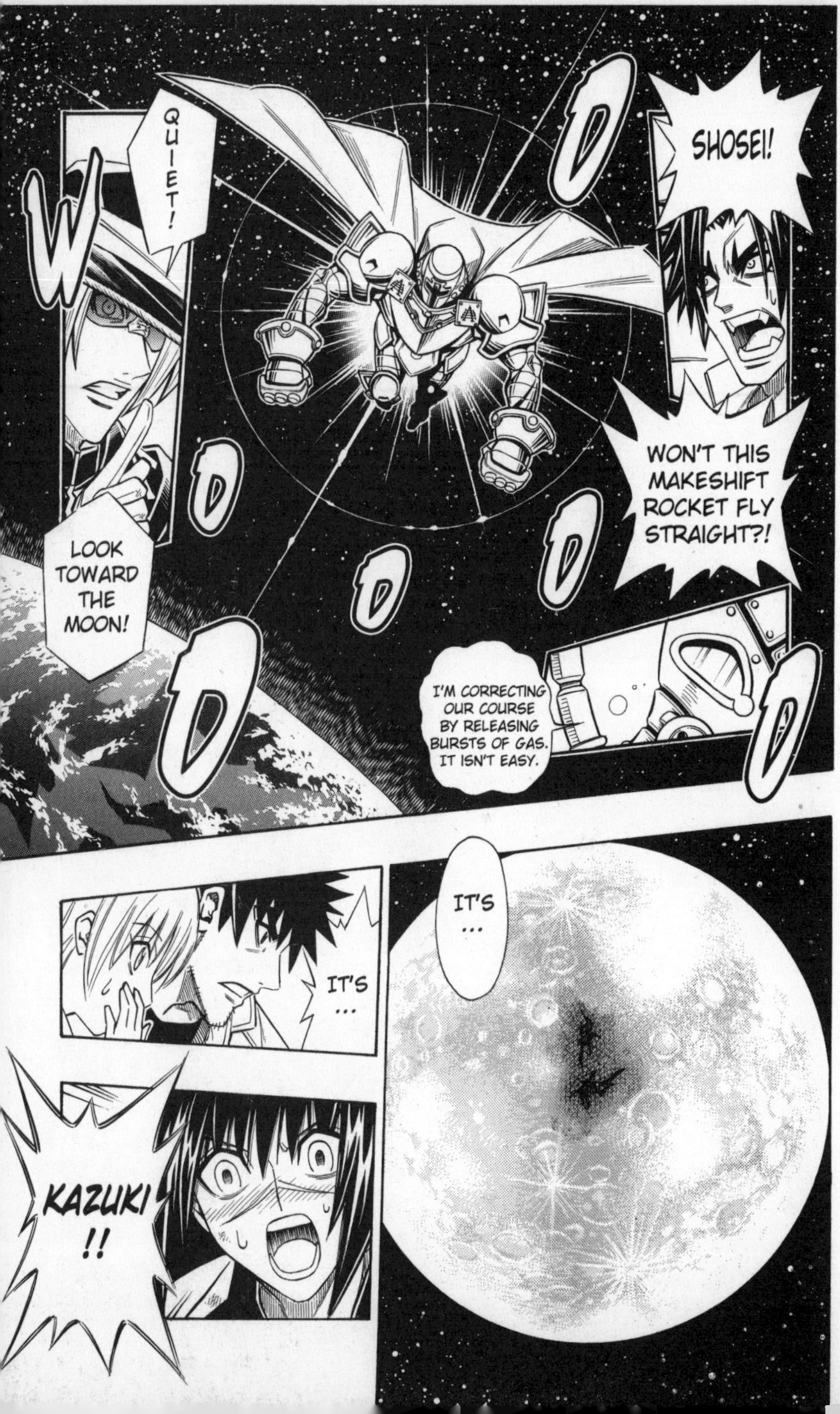
D
SHOSEI!
WON'T THIS MAKESHIFT ROCKET FLY STRAIGHT?!
D
I'M CORRECTING OUR COURSE BY RELEASING BURSTS OF GAS. IT ISN'T EASY.
D
D
D
D
QUIET!
W
LOOK TOWARD THE MOON!
IT'S ...
IT'S ...
KAZUKI!!

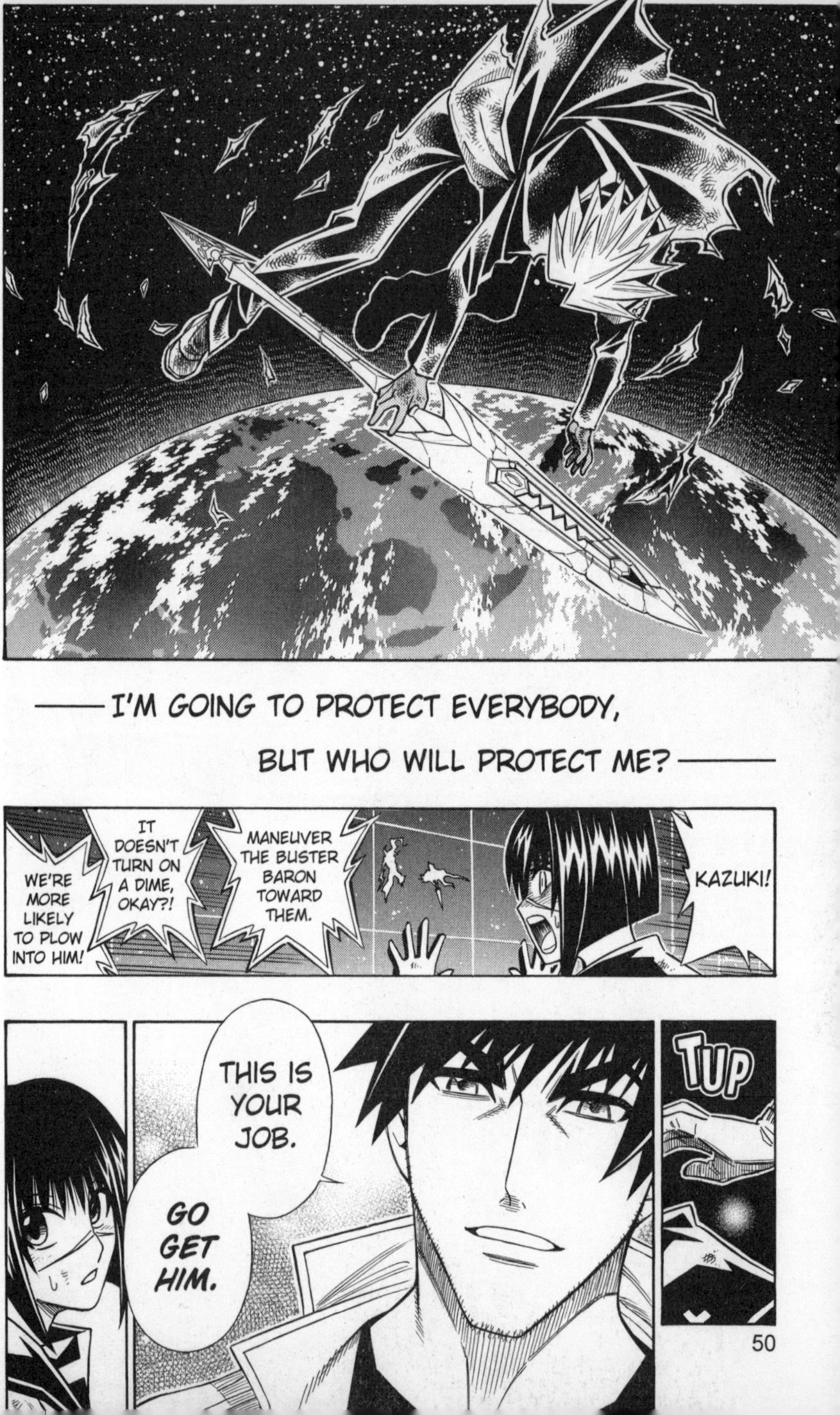
——I'M GOING TO PROTECT EVERYBODY,
BUT WHO WILL PROTECT ME?——
KAZUKI!
MANEUVER THE BUSTER BARON TOWARD THEM.
IT DOESN'T TURN ON A DIME, OKAY?!
WE'RE MORE LIKELY TO PLOW INTO HIM!
TUP
THIS IS YOUR JOB.
GO GET HIM.

READ THIS WAY

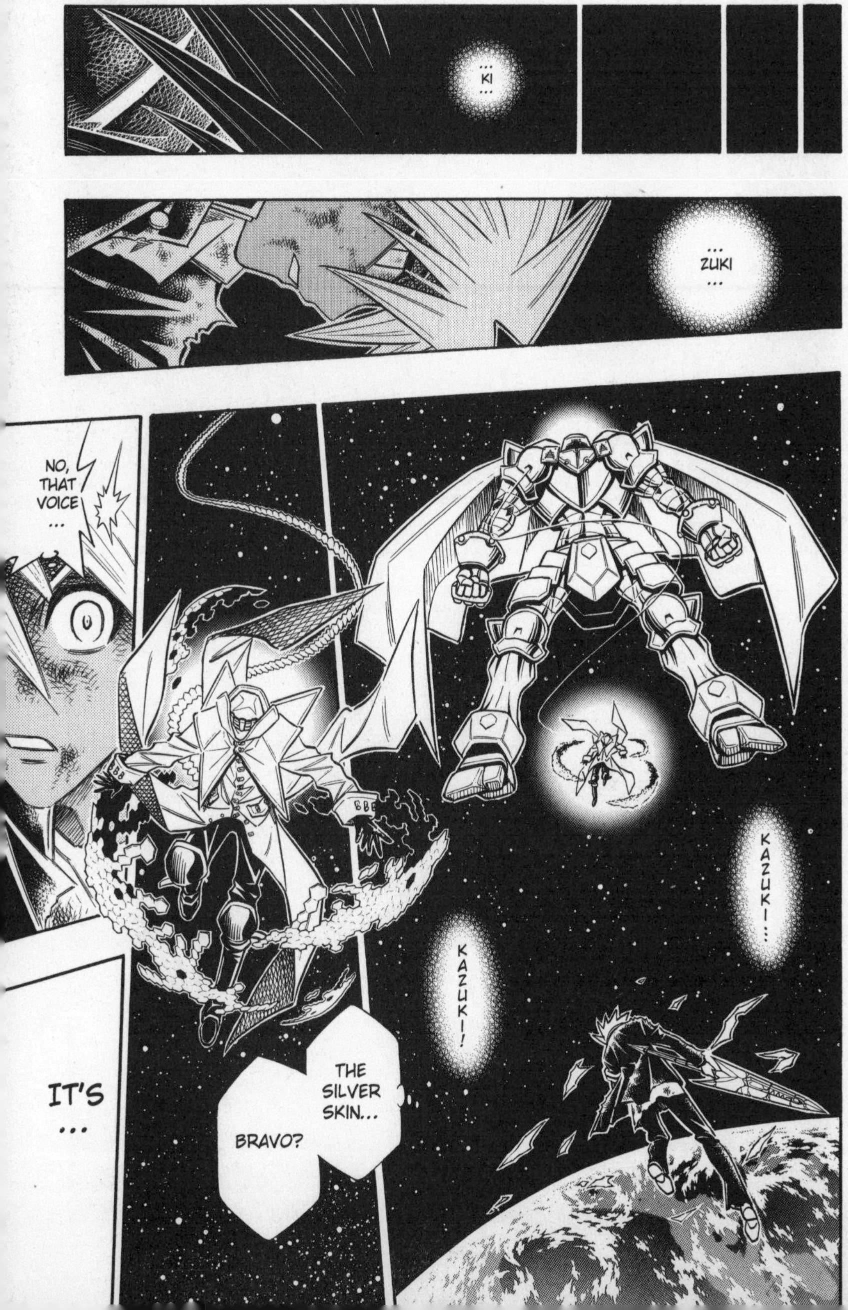

...KI...
...ZUKI...
KAZUKI...
KAZUKI!
THE SILVER SKIN...
BRAVO?
NO, THAT VOICE...
IT'S...

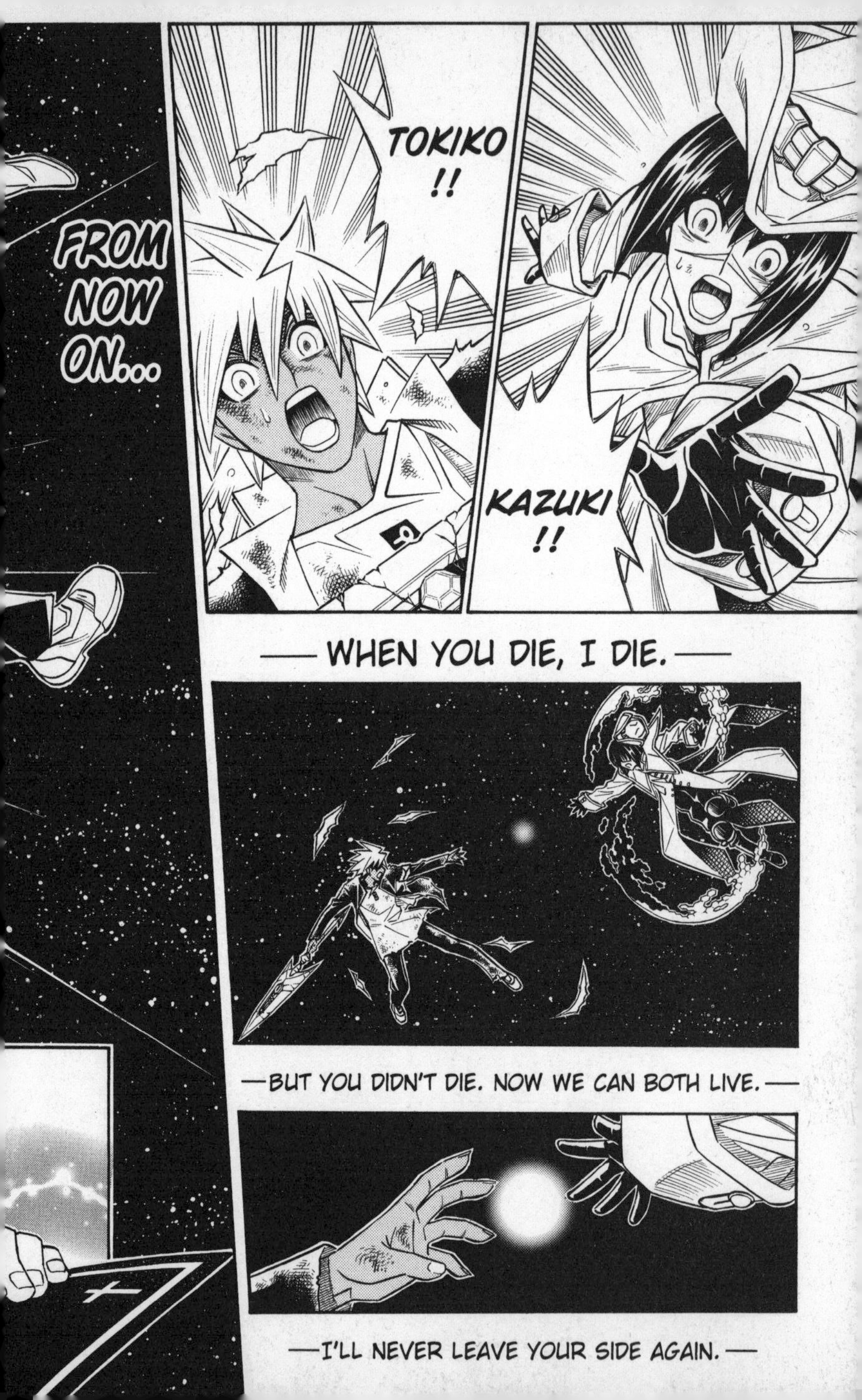
KAZUKI !!
TOKIKO !!
—WHEN YOU DIE, I DIE.—
—BUT YOU DIDN'T DIE. NOW WE CAN BOTH LIVE.—
—I'LL NEVER LEAVE YOUR SIDE AGAIN.—
FROM NOW ON...

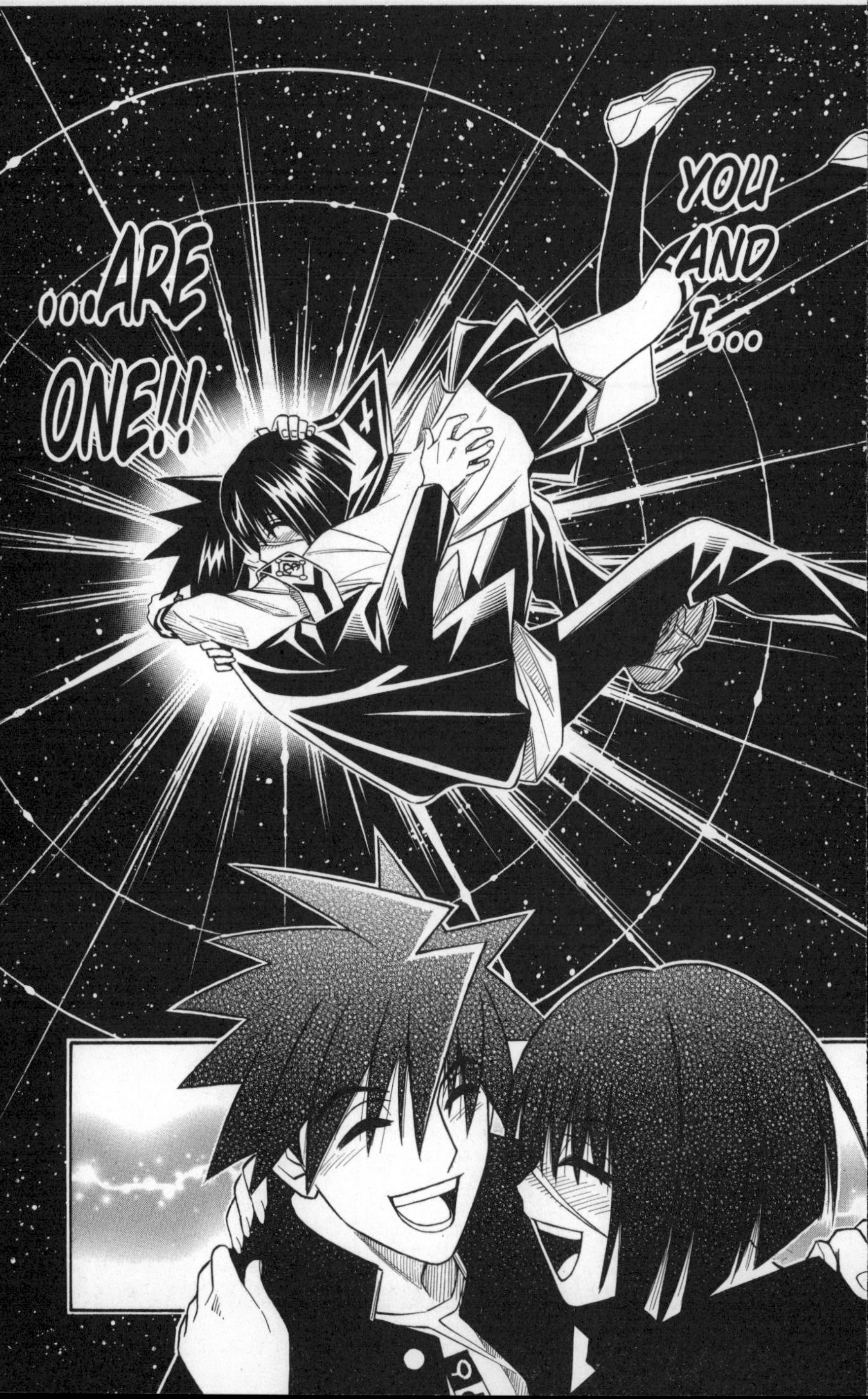
YOU AND I...
...ARE ONE!!

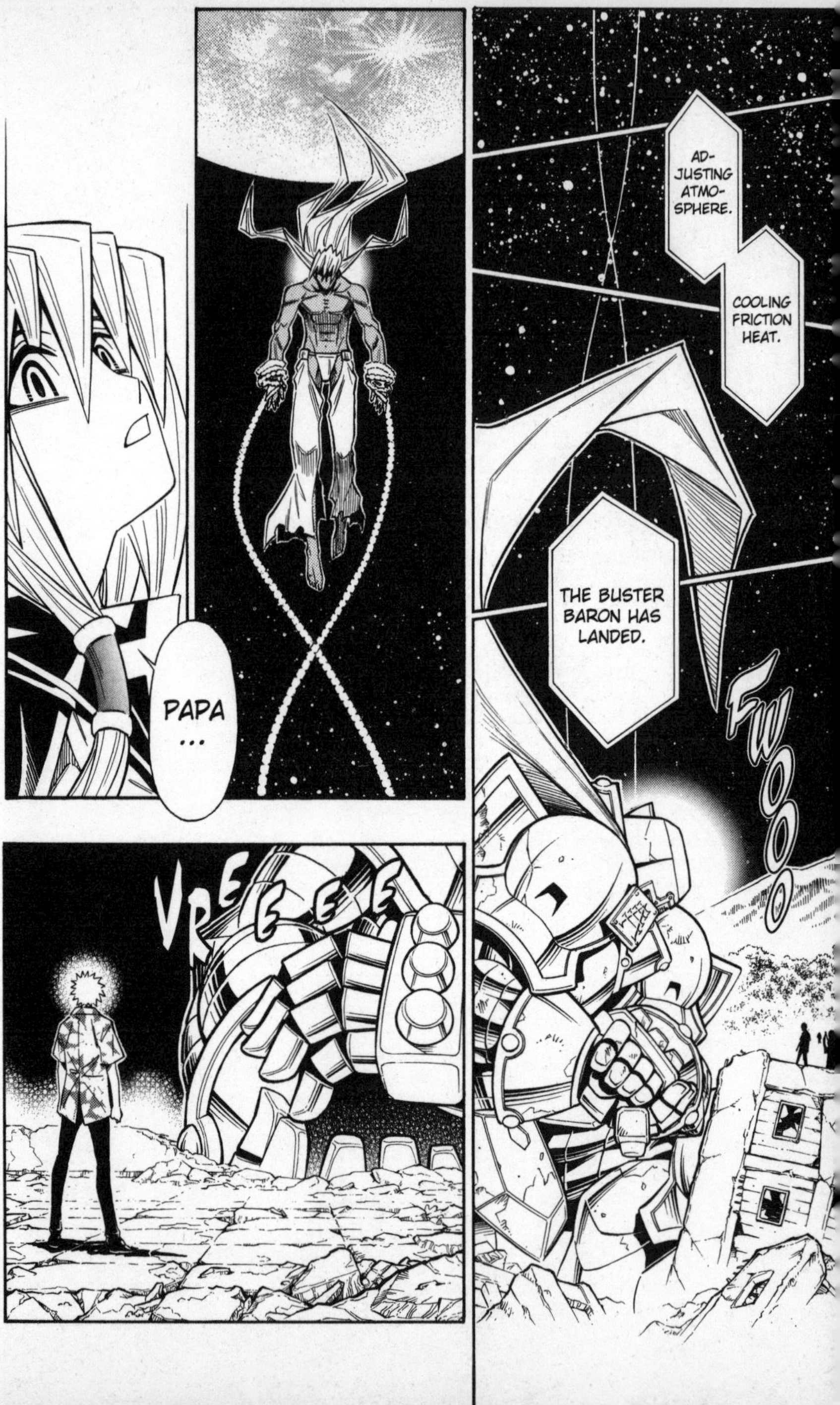
AD-JUSTING ATMO-SPHERE.
COOLING FRICTION HEAT.
THE BUSTER BARON HAS LANDED.
FWOOOO
PAPA ...
VREEEEE

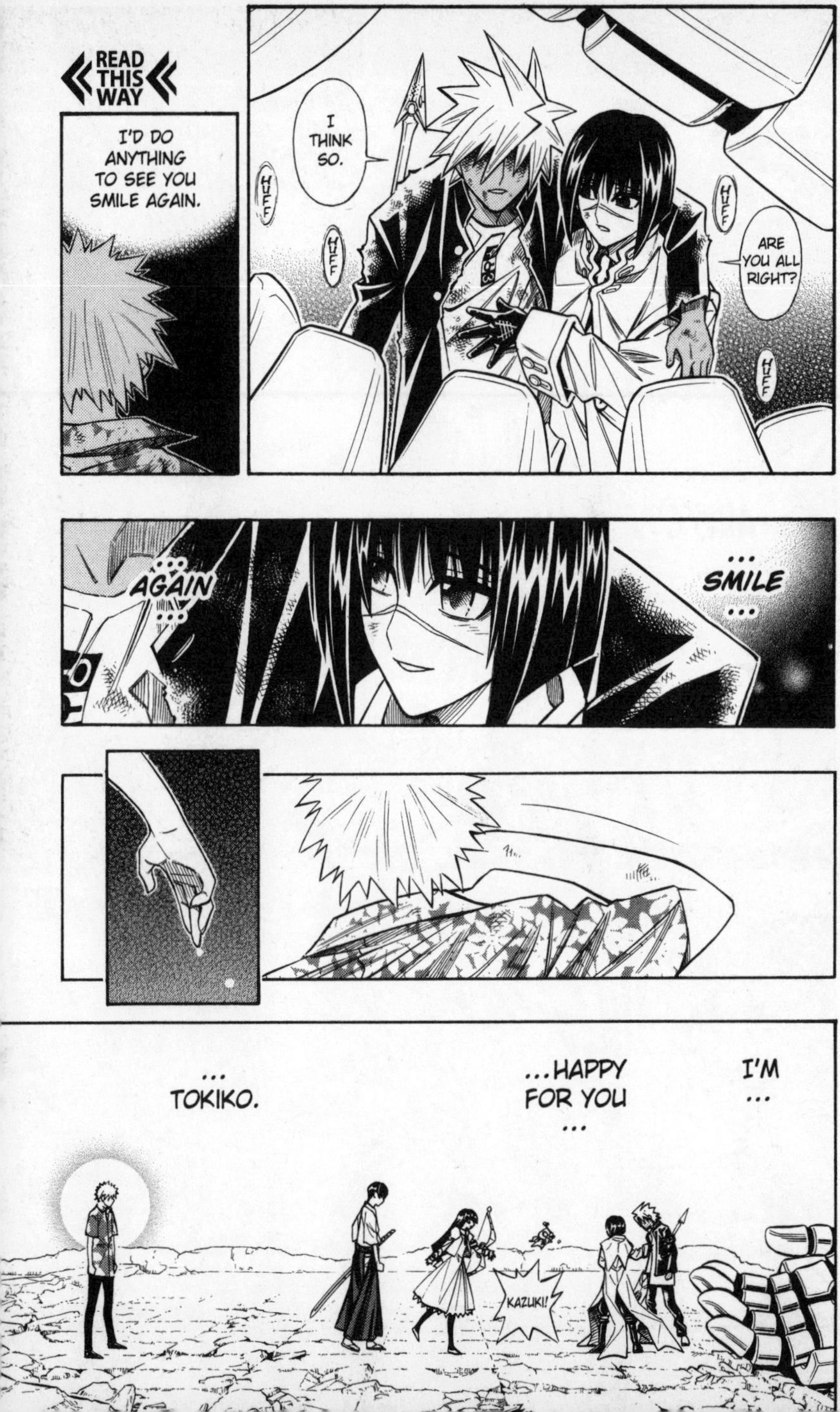
READ THIS WAY
HUFF
ARE YOU ALL RIGHT?
HUFF
I THINK SO.
HUFF
HUFF
I'D DO ANYTHING TO SEE YOU SMILE AGAIN.
...SMILE...
...AGAIN...
I'M...
...HAPPY FOR YOU...
...TOKIKO.
KAZUKI!

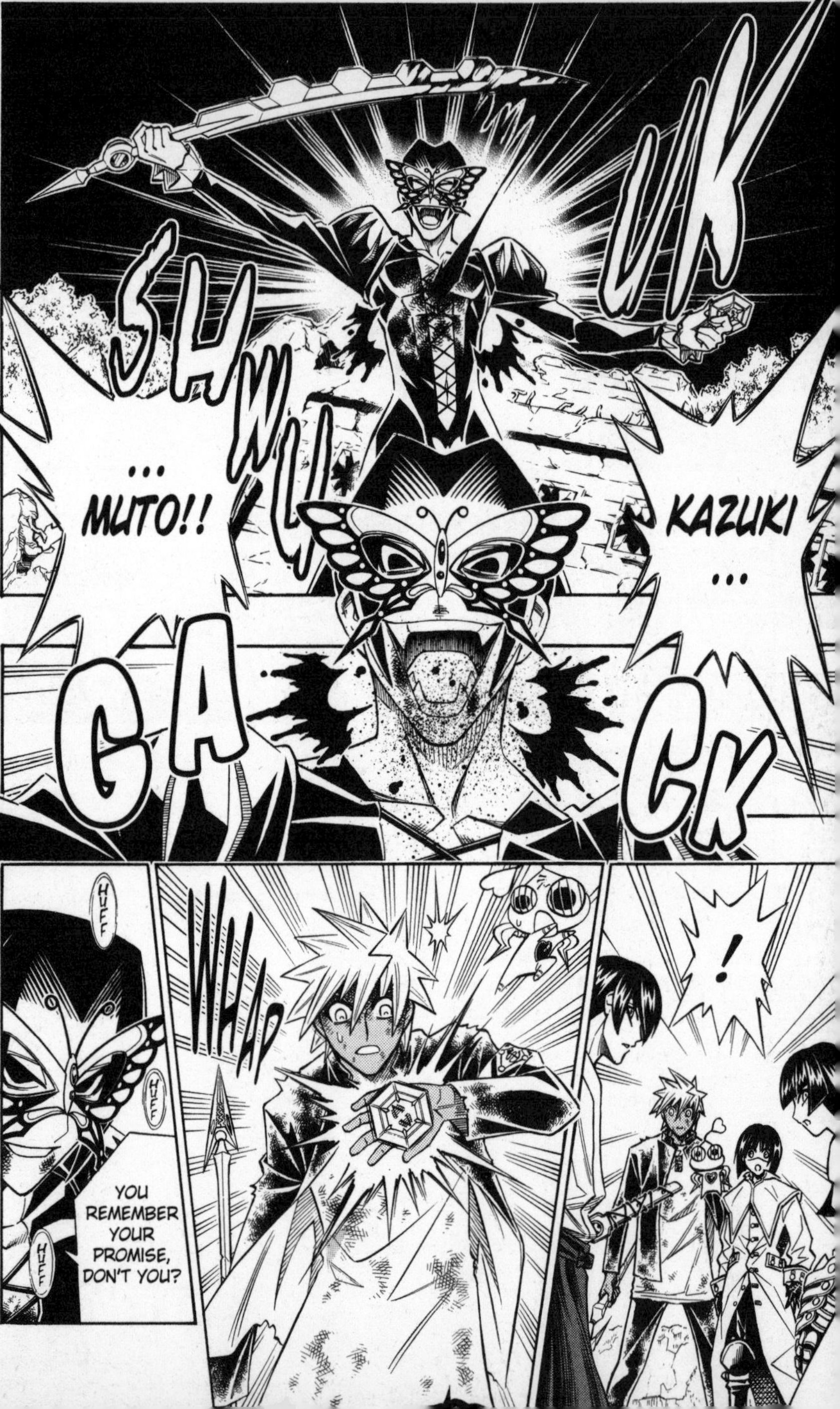
SHWUUK
KAZUKI ...
... MUTO!!
GACK
!
WHAP
HUFF
HUFF
HUFF
YOU REMEMBER YOUR PROMISE, DON'T YOU?

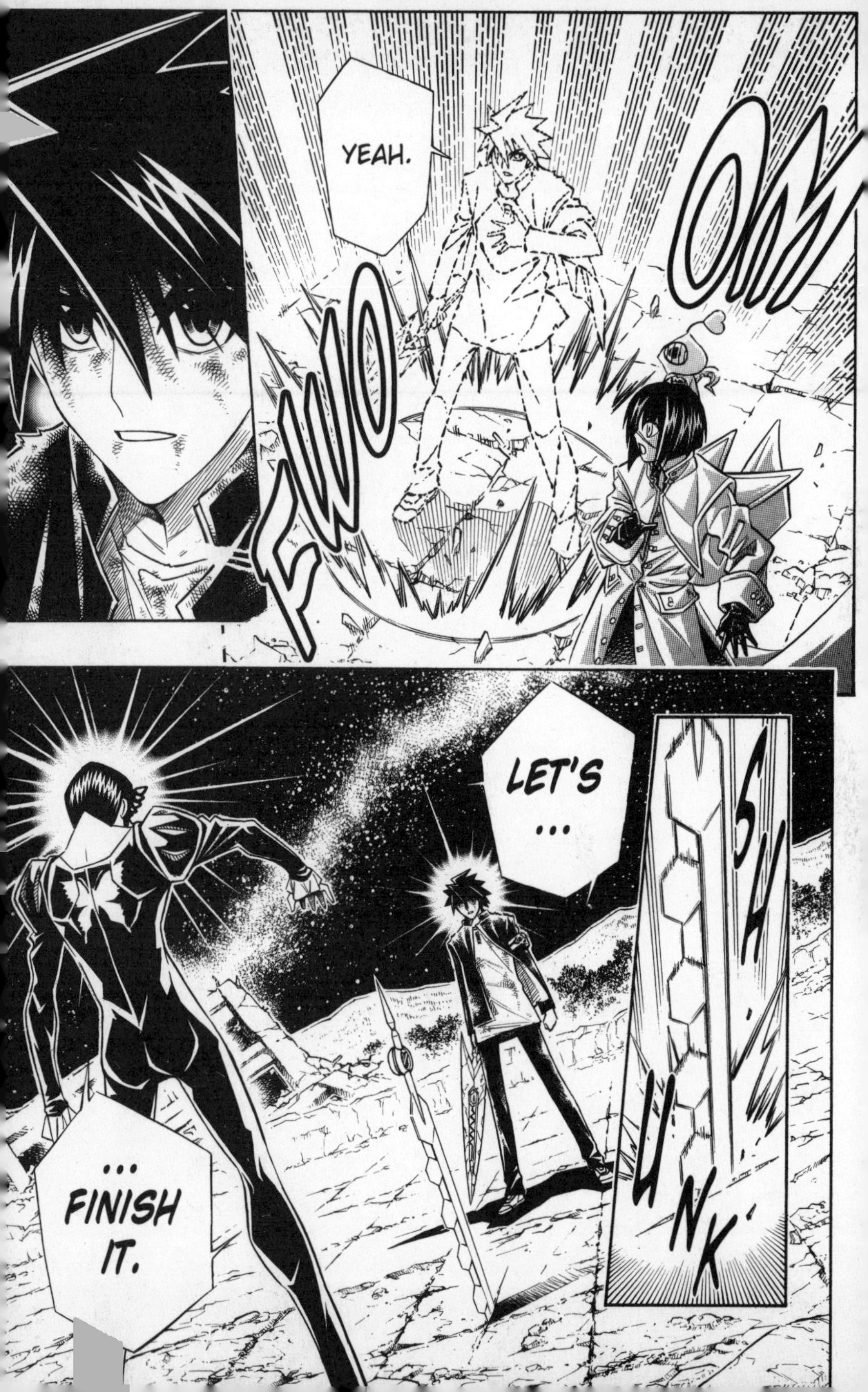
YEAH.
FWOOM
SHUNK
LET'S...
...FINISH IT.

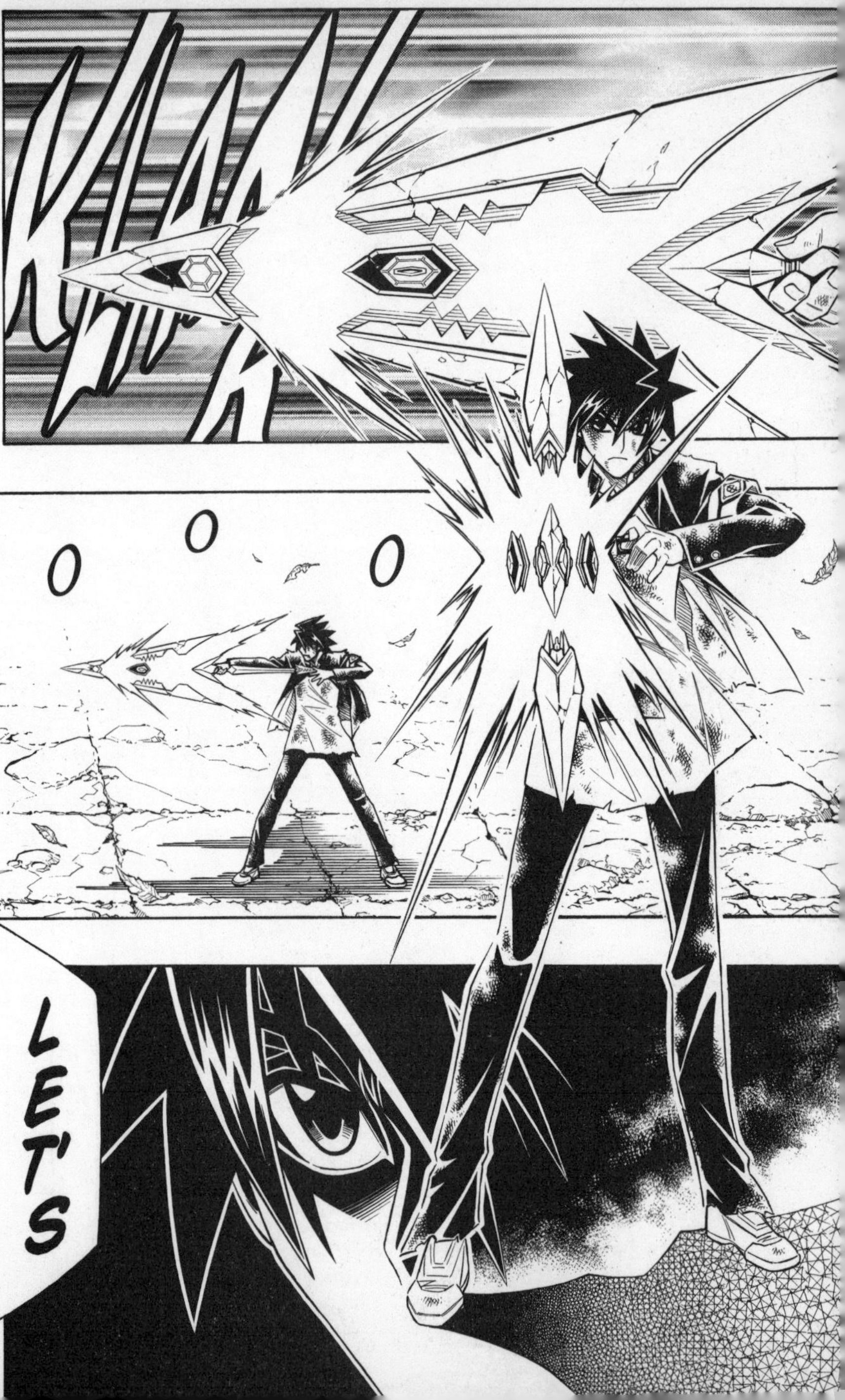
O O O
LET'S

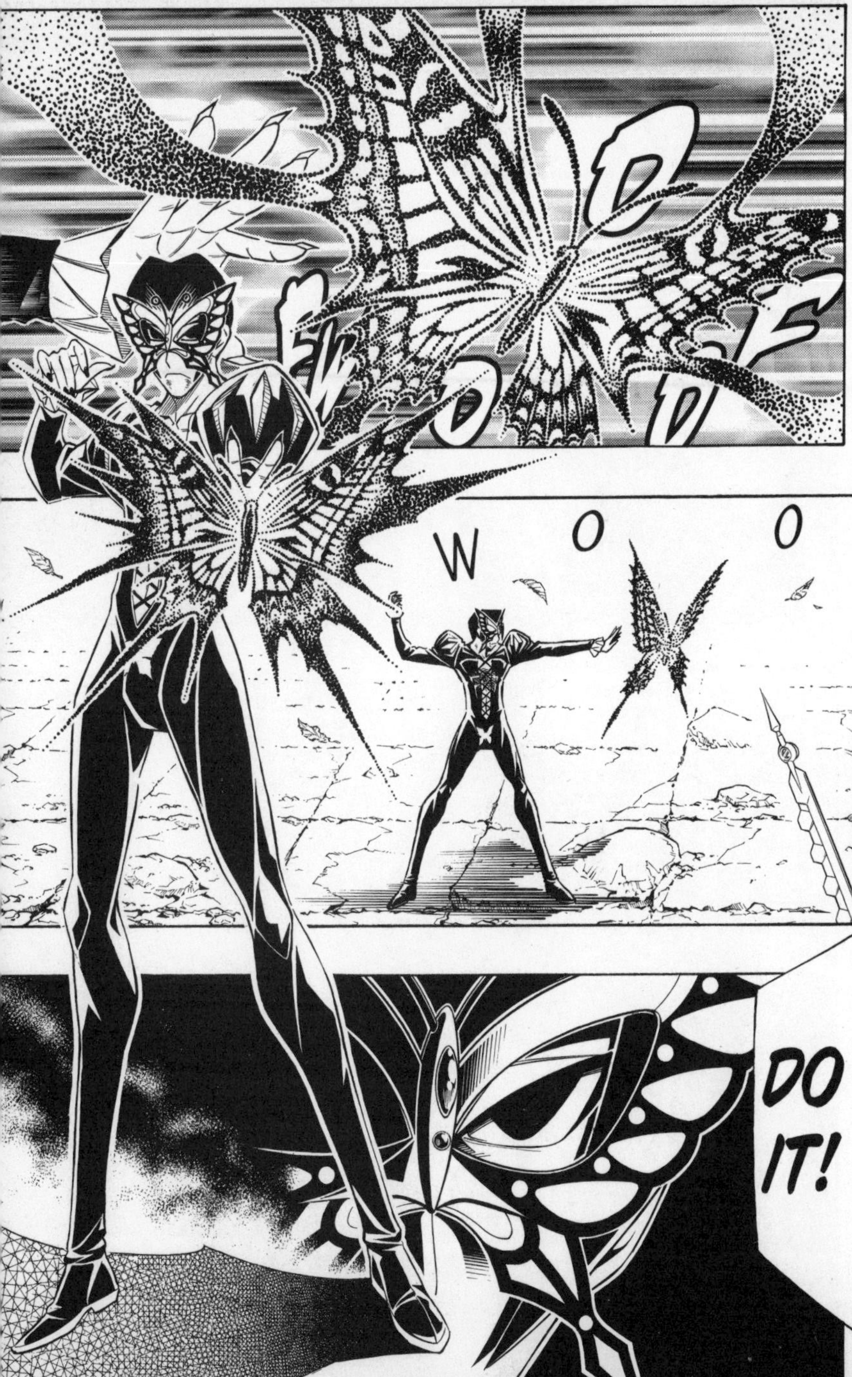
WOO
DO IT!

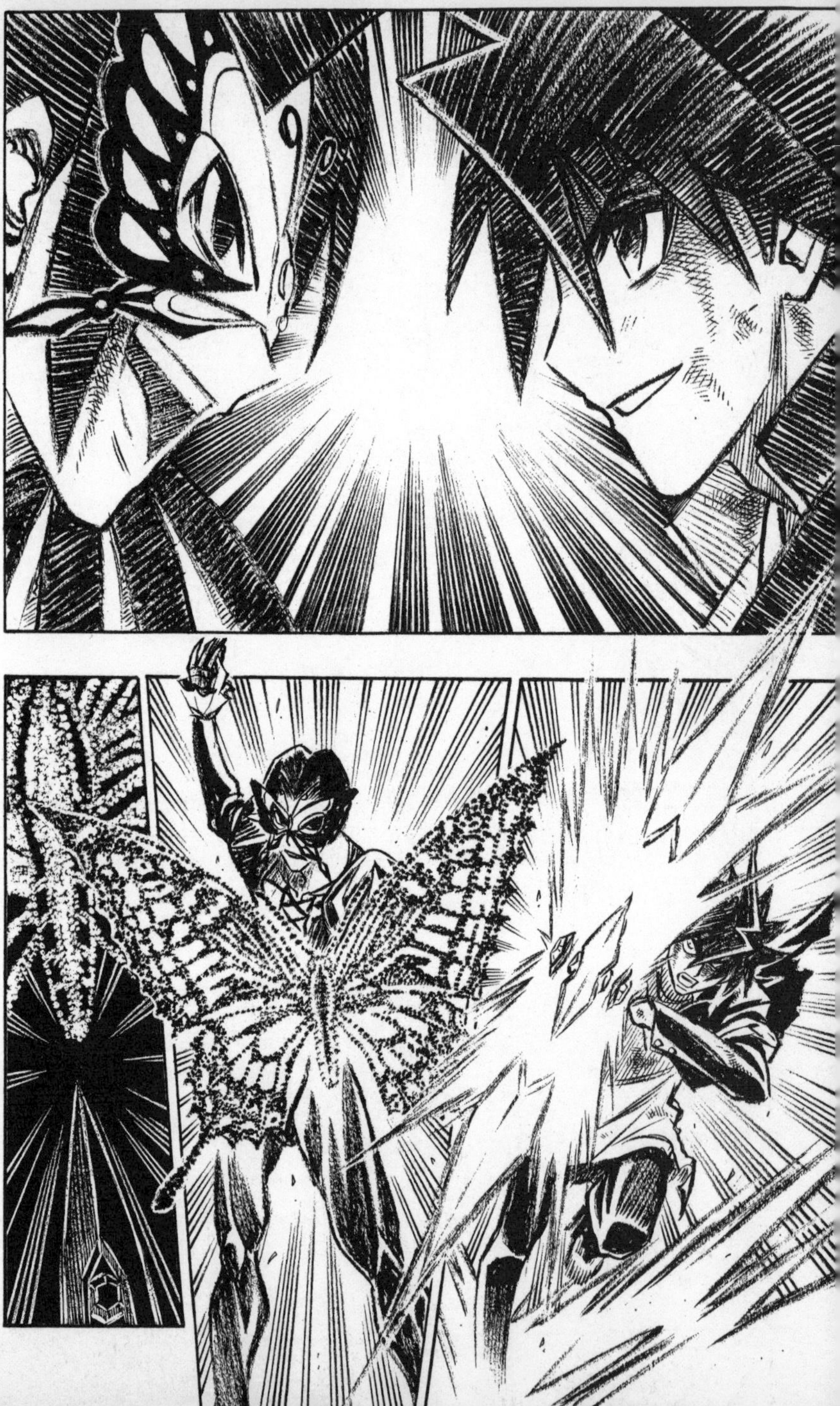

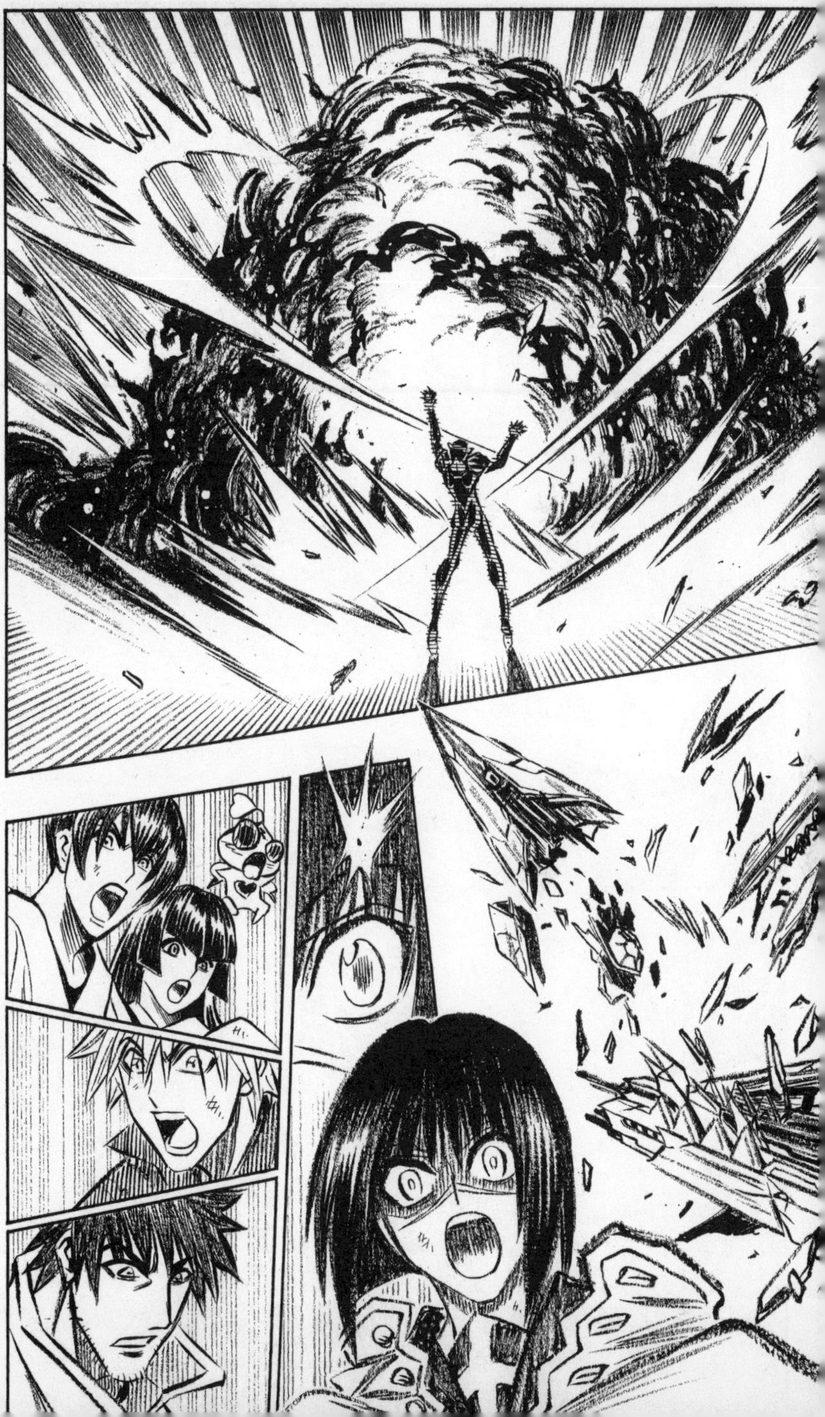

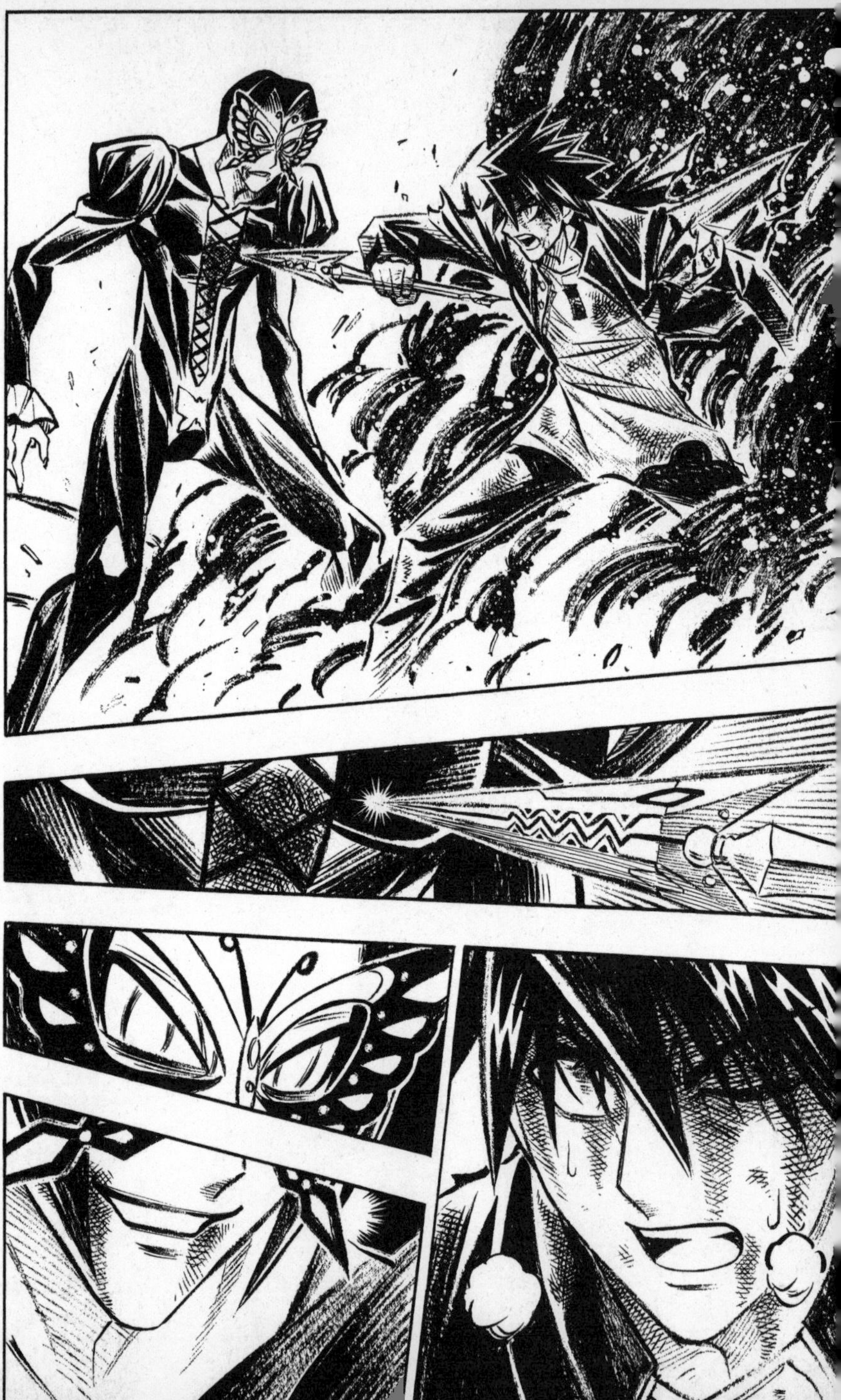

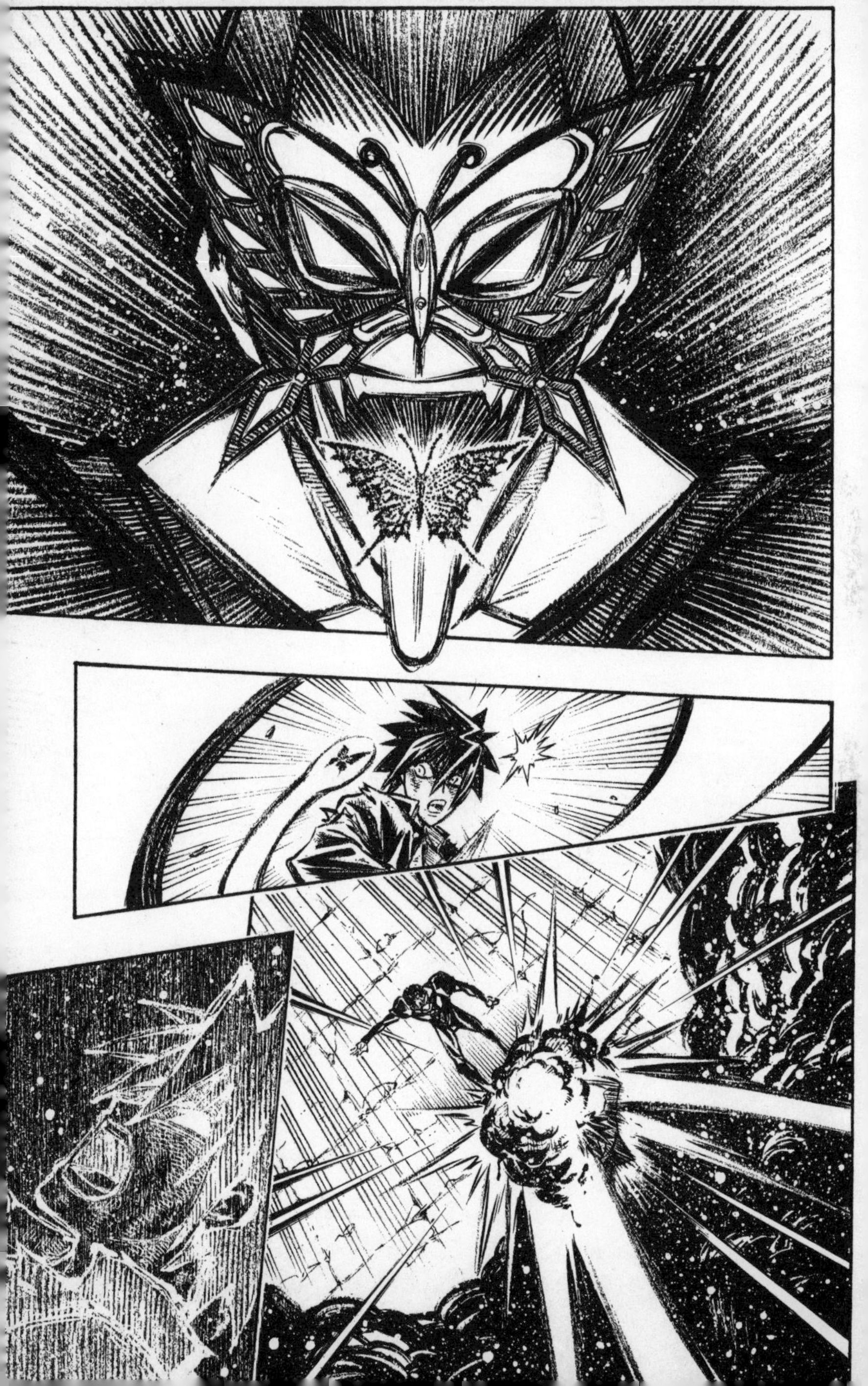

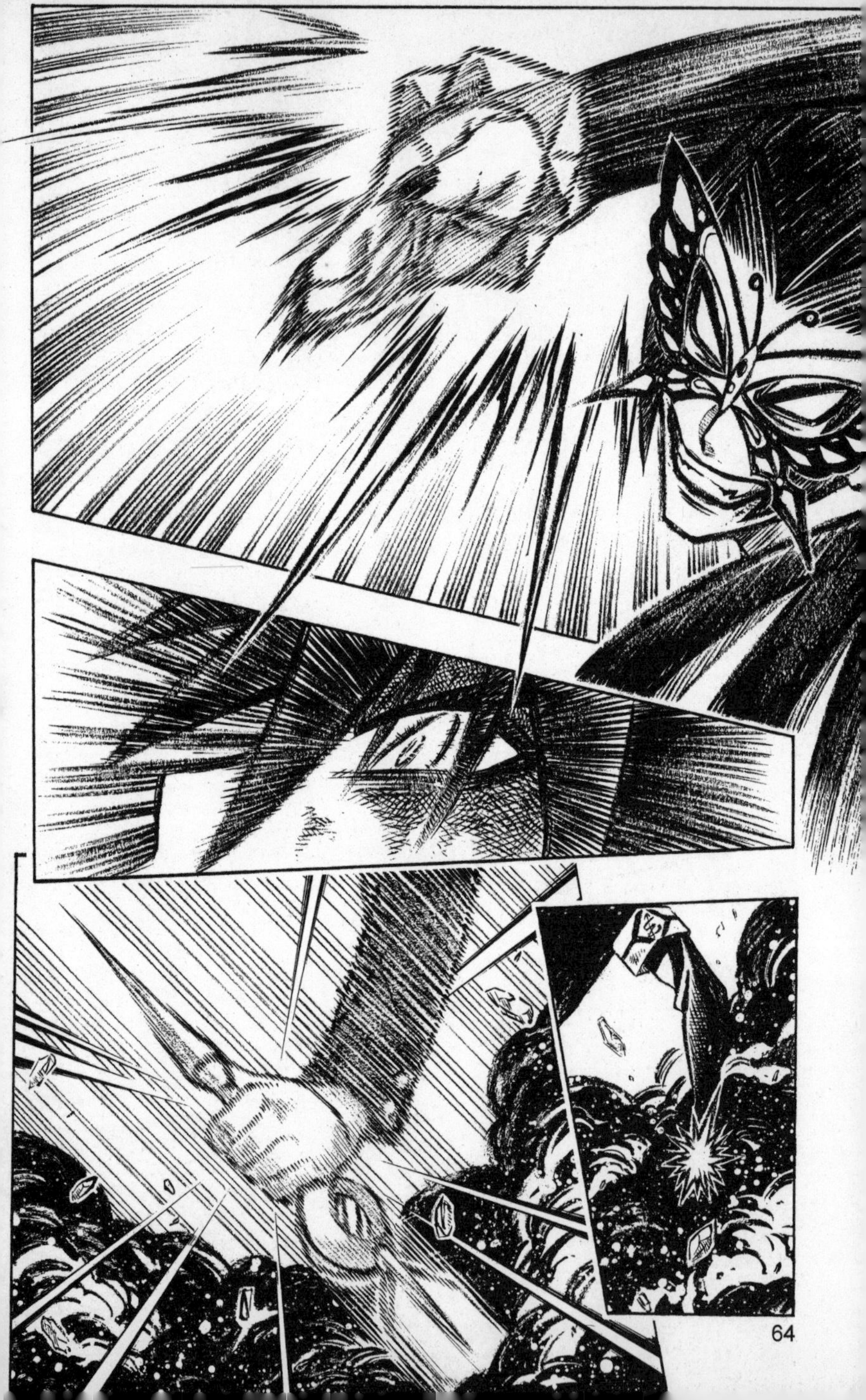

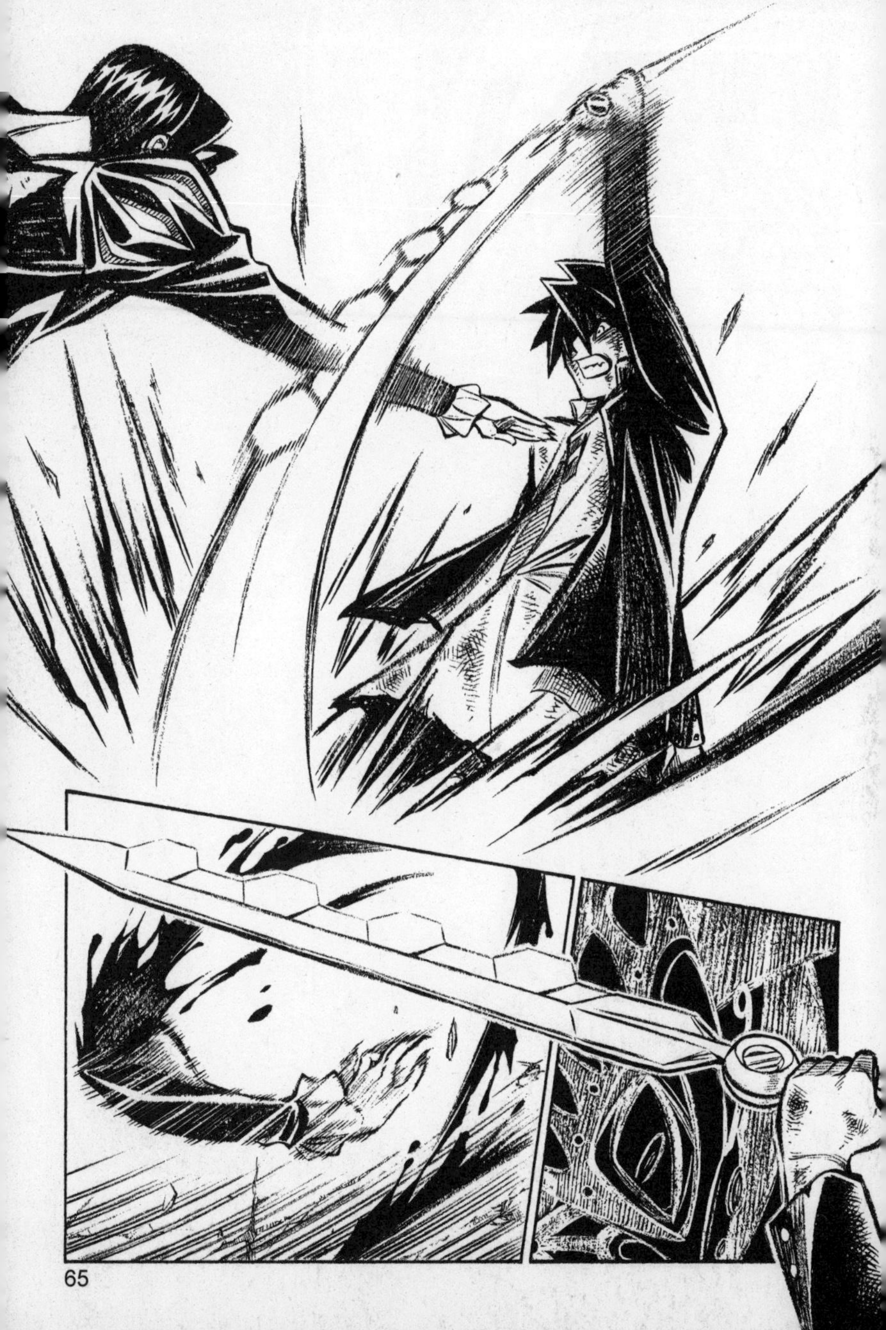

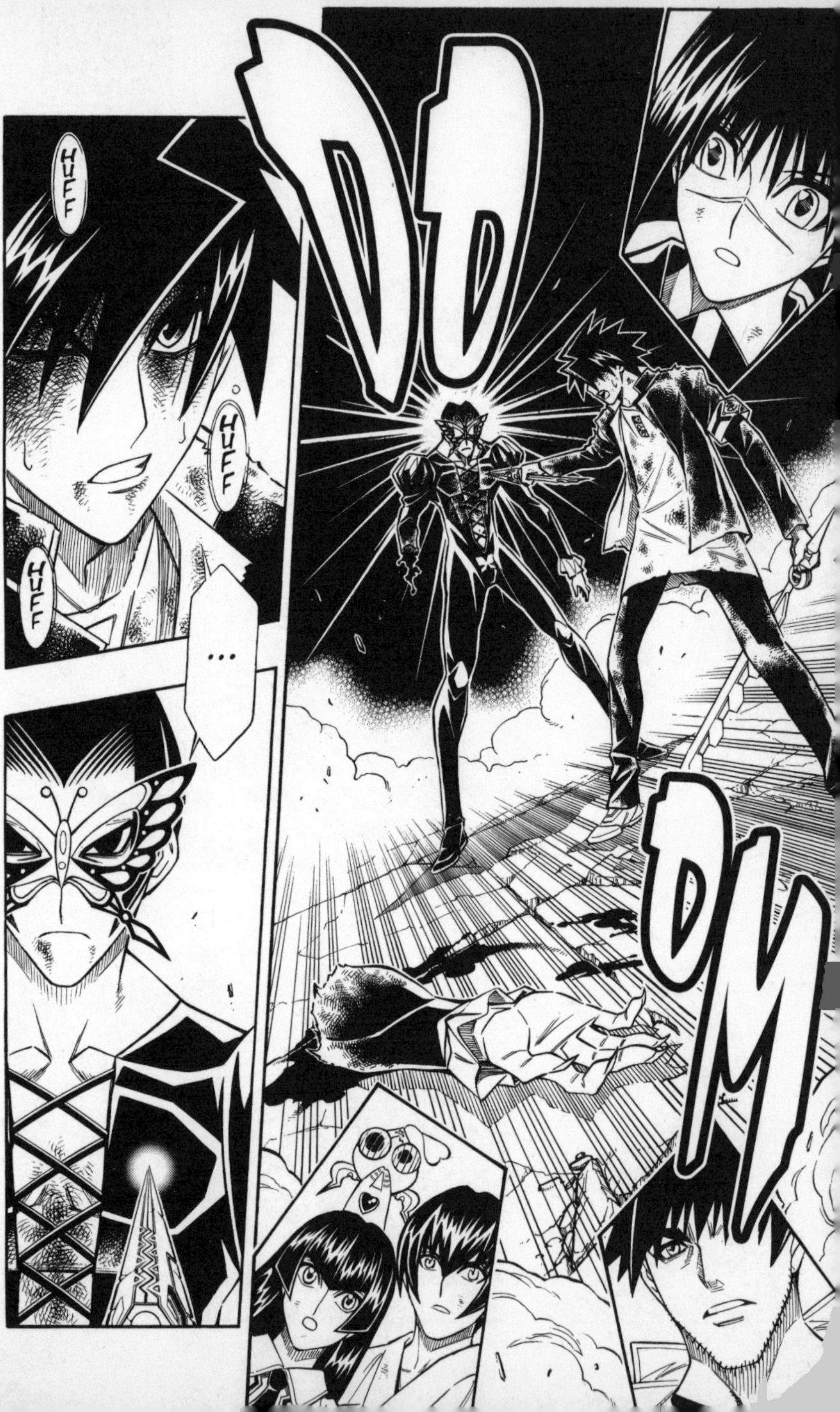
HUFF
HUFF
HUFF
...

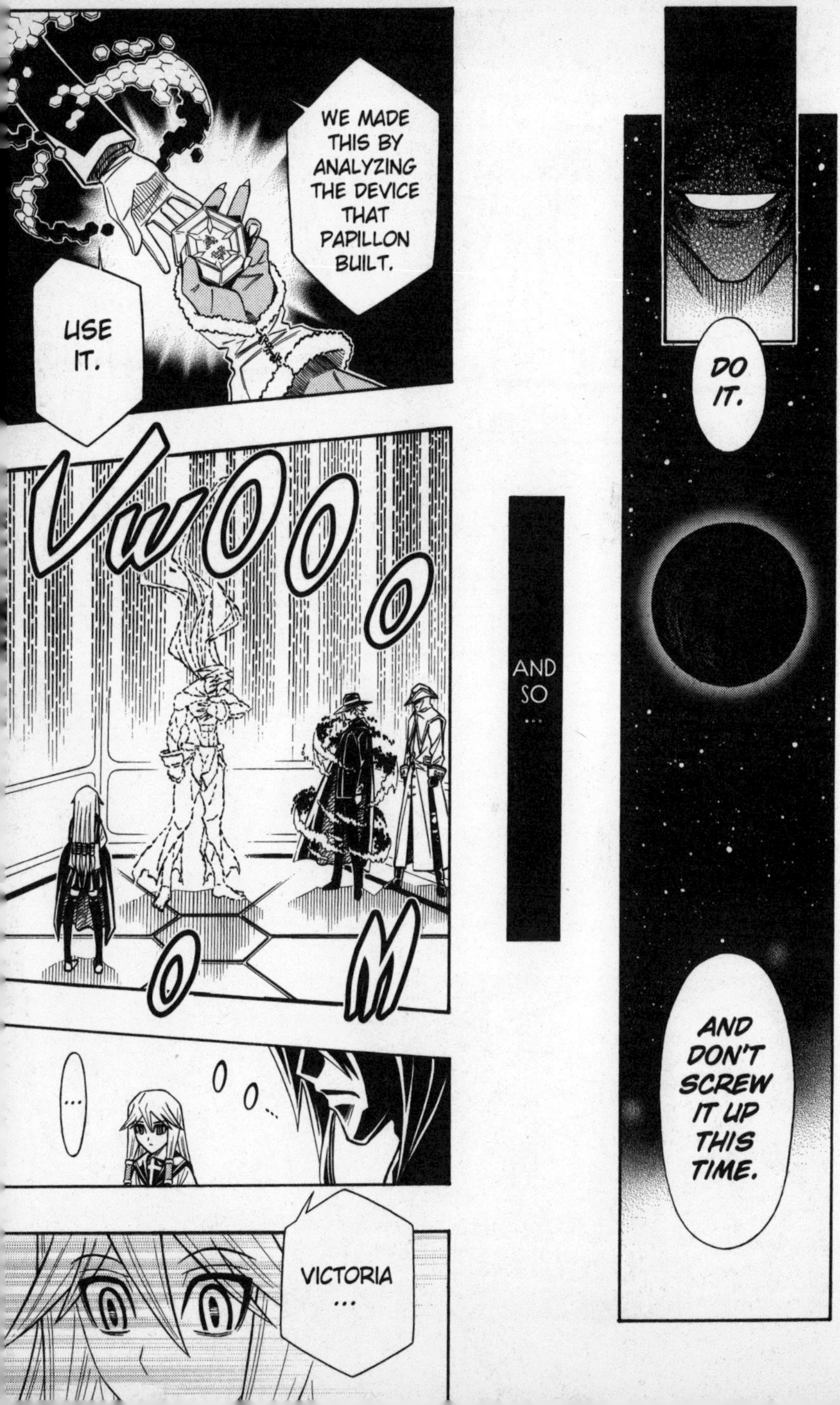
DO IT.
AND DON'T SCREW IT UP THIS TIME.
AND SO...
WE MADE THIS BY ANALYZING THE DEVICE THAT PAPILLON BUILT.
USE IT.
VWOOOOOOOM
OO...
...
VICTORIA...

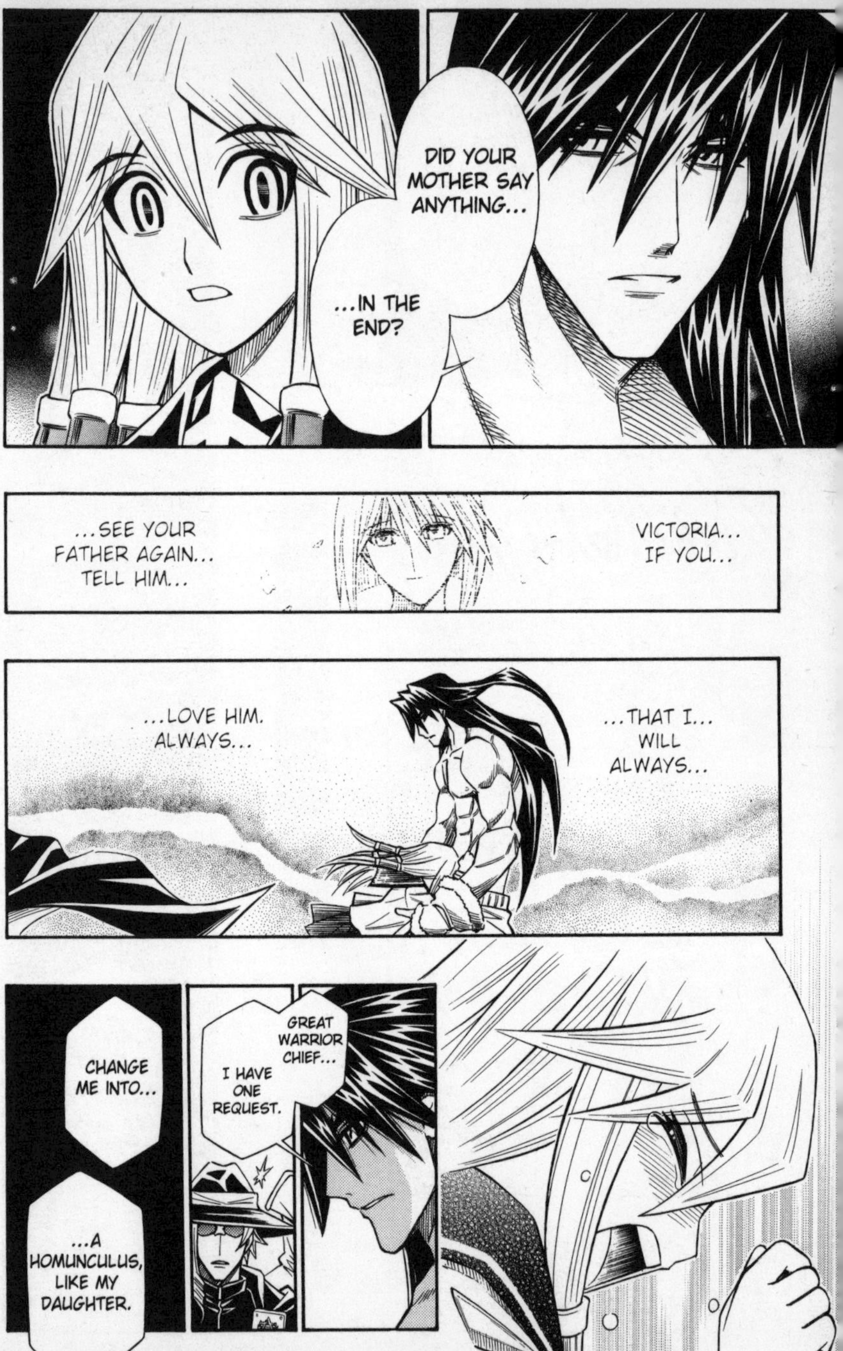
DID YOUR MOTHER SAY ANYTHING...
...IN THE END?
VICTORIA... IF YOU...
...SEE YOUR FATHER AGAIN... TELL HIM...
...THAT I... WILL ALWAYS...
...LOVE HIM. ALWAYS...
GREAT WARRIOR CHIEF...
I HAVE ONE REQUEST.
CHANGE ME INTO...
...A HOMUNCULUS, LIKE MY DAUGHTER.

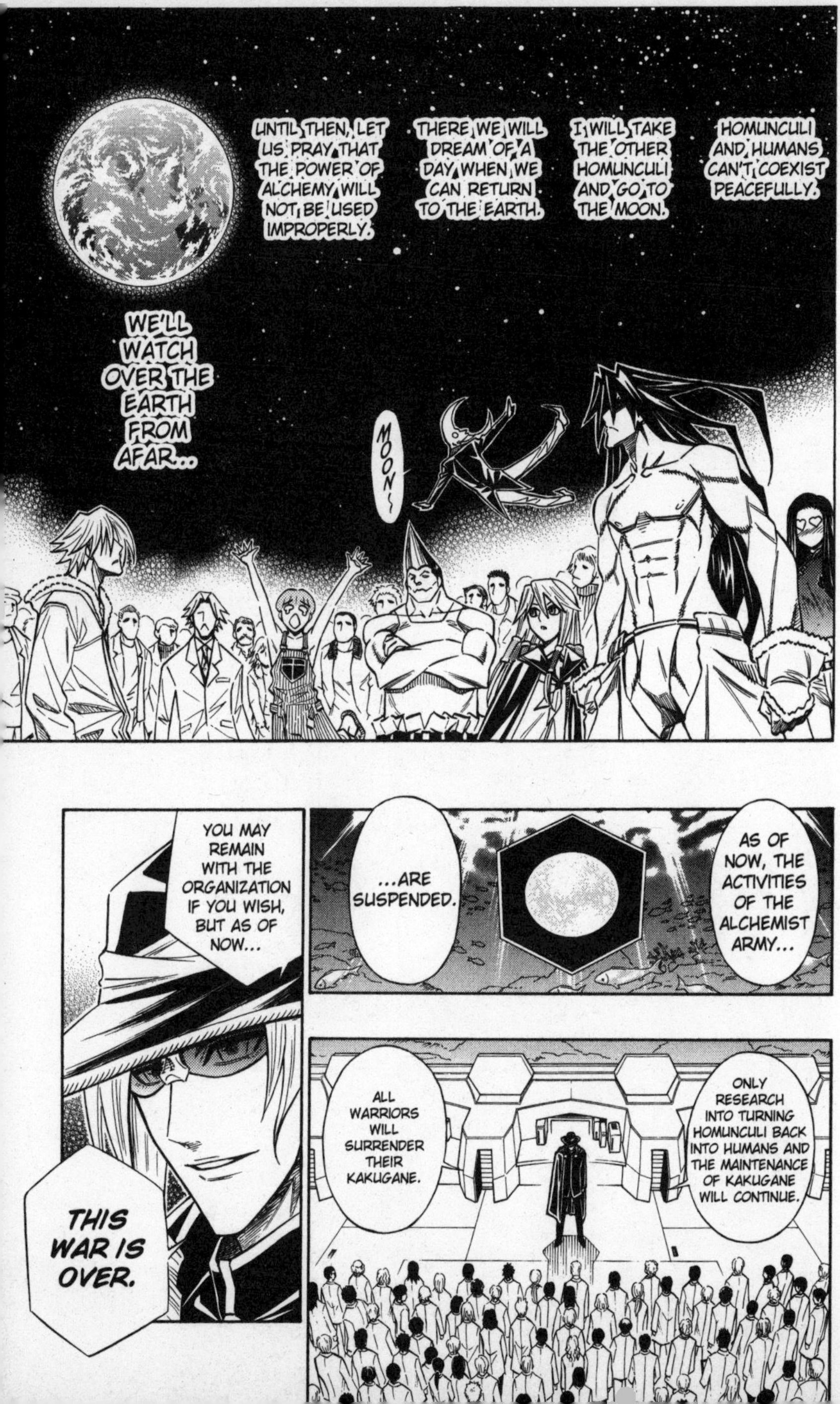
HOMUNCULI AND HUMANS CAN'T COEXIST PEACEFULLY.
I WILL TAKE THE OTHER HOMUNCULI AND GO TO THE MOON.
THERE WE WILL DREAM OF A DAY WHEN WE CAN RETURN TO THE EARTH.
UNTIL THEN, LET US PRAY THAT THE POWER OF ALCHEMY WILL NOT BE USED IMPROPERLY.
WE'LL WATCH OVER THE EARTH FROM AFAR...
MOON~
AS OF NOW, THE ACTIVITIES OF THE ALCHEMIST ARMY...
...ARE SUSPENDED.
ONLY RESEARCH INTO TURNING HOMUNCULI BACK INTO HUMANS AND THE MAINTENANCE OF KAKUGANE WILL CONTINUE.
ALL WARRIORS WILL SURRENDER THEIR KAKUGANE.
YOU MAY REMAIN WITH THE ORGANIZATION IF YOU WISH, BUT AS OF NOW...
THIS WAR IS OVER.

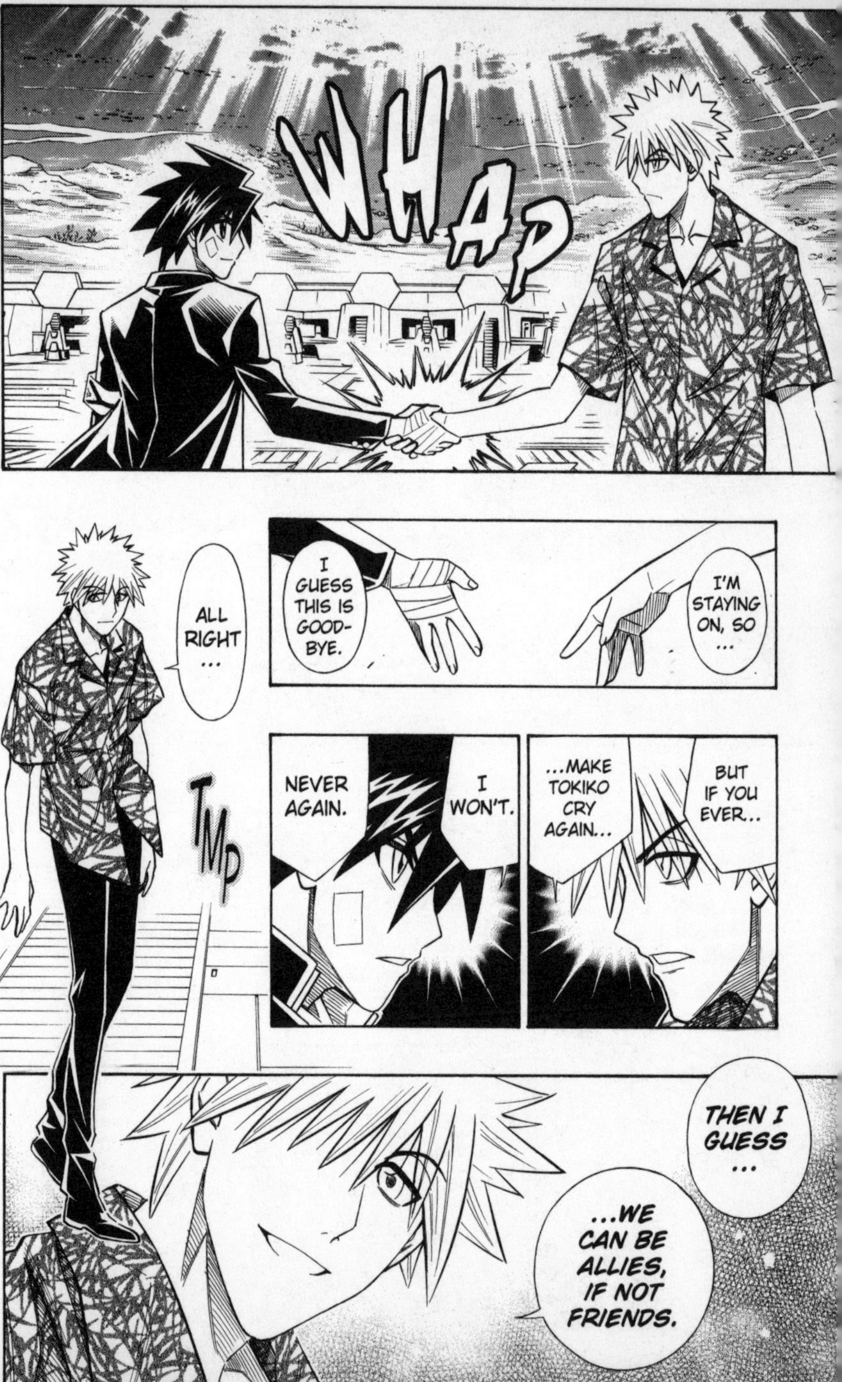
WHAP
I'M STAYING ON, SO ...
I GUESS THIS IS GOOD-BYE.
ALL RIGHT ...
BUT IF YOU EVER...
...MAKE TOKIKO CRY AGAIN...
I WON'T.
NEVER AGAIN.
TMP
THEN I GUESS ...
...WE CAN BE ALLIES, IF NOT FRIENDS.

READ THIS WAY

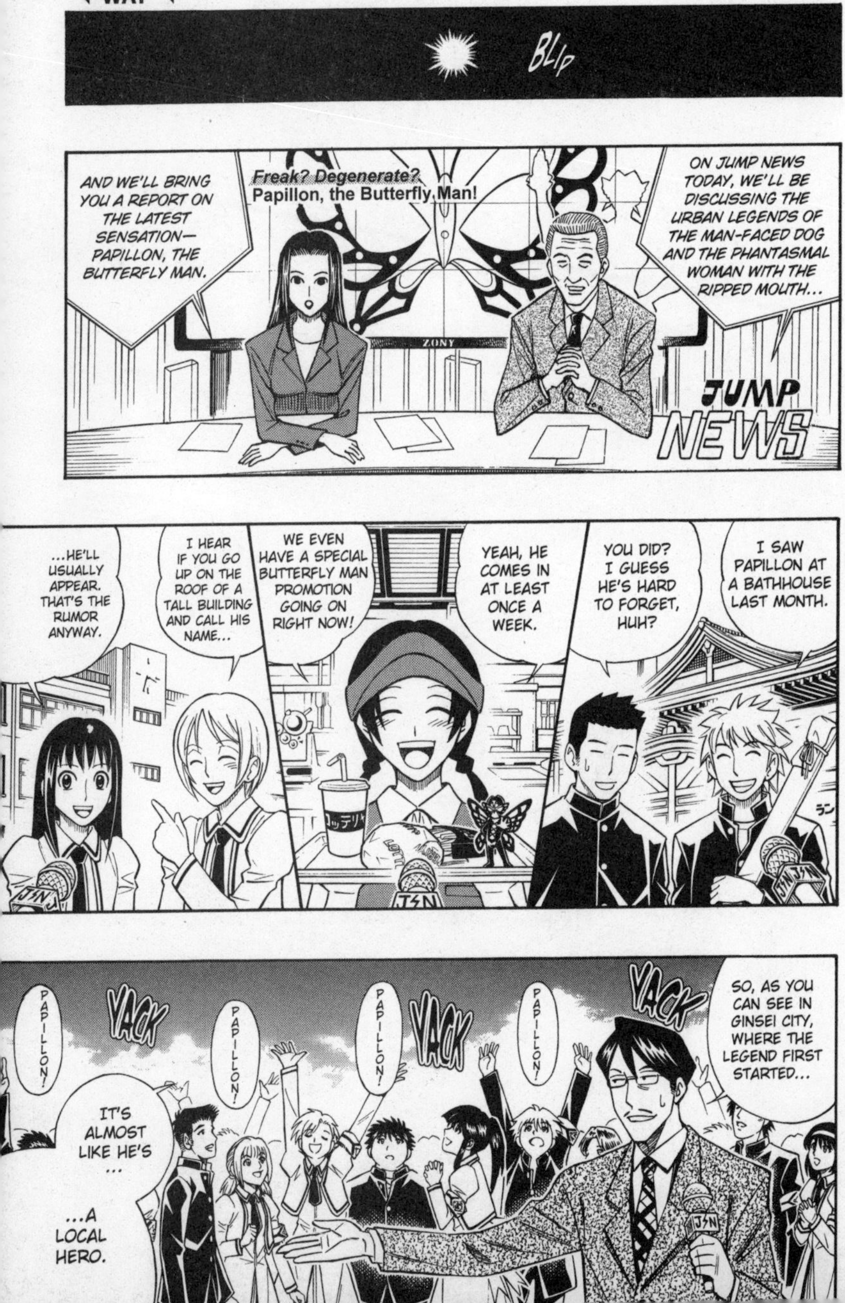
BLIP
ON JUMP NEWS TODAY, WE'LL BE DISCUSSING THE URBAN LEGENDS OF THE MAN-FACED DOG AND THE PHANTASMAL WOMAN WITH THE RIPPED MOUTH...
Freak? Degenerate? Papillon, the Butterfly Man!
AND WE'LL BRING YOU A REPORT ON THE LATEST SENSATION— PAPILLON, THE BUTTERFLY MAN.
ZONY
JUMP NEWS
I SAW PAPILLON AT A BATHHOUSE LAST MONTH.
YOU DID? I GUESS HE'S HARD TO FORGET, HUH?
YEAH, HE COMES IN AT LEAST ONCE A WEEK.
WE EVEN HAVE A SPECIAL BUTTERFLY MAN PROMOTION GOING ON RIGHT NOW!
I HEAR IF YOU GO UP ON THE ROOF OF A TALL BUILDING AND CALL HIS NAME...
...HE'LL USUALLY APPEAR. THAT'S THE RUMOR ANYWAY.
SO, AS YOU CAN SEE IN GINSEI CITY, WHERE THE LEGEND FIRST STARTED...
YACK
PAPILLON!
YACK
PAPILLON!
PAPILLON!
YACK
PAPILLON!
IT'S ALMOST LIKE HE'S ...
...A LOCAL HERO.

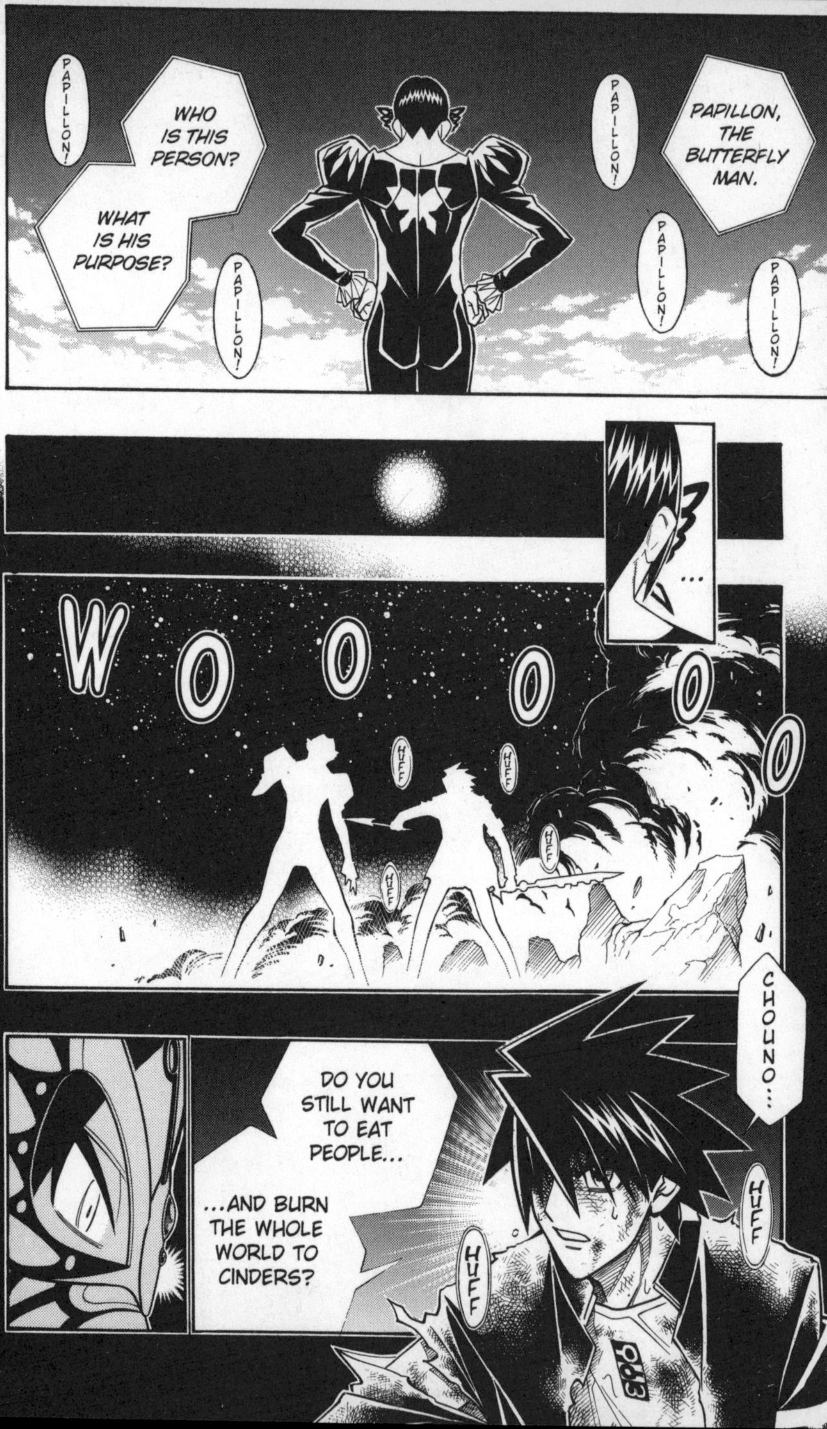
PAPILLON, THE BUTTERFLY MAN.
PAPILLON!
PAPILLON!
PAPILLON!
PAPILLON!
WHO IS THIS PERSON?
WHAT IS HIS PURPOSE?
PAPILLON!
...
WOOOOOO
HUFF
HUFF
HUFF
HUFF
CHOUNO...
DO YOU STILL WANT TO EAT PEOPLE...
...AND BURN THE WHOLE WORLD TO CINDERS?
HUFF
HUFF

READ THIS WAY

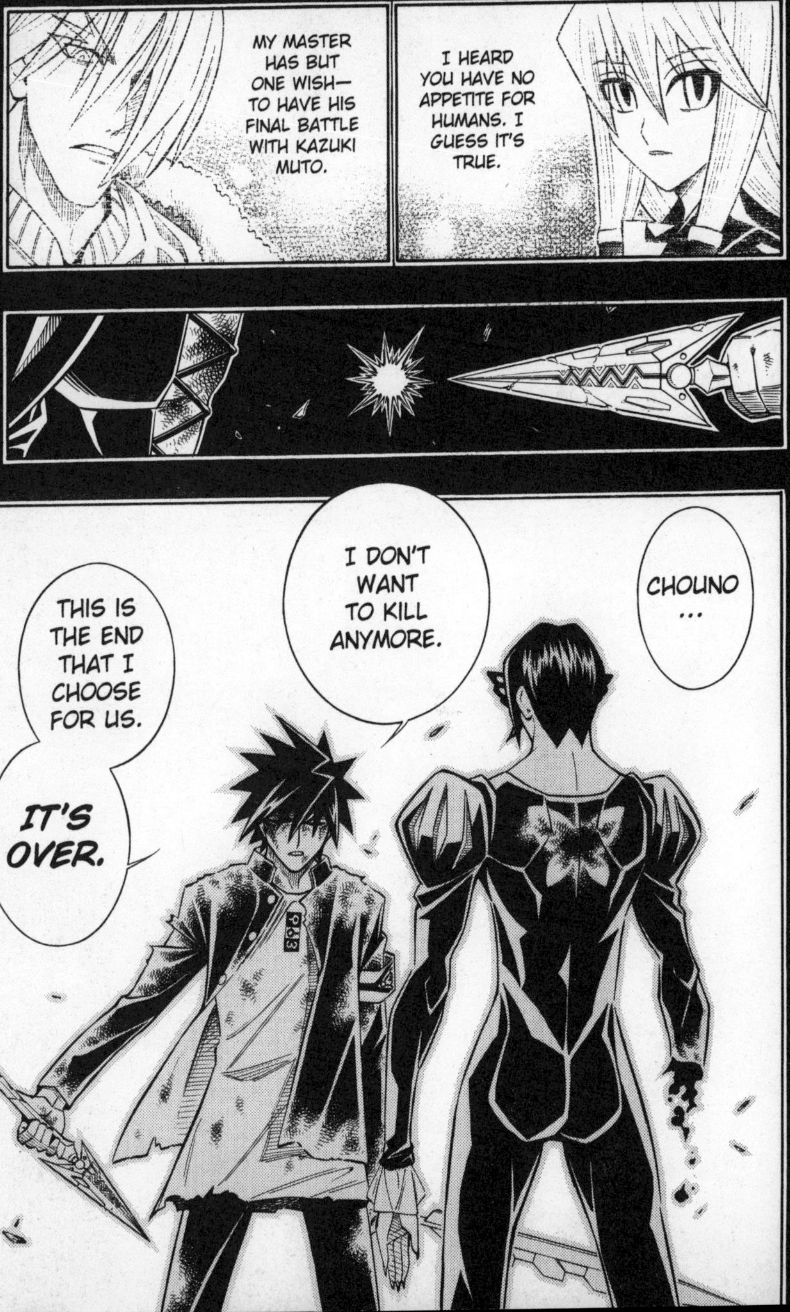
I HEARD YOU HAVE NO APPETITE FOR HUMANS. I GUESS IT'S TRUE.
MY MASTER HAS BUT ONE WISH— TO HAVE HIS FINAL BATTLE WITH KAZUKI MUTO.
CHOUNO ...
I DON'T WANT TO KILL ANYMORE.
THIS IS THE END THAT I CHOOSE FOR US.
IT'S OVER.

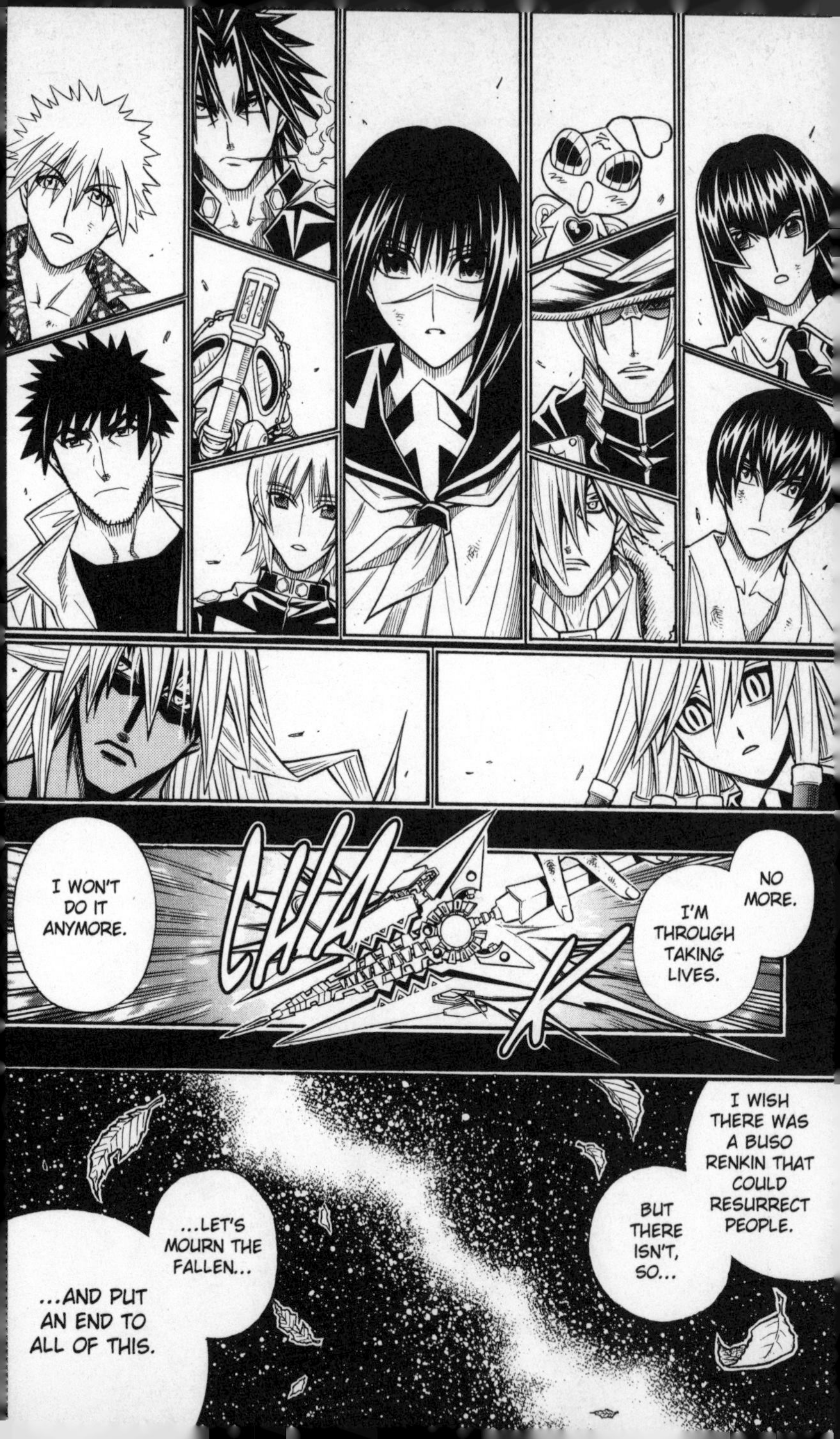
NO MORE.
I'M THROUGH TAKING LIVES.
CHAK
I WON'T DO IT ANYMORE.
I WISH THERE WAS A BUSO RENKIN THAT COULD RESURRECT PEOPLE.
BUT THERE ISN'T, SO...
...LET'S MOURN THE FALLEN...
...AND PUT AN END TO ALL OF THIS.

READ THIS WAY

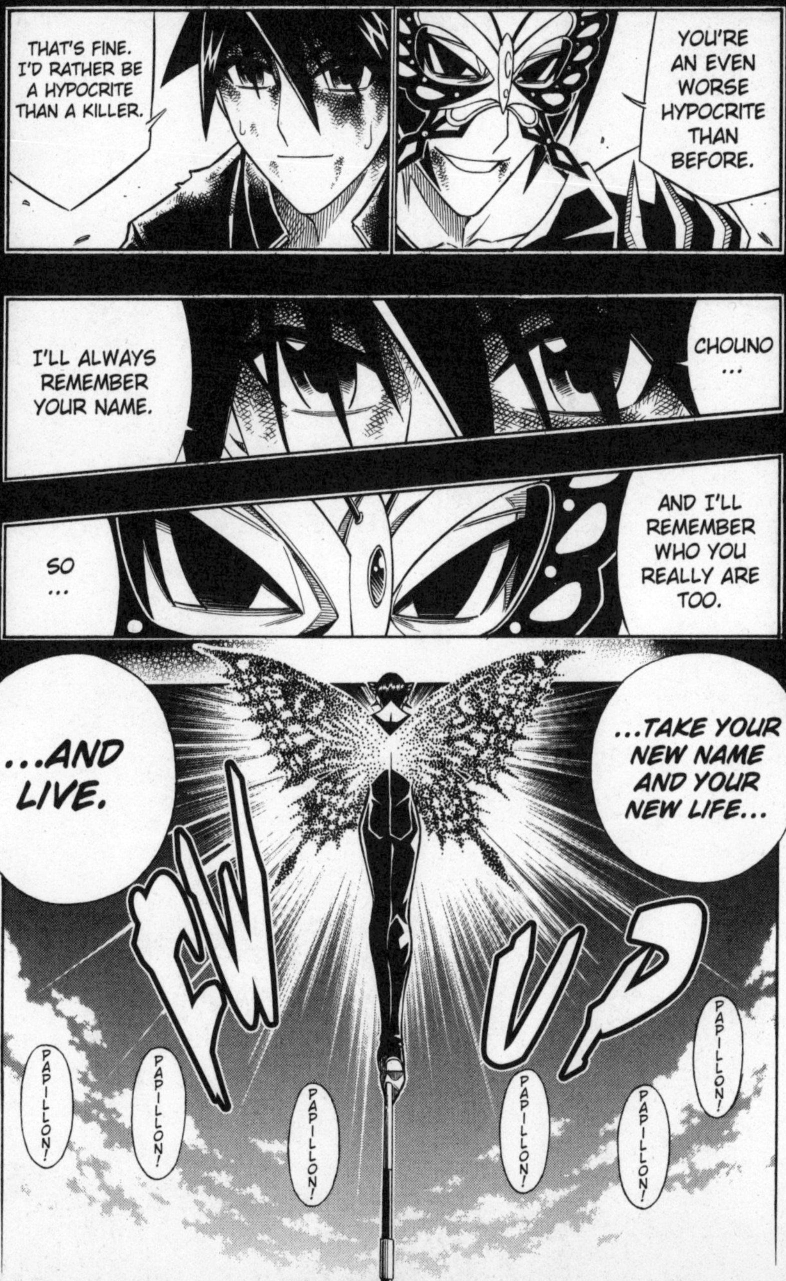

YOU'RE AN EVEN WORSE HYPOCRITE THAN BEFORE.
THAT'S FINE. I'D RATHER BE A HYPOCRITE THAN A KILLER.
CHOUNO ...
I'LL ALWAYS REMEMBER YOUR NAME.
AND I'LL REMEMBER WHO YOU REALLY ARE TOO.
SO ...
...TAKE YOUR NEW NAME AND YOUR NEW LIFE...
...AND LIVE.
PAPILLON!
PAPILLON!
PAPILLON!
PAPILLON!
PAPILLON!
PAPILLON!

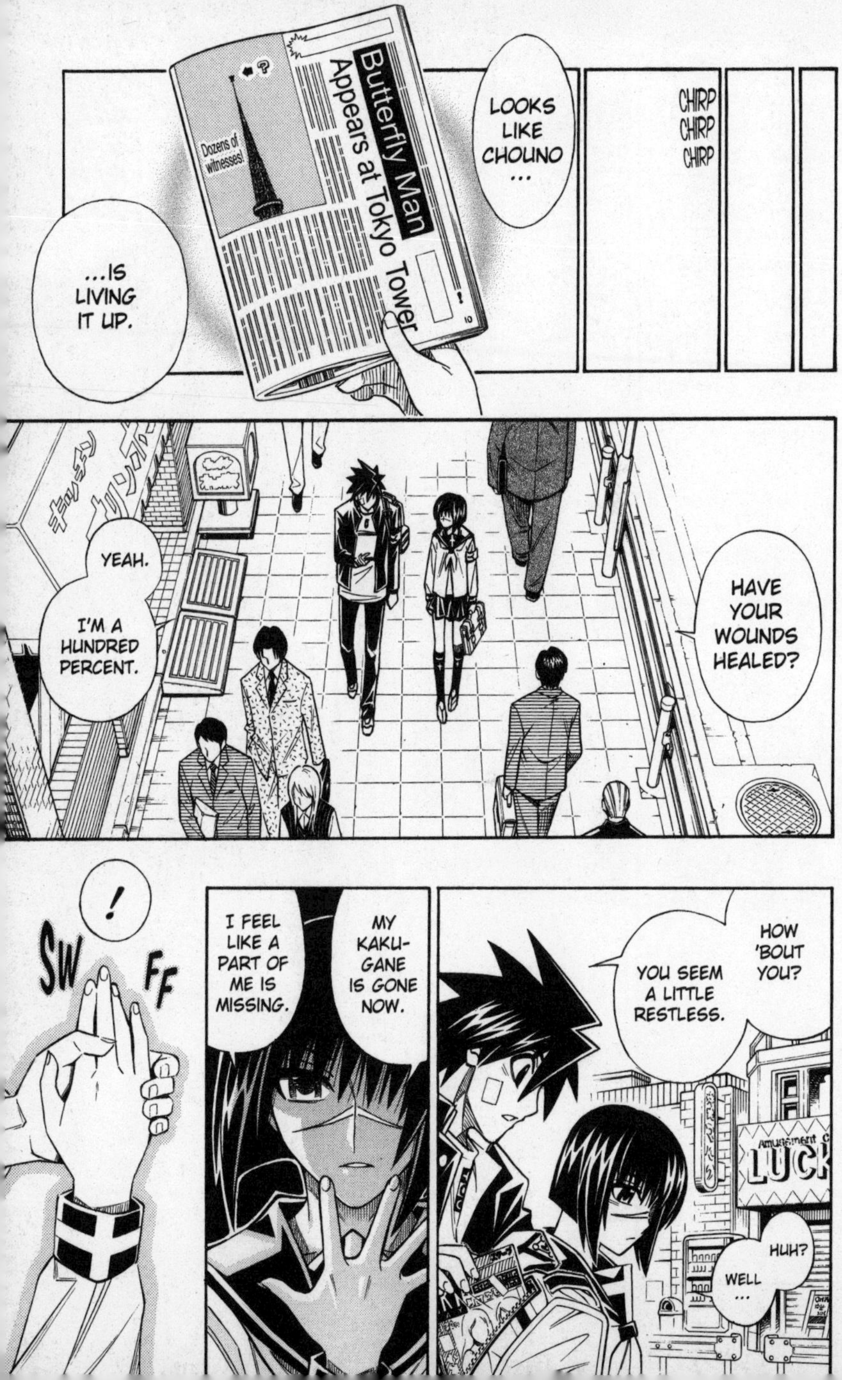
CHIRP CHIRP CHIRP
LOOKS LIKE CHOUNO...
Butterfly Man Appears at Tokyo Tower
Dozens of witnesses!
...IS LIVING IT UP.
HAVE YOUR WOUNDS HEALED?
YEAH.
I'M A HUNDRED PERCENT.
HOW 'BOUT YOU?
YOU SEEM A LITTLE RESTLESS.
HUH?
WELL...
MY KAKU-GANE IS GONE NOW.
I FEEL LIKE A PART OF ME IS MISSING.
!
SWFF

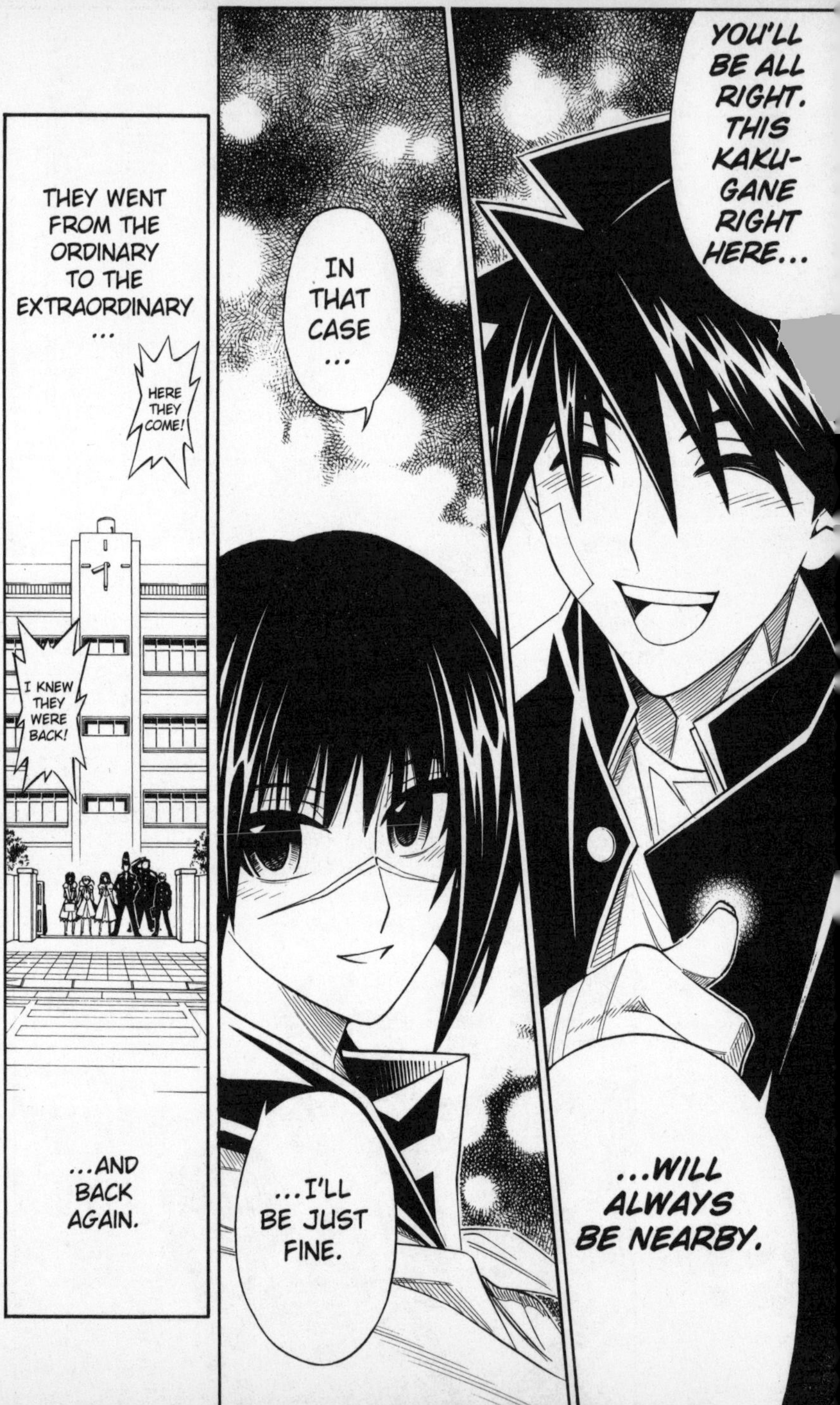
YOU'LL BE ALL RIGHT. THIS KAKU-GANE RIGHT HERE...
...WILL ALWAYS BE NEARBY.
IN THAT CASE...
...I'LL BE JUST FINE.
THEY WENT FROM THE ORDINARY TO THE EXTRAORDINARY...
HERE THEY COME!
I KNEW THEY WERE BACK!
...AND BACK AGAIN.

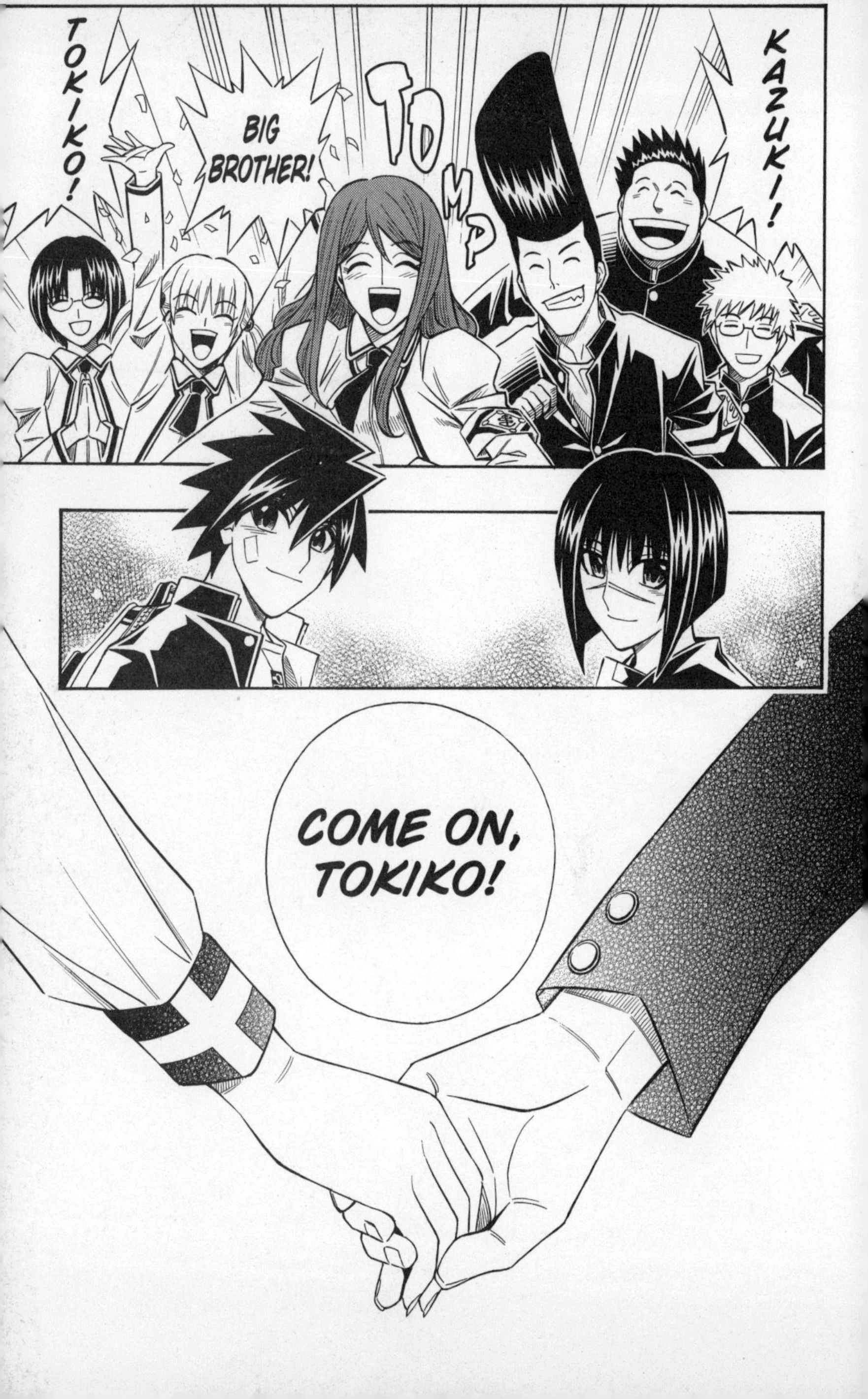
KAZUKI!
TOMP
BIG BROTHER!
TOKIKO!
COME ON, TOKIKO!

BUSO RENKIN

THE END

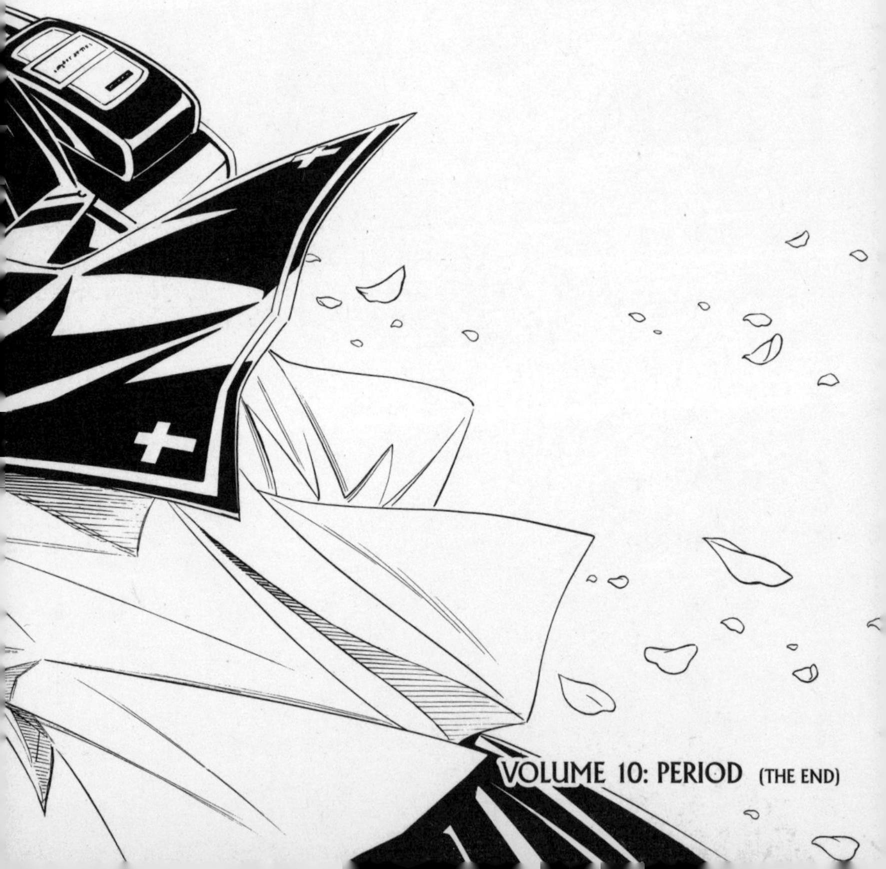

VOLUME 10: PERIOD (THE END)

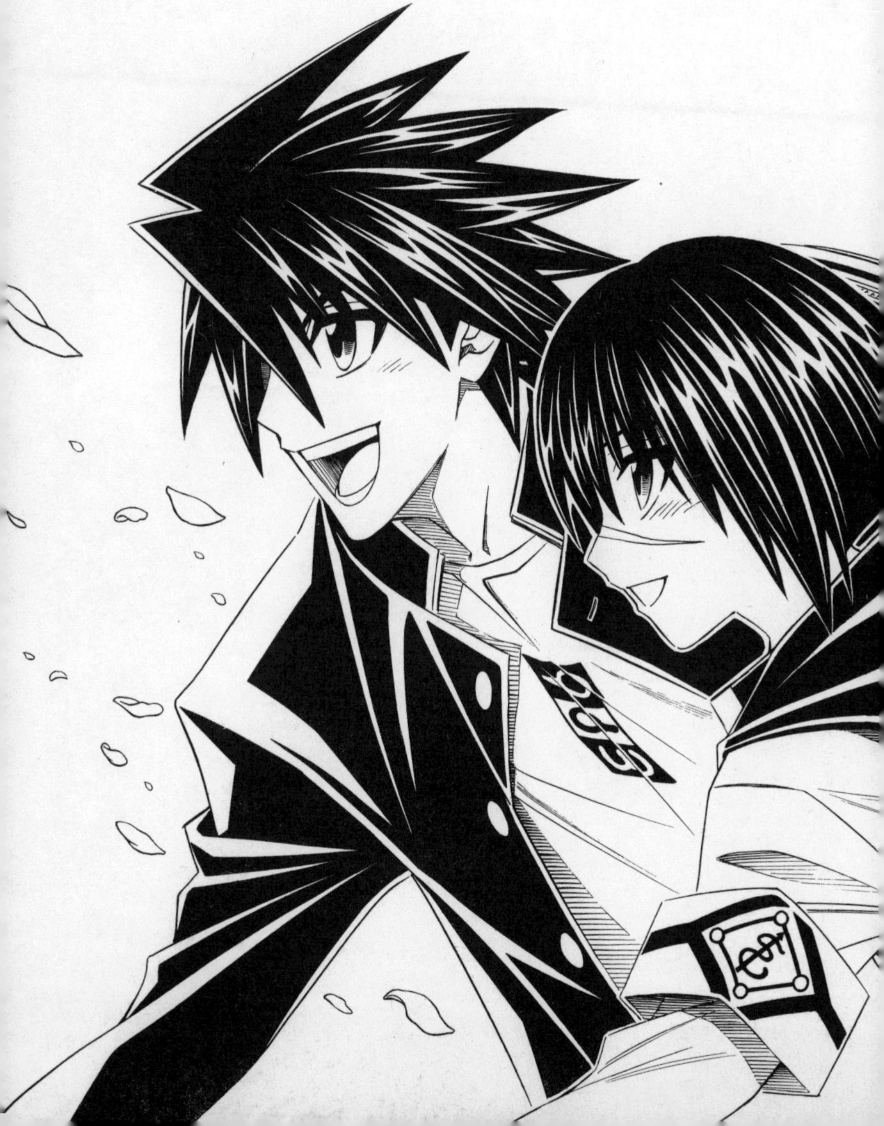

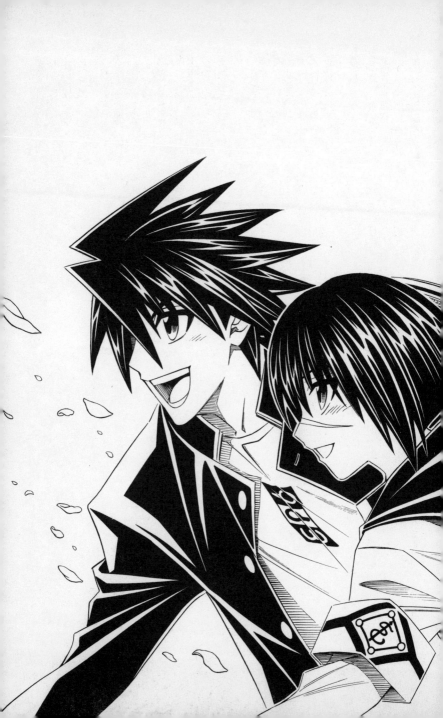

- Height: 169 cm; Weight: 47 kg
- Measurements: 85-57-88
- Born: July 4; Cancer; Blood Type: A; Age: 26
- Likes: Reconnaissance, household chores
- Dislikes: Combat, gambling
- Hobby: Cosplay (She denies it.)
- Special Ability: Peeling apples
- Affiliations: Alchemist Army, Re-Extermination Squad

Character File No. 34

CHITOSE TATEYAMA

Author's Notes

- This is the character I came up with when I decided to do an "adult woman."
- Since she was older, I decided she had been in a unit with Bravo and Hiwatari in the past.
- As member Number One of the Re-Extermination Squad, I wanted her to be more of a tactician than a fighter. Then the series was cancelled and I had to scrap all that, unfortunately.
- She seems to be overshadowed by Bravo and Hiwatari, but the only way she could keep going after the humiliating failure of her mission was to become a kind of human machine. At least that was what I had planned for her. I'm going to use this idea again someday.
- Since she was supposed to be a grown woman, I gave her short hair so that it wouldn't look too manga-like. It looks like hair you might see anywhere. Originally I was going to put a bit of gradation in her eyes, but time constraints made it impossible. I tried to give her an unusual nose. Her uniform is based on the Re-Extermination Squad's, only with a tight skirt like a businesswoman might wear. There's nothing about her that's really earth-shattering, but I like her anyway.

· Height: 145 cm; Weight: 32 kg
· Measurements: 70-54-73
· Born: August 28; Virgo; Blood Type: AB; Age: 16
· Likes: Clean air, quiet places
· Dislikes: Polluted air, crowds
· Hobbies: Walking in the woods, aromatherapy
· Special Ability: Able to accurately measure the oxygen
                   content of the air
· Affiliations: Alchemist Army, Re-Extermination Squad

Character File No. 35

HANAKA BUSUJIMA

Author's Notes

· As with other members of the Re-Extermination Squad, Busujima's design was some-what haphazard. You can't even tell if she's male or female with that gas mask Buso Renkin.
· As the story progressed, I started thinking, "This character looks a little feminine." So I decided that she was an extremely shy young girl, hopelessly in love with Hiwatari, who hides her face behind a gas mask. Cheesy, huh?
· But cheesy or not, you get attached to the characters you create, so I can't help wishing I'd been able to explore this character further.
· And so, the story ends and we never get to see her face. Ah, well…

· Height: 186 cm; Weight: 80 kg
· Born: March 14; Pisces; Blood Type: O; Age: 36
· Likes: Peace, ancient traditions
· Dislikes: Those who disrupt peace or ignore tradition
· Hobbies: Collecting sunglasses, praying
· Special Ability: Able to laugh as he disciplines his
   subordinates
· Affiliations: Alchemist Army, Great Warrior Chief–Asian
   Sector

Character File No. 36

SHOSEI SAKAGUCHI

Author's Notes

· Originally, this character was supposed to replace the dead Captain Bravo, but that storyline was dropped. In the beginning, he was supposed to be a thug with a heart of gold.
· Because of the way the story progressed in volume 8, this character was put on hold. So, when I needed a Great Warrior Chief, I decided to use this character.
· But since he was the Great Warrior Chief, I had to change his looks and personality. So I went completely the other direction and made him look and talk a bit like a priest. I guess a thuggish version will have to show up somewhere else.
· This character had the unfortunate task of having to account for the past and present actions of the Alchemist Warriors.
· The design was based on a priest's outfit, which I altered. Then I added a hat, sunglasses and a cape. Looking at it now, it seems a little busy. I think the best characters and stories are often simple on the surface, but have hidden depths.

- Height: 150 cm; Weight: 37 kg
- Measurements: 79-58-81
- Born: November 11; Scorpio; Blood Type: A; Age: 13
- Likes: Her parents, meat pies
- Dislikes: Alchemy, Alchemist Army
- Hobby: Making meat pies
- Special Ability: Delivering verbal abuse
- Affiliations: Former Alchemist Army, Victor Hunting Squad

Character File No. 37

VICTORIA POWERED

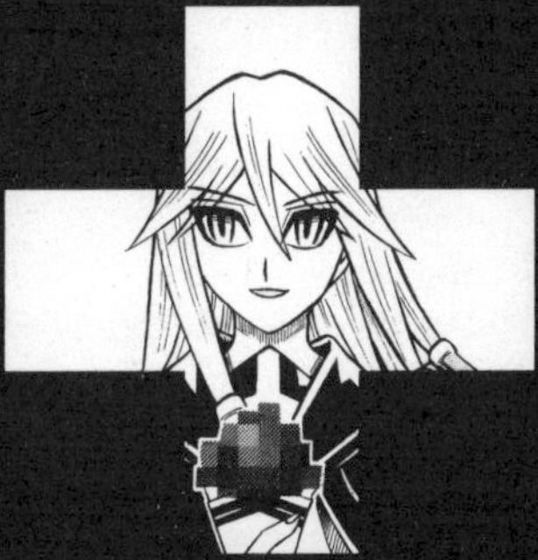

Author's Notes

- Originally, Victoria was only supposed to show up in Victor's flashbacks as the first victim of the black kakugane. (Victor was to have unintentionally killed his daughter with his energy drain.)
- But as it turned out, she and her mother were needed in the present to introduce the masked man (Rurio Head) and the secret laboratory at Newton Apple Academy for Girls.
- Looking back on the choice, I think it was the right one as Victoria provided a reason for Victor to want to live, and vice versa.
- Although I had this character planned out well before her appearance, she evolved into an adult woman with the appearance of a little girl and a sharp tongue. She was a lot of fun to write and to draw. I think this type of character needs to come up again in my work.
- I designed her look without much planning. Now I wish I'd spent more time on her hair. But I'm pretty happy with the sailor suit and cape combo I put her in.

A Secret Room for a Secret Family

Buso Renkin File No. 19

アンダーグラウンドサーチライト

UNDERGROUND SEARCHLIGHT

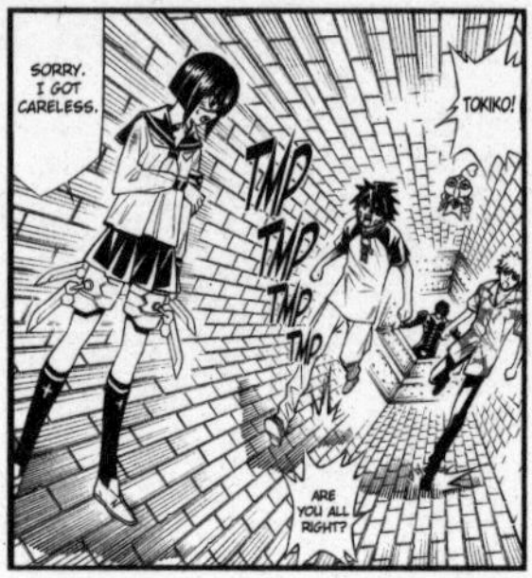
TOKIKO!
SORRY. I GOT CARELESS.
TMP TMP TMP TMP
ARE YOU ALL RIGHT?

- ○ Kakugane Serial Number: LI (51)
- ○ Creator: Victoria Powered
- ○ Form: Shelter
- ○ Main Colors: Ivory and Light Green
- ○ Special Abilities: · Creates a hidden shelter behind any wall or floor
- ○ Special Traits:
  - · The shelter resides in another dimension and its entrance is virtually impossible to detect when the hatch is closed.
  - · The size and décor can be changed at will, but the larger and more complex the interior, the greater the drain on the creator.
  - · Plumbing and electricity are obtained by tapping into existing systems in the real world. In an emergency, the shelter can generate power and store about a month's supply of water.

○ Author's Notes:

- · This Buso Renkin was necessary because I needed a place where Victoria and Alexandria could remain hidden and conduct their research for the last hundred years.
- · The basic design was an octagonal shape that I gave a '60s or '70s science fiction movie feel to.
- · It looks more like something out of *Doraemon* than a Buso Renkin.
- · The name comes from the Kinniku Shojo Tai song "Underground Searchlight." I really like the sound and message behind that song.

UNDERGROUND SEARCHLIGHT

BUSTER BARON

○ Kakugane Serial Number: XVII (17)

○ Creator: Shosei Sakaguchi

○ Form: Full Plate Armor

○ Main Colors: Silver, Gold, and Gun Metal Blue

○ Special Abilities: · Able to replicate and amplify the powers of other Buso Renkin

○ Special Traits: · It's a 57-meter-tall, 550-ton giant robot. It's not only the most powerful Buso Renkin around, but the most powerful conventional weapon too. Unfortunately, this weapon is limited by its great size.
· Hands and feet can detach for independent use. But again, because of their enormous size, their use may be rather limited.
· The maximum number of Buso Renkin it can use at one time is five.
· The rocket pack on its back allows it to fly for short periods of time. (It's normally used for charging attacks.)

○ Author's Notes:
· This was conceived when somebody said to me, "You gotta have a giant robot." Whether it's Honda's ASIMO, or Tmsuk's Enryu, or Getter Robo, or the Iron Giant, I love robots.
· The design is based on Armor Baron from my previous series, *Gun Blaze West*. I increased the amount of detail in the design. It was half play, half recycling a character I was used to drawing. But I knew that once this thing showed up, the series would be coming to an end, so…farewell, Baron.
· I really like designing armor and robots, but they're not easy to draw. Again I find myself marveling at animators.

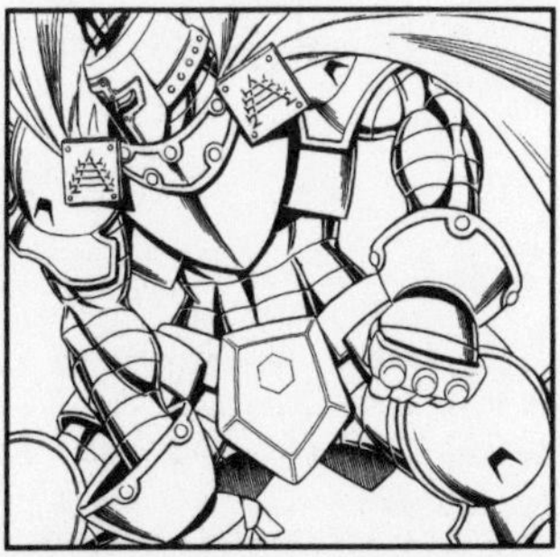

Buso Renkin File No. 20

バスター
バロン

BUSTER BARON

The Baron is Undefeatable!!

The Strongest within the Atmosphere?

Buso Renkin File No. 21

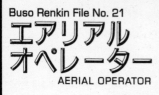

エアリアルオペレーター

AERIAL OPERATOR

SHOOOOO

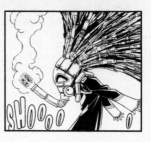

- Kakugane Serial Number: XXXIX (39)
- Creator: Hanaka Busujima
- Form: Gas Mask
- Main Color: Brass Color
- Special Abilities: · Atmospheric Control
- Special Traits:
  - · Able to alter and mix various gases to make new ones
  - · Able to create gases such as oxygen, poison gas, knockout gas, laughing gas, etc.
  - · Once expelled, the gas needs to reach a certain level of strength before it can be mixed again.
  - · The tube in the gas mask has a filtration unit that protects the user from the gases she creates.
  - · The goggles can function as binoculars, a microscope, night-vision goggles, and eye protection when working in a gaseous environment.

- Author's Notes:

· I knew I wanted a Buso Renkin like this one for the Re-Extermination Squad, but I didn't really know what to do with it until I read that napalm was used to clear poisonous gas. So Busujima complements Hiwatari. But in the end, it was all for nothing.

· I'm happy that Busujima got to use her powers to help the others reach Kazuki in outer space.

· The name was something I came up with on the spot. It's the kind of gas mask you'd see in a movie set in the 19th century in which an evil corporation releases toxic gases into the atmosphere. I love the retro feel of the chimney-like respirator that comes off the mouth of the mask.

AERIAL OPERATOR

○ Kakugane Serial Number: XCV (95)

○ Creator: Chitose Tateyama

○ Form: Radar

○ Main Colors: Chrome and Dark Blue

○ Special Abilities: · Reconnaissance of a target and teleportation

○ Special Traits:
- · Reconnaissance is limited to people the user knows.
- · Range and frequency of teleportation are dependant on the user's willpower and stamina.
- · The maximum weight that can be teleported is 100 kilograms (220 lbs.), or roughly two small adults.
- · The Buso Renkin itself is very sturdy and can be used as a shield or a small impact weapon.

○ Author's Notes:

· Originally, I had a completely different Buso Renkin in mind for Chitose. It was going to be a small dagger called "Chrome Cradle to Grave" that would allow her to change her age. In volume 7, there's a panel where you see Chitose in the uniform of Newton Apple Academy for Girls. She hadn't dressed up like a school girl; she'd actually changed her age in order to infiltrate the school, but…

· With the series coming to an end, I needed her to have a Buso Renkin that could teleport. So, unfortunately for Chitose, she became a grown woman who likes to cosplay in high school girl uniforms. How sad.

· The design for this Buso Renkin was improvised. It's basically an octagon plus radar. Kaoru Kurosaki provided the name.

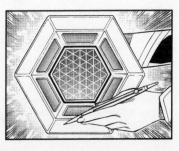

Buso Renkin File No. 22

ヘルメス
ドライブ

HERMES DRIVE

I Can Find You Anywhere!

Its Power to Attract Affects Destiny!

Buso Renkin File No. 23

フェイタル
アトラクション

FATAL ATTRACTION

○ Kakugane Serial Number: I (Black Kakugane)
○ Creator: Victor Powered
○ Form: Great Axe
○ Main Colors: Red, Silver, and Black
○ Special Abilities: · Gravitational control

○ Special Traits: · At the point of impact, the weapon's momentum can be altered to control the amount of damage.
· By applying maximum force to opposing gravitational fields, it can momentarily create a miniature black hole, thereby destroying anything it comes in contact with.
· The great axe can be separated to form two smaller tomahawks.

○ Author's Notes:
· The truth is, I really didn't think about this Buso Renkin's special ability when I designed it. But since it was for a major character, it needed to have a really powerful attack. What came to mind was gravity, and this is what came of it.
· The design motif comes from Divebomb's weapon in *Transformers: Energon*. When I first saw it, I fell in love with the design.
· I made minor changes to this weapon as the series progressed.
· Think of the changes in Victor's Buso Renkin as being like the changes to Kazuki's Sunlight Heart. Please accept this explanation and move along.
· The name comes from the famous storyline in the American comic book *X-Men*. Sorry.

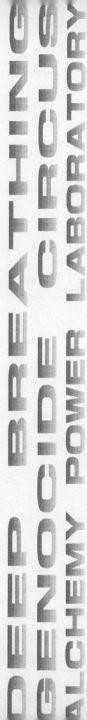

DEEP BREATHING
GENOCIDE CIRCUS
ALCHEMY POWER LABORATORY

Buso Renkin File No. 24

ディープブレッシング

DEEP BREATHING

○Kakugane Serial Number: LXXVII (77)
○Creator: The Captain (real name unknown)
○Form: Submarine
○Main Colors: Deep Blue and Yellow
○Special Abilities: · A submarine with ramming capability

Buso Renkin File No. 25

ジェノサイド　サーカス

GENOCIDE CIRCUS

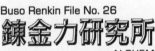

○Kakugane Serial Number: LXVI (66)
○Creator: Unknown
○Form: Missile Pod
○Main Color: Khaki
○Special Abilities: · Never-ending supply of missiles

Buso Renkin File No. 26

錬金力研究所

ALCHEMY-POWERED LABORATORY

○Kakugane Serial Number: XI (11)
○Creator: Unknown
○Form: Secret Base
○Main Colors: Ivory and Silver
○Special Abilities: · Electronic camouflage and stealth capabilities

○Author's Note:
· The whole story of *Buse Renkin* was created through improvisation. I didn't think about it too much.

There are so many more Buso Renkin!!

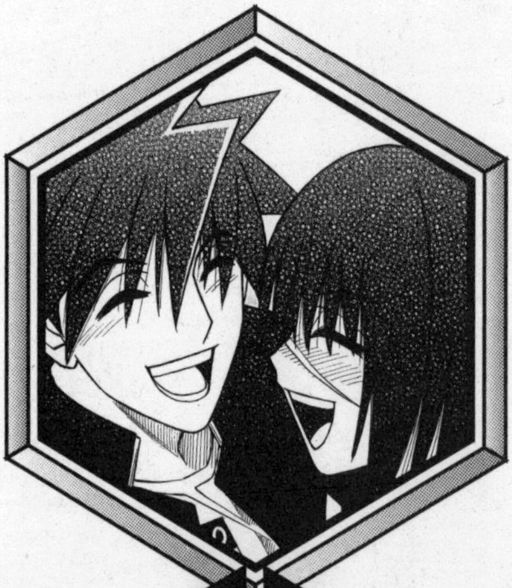

Buso Renkin

ブソウレンキン

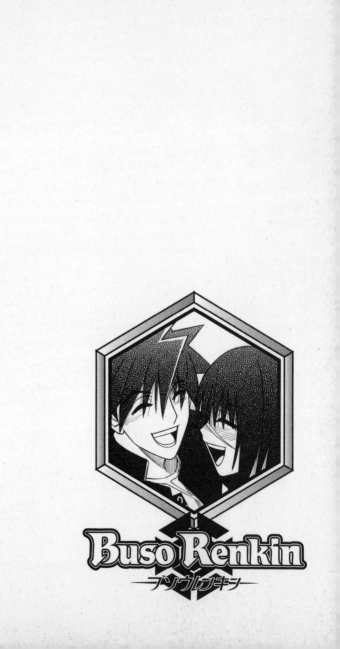

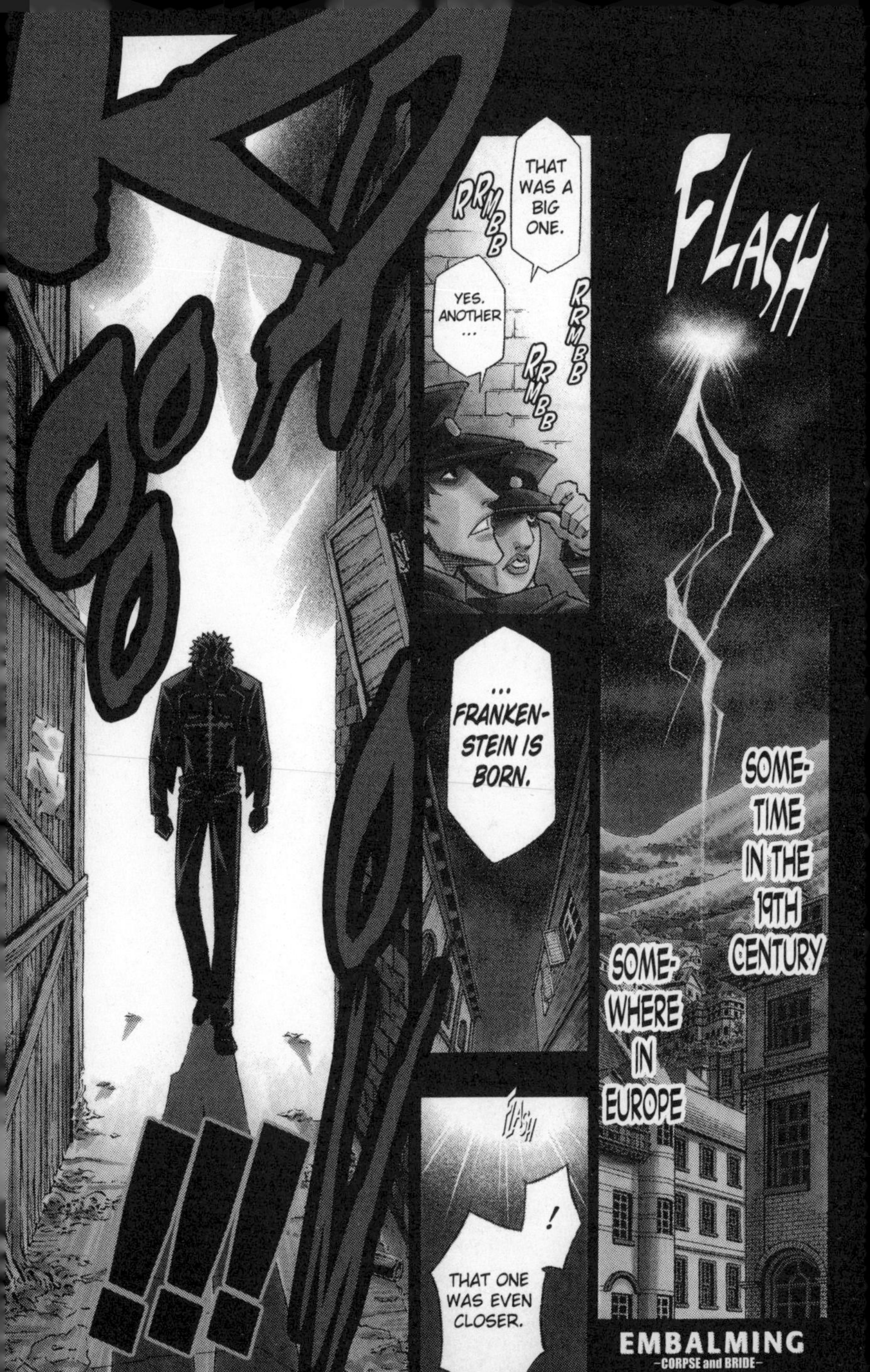
FLASH
SOME-TIME IN THE 19TH CENTURY
SOME-WHERE IN EUROPE
THAT WAS A BIG ONE.
RRMBB
YES. ANOTHER ...
RRMBB
RRMBB
... FRANKEN-STEIN IS BORN.
FLASH
!
THAT ONE WAS EVEN CLOSER.
!!!

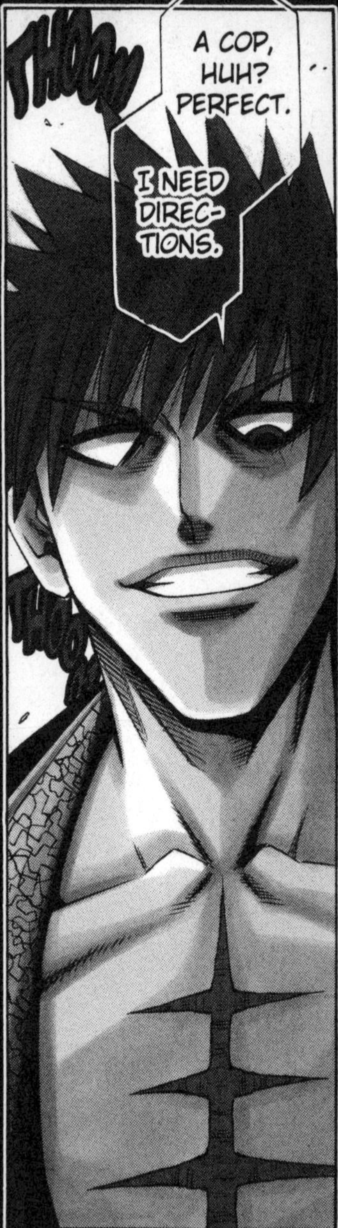
THOOM
A COP, HUH? PERFECT.
I NEED DIRECTIONS.

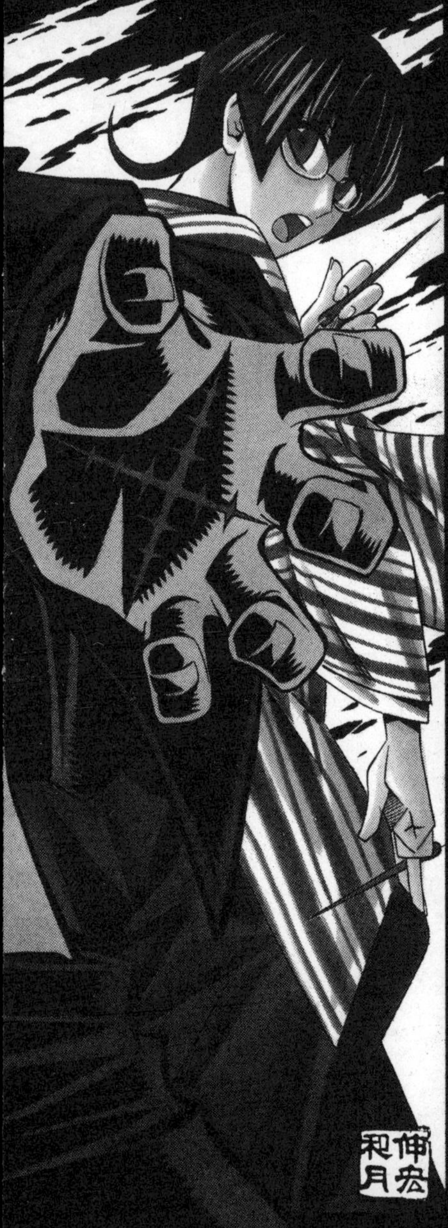
伸宏
和月

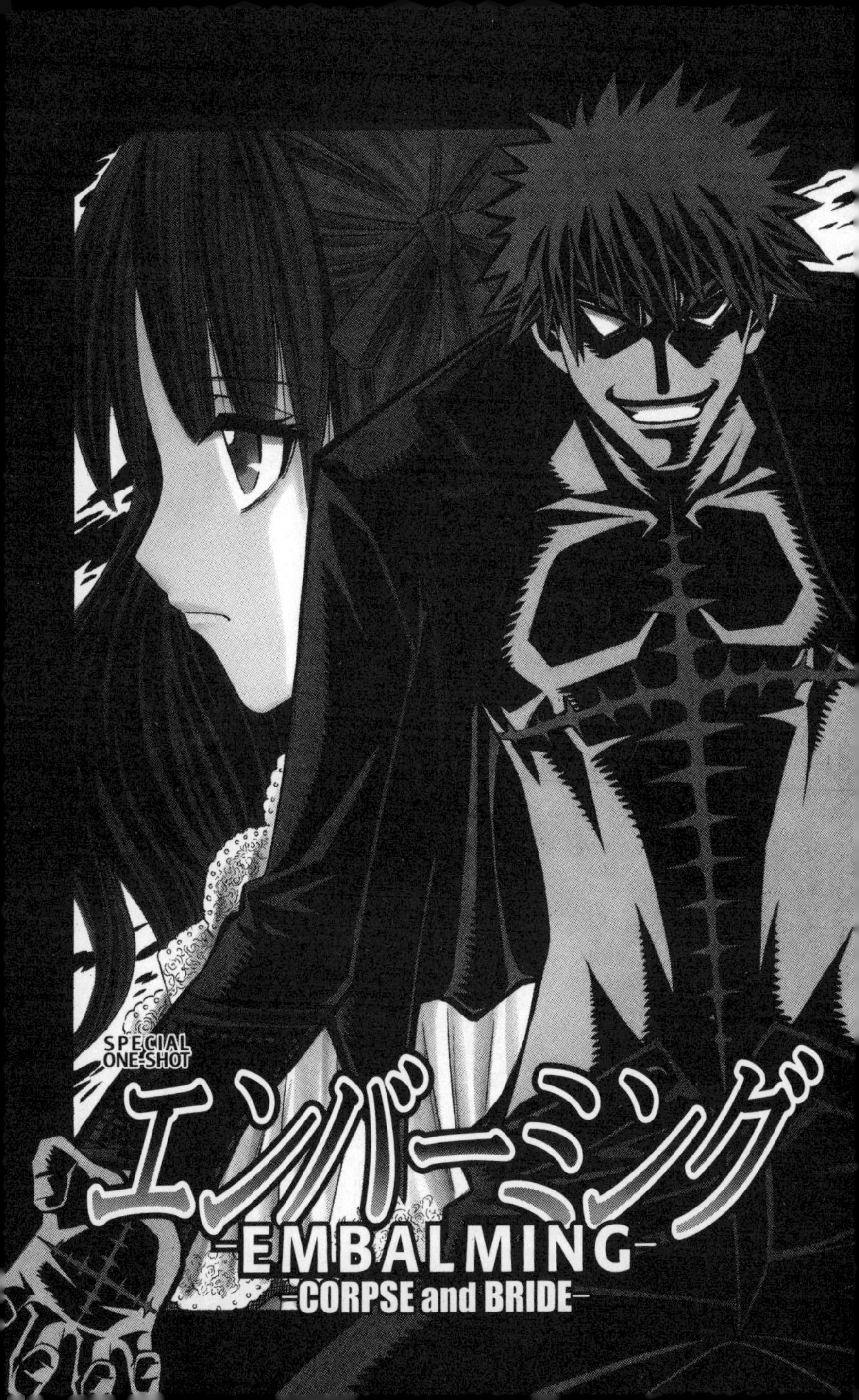
SPECIAL ONE-SHOT
エンバーミング
-EMBALMING-
-CORPSE and BRIDE-

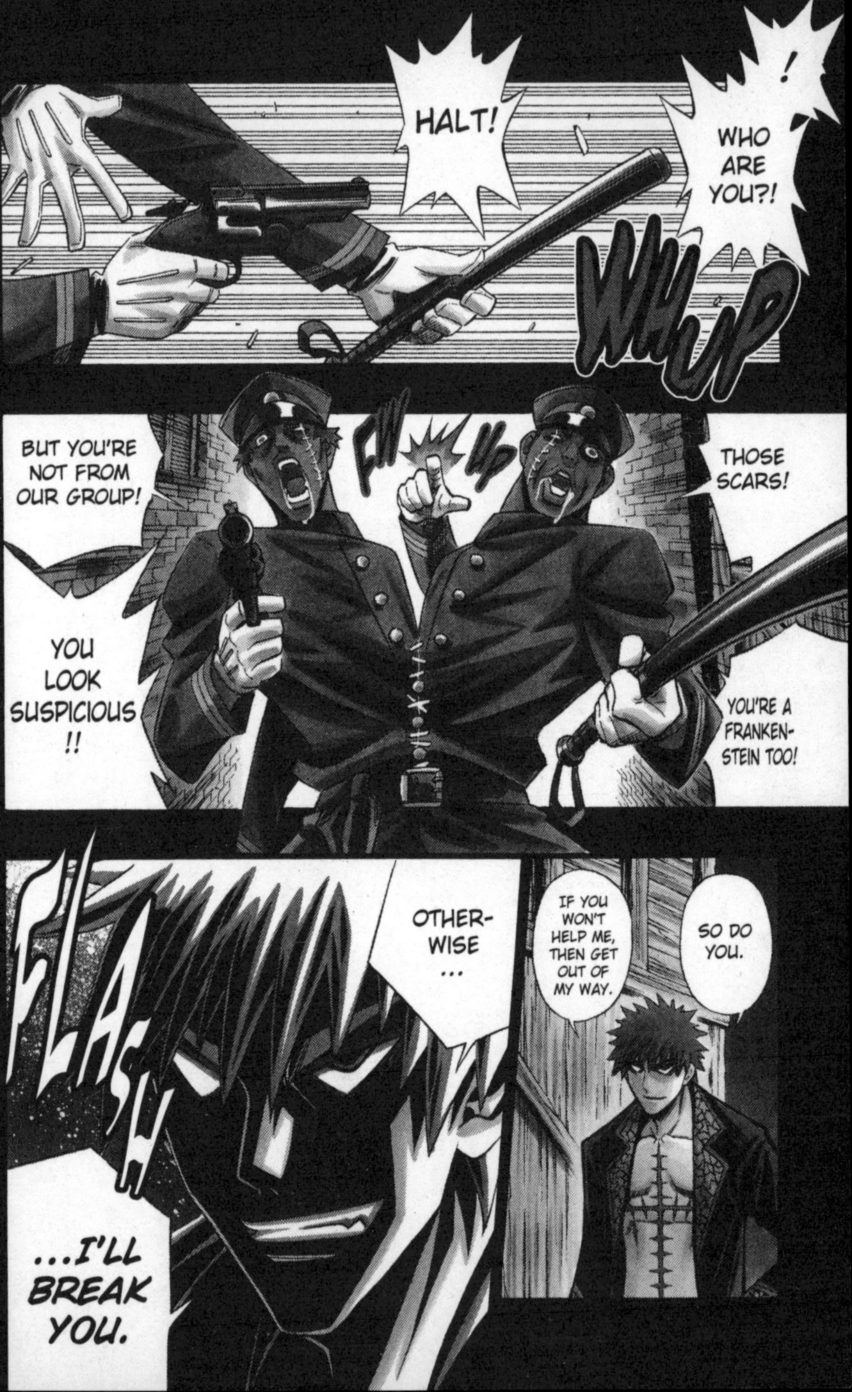
!
WHO ARE YOU?!
HALT!
WHUP
THOSE SCARS!
YOU'RE A FRANKEN-STEIN TOO!
BUT YOU'RE NOT FROM OUR GROUP!
YOU LOOK SUSPICIOUS!!
SO DO YOU.
IF YOU WON'T HELP ME, THEN GET OUT OF MY WAY.
OTHER-WISE ...
FLASH
...I'LL BREAK YOU.

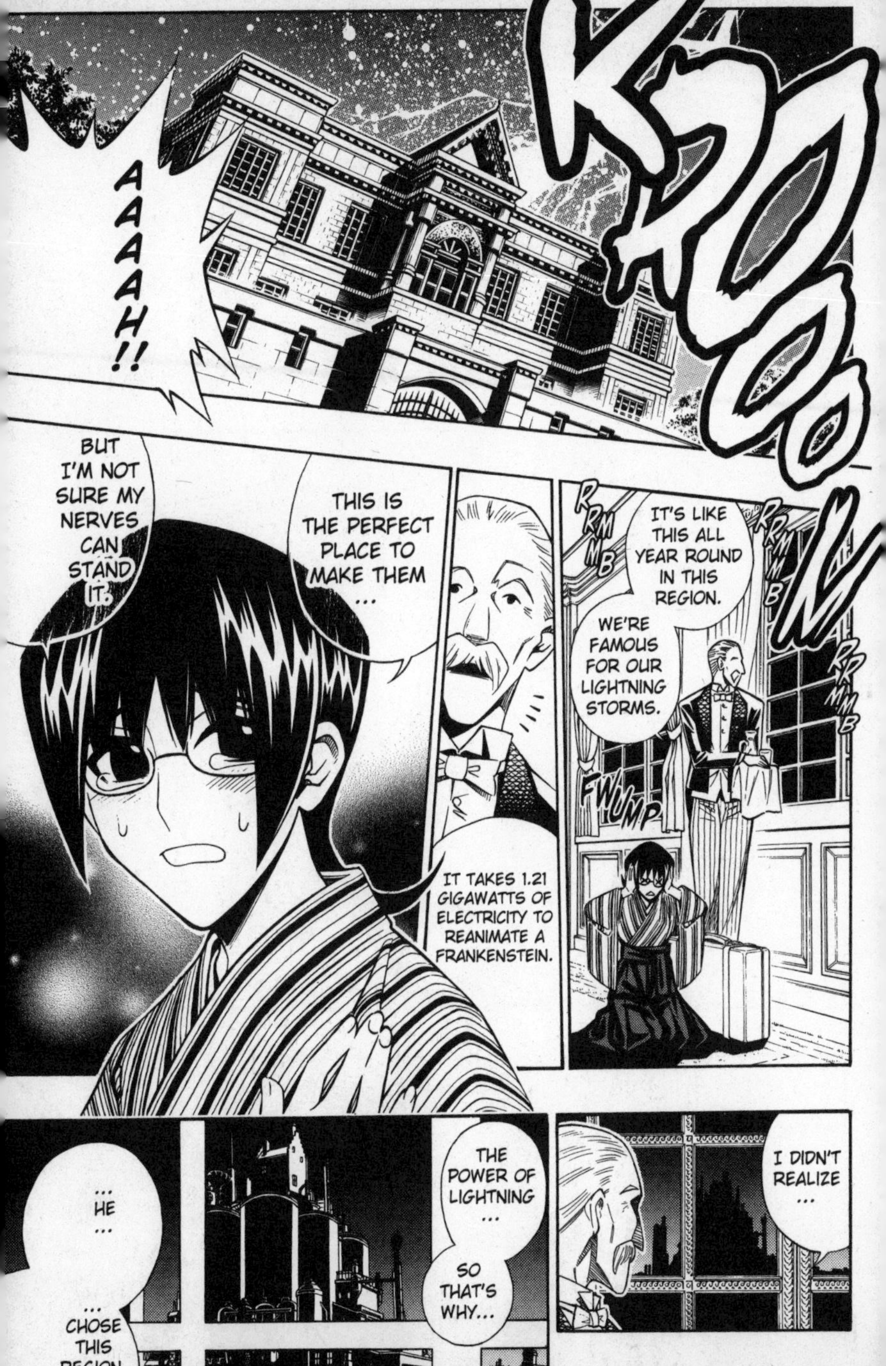
AAAAAH!!
RRMB
IT'S LIKE THIS ALL YEAR ROUND IN THIS REGION.
WE'RE FAMOUS FOR OUR LIGHTNING STORMS.
RRMMB
RRMMB
FWUMP
IT TAKES 1.21 GIGAWATTS OF ELECTRICITY TO REANIMATE A FRANKENSTEIN.
THIS IS THE PERFECT PLACE TO MAKE THEM...
BUT I'M NOT SURE MY NERVES CAN STAND IT.
I DIDN'T REALIZE...
THE POWER OF LIGHTNING...
SO THAT'S WHY...
...HE...
...CHOSE THIS REGION.

"ARTIFICIAL HUMAN" FRANKENSTEIN

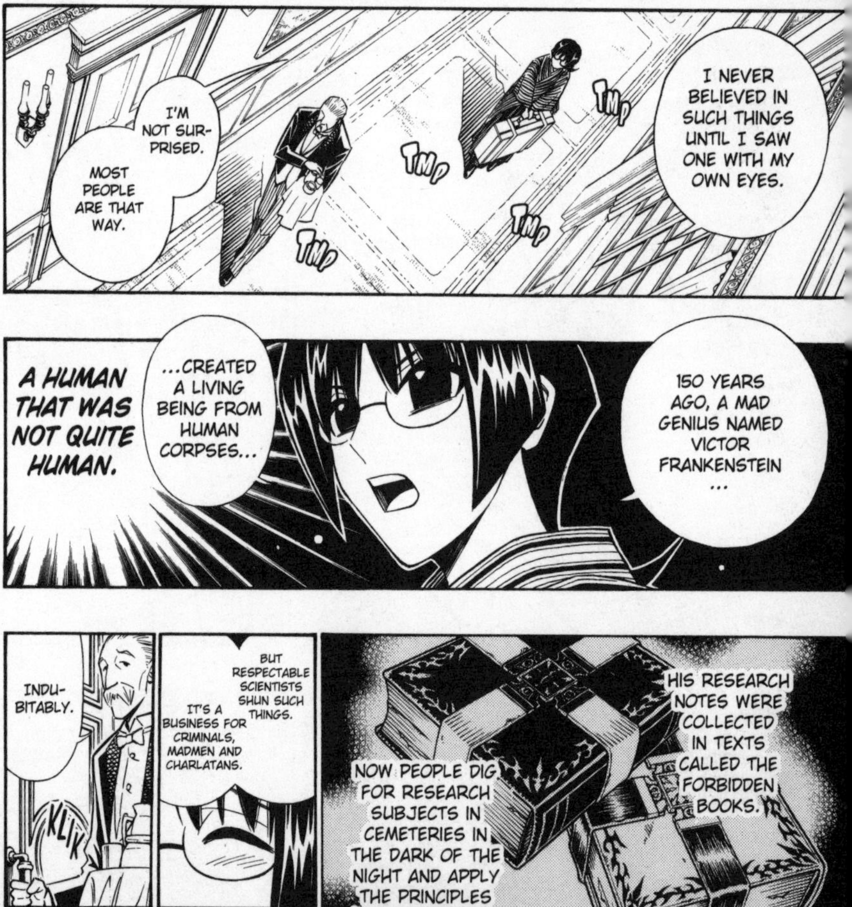
I NEVER BELIEVED IN SUCH THINGS UNTIL I SAW ONE WITH MY OWN EYES.
TMP
TMP
TMP
TMP
I'M NOT SUR-PRISED.
MOST PEOPLE ARE THAT WAY.
150 YEARS AGO, A MAD GENIUS NAMED VICTOR FRANKENSTEIN...
...CREATED A LIVING BEING FROM HUMAN CORPSES...
A HUMAN THAT WAS NOT QUITE HUMAN.
HIS RESEARCH NOTES WERE COLLECTED IN TEXTS CALLED THE FORBIDDEN BOOKS.
NOW PEOPLE DIG FOR RESEARCH SUBJECTS IN CEMETERIES IN THE DARK OF THE NIGHT AND APPLY THE PRINCIPLES IN THOSE BOOKS.
BUT RESPECTABLE SCIENTISTS SHUN SUCH THINGS.
IT'S A BUSINESS FOR CRIMINALS, MADMEN AND CHARLATANS.
INDU-BITABLY.
KLIK

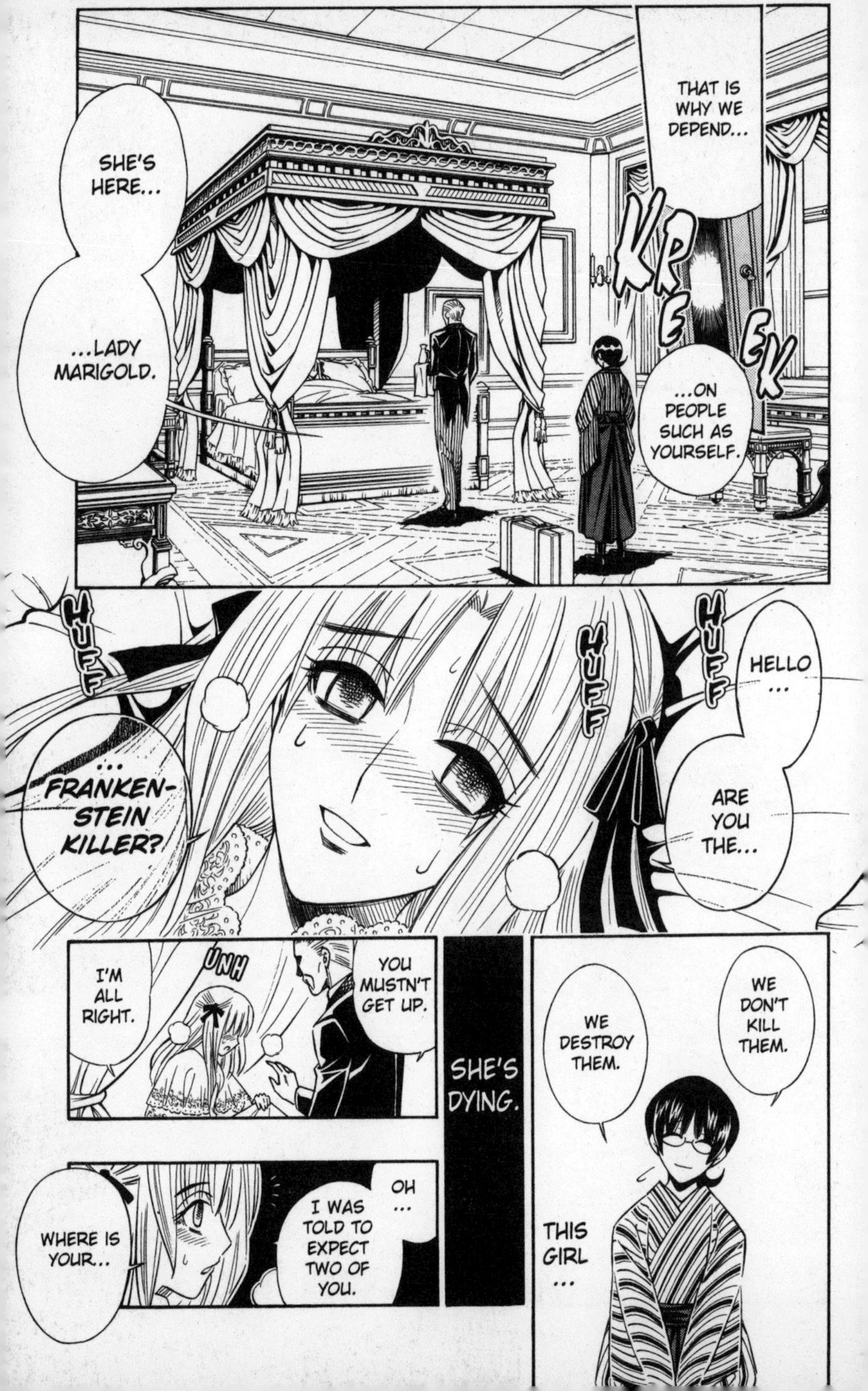
THAT IS WHY WE DEPEND...
KREEEK
...ON PEOPLE SUCH AS YOURSELF.
SHE'S HERE...
...LADY MARIGOLD.
HUFF HUFF
HELLO ...
ARE YOU THE...
HUFF
... FRANKEN-STEIN KILLER?
WE DON'T KILL THEM.
WE DESTROY THEM.
THIS GIRL ...
SHE'S DYING.
YOU MUSTN'T GET UP.
UNH
I'M ALL RIGHT.
OH ...
I WAS TOLD TO EXPECT TWO OF YOU.
WHERE IS YOUR...

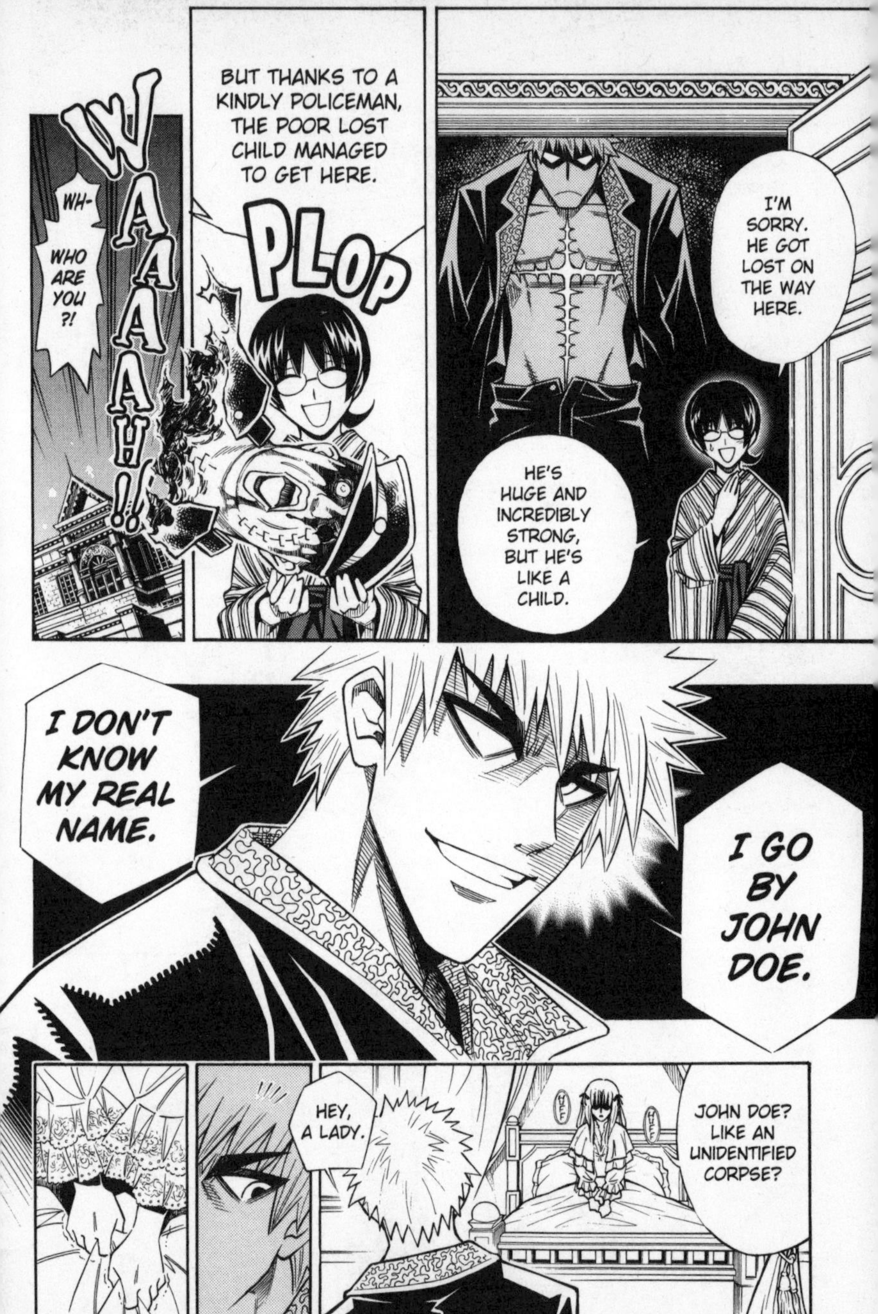
I'M SORRY. HE GOT LOST ON THE WAY HERE.
HE'S HUGE AND INCREDIBLY STRONG, BUT HE'S LIKE A CHILD.
BUT THANKS TO A KINDLY POLICEMAN, THE POOR LOST CHILD MANAGED TO GET HERE.
PLOP
WAAAAH!!
WH- WHO ARE YOU?!
I DON'T KNOW MY REAL NAME.
I GO BY JOHN DOE.
JOHN DOE? LIKE AN UNIDENTIFIED CORPSE?
HEY, A LADY.

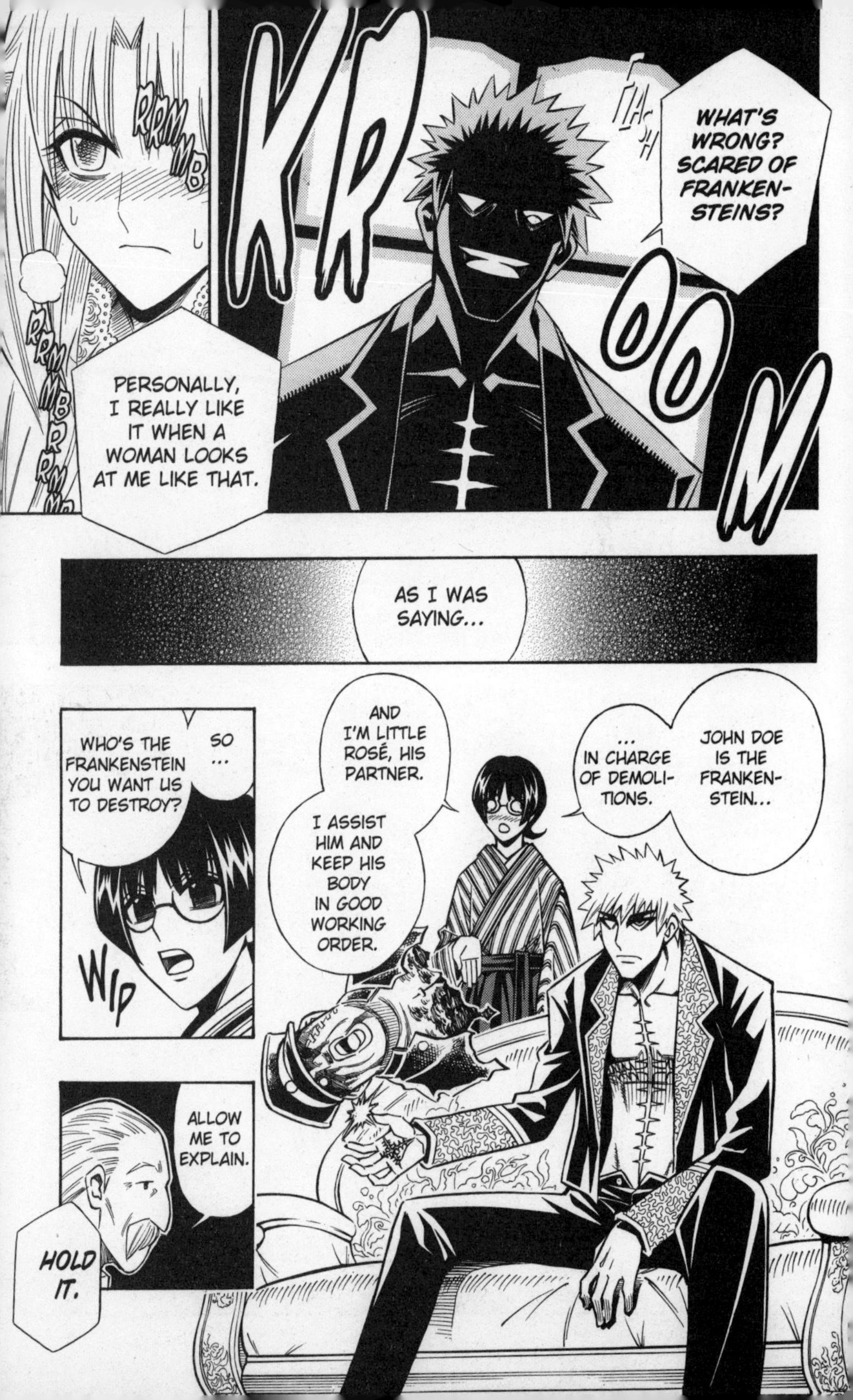
FLASH
WHAT'S WRONG? SCARED OF FRANKEN-STEINS?
KR
OOM
PERSONALLY, I REALLY LIKE IT WHEN A WOMAN LOOKS AT ME LIKE THAT.
RRMMB
RRMMBRRRMMB
AS I WAS SAYING...
JOHN DOE IS THE FRANKEN-STEIN...
... IN CHARGE OF DEMOLI-TIONS.
AND I'M LITTLE ROSÉ, HIS PARTNER.
I ASSIST HIM AND KEEP HIS BODY IN GOOD WORKING ORDER.
SO...
WHO'S THE FRANKENSTEIN YOU WANT US TO DESTROY?
WIP
ALLOW ME TO EXPLAIN.
HOLD IT.

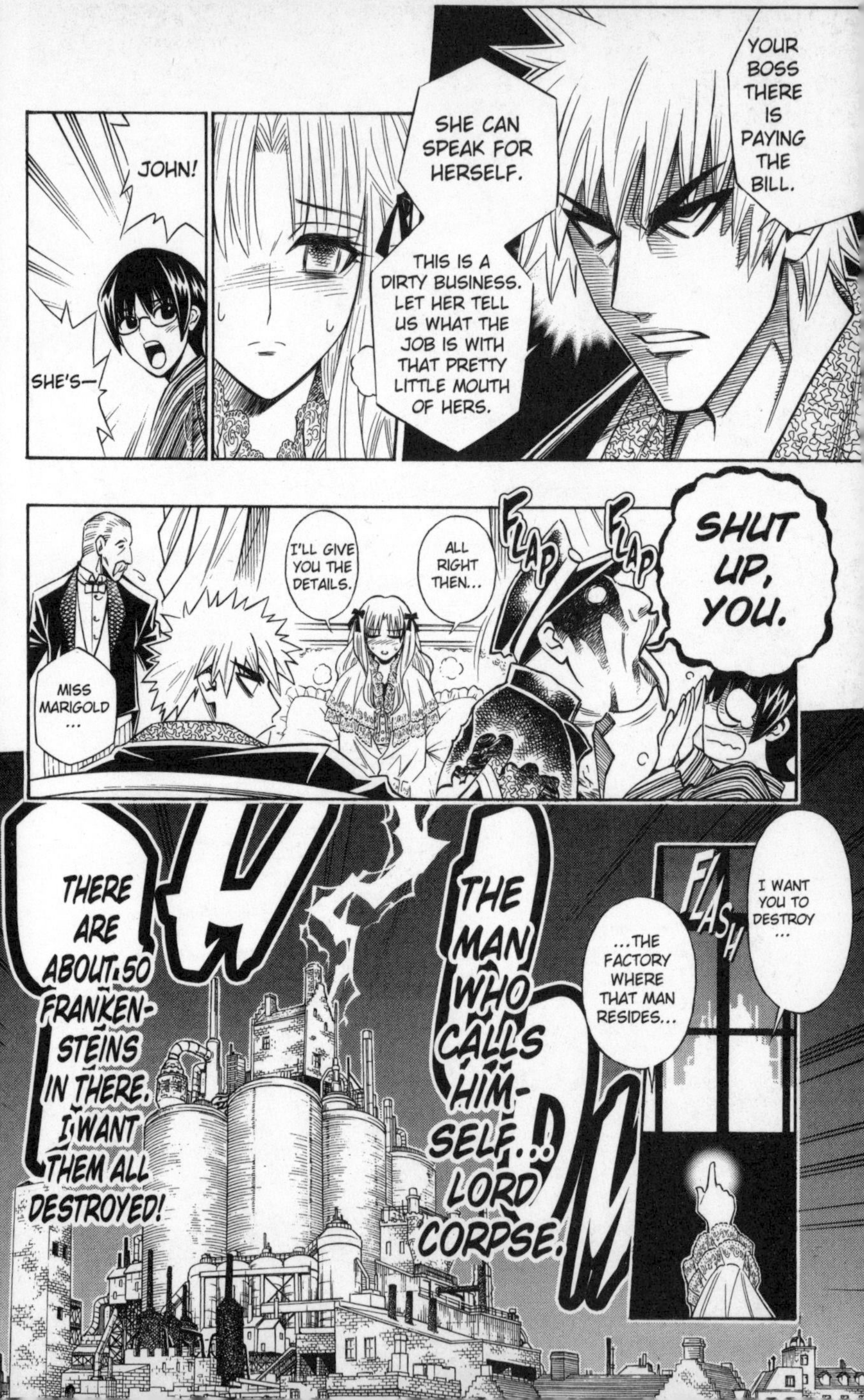
YOUR BOSS THERE IS PAYING THE BILL.
SHE CAN SPEAK FOR HERSELF.
THIS IS A DIRTY BUSINESS. LET HER TELL US WHAT THE JOB IS WITH THAT PRETTY LITTLE MOUTH OF HERS.
JOHN!
SHE'S—
SHUT UP, YOU.
FLAP FLAP
ALL RIGHT THEN...
I'LL GIVE YOU THE DETAILS.
MISS MARIGOLD ...
FLASH
I WANT YOU TO DESTROY ...
...THE FACTORY WHERE THAT MAN RESIDES...
THE MAN WHO CALLS HIM-SELF...! LORD CORPSE.
THERE ARE ABOUT 50 FRANKEN-STEINS IN THERE. I WANT THEM ALL DESTROYED!

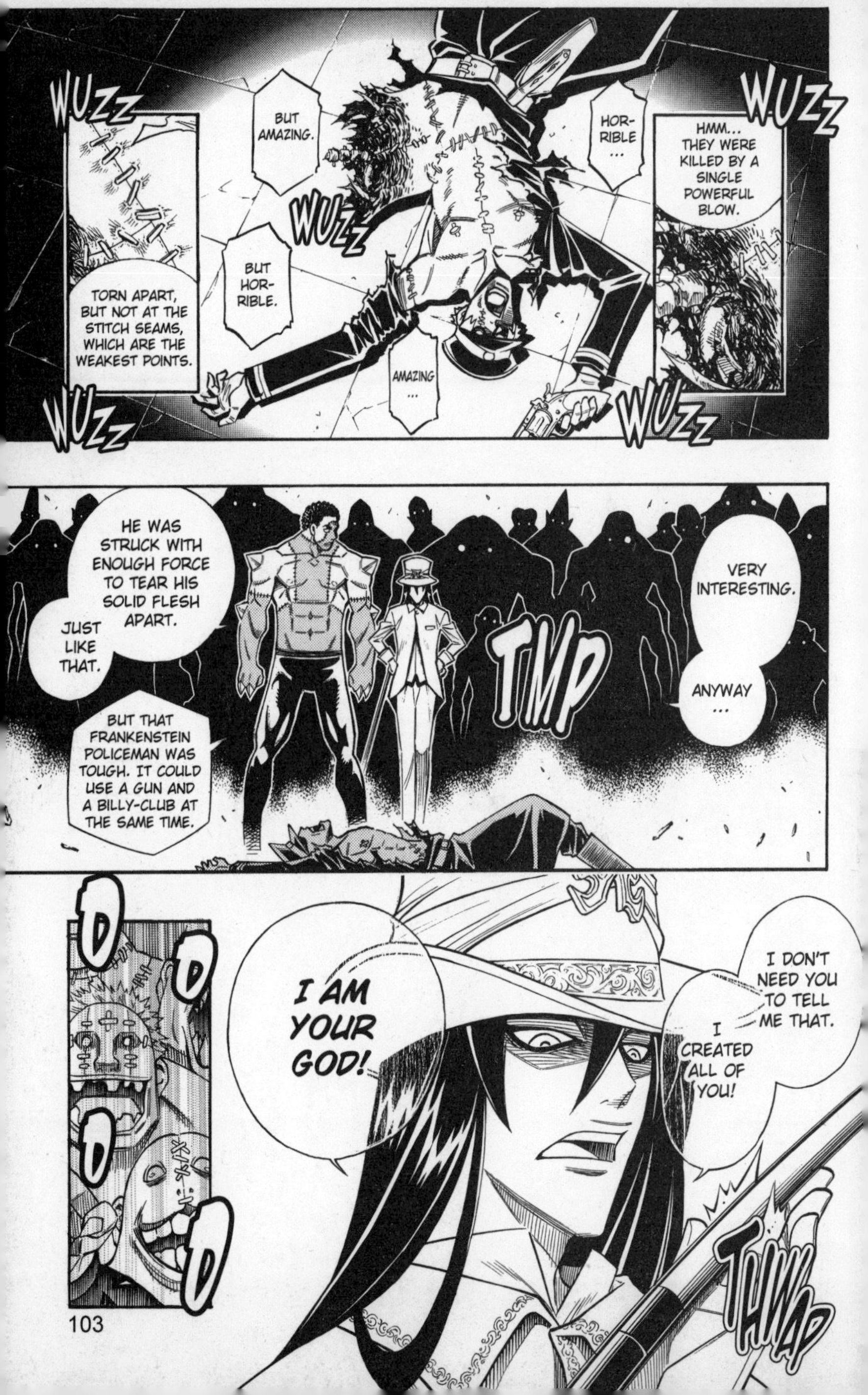
WUZZ
HMM... THEY WERE KILLED BY A SINGLE POWERFUL BLOW.
HOR-RIBLE ...
BUT AMAZING.
WUZZ
BUT HOR-RIBLE.
AMAZING ...
WUZZ
WUZZ
TORN APART, BUT NOT AT THE STITCH SEAMS, WHICH ARE THE WEAKEST POINTS.
WUZZ
VERY INTERESTING.
ANYWAY ...
TMP
HE WAS STRUCK WITH ENOUGH FORCE TO TEAR HIS SOLID FLESH APART.
JUST LIKE THAT.
BUT THAT FRANKENSTEIN POLICEMAN WAS TOUGH. IT COULD USE A GUN AND A BILLY-CLUB AT THE SAME TIME.
I DON'T NEED YOU TO TELL ME THAT.
I CREATED ALL OF YOU!
I AM YOUR GOD!
THWAP
D
D
D
D

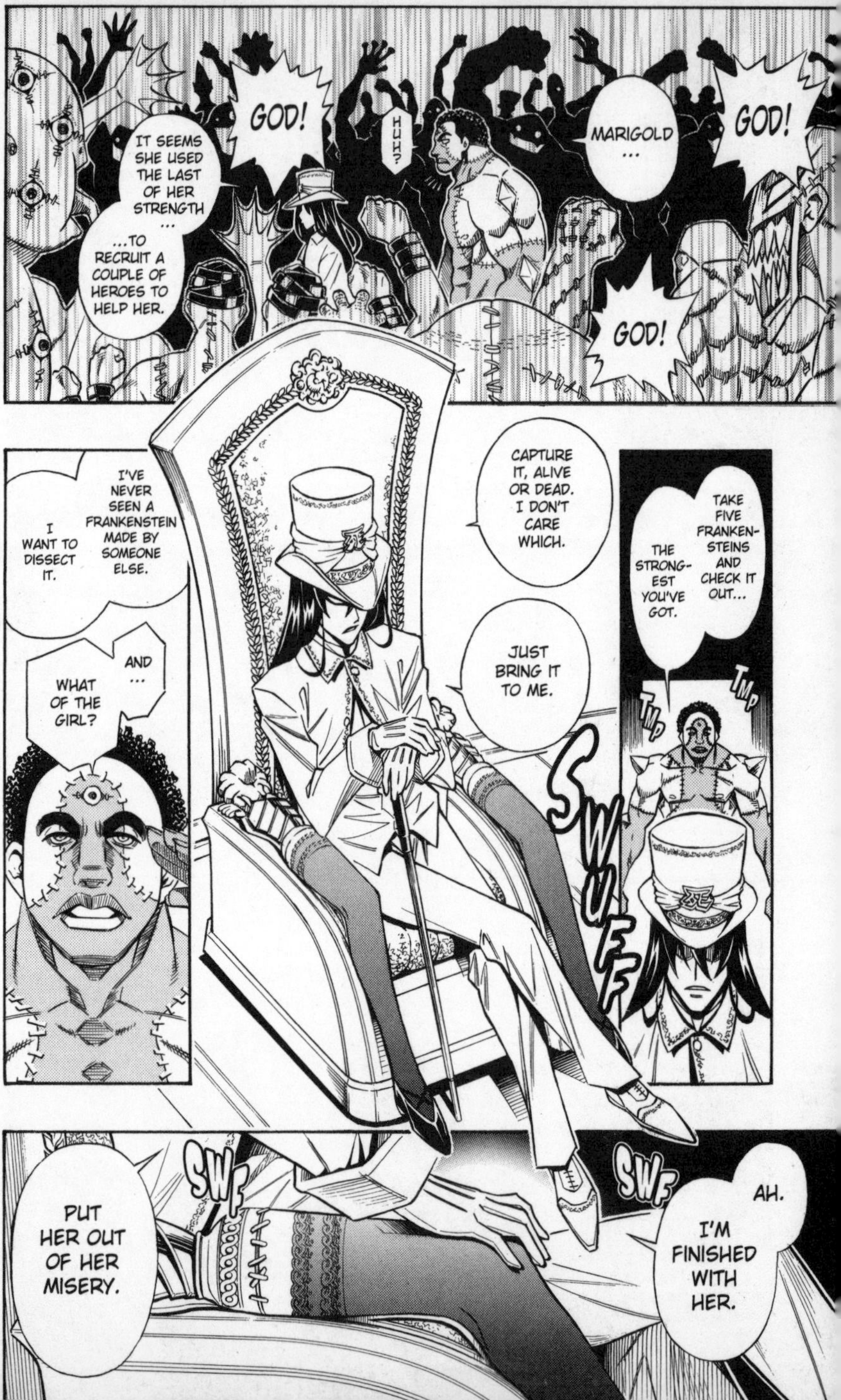
GOD!
MARIGOLD ...
GOD!
HUH?
GOD!
IT SEEMS SHE USED THE LAST OF HER STRENGTH ...
...TO RECRUIT A COUPLE OF HEROES TO HELP HER.
TMP
TMP
TAKE FIVE FRANKEN-STEINS AND CHECK IT OUT...
THE STRONG-EST YOU'VE GOT.
SWUFF
CAPTURE IT, ALIVE OR DEAD. I DON'T CARE WHICH.
JUST BRING IT TO ME.
I'VE NEVER SEEN A FRANKENSTEIN MADE BY SOMEONE ELSE.
I WANT TO DISSECT IT.
AND ...
WHAT OF THE GIRL?
SWF
AH.
I'M FINISHED WITH HER.
SWF
PUT HER OUT OF HER MISERY.

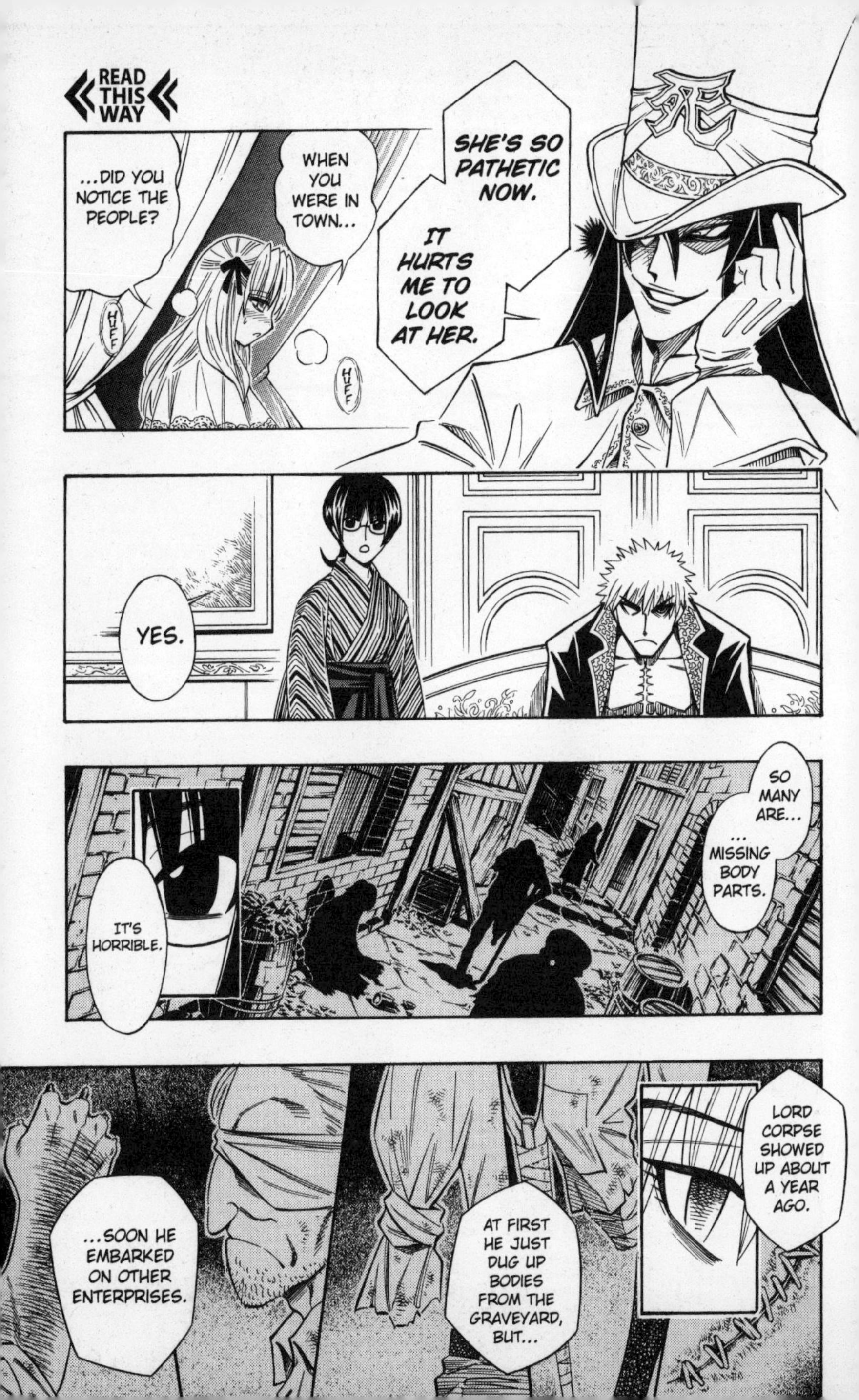
READ THIS WAY
SHE'S SO PATHETIC NOW.
IT HURTS ME TO LOOK AT HER.
WHEN YOU WERE IN TOWN...
...DID YOU NOTICE THE PEOPLE?
HUFF
HUFF
YES.
SO MANY ARE...
... MISSING BODY PARTS.
IT'S HORRIBLE.
LORD CORPSE SHOWED UP ABOUT A YEAR AGO.
AT FIRST HE JUST DUG UP BODIES FROM THE GRAVEYARD, BUT...
...SOON HE EMBARKED ON OTHER ENTERPRISES.

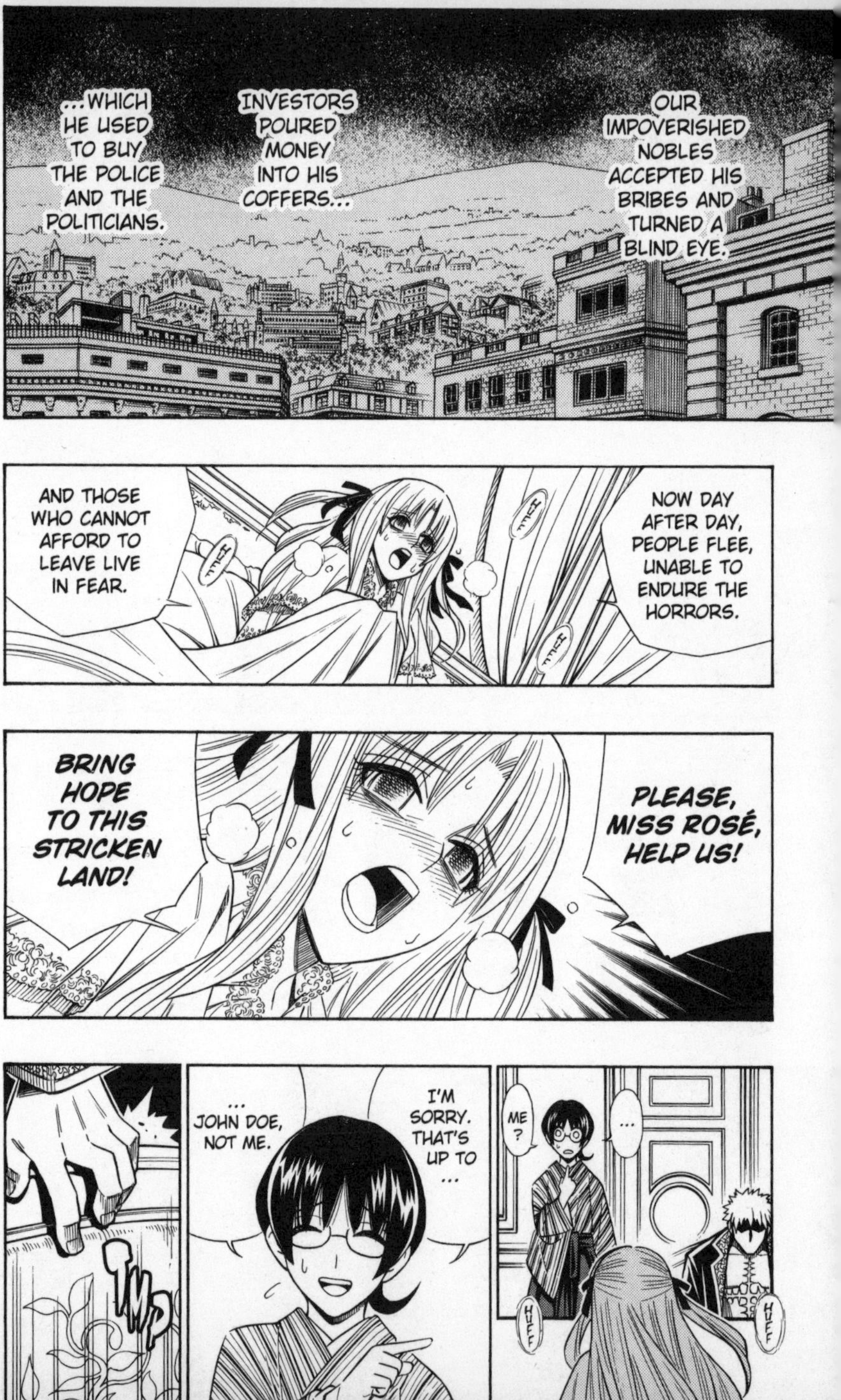
OUR IMPOVERISHED NOBLES ACCEPTED HIS BRIBES AND TURNED A BLIND EYE.
INVESTORS POURED MONEY INTO HIS COFFERS...
...WHICH HE USED TO BUY THE POLICE AND THE POLITICIANS.
NOW DAY AFTER DAY, PEOPLE FLEE, UNABLE TO ENDURE THE HORRORS.
AND THOSE WHO CANNOT AFFORD TO LEAVE LIVE IN FEAR.
PLEASE, MISS ROSÉ, HELP US!
BRING HOPE TO THIS STRICKEN LAND!
...
ME ?
HUFF
HUFF
I'M SORRY. THAT'S UP TO ...
... JOHN DOE, NOT ME.
TMP

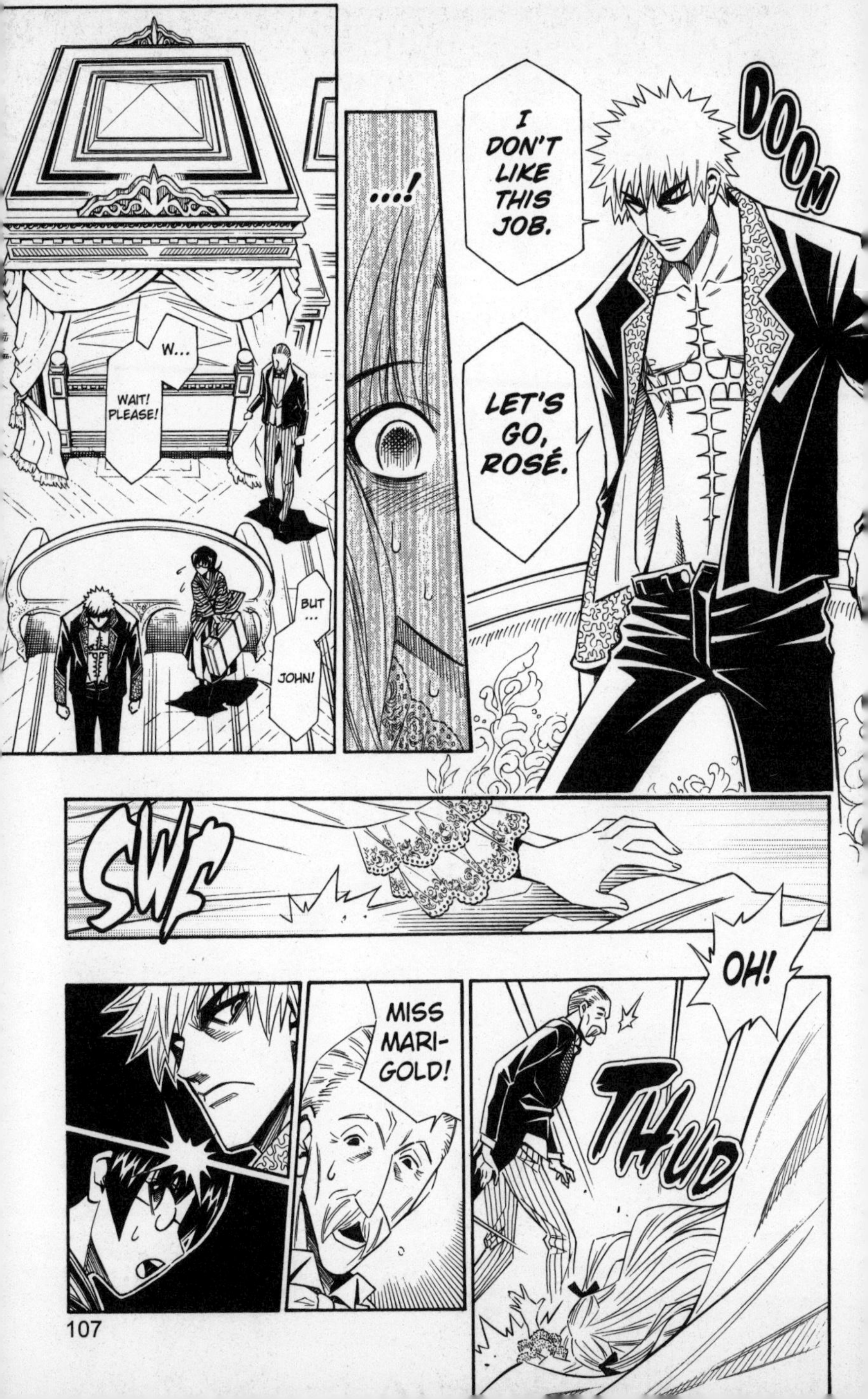
DOOM
I DON'T LIKE THIS JOB.
LET'S GO, ROSÉ.
...!
W...
WAIT! PLEASE!
BUT ...
JOHN!
SWF
OH!
THUD
MISS MARI-GOLD!

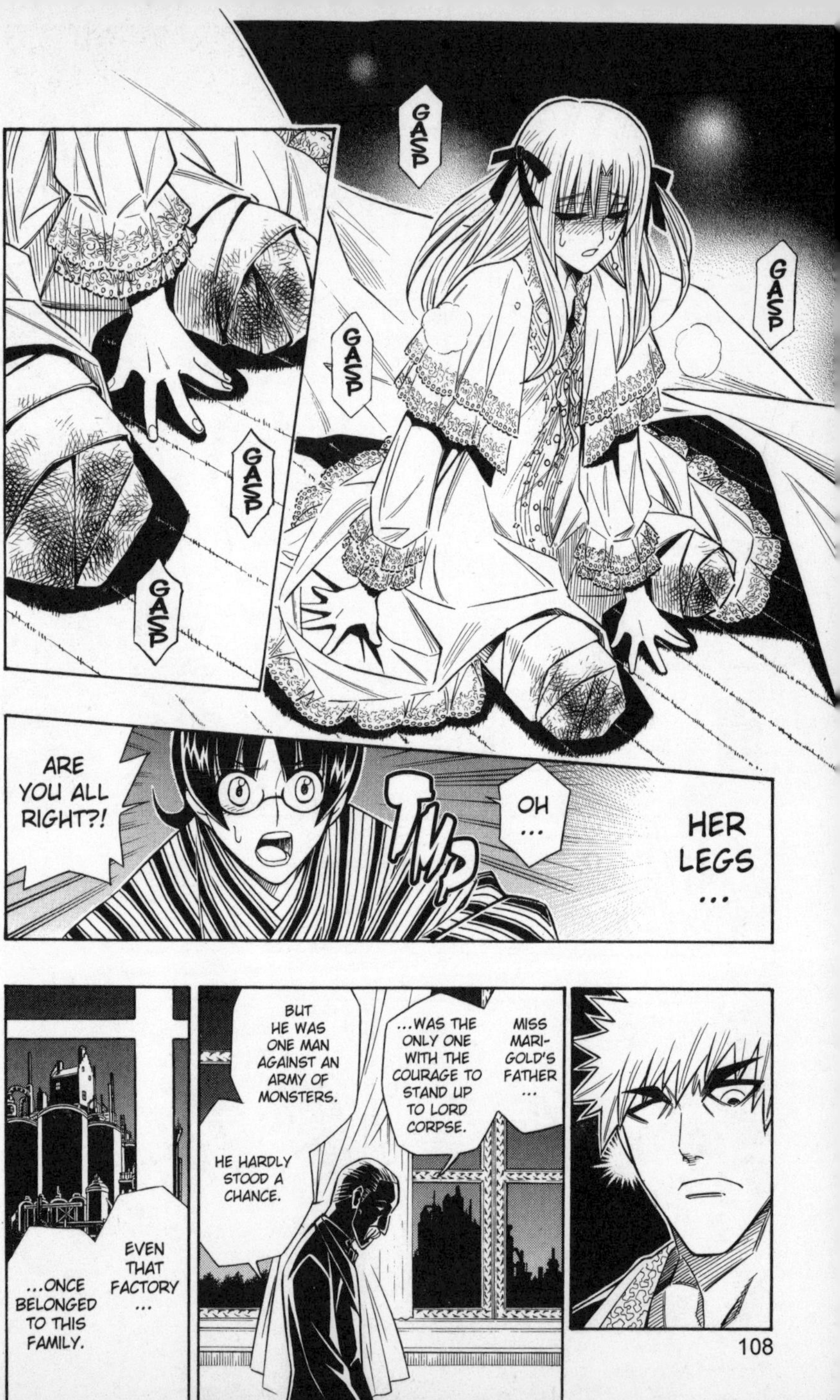
GASP
GASP
GASP
GASP
GASP
HER LEGS ...
OH ...
TMP
ARE YOU ALL RIGHT?!
MISS MARI-GOLD'S FATHER ...
...WAS THE ONLY ONE WITH THE COURAGE TO STAND UP TO LORD CORPSE.
BUT HE WAS ONE MAN AGAINST AN ARMY OF MONSTERS.
HE HARDLY STOOD A CHANCE.
EVEN THAT FACTORY ...
...ONCE BELONGED TO THIS FAMILY.

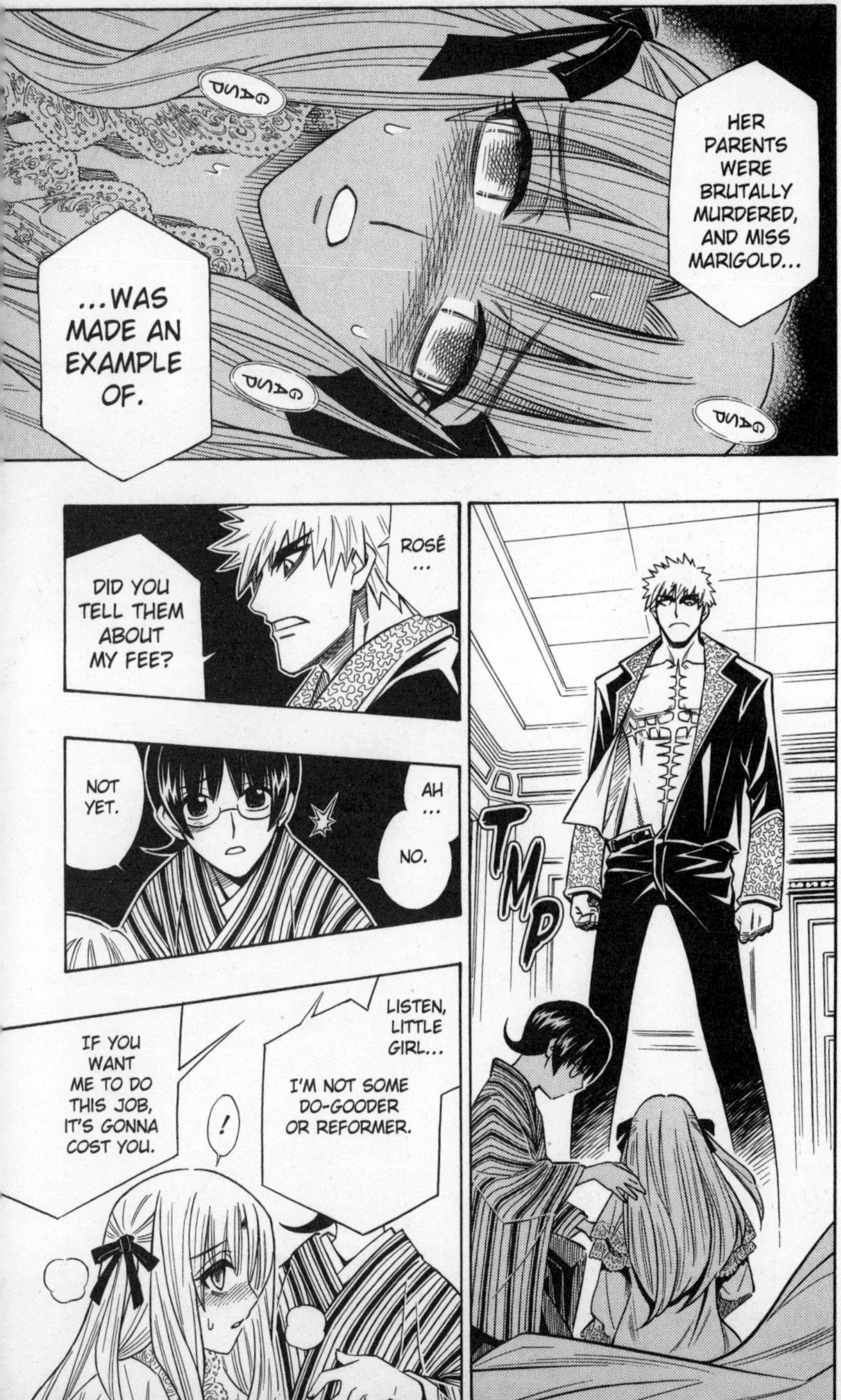
HER PARENTS WERE BRUTALLY MURDERED, AND MISS MARIGOLD...
...WAS MADE AN EXAMPLE OF.
TMP
ROSÉ...
DID YOU TELL THEM ABOUT MY FEE?
AH... NO.
NOT YET.
LISTEN, LITTLE GIRL...
I'M NOT SOME DO-GOODER OR REFORMER.
!
IF YOU WANT ME TO DO THIS JOB, IT'S GONNA COST YOU.

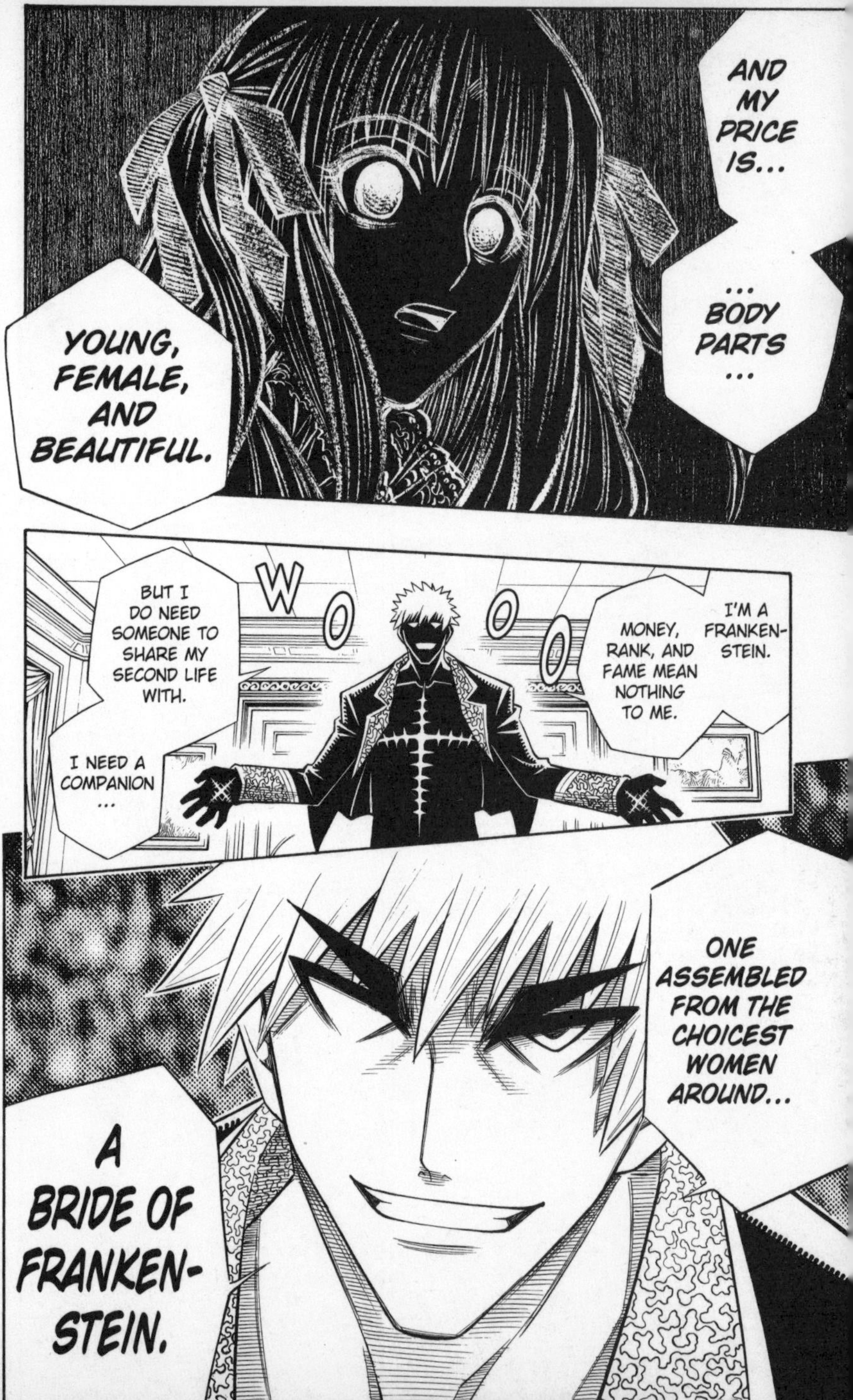
AND MY PRICE IS...
... BODY PARTS ...
YOUNG, FEMALE, AND BEAUTIFUL.
I'M A FRANKEN-STEIN.
MONEY, RANK, AND FAME MEAN NOTHING TO ME.
WOOO
BUT I DO NEED SOMEONE TO SHARE MY SECOND LIFE WITH.
I NEED A COMPANION ...
ONE ASSEMBLED FROM THE CHOICEST WOMEN AROUND...
A BRIDE OF FRANKEN-STEIN.

READ THIS WAY

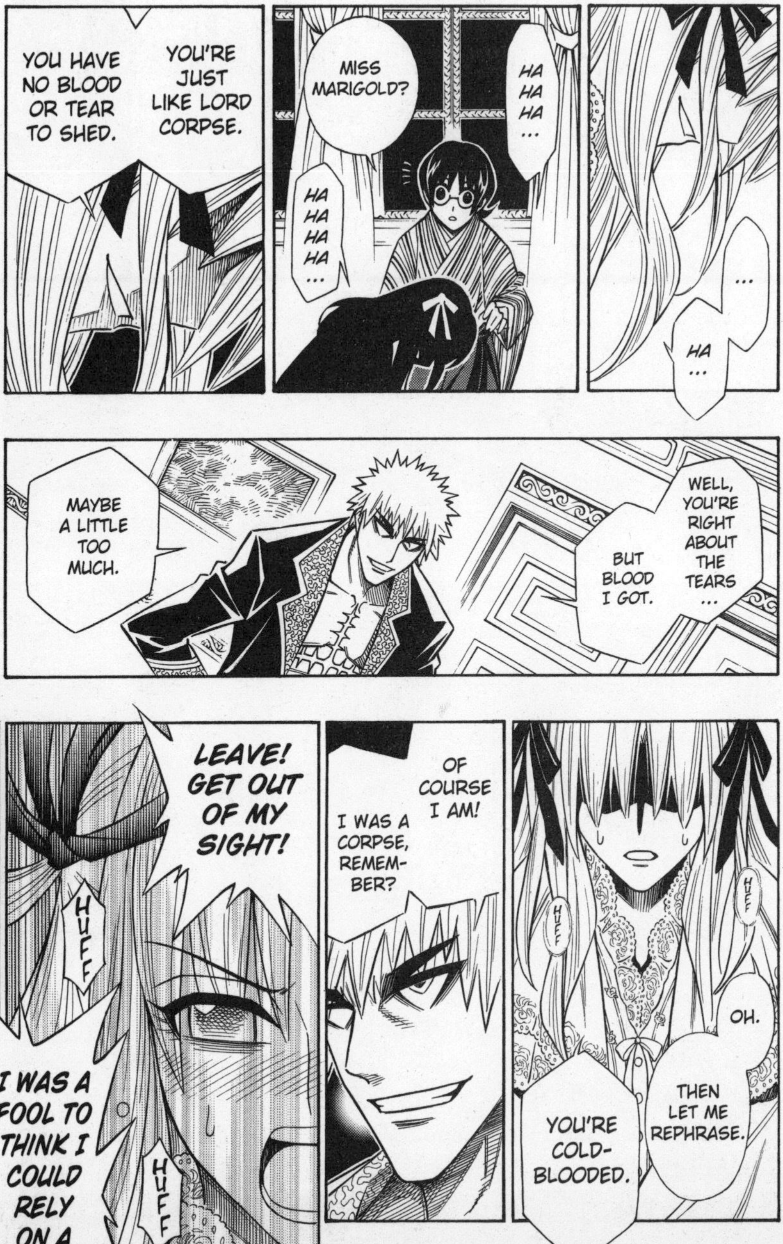
...
HA ...
HA HA HA ...
MISS MARIGOLD?
HA HA HA HA ...
YOU'RE JUST LIKE LORD CORPSE.
YOU HAVE NO BLOOD OR TEAR TO SHED.
WELL, YOU'RE RIGHT ABOUT THE TEARS ...
BUT BLOOD I GOT.
MAYBE A LITTLE TOO MUCH.
HUFF
HUFF
OH.
THEN LET ME REPHRASE.
YOU'RE COLD-BLOODED.
OF COURSE I AM!
I WAS A CORPSE, REMEMBER?
LEAVE! GET OUT OF MY SIGHT!
HUFF
HUFF
I WAS A FOOL TO THINK I COULD RELY ON A FRANKEN—

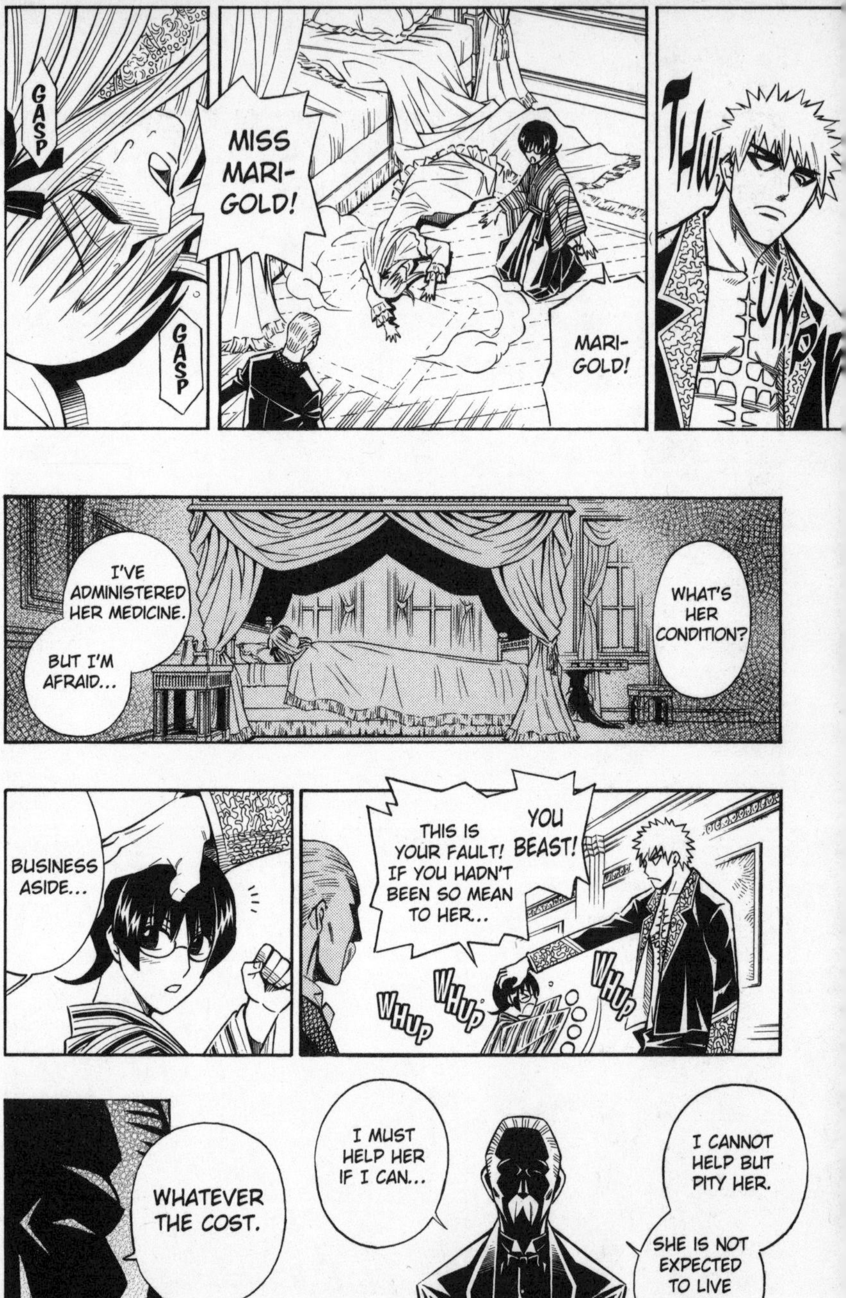
THUMP
MARIGOLD!
MISS MARIGOLD!
GASP
GASP
WHAT'S HER CONDITION?
I'VE ADMINISTERED HER MEDICINE.
BUT I'M AFRAID...
YOU BEAST!
THIS IS YOUR FAULT! IF YOU HADN'T BEEN SO MEAN TO HER...
WHUP
WHUP
WHUP
BUSINESS ASIDE...
I CANNOT HELP BUT PITY HER.
SHE IS NOT EXPECTED TO LIVE MUCH LONGER.
I MUST HELP HER IF I CAN...
WHATEVER THE COST.

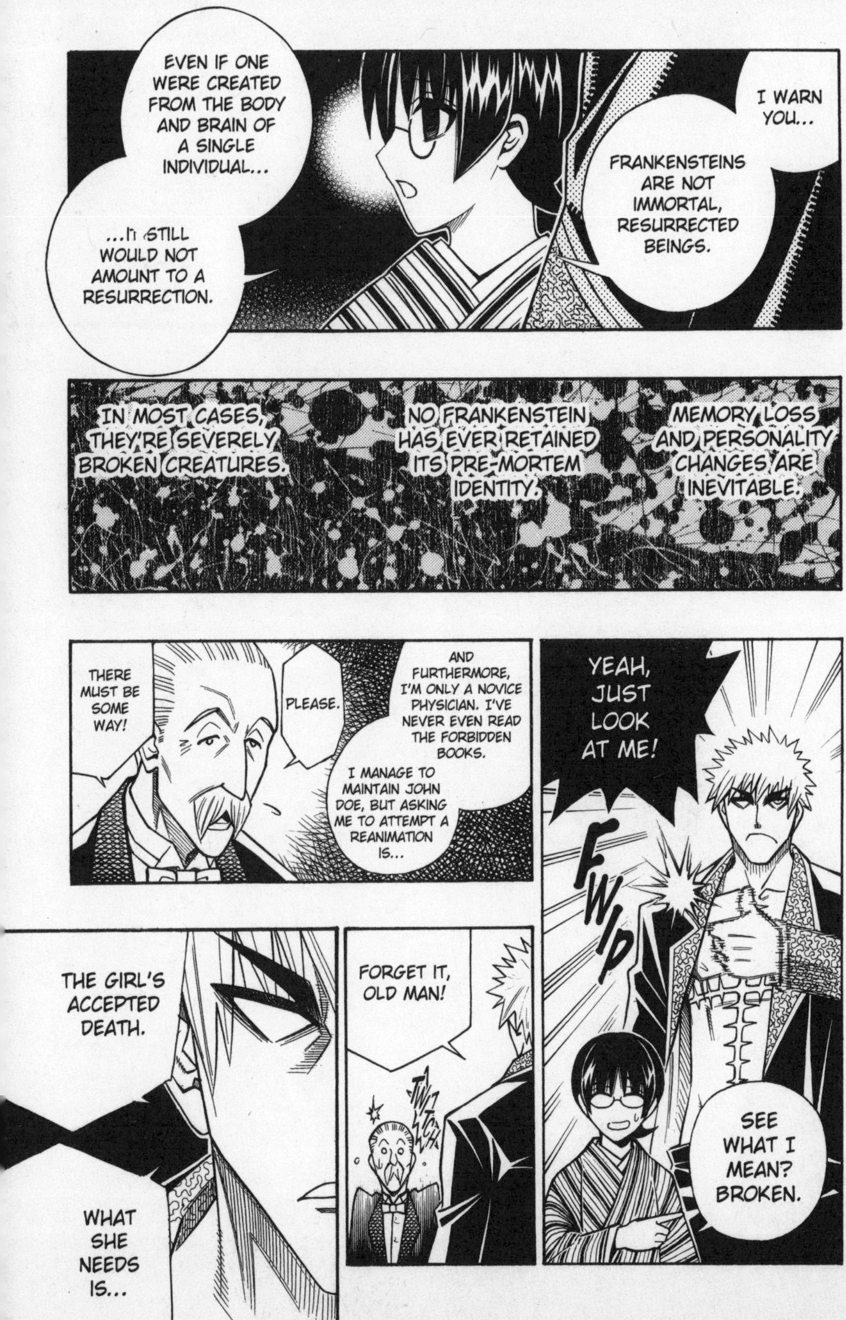
I WARN YOU...
FRANKENSTEINS ARE NOT IMMORTAL, RESURRECTED BEINGS.
EVEN IF ONE WERE CREATED FROM THE BODY AND BRAIN OF A SINGLE INDIVIDUAL...
...IT STILL WOULD NOT AMOUNT TO A RESURRECTION.
MEMORY LOSS AND PERSONALITY CHANGES ARE INEVITABLE.
NO FRANKENSTEIN HAS EVER RETAINED ITS PRE-MORTEM IDENTITY.
IN MOST CASES, THEY'RE SEVERELY BROKEN CREATURES.
YEAH, JUST LOOK AT ME!
FWIP
SEE WHAT I MEAN? BROKEN.
AND FURTHERMORE, I'M ONLY A NOVICE PHYSICIAN. I'VE NEVER EVEN READ THE FORBIDDEN BOOKS.
I MANAGE TO MAINTAIN JOHN DOE, BUT ASKING ME TO ATTEMPT A REANIMATION IS...
PLEASE.
THERE MUST BE SOME WAY!
FORGET IT, OLD MAN!
TWITCH
THE GIRL'S ACCEPTED DEATH.
WHAT SHE NEEDS IS...

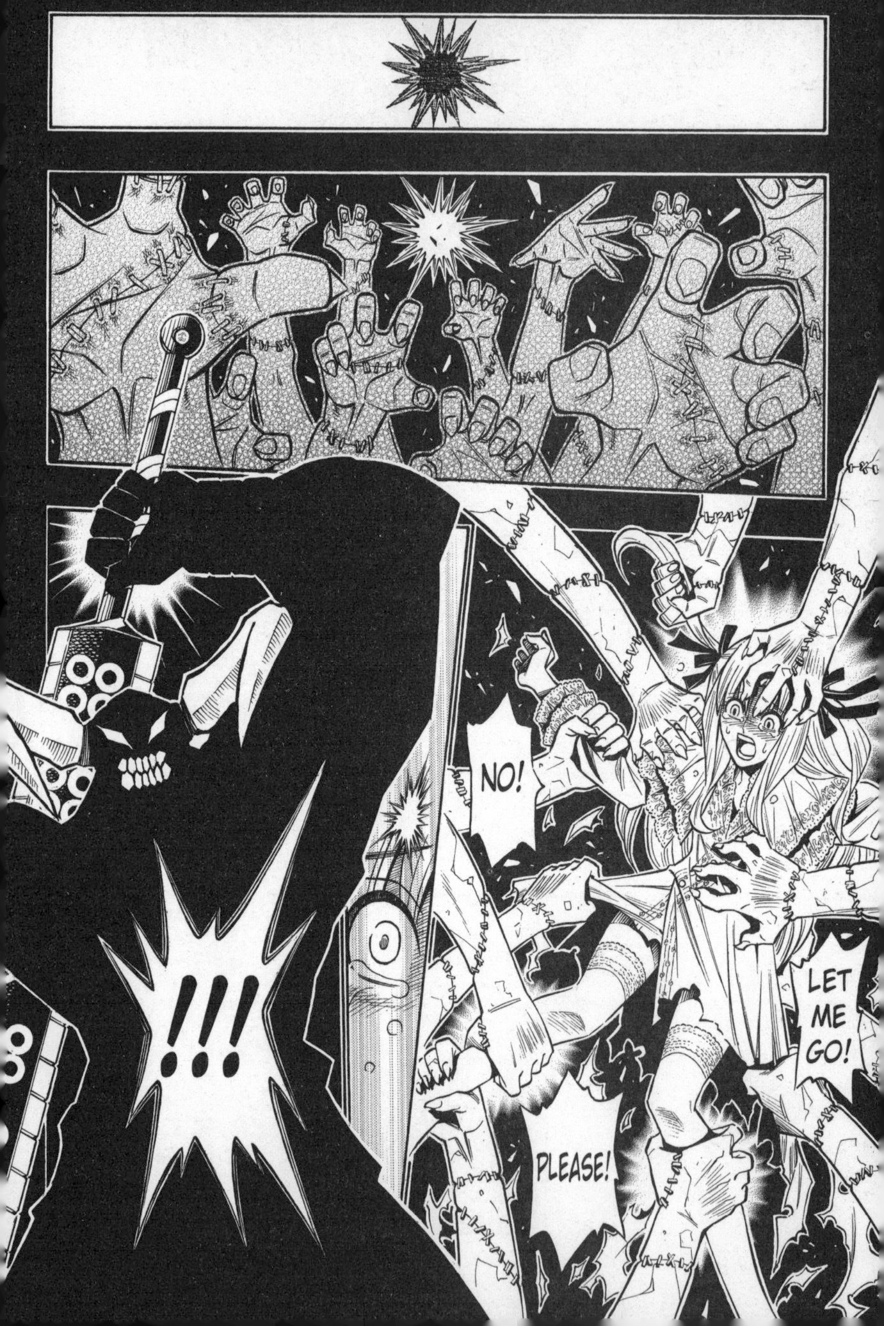
LET ME GO!
NO!
PLEASE!
!!!

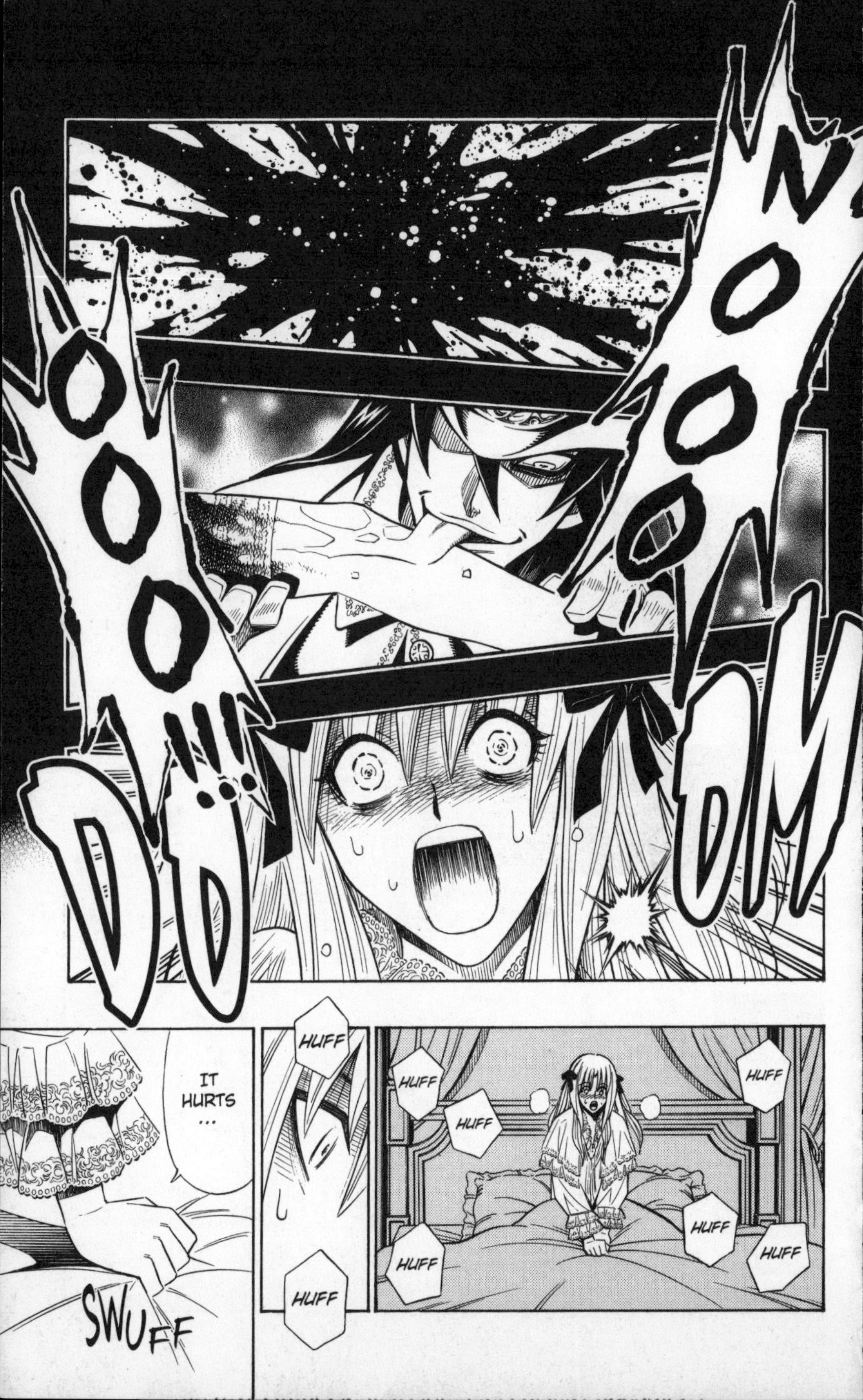
HUFF
HUFF
HUFF
HUFF
HUFF
HUFF
HUFF
HUFF
IT HURTS ...
SWUFF

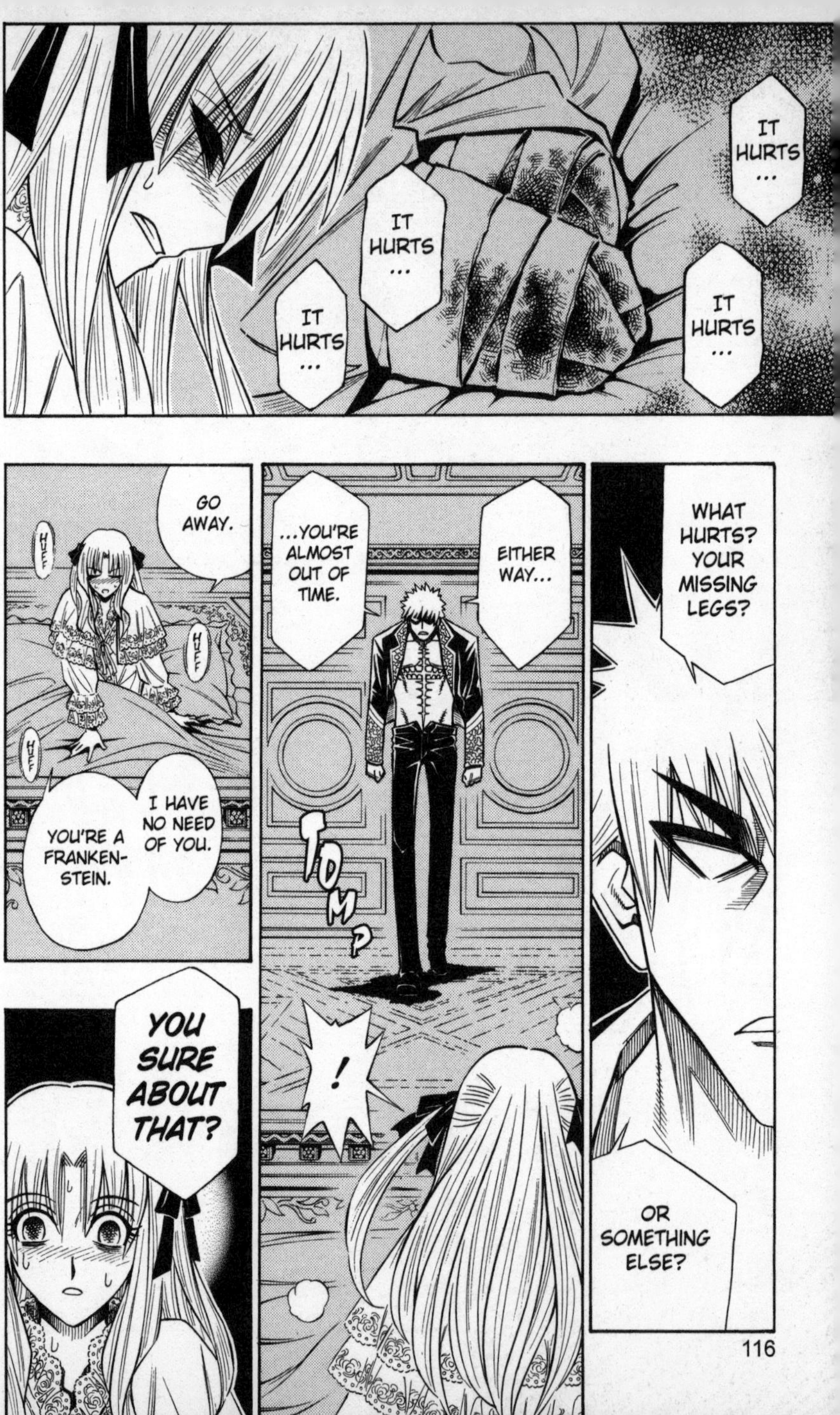
IT HURTS...
IT HURTS...
IT HURTS...
IT HURTS...
WHAT HURTS? YOUR MISSING LEGS?
OR SOMETHING ELSE?
EITHER WAY...
...YOU'RE ALMOST OUT OF TIME.
TOMP
!
GO AWAY.
HUFF
HUFF
HUFF
I HAVE NO NEED OF YOU.
YOU'RE A FRANKEN-STEIN.
YOU SURE ABOUT THAT?

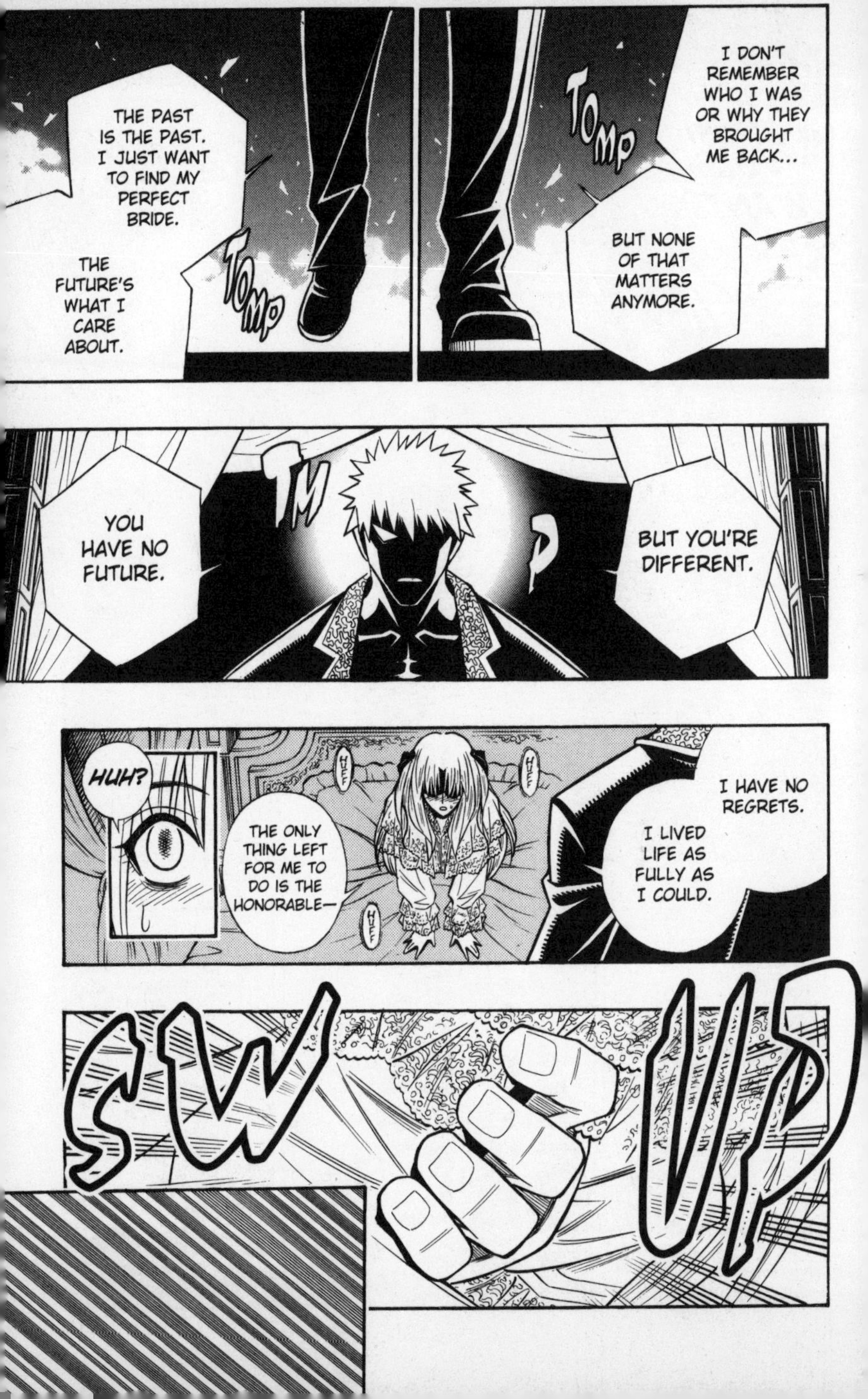
I DON'T REMEMBER WHO I WAS OR WHY THEY BROUGHT ME BACK...
TOMP
BUT NONE OF THAT MATTERS ANYMORE.
THE PAST IS THE PAST. I JUST WANT TO FIND MY PERFECT BRIDE.
TOMP
THE FUTURE'S WHAT I CARE ABOUT.
BUT YOU'RE DIFFERENT.
TMP
YOU HAVE NO FUTURE.
I HAVE NO REGRETS.
I LIVED LIFE AS FULLY AS I COULD.
HUFF
HUFF
THE ONLY THING LEFT FOR ME TO DO IS THE HONORABLE—
HUFF
HUH?
SWUP

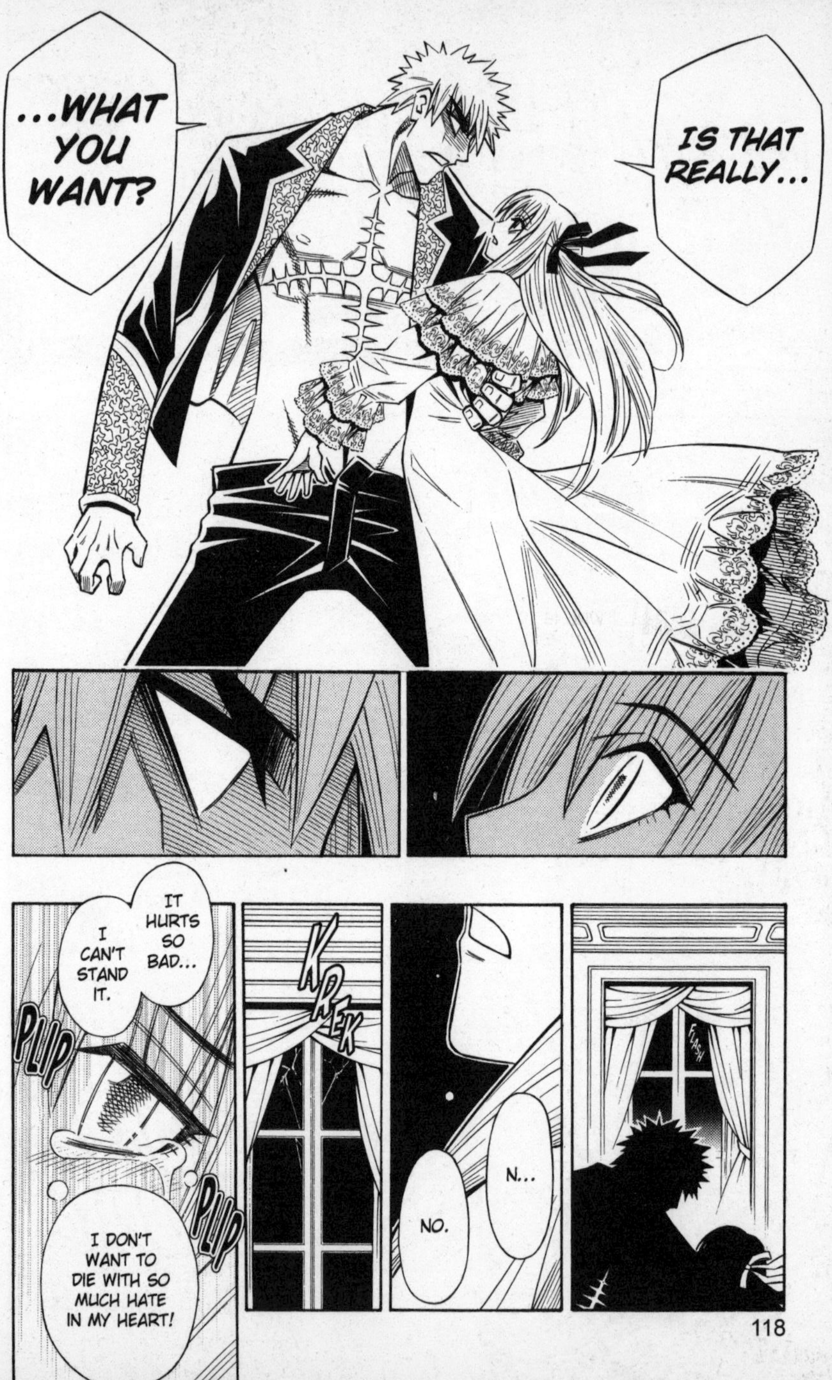
IS THAT REALLY...
...WHAT YOU WANT?
FLASH
N...
NO.
KREK
IT HURTS SO BAD...
I CAN'T STAND IT.
PLIP
PLIP
I DON'T WANT TO DIE WITH SO MUCH HATE IN MY HEART!

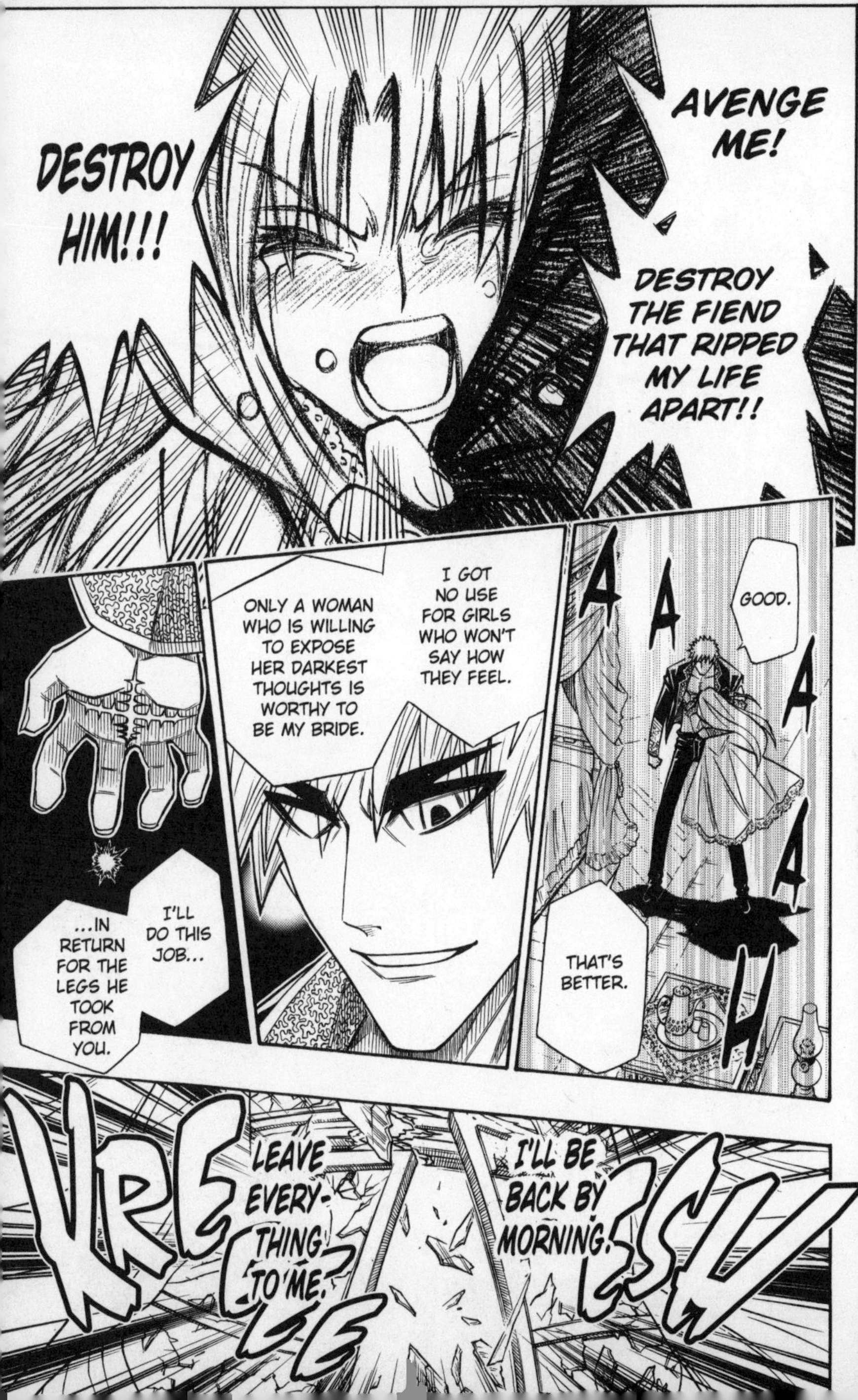
AVENGE ME!
DESTROY THE FIEND THAT RIPPED MY LIFE APART!!
DESTROY HIM!!!
AAAAAH
GOOD.
THAT'S BETTER.
I GOT NO USE FOR GIRLS WHO WON'T SAY HOW THEY FEEL.
ONLY A WOMAN WHO IS WILLING TO EXPOSE HER DARKEST THOUGHTS IS WORTHY TO BE MY BRIDE.
I'LL DO THIS JOB...
...IN RETURN FOR THE LEGS HE TOOK FROM YOU.
I'LL BE BACK BY MORNING.
LEAVE EVERY-THING TO ME?

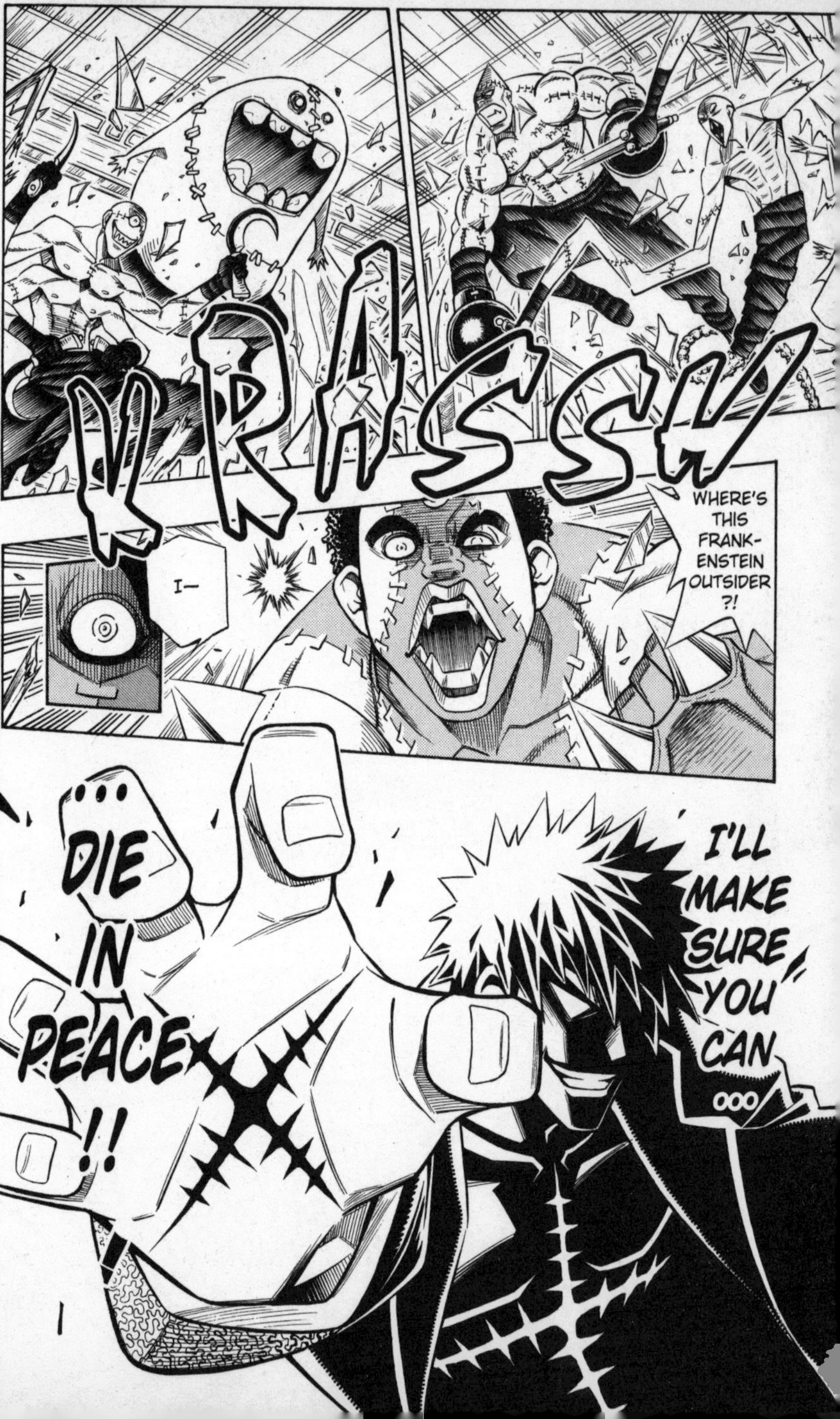

KRASSH
WHERE'S THIS FRANKENSTEIN OUTSIDER?!
I—
I'LL MAKE SURE YOU CAN...
...DIE IN PEACE!!

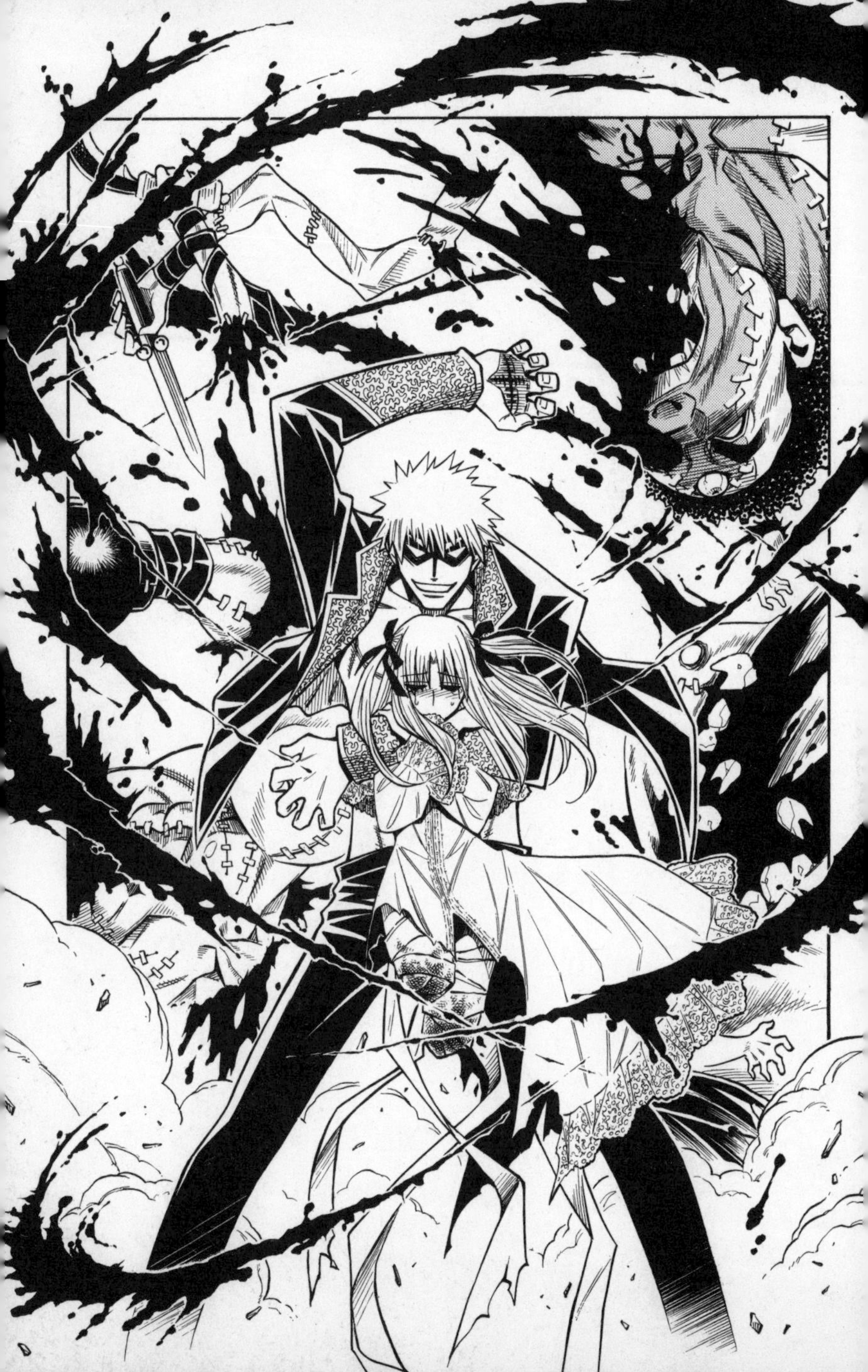

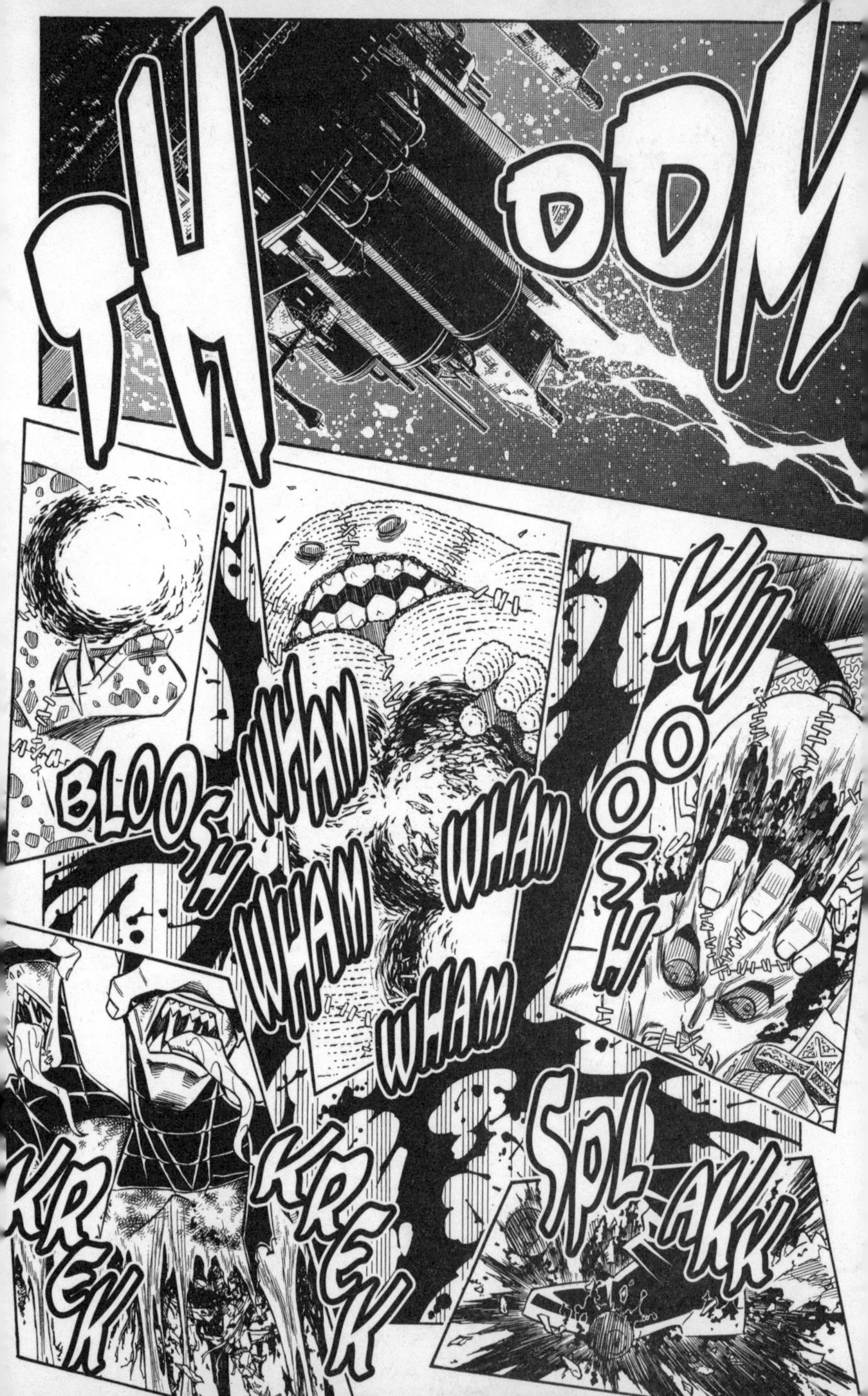
THOOM
KWOOOSH
WHAM
WHAM
WHAM
WHAM
BLOOSH
SPLAKK
KRECK
KRECK

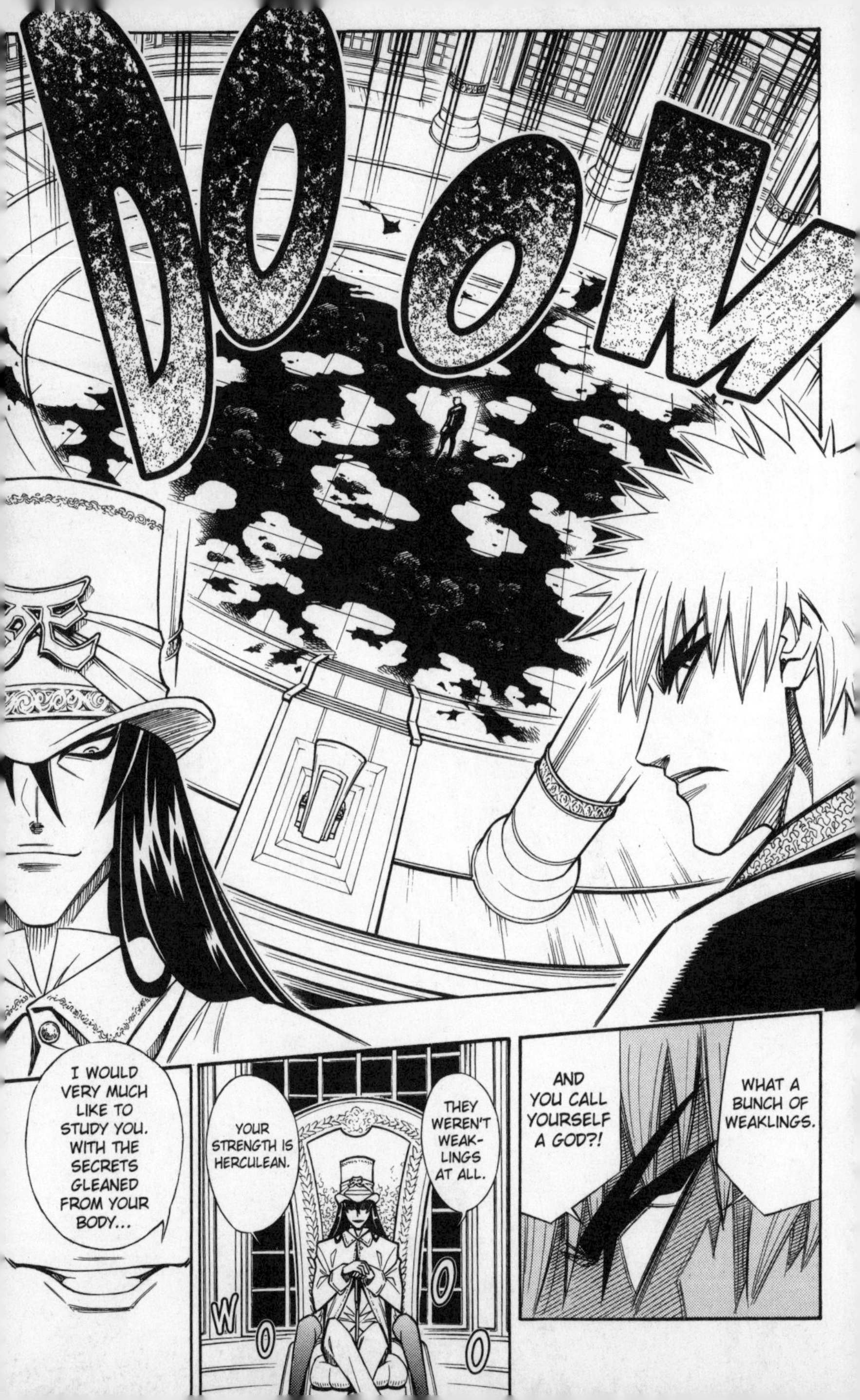
DOOM
WHAT A BUNCH OF WEAKLINGS.
AND YOU CALL YOURSELF A GOD?!
THEY WEREN'T WEAK-LINGS AT ALL.
YOUR STRENGTH IS HERCULEAN.
WOOO
I WOULD VERY MUCH LIKE TO STUDY YOU. WITH THE SECRETS GLEANED FROM YOUR BODY...

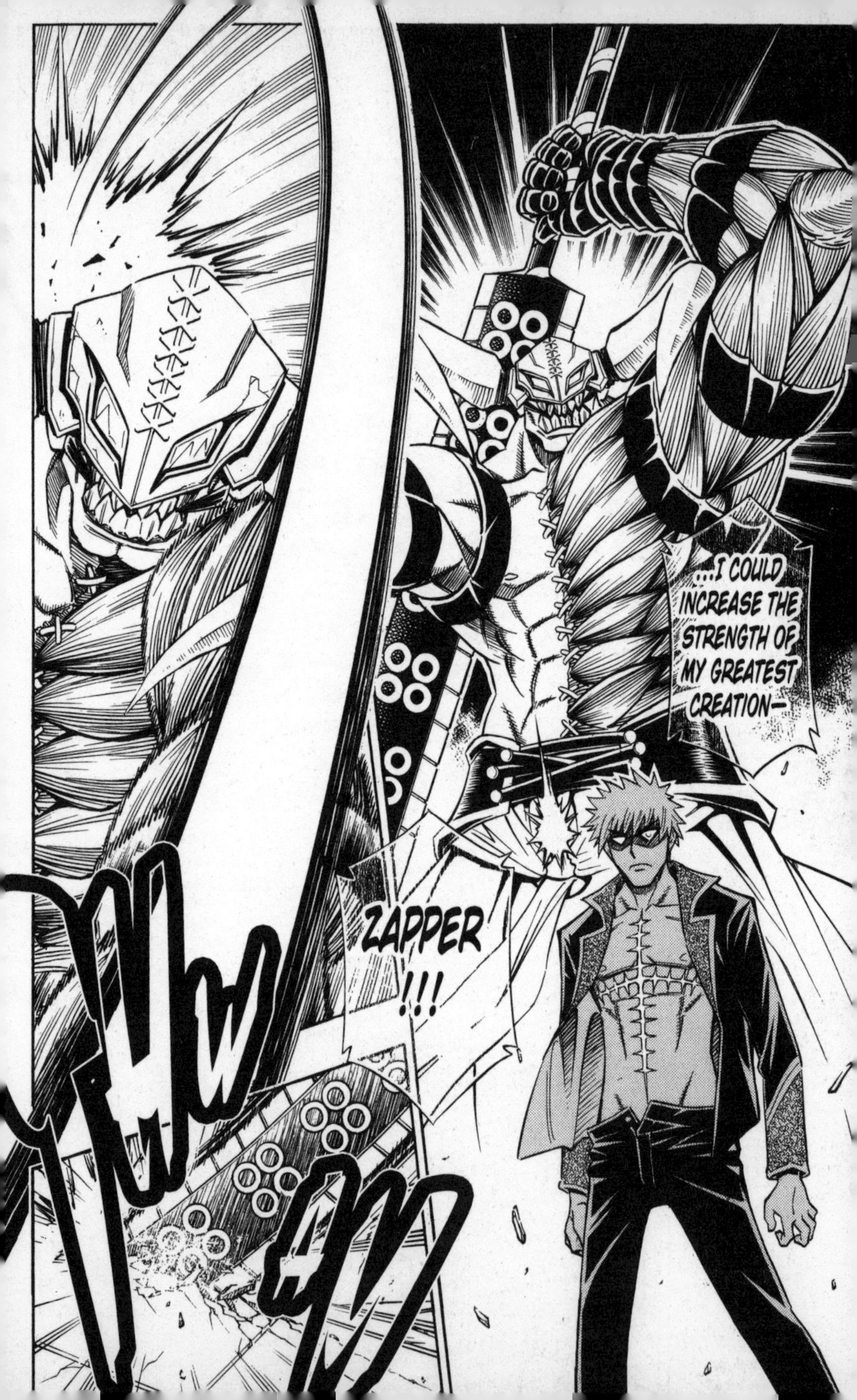
...I COULD INCREASE THE STRENGTH OF MY GREATEST CREATION–
ZAPPER !!!

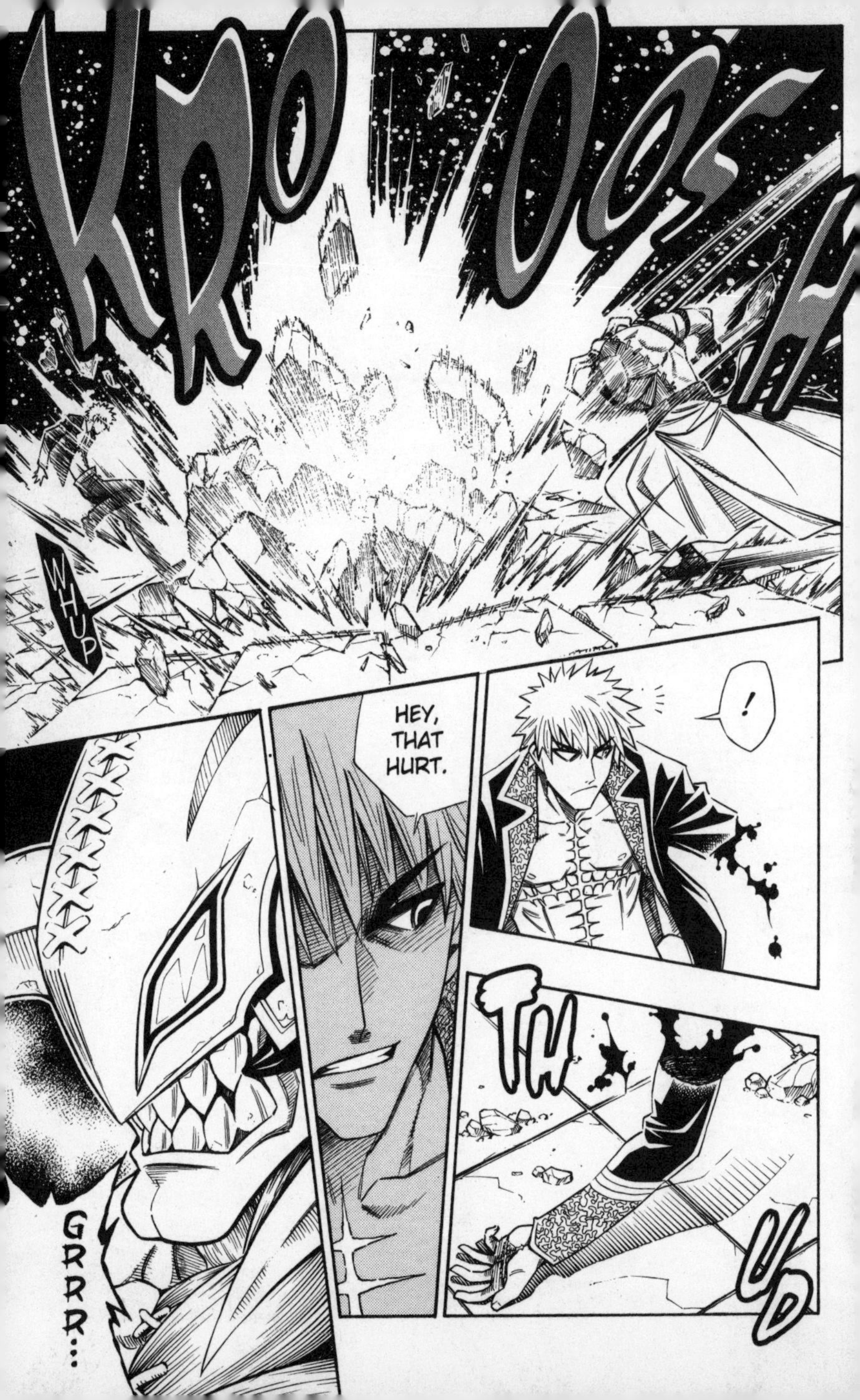
KROOOSH
WHUP
!
THUD
HEY, THAT HURT.
GRRRR...

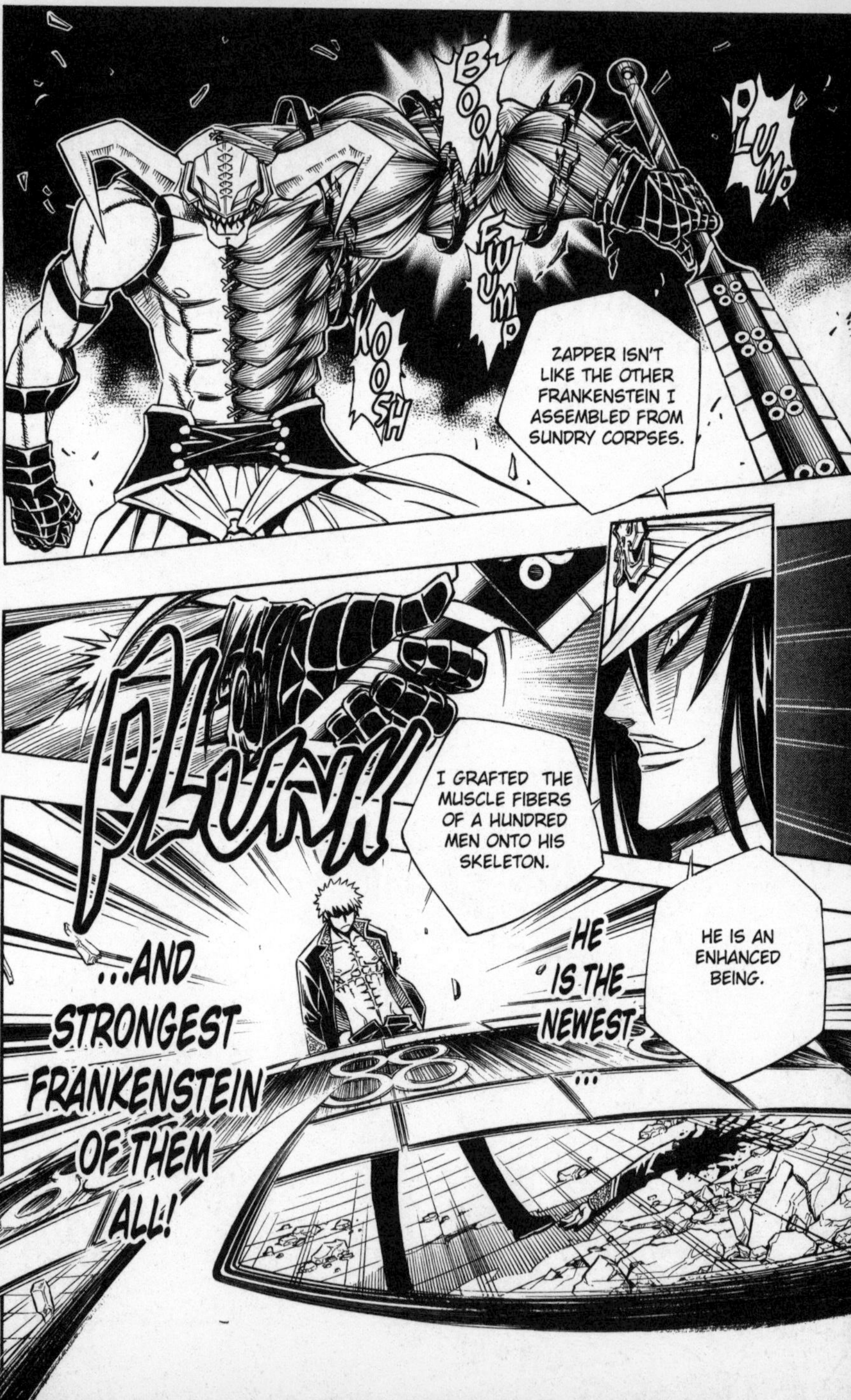
PLUMP
BOOM
FWUMP
KOOSH
ZAPPER ISN'T LIKE THE OTHER FRANKENSTEIN I ASSEMBLED FROM SUNDRY CORPSES.
I GRAFTED THE MUSCLE FIBERS OF A HUNDRED MEN ONTO HIS SKELETON.
PLUNK
HE IS AN ENHANCED BEING.
HE IS THE NEWEST...
...AND STRONGEST FRANKENSTEIN OF THEM ALL!

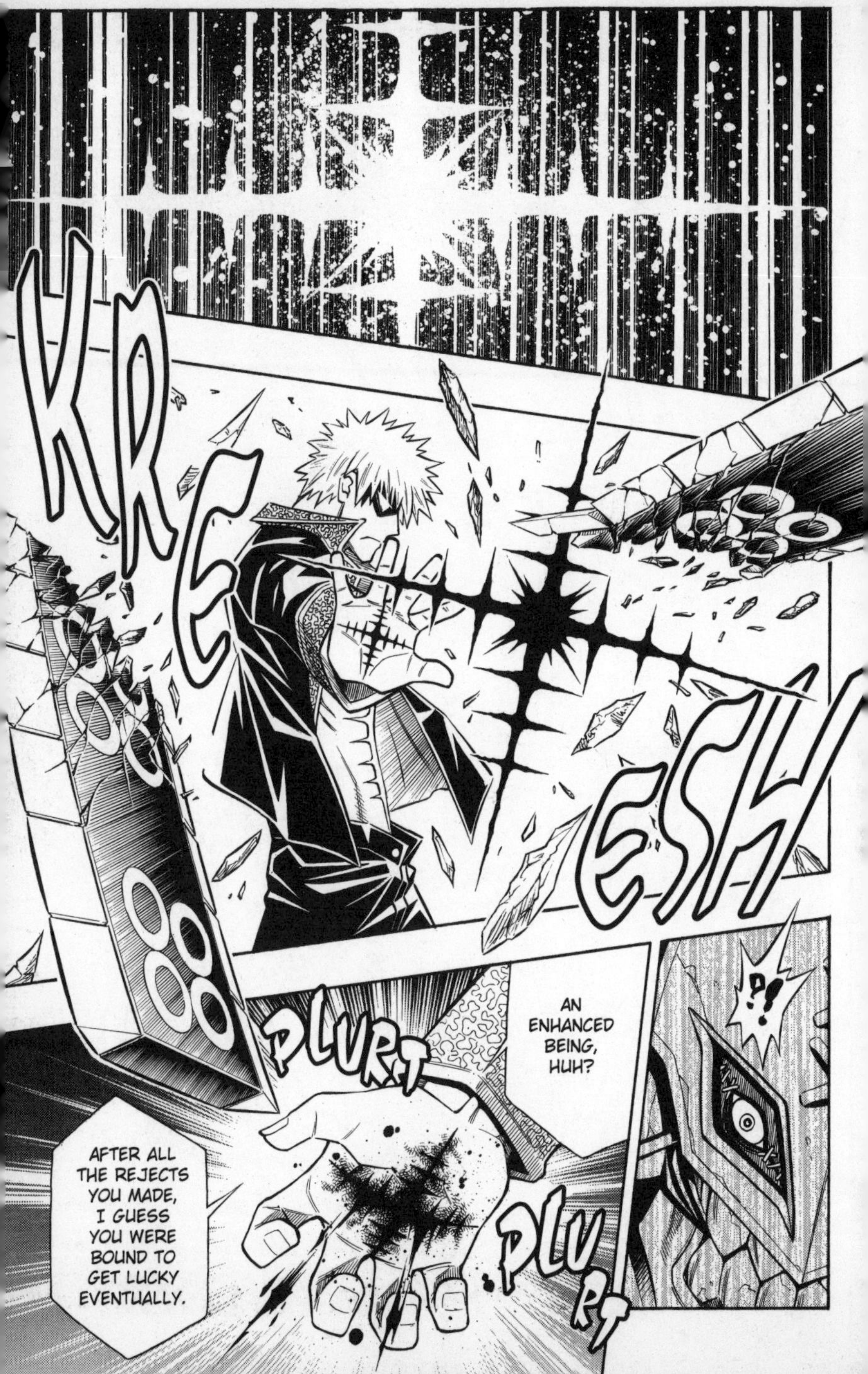
KRESH
?!
AN ENHANCED BEING, HUH?
PLURT
AFTER ALL THE REJECTS YOU MADE, I GUESS YOU WERE BOUND TO GET LUCKY EVENTUALLY.
PLURT

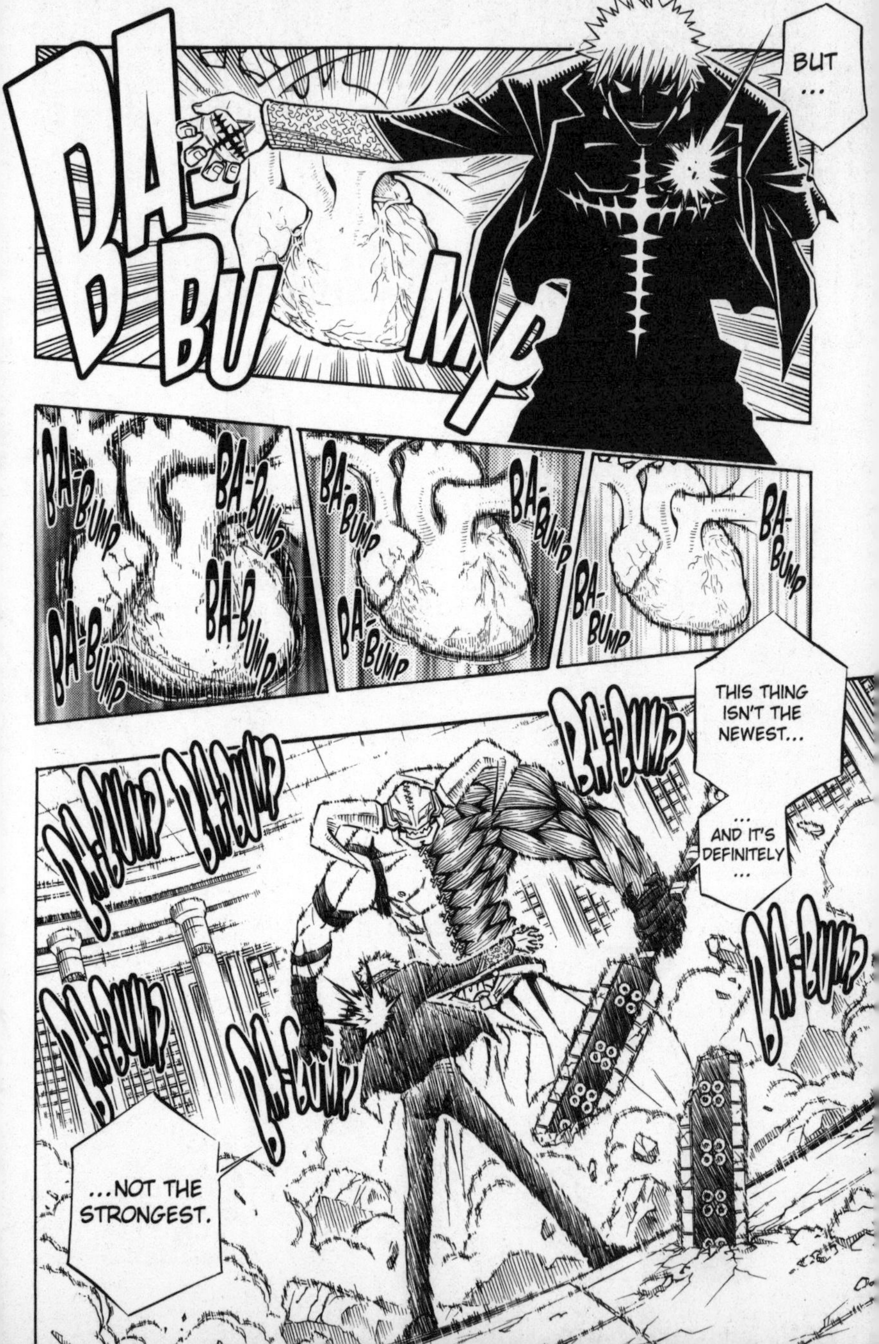
BUT ...
BA-BUMP
BA-BUMP
BA-BUMP
BA-BUMP
BA-BUMP
BA-BUMP
BA-BUMP
BA-BUMP
BA-BUMP
THIS THING ISN'T THE NEWEST...
... AND IT'S DEFINITELY ...
BA-BUMP
BA-BUMP
BA-BUMP
BA-BUMP
BA-BUMP
BA-BUMP
...NOT THE STRONGEST.

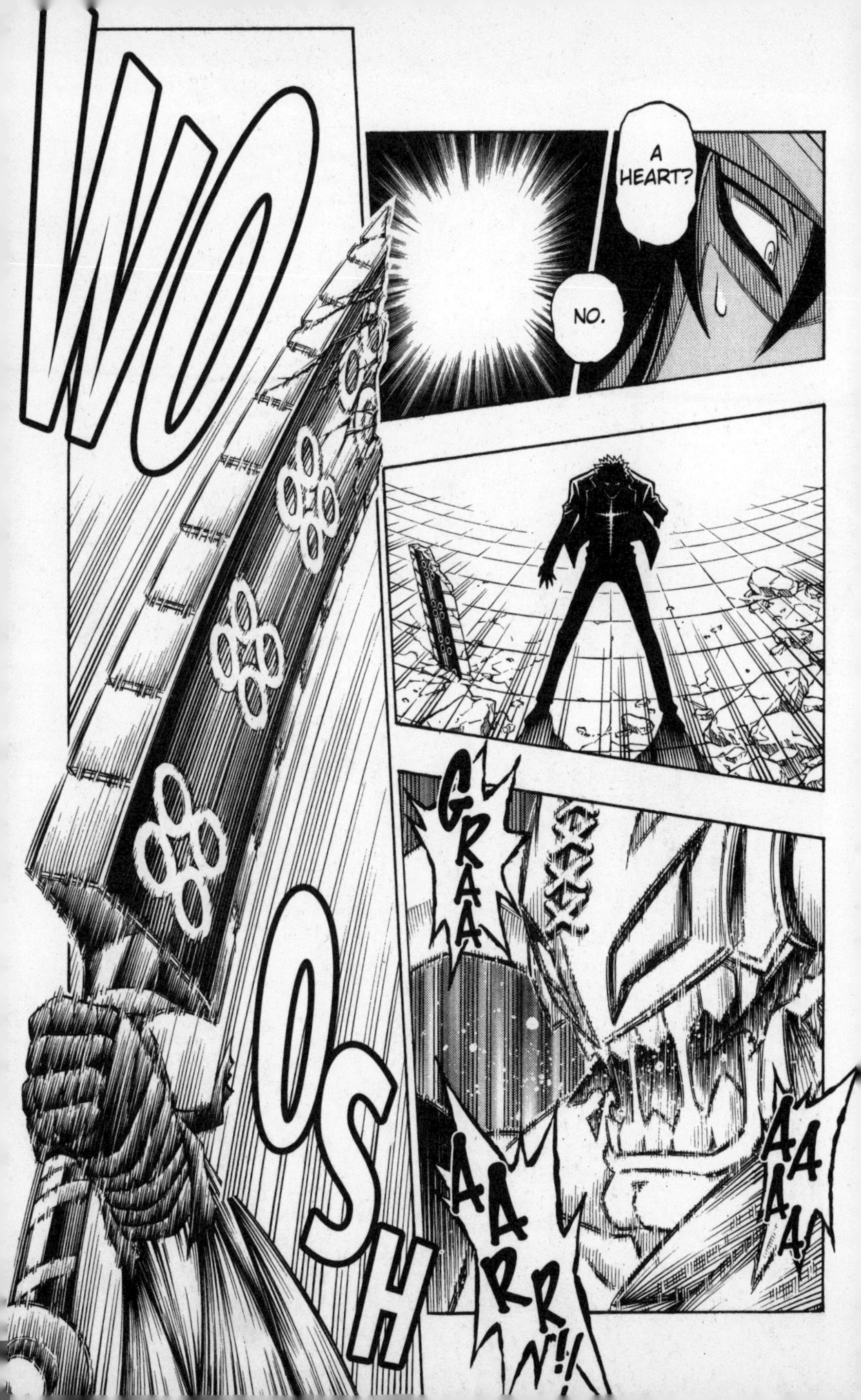
A HEART?
NO.
GRAAA
AAAA!
AARRN!!
WOOOSH

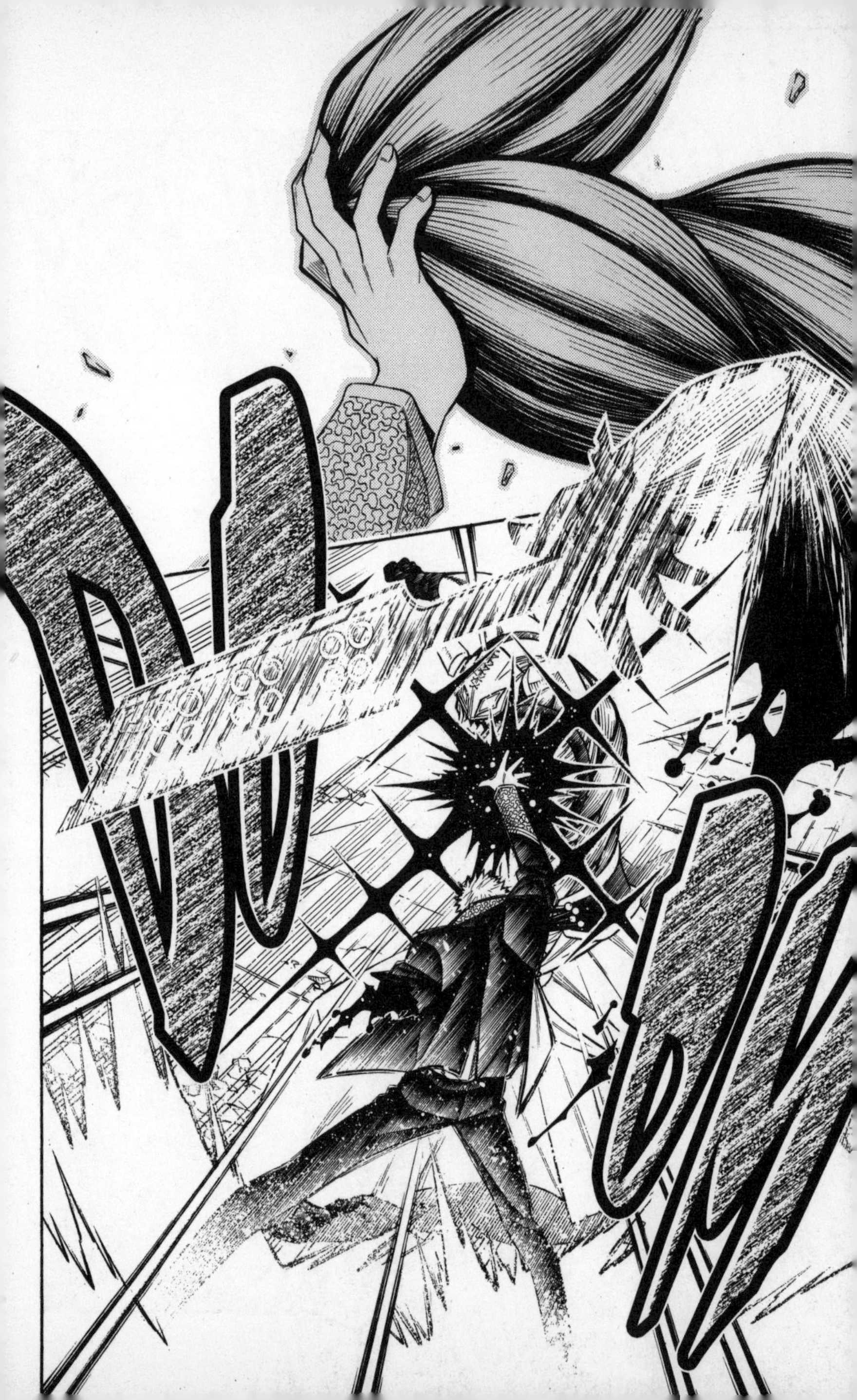

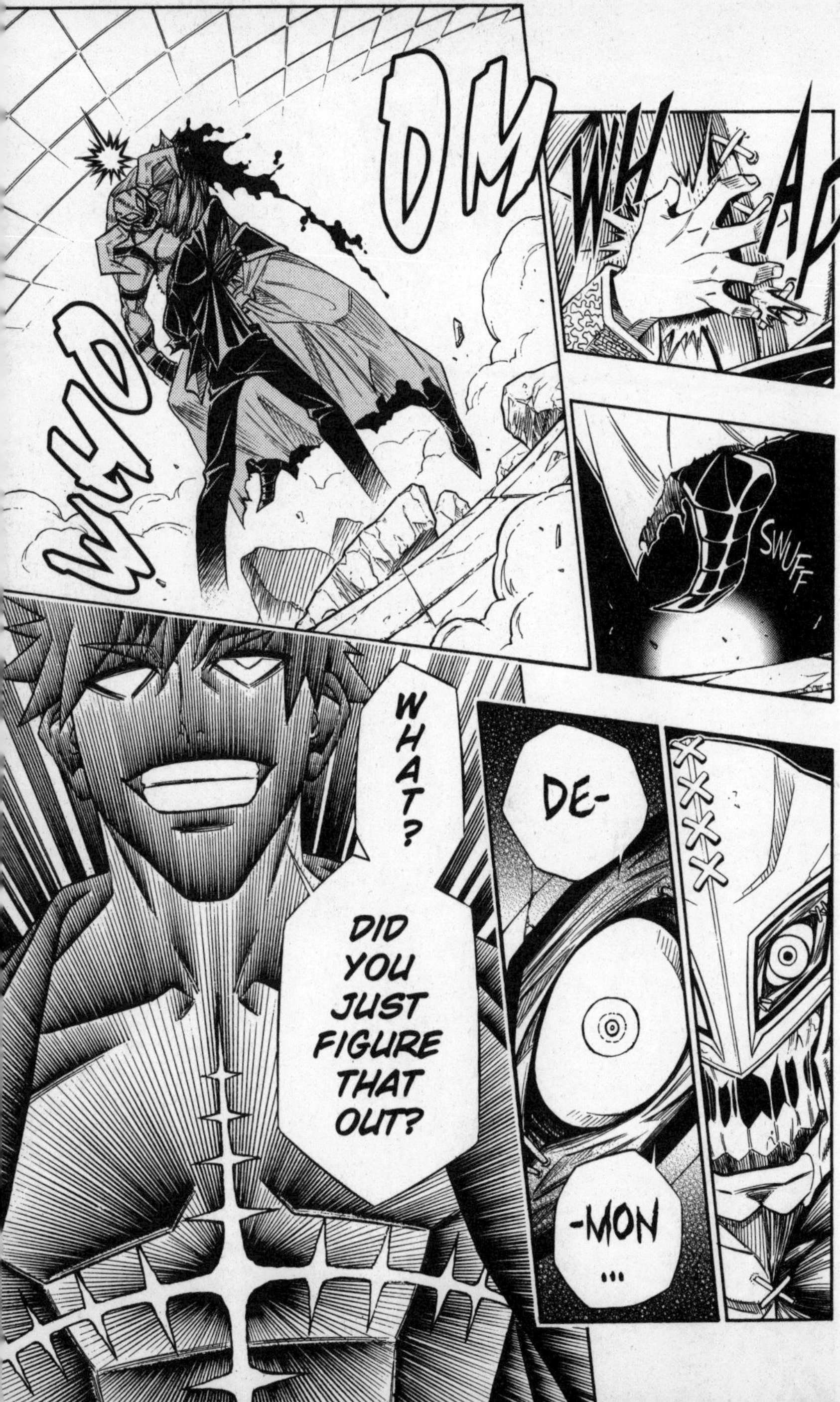

DMWHAP
SWUFF
WHUD
DE-
-MON...
WHAT?
DID YOU JUST FIGURE THAT OUT?

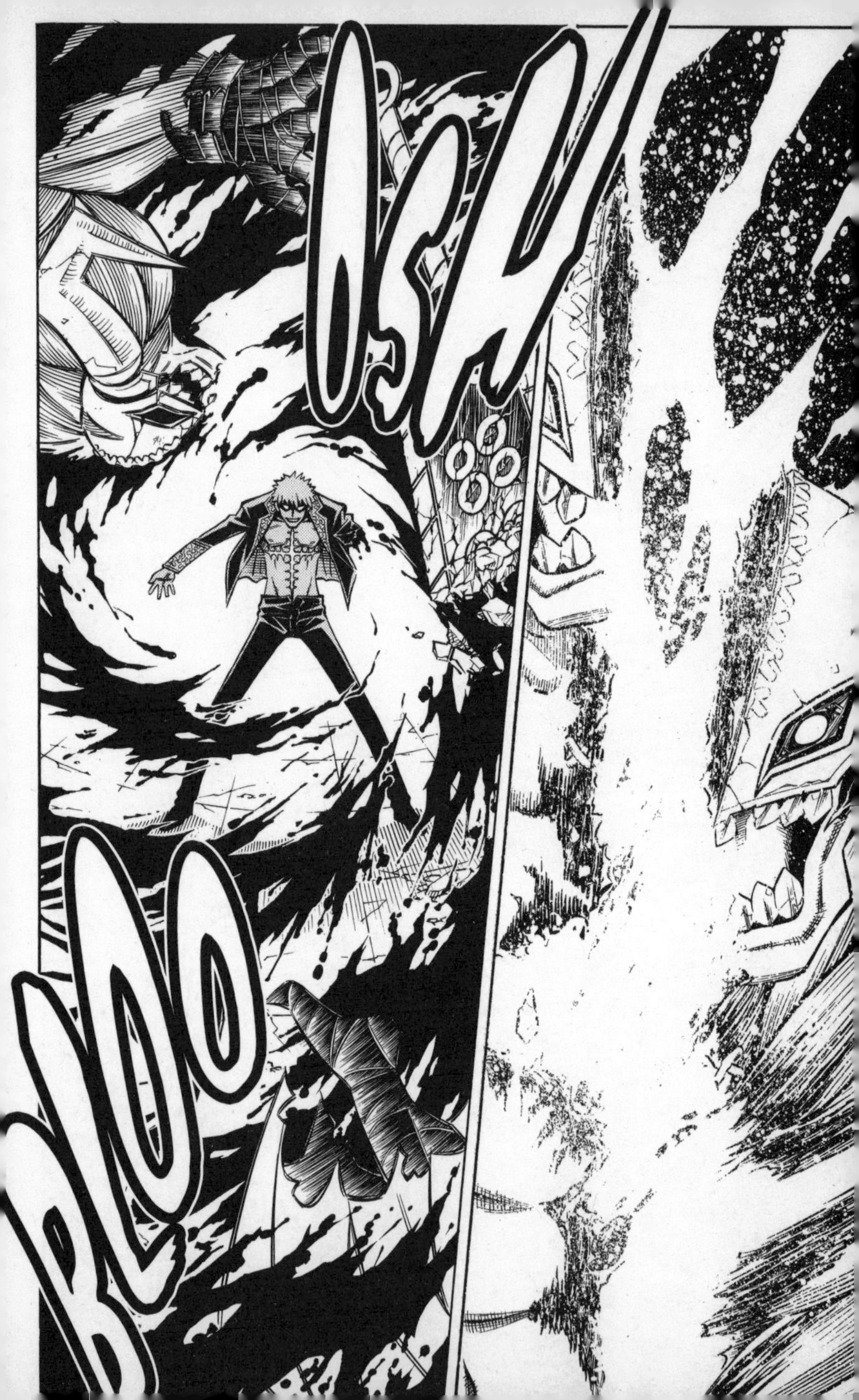

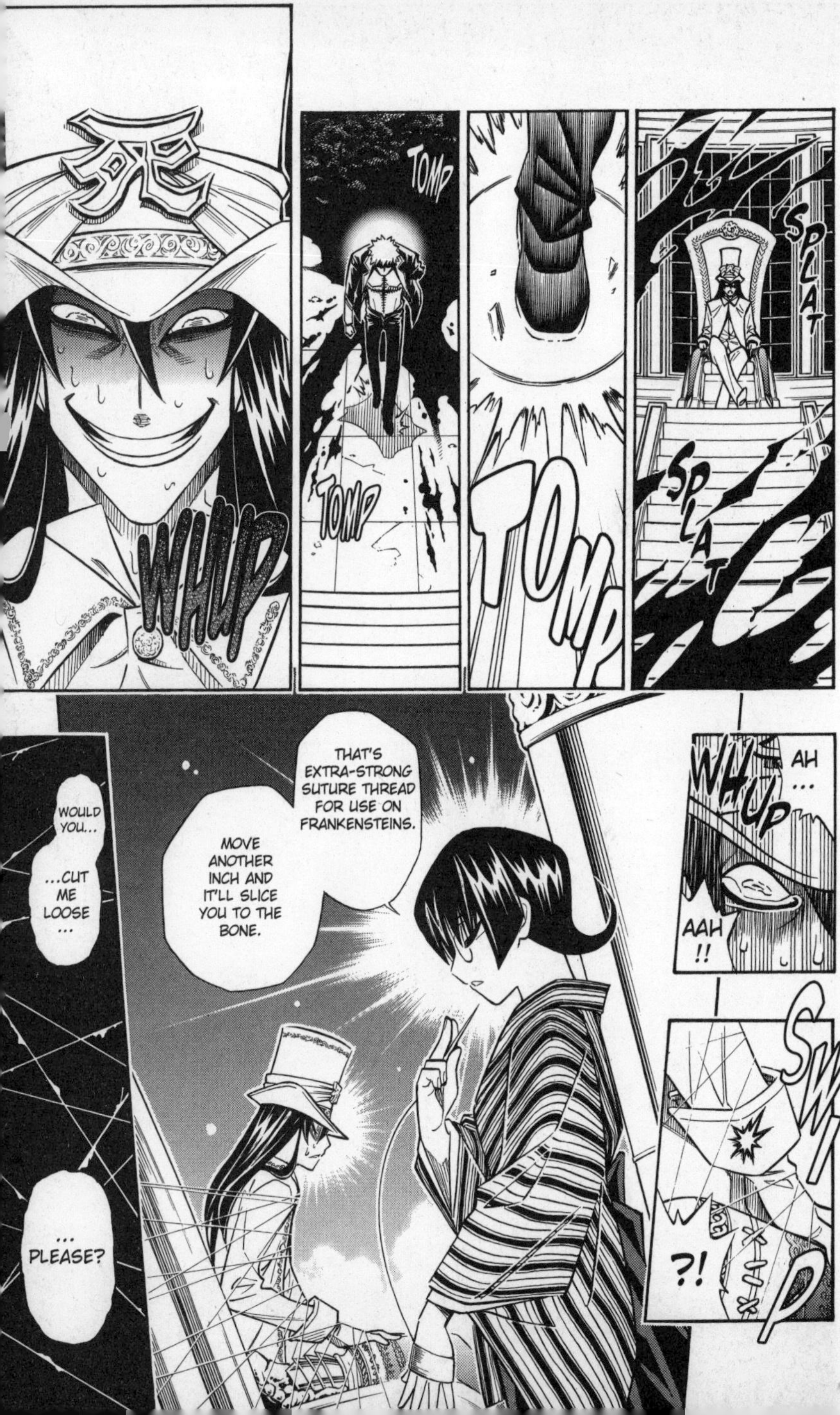
SPLAT
SPLAT
TOMP
TOMP
TOMP
WHUP
WHUP
AH...
AAH!!
SWIP
?!
THAT'S EXTRA-STRONG SUTURE THREAD FOR USE ON FRANKENSTEINS.
MOVE ANOTHER INCH AND IT'LL SLICE YOU TO THE BONE.
WOULD YOU...
...CUT ME LOOSE...
...PLEASE?

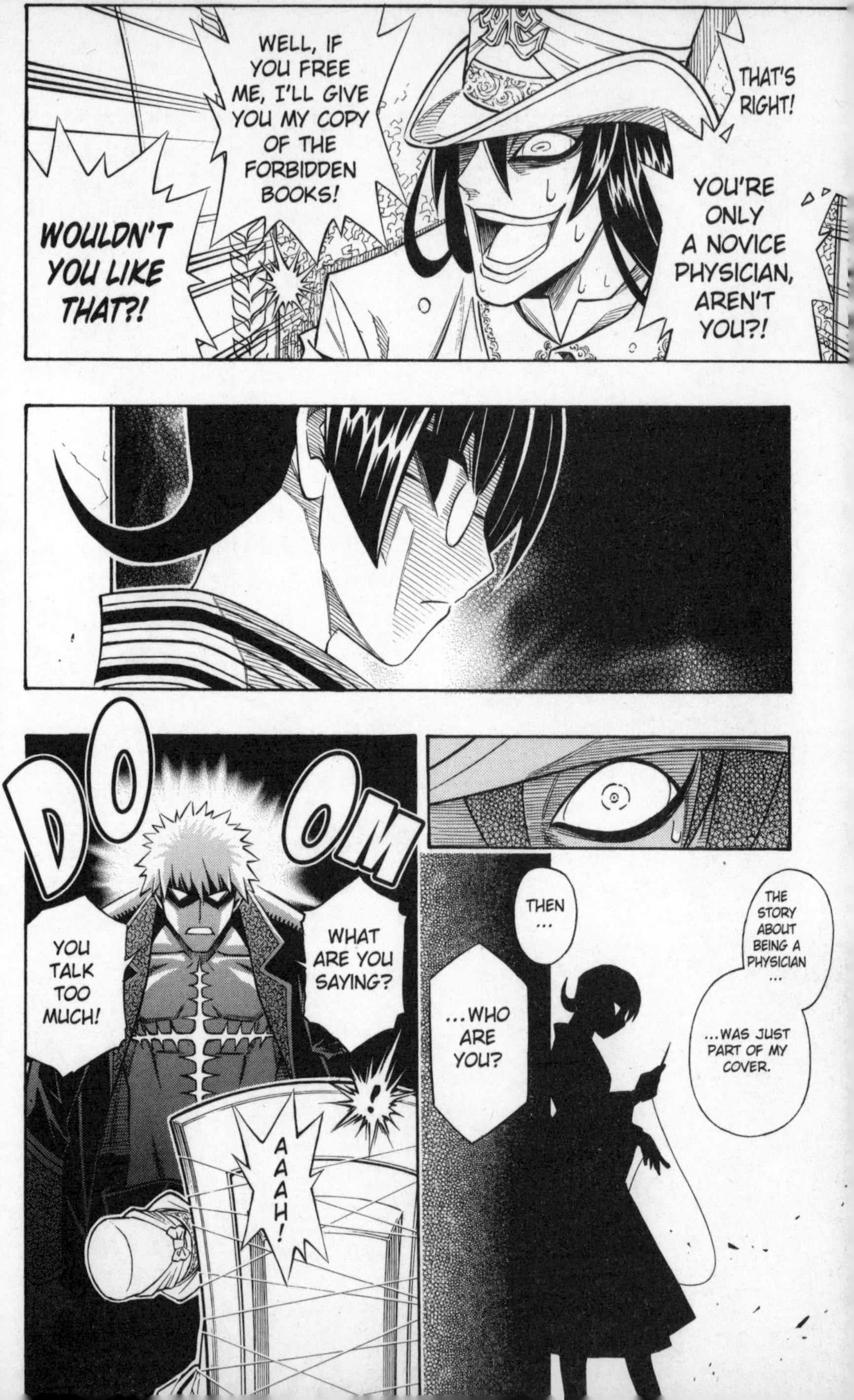
THAT'S RIGHT!
YOU'RE ONLY A NOVICE PHYSICIAN, AREN'T YOU?!
WELL, IF YOU FREE ME, I'LL GIVE YOU MY COPY OF THE FORBIDDEN BOOKS!
WOULDN'T YOU LIKE THAT?!
THE STORY ABOUT BEING A PHYSICIAN ...
...WAS JUST PART OF MY COVER.
THEN ...
...WHO ARE YOU?
DOOM
WHAT ARE YOU SAYING?
YOU TALK TOO MUCH!
!
AAAAH!

READ THIS WAY

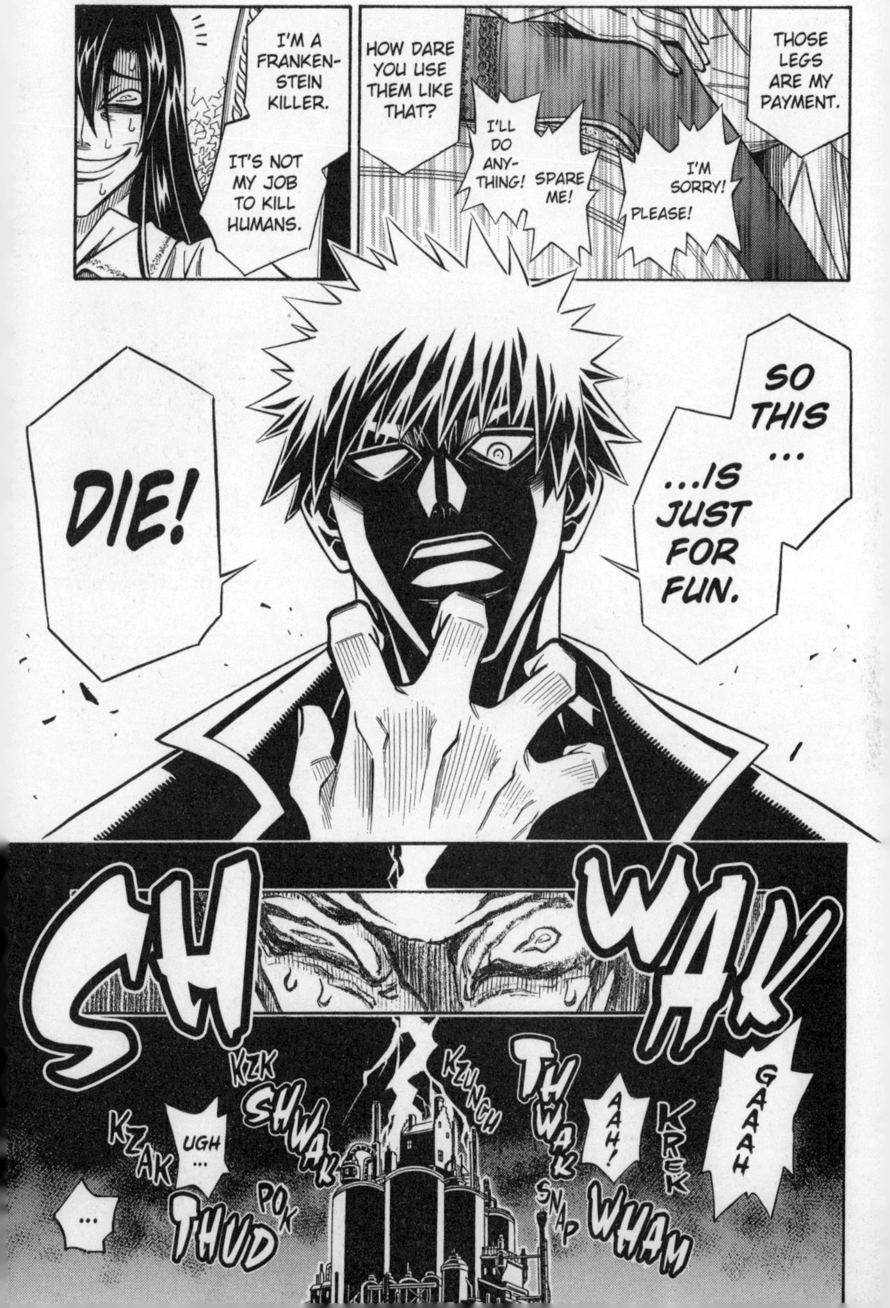
THOSE LEGS ARE MY PAYMENT.
HOW DARE YOU USE THEM LIKE THAT?
I'M SORRY!
PLEASE!
SPARE ME!
I'LL DO ANY-THING!
I'M A FRANKEN-STEIN KILLER.
IT'S NOT MY JOB TO KILL HUMANS.
SO THIS ...
...IS JUST FOR FUN.
DIE!
SH
WAK
GAAAH
KREK
WHAM
AAAH!
THWAK
SNAP
KZUNCH
KZK
SHWAK
POK
THUD
UGH ...
KZAK
...

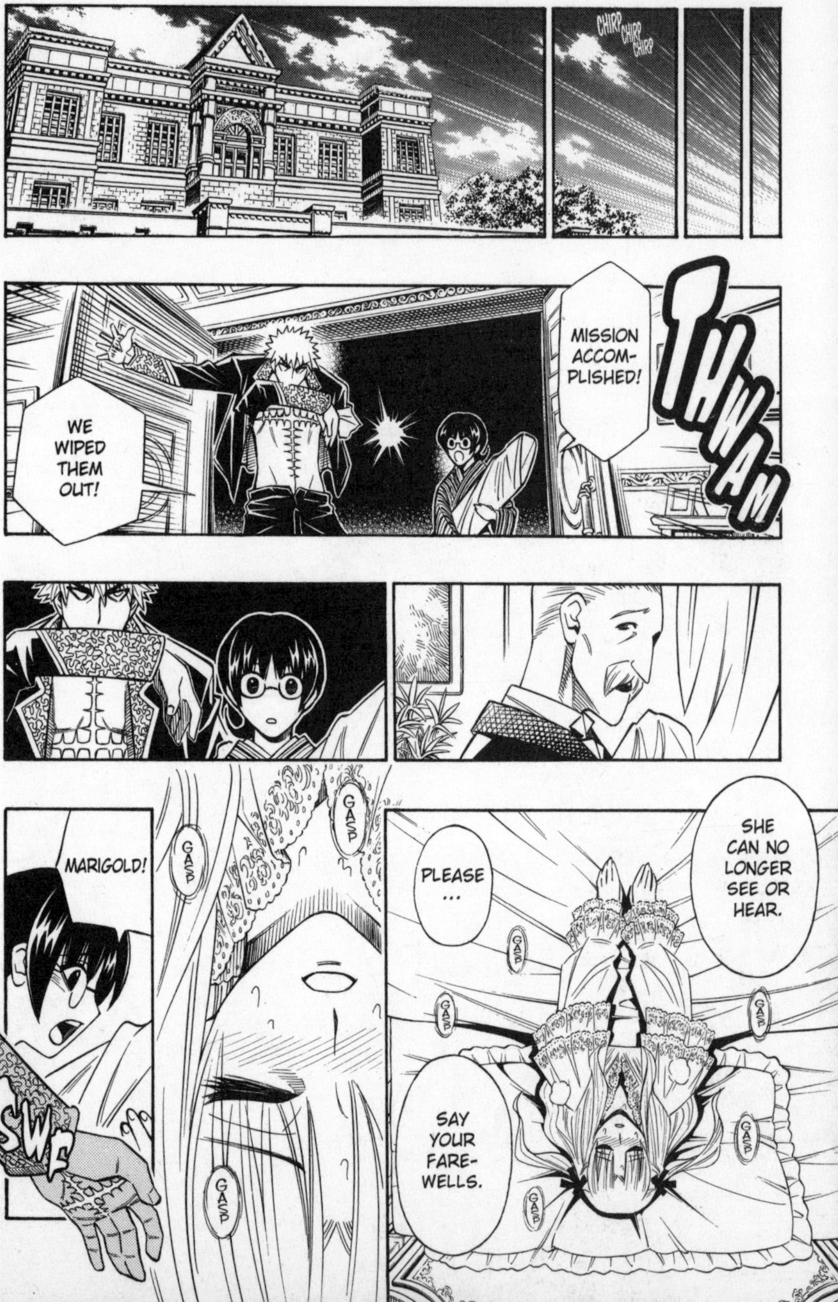
CHIRP CHIRP CHIRP
THWAM
MISSION ACCOM-PLISHED!
WE WIPED THEM OUT!
SHE CAN NO LONGER SEE OR HEAR.
PLEASE ...
GASP
GASP
GASP
GASP
GASP
SAY YOUR FARE-WELLS.
GASP
GASP
GASP
GASP
MARIGOLD!
SWF

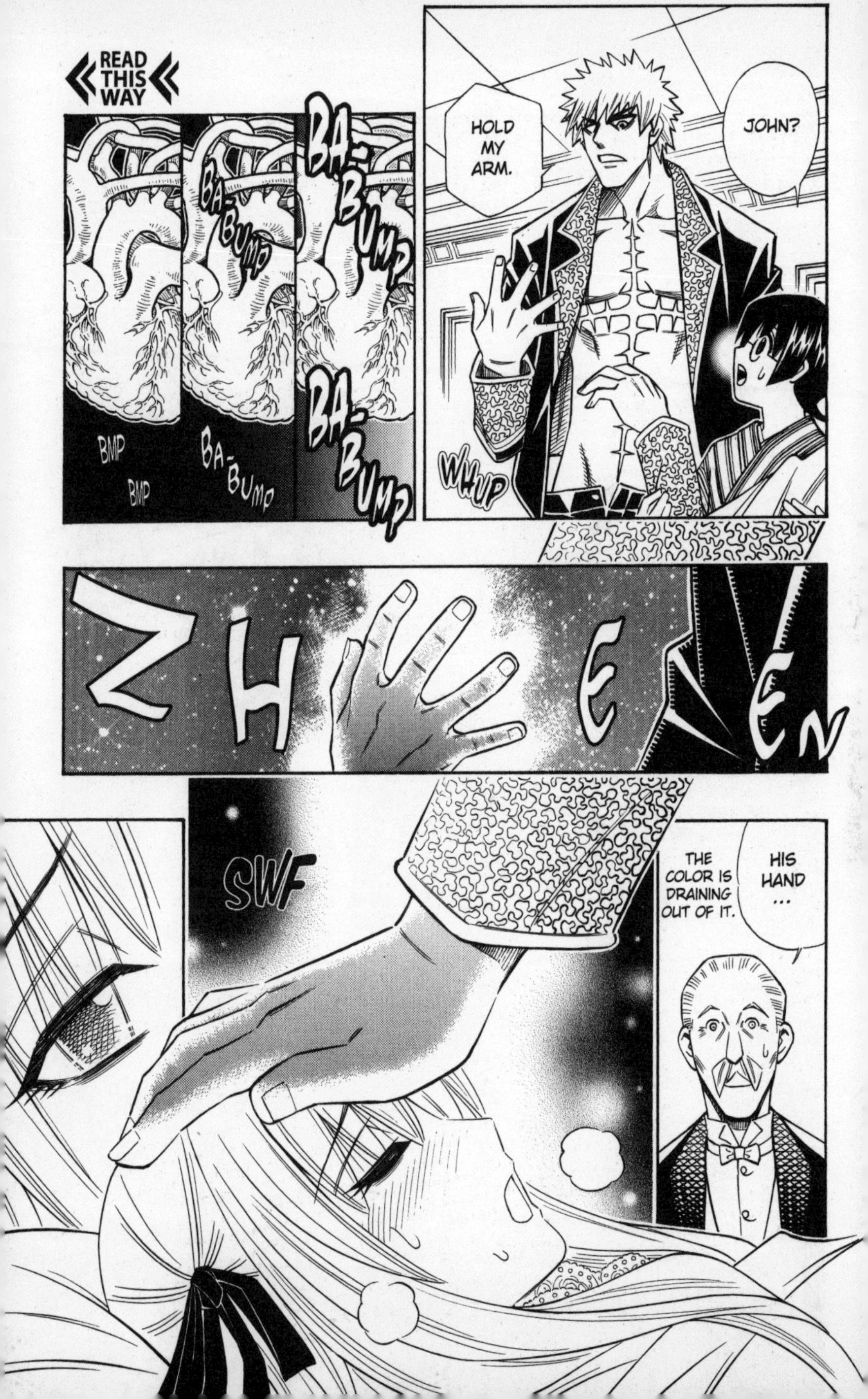
READ THIS WAY
JOHN?
HOLD MY ARM.
WHUP
BA-BUMP
BA-BUMP
BA-BUMP
BA-BUMP
BMP
BMP
ZHEEN
HIS HAND ...
THE COLOR IS DRAINING OUT OF IT.
SWF

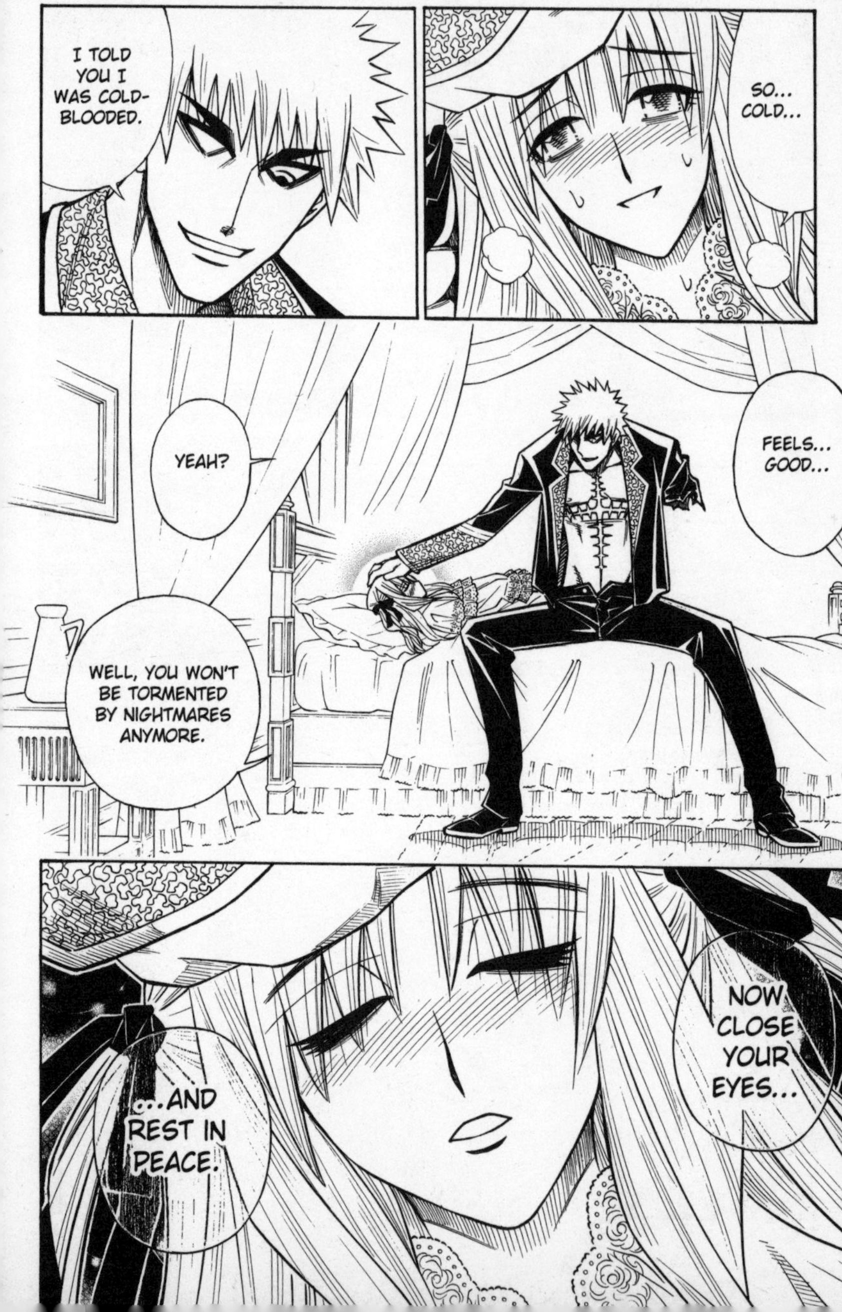
SO... COLD...
I TOLD YOU I WAS COLD-BLOODED.
FEELS... GOOD...
YEAH?
WELL, YOU WON'T BE TORMENTED BY NIGHTMARES ANYMORE.
NOW CLOSE YOUR EYES...
...AND REST IN PEACE.

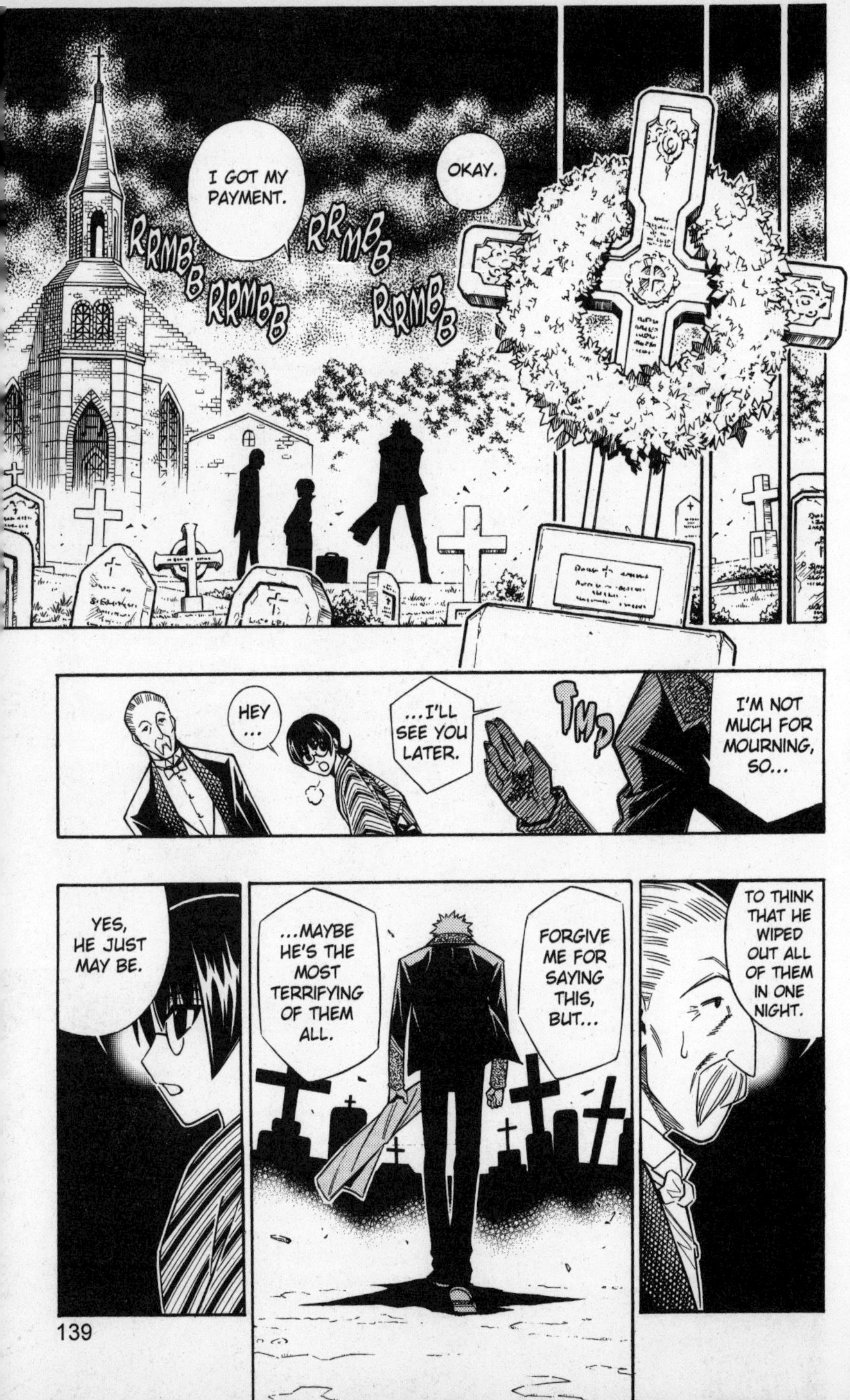
OKAY.
I GOT MY PAYMENT.
RRMBB RRMBB RRMBB RRMBB
I'M NOT MUCH FOR MOURNING, SO...
THP
...I'LL SEE YOU LATER.
HEY ...
TO THINK THAT HE WIPED OUT ALL OF THEM IN ONE NIGHT.
FORGIVE ME FOR SAYING THIS, BUT...
...MAYBE HE'S THE MOST TERRIFYING OF THEM ALL.
YES, HE JUST MAY BE.

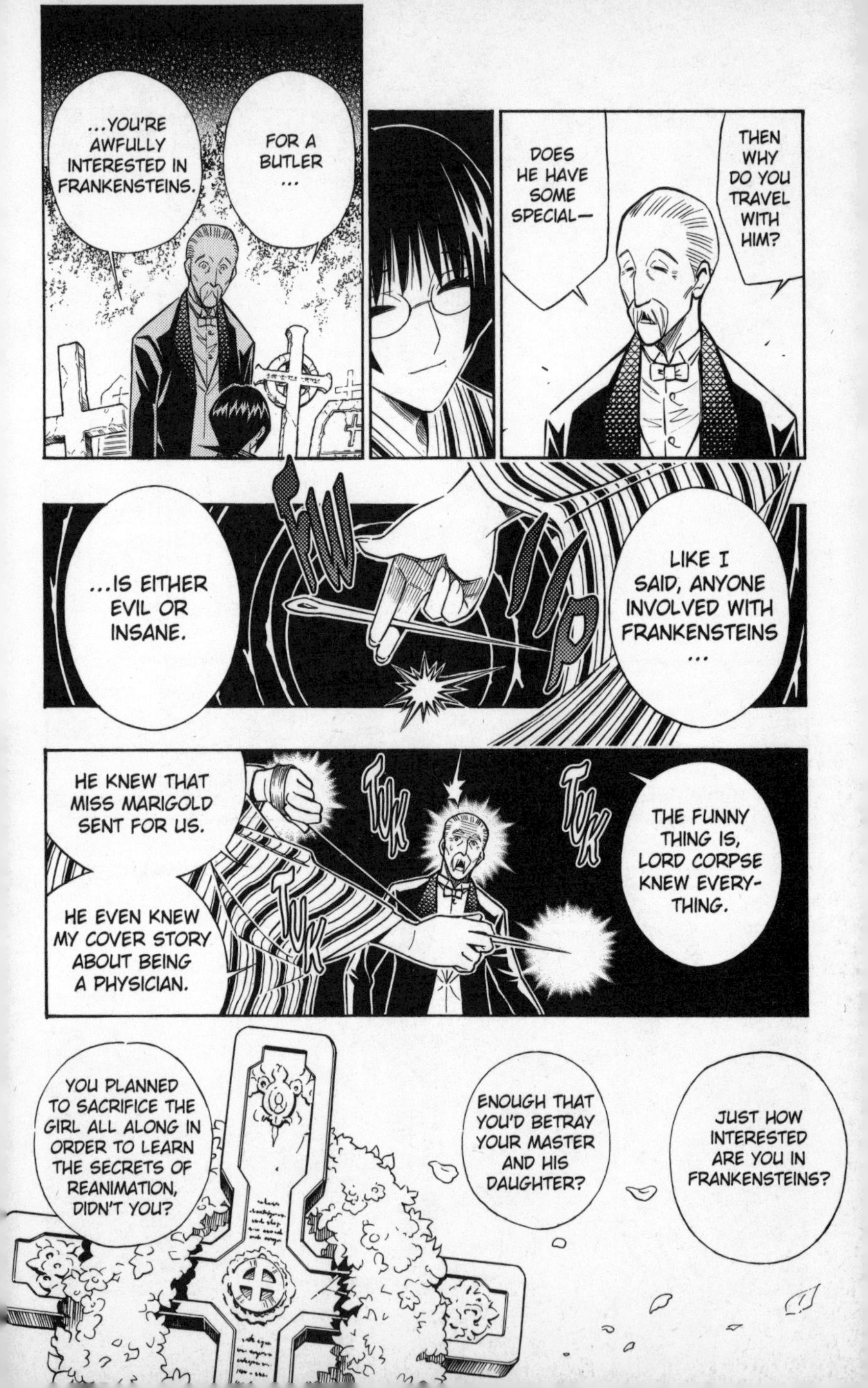
THEN WHY DO YOU TRAVEL WITH HIM?
DOES HE HAVE SOME SPECIAL—
FOR A BUTLER ...
...YOU'RE AWFULLY INTERESTED IN FRANKENSTEINS.
FWWIP
LIKE I SAID, ANYONE INVOLVED WITH FRANKENSTEINS ...
...IS EITHER EVIL OR INSANE.
TUK
TUK
TUK
THE FUNNY THING IS, LORD CORPSE KNEW EVERY-THING.
HE KNEW THAT MISS MARIGOLD SENT FOR US.
HE EVEN KNEW MY COVER STORY ABOUT BEING A PHYSICIAN.
JUST HOW INTERESTED ARE YOU IN FRANKENSTEINS?
ENOUGH THAT YOU'D BETRAY YOUR MASTER AND HIS DAUGHTER?
YOU PLANNED TO SACRIFICE THE GIRL ALL ALONG IN ORDER TO LEARN THE SECRETS OF REANIMATION, DIDN'T YOU?

READ THIS WAY

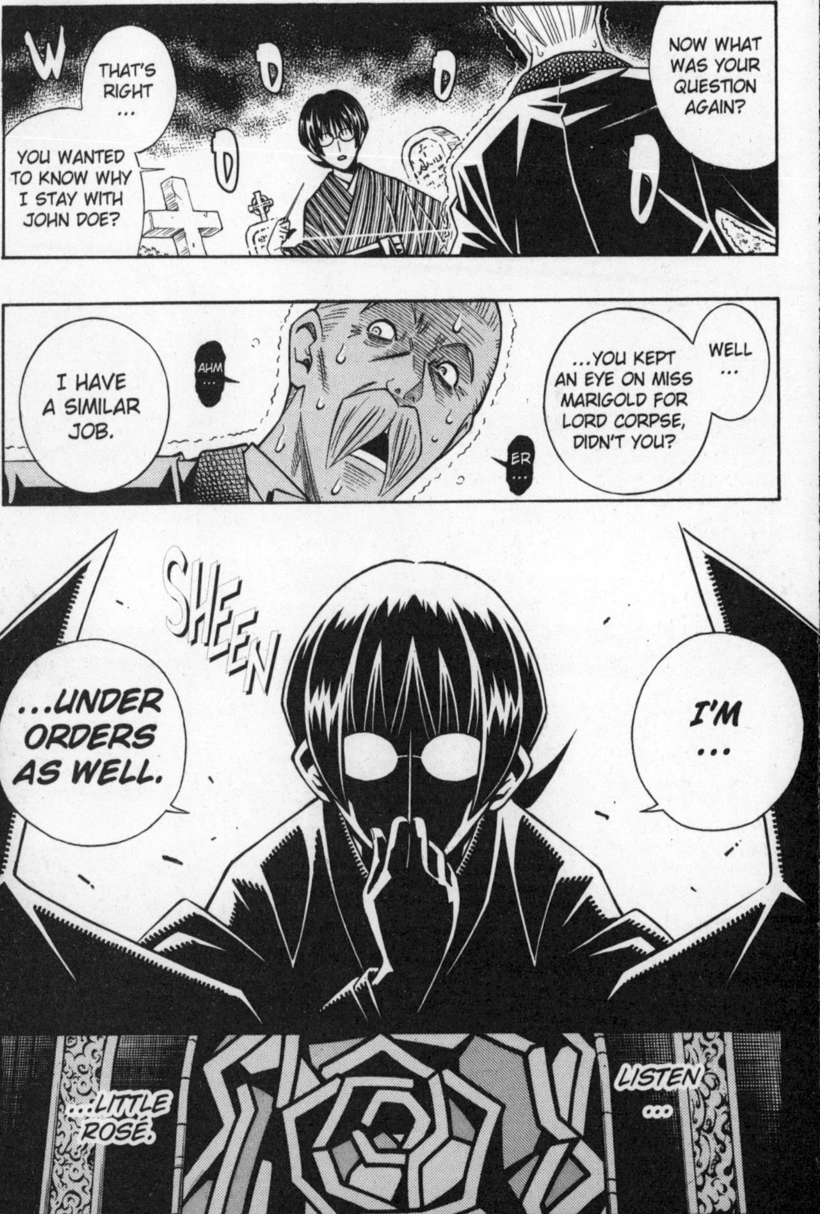

NOW WHAT WAS YOUR QUESTION AGAIN?
THAT'S RIGHT ...
YOU WANTED TO KNOW WHY I STAY WITH JOHN DOE?
WELL ...
...YOU KEPT AN EYE ON MISS MARIGOLD FOR LORD CORPSE, DIDN'T YOU?
ER ...
AHM ...
I HAVE A SIMILAR JOB.
I'M ...
SHEEN
...UNDER ORDERS AS WELL.
LISTEN ...
...LITTLE ROSE.

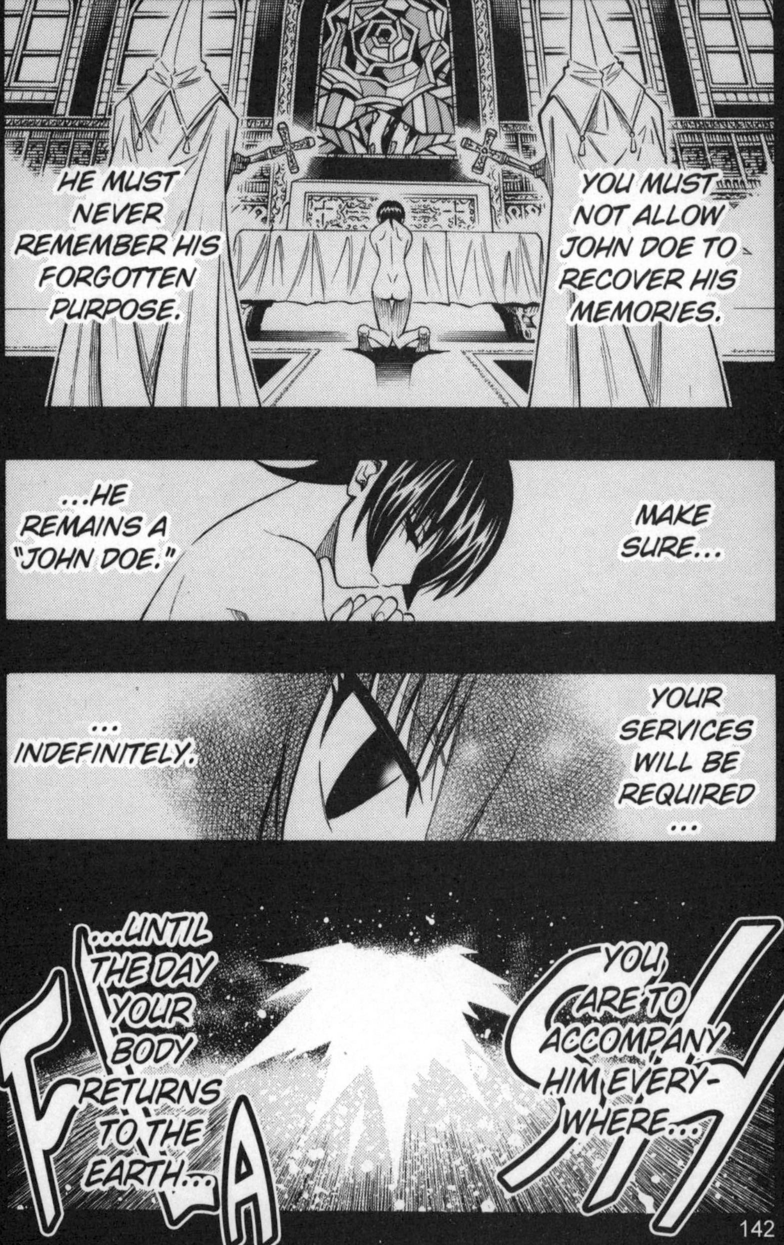
YOU MUST NOT ALLOW JOHN DOE TO RECOVER HIS MEMORIES.
HE MUST NEVER REMEMBER HIS FORGOTTEN PURPOSE.
MAKE SURE...
...HE REMAINS A "JOHN DOE."
YOUR SERVICES WILL BE REQUIRED ...
... INDEFINITELY.
YOU ARE TO ACCOMPANY HIM EVERY-WHERE...
...UNTIL THE DAY YOUR BODY RETURNS TO THE EARTH...
FLASH

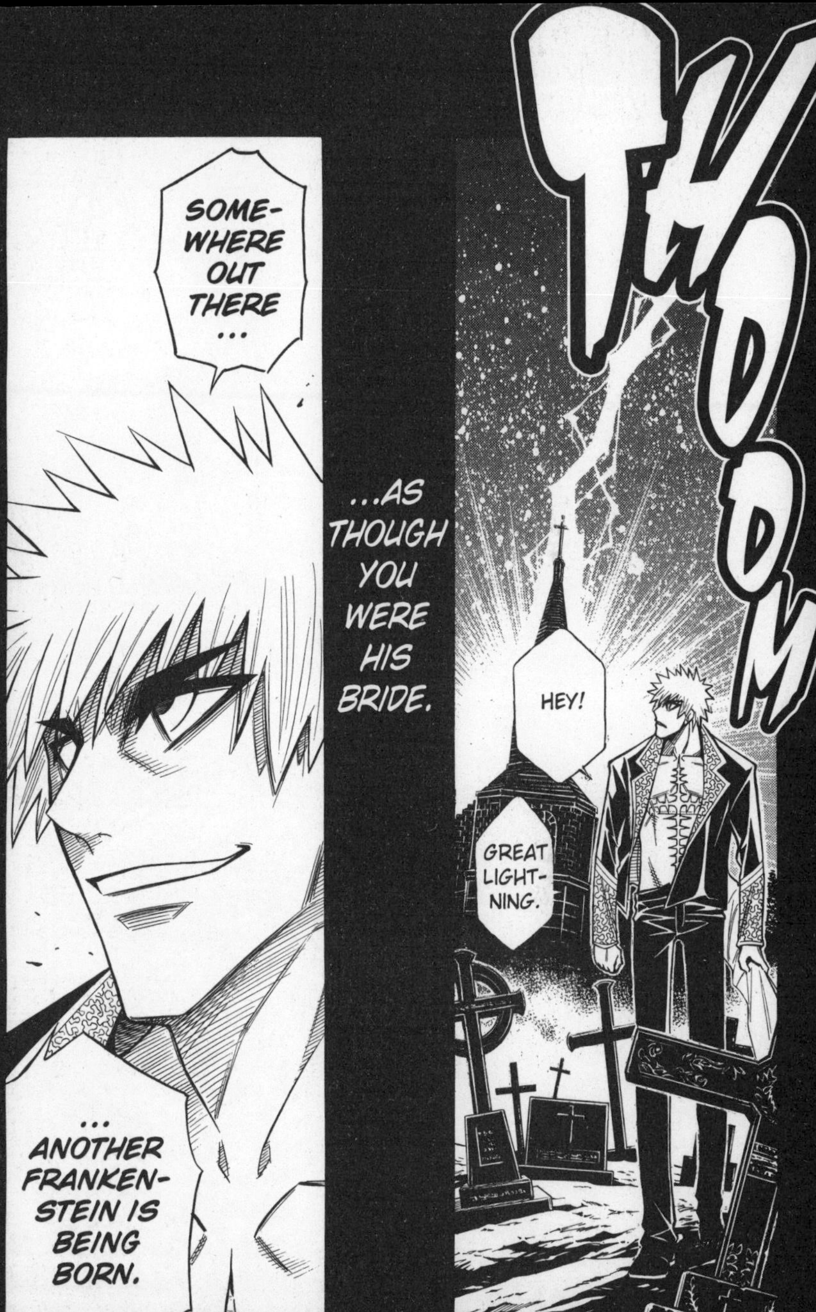
HEY!
GREAT LIGHT-NING.
...AS THOUGH YOU WERE HIS BRIDE.
SOME-WHERE OUT THERE...
...ANOTHER FRANKEN-STEIN IS BEING BORN.

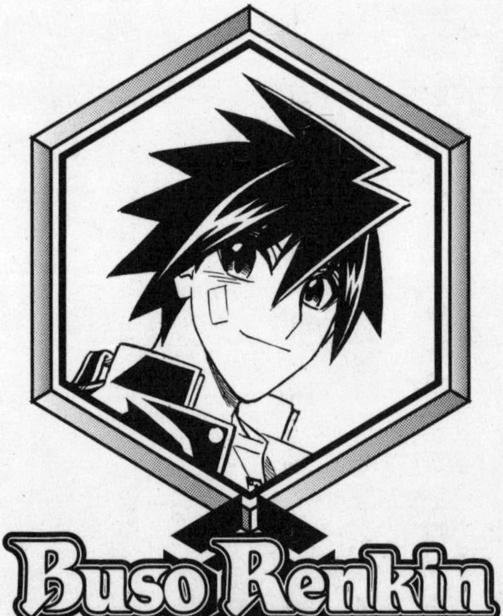
Buso Renkin
ブソウレンキン

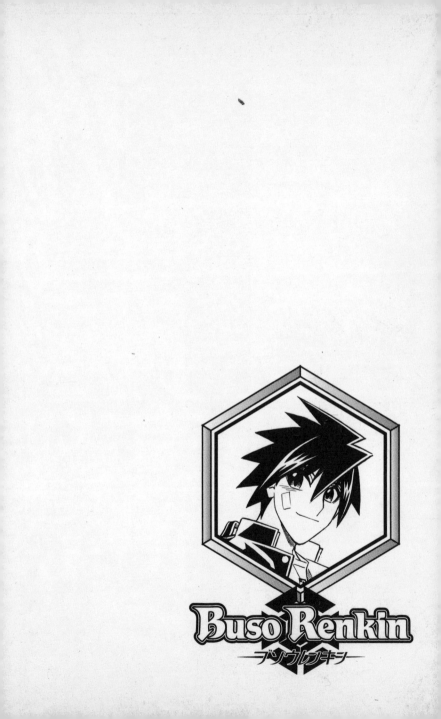

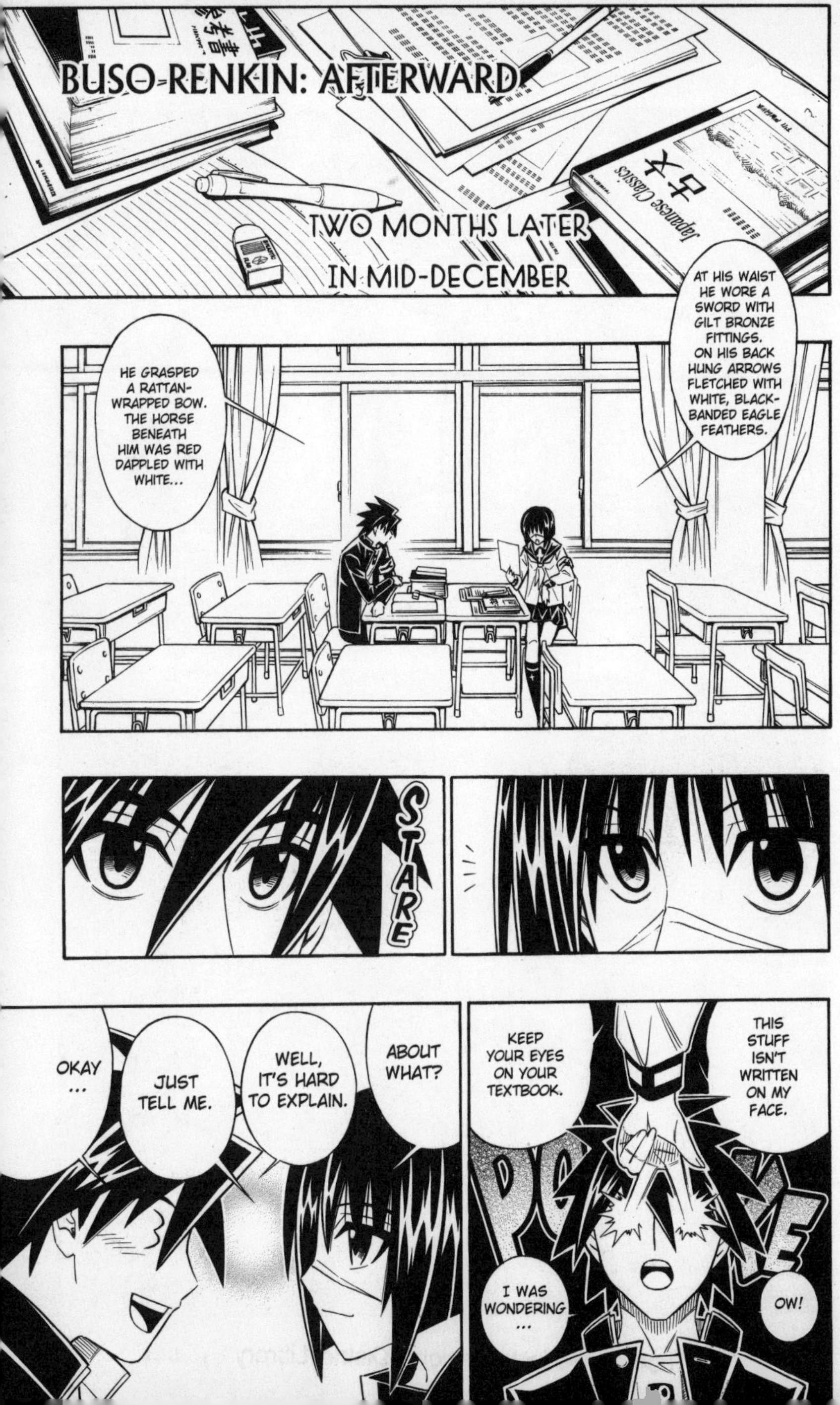
BUSO-RENKIN: AFTERWARD
Japanese Classics
TWO MONTHS LATER
IN MID-DECEMBER
AT HIS WAIST HE WORE A SWORD WITH GILT BRONZE FITTINGS. ON HIS BACK HUNG ARROWS FLETCHED WITH WHITE, BLACK-BANDED EAGLE FEATHERS.
HE GRASPED A RATTAN-WRAPPED BOW. THE HORSE BENEATH HIM WAS RED DAPPLED WITH WHITE...
STARE
THIS STUFF ISN'T WRITTEN ON MY FACE.
KEEP YOUR EYES ON YOUR TEXTBOOK.
OW!
I WAS WONDERING ...
ABOUT WHAT?
WELL, IT'S HARD TO EXPLAIN.
JUST TELL ME.
OKAY ...

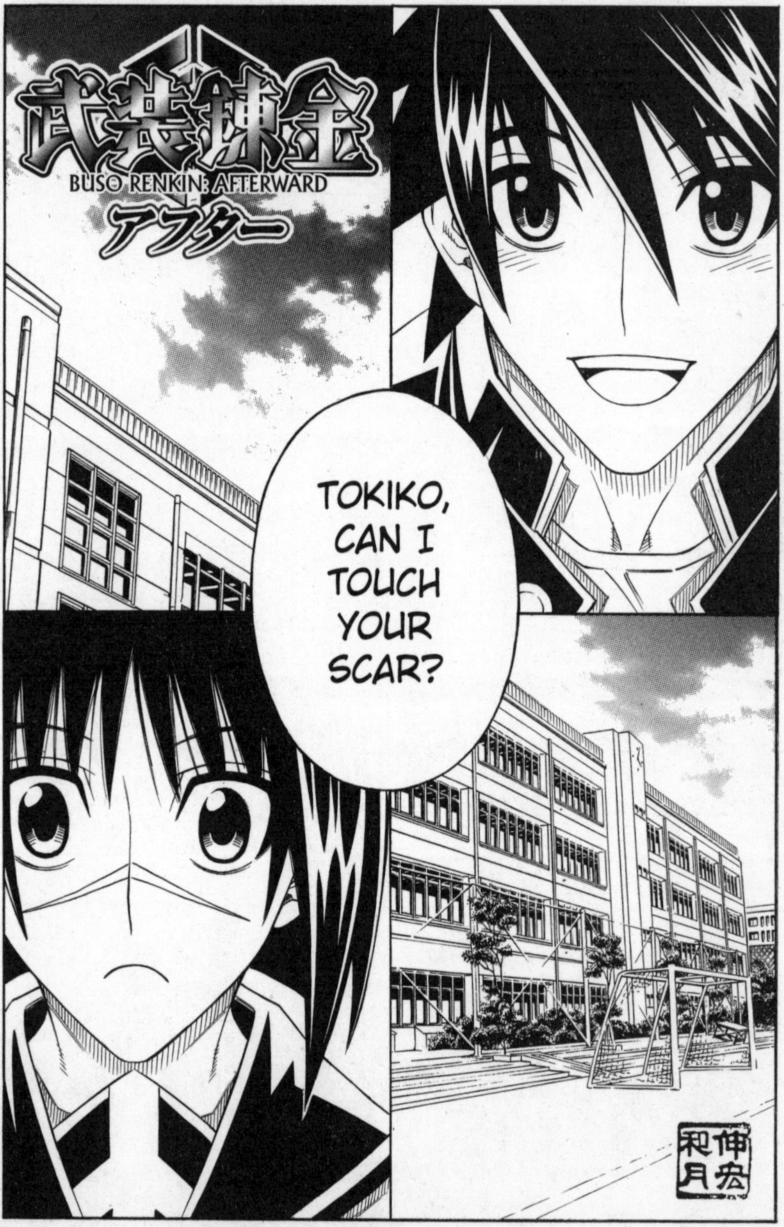
TOKIKO, CAN I TOUCH YOUR SCAR?
武装錬金
BUSO RENKIN: AFTERWARD
アフター
伸宏和月

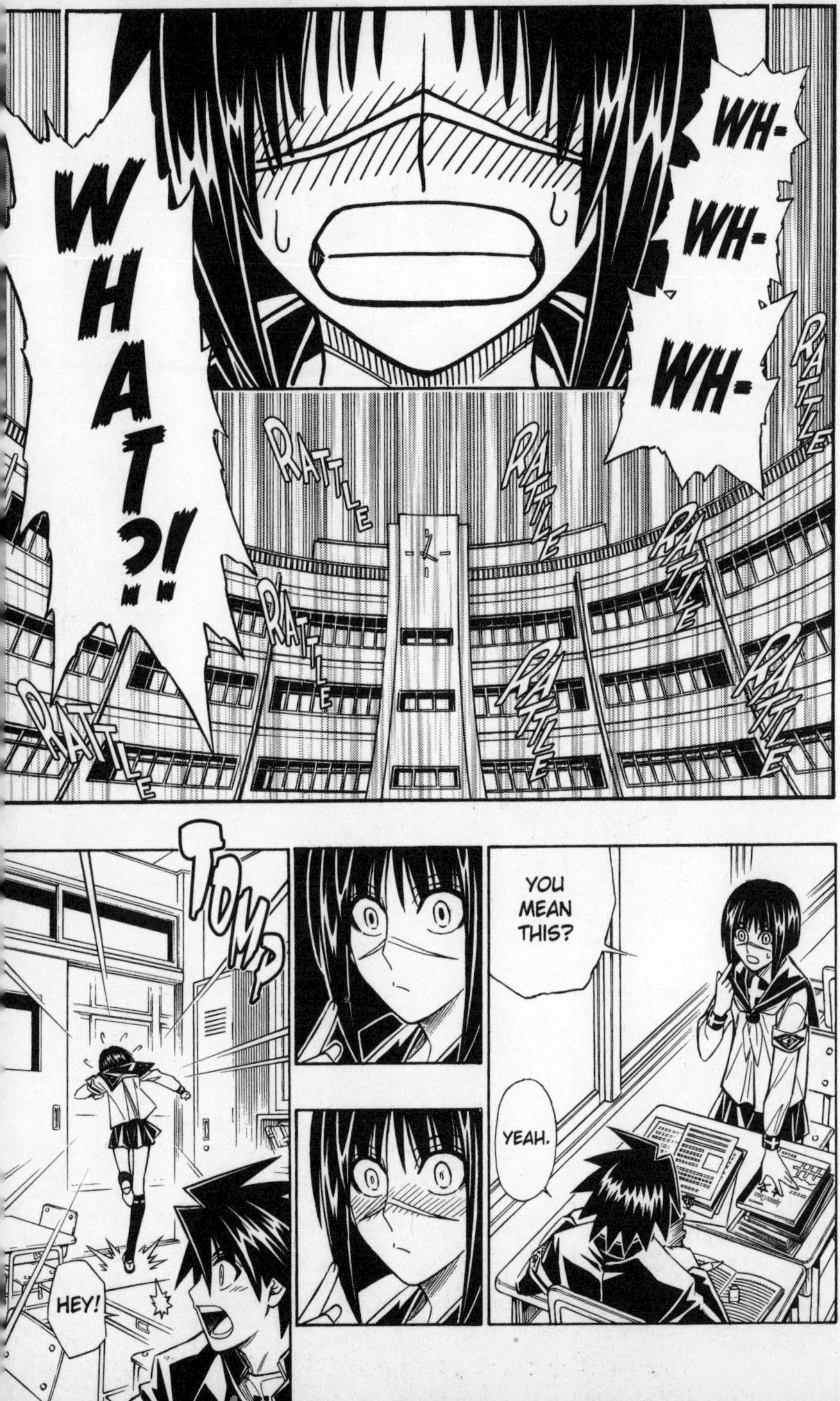
WH- WH- WH-
WHAT?!
RATTLE
RATTLE
RATTLE
RATTLE
RATTLE
RATTLE
RATTLE
RATTLE
YOU MEAN THIS?
YEAH.
TOMP
HEY!

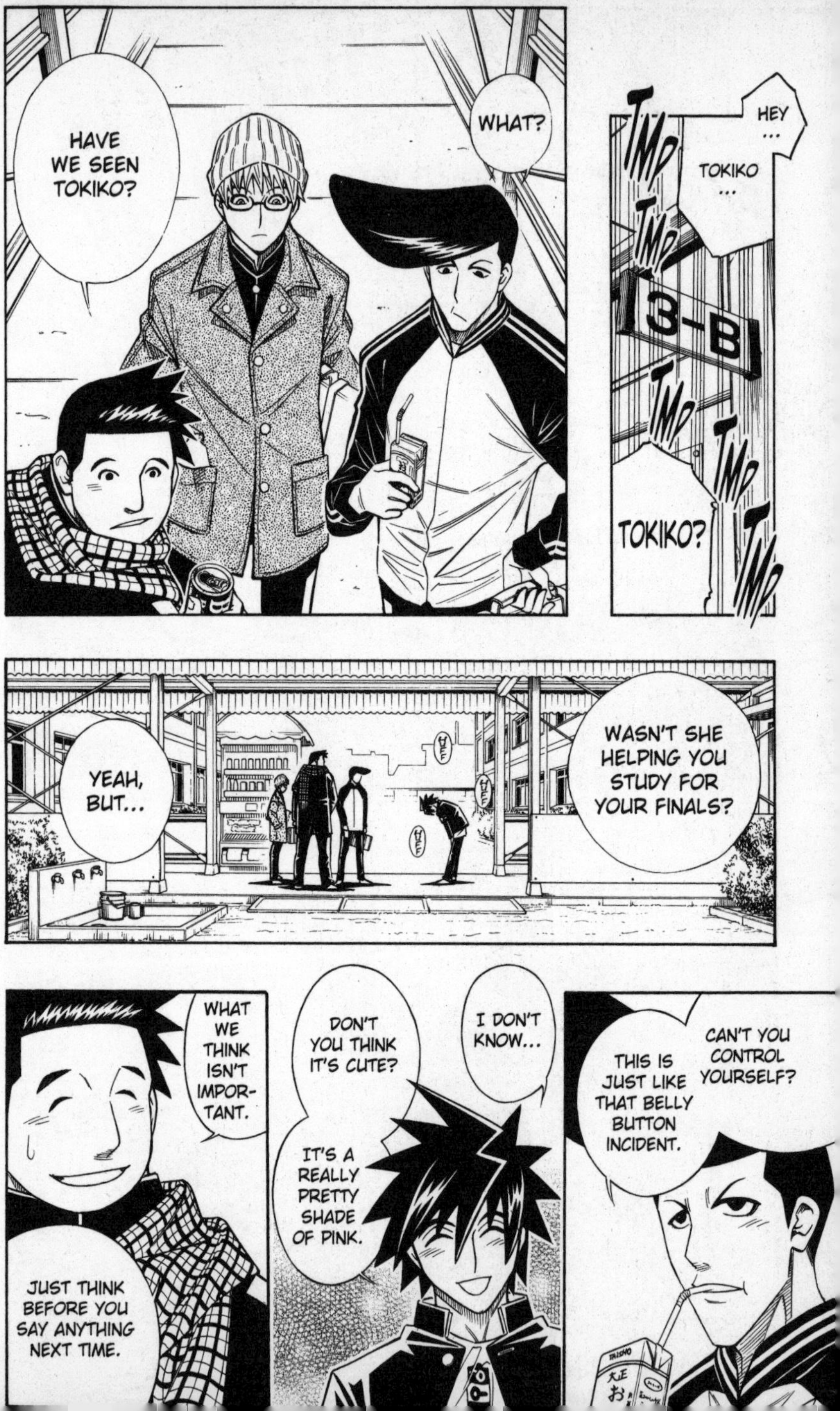
HEY...
TOKIKO...
TMP TMP TMP
TOKIKO?
TMP TMP TMP
WHAT?
HAVE WE SEEN TOKIKO?
WASN'T SHE HELPING YOU STUDY FOR YOUR FINALS?
HUFF
HUFF
HUFF
YEAH, BUT...
CAN'T YOU CONTROL YOURSELF?
THIS IS JUST LIKE THAT BELLY BUTTON INCIDENT.
I DON'T KNOW...
DON'T YOU THINK IT'S CUTE?
IT'S A REALLY PRETTY SHADE OF PINK.
WHAT WE THINK ISN'T IMPOR-TANT.
JUST THINK BEFORE YOU SAY ANYTHING NEXT TIME.

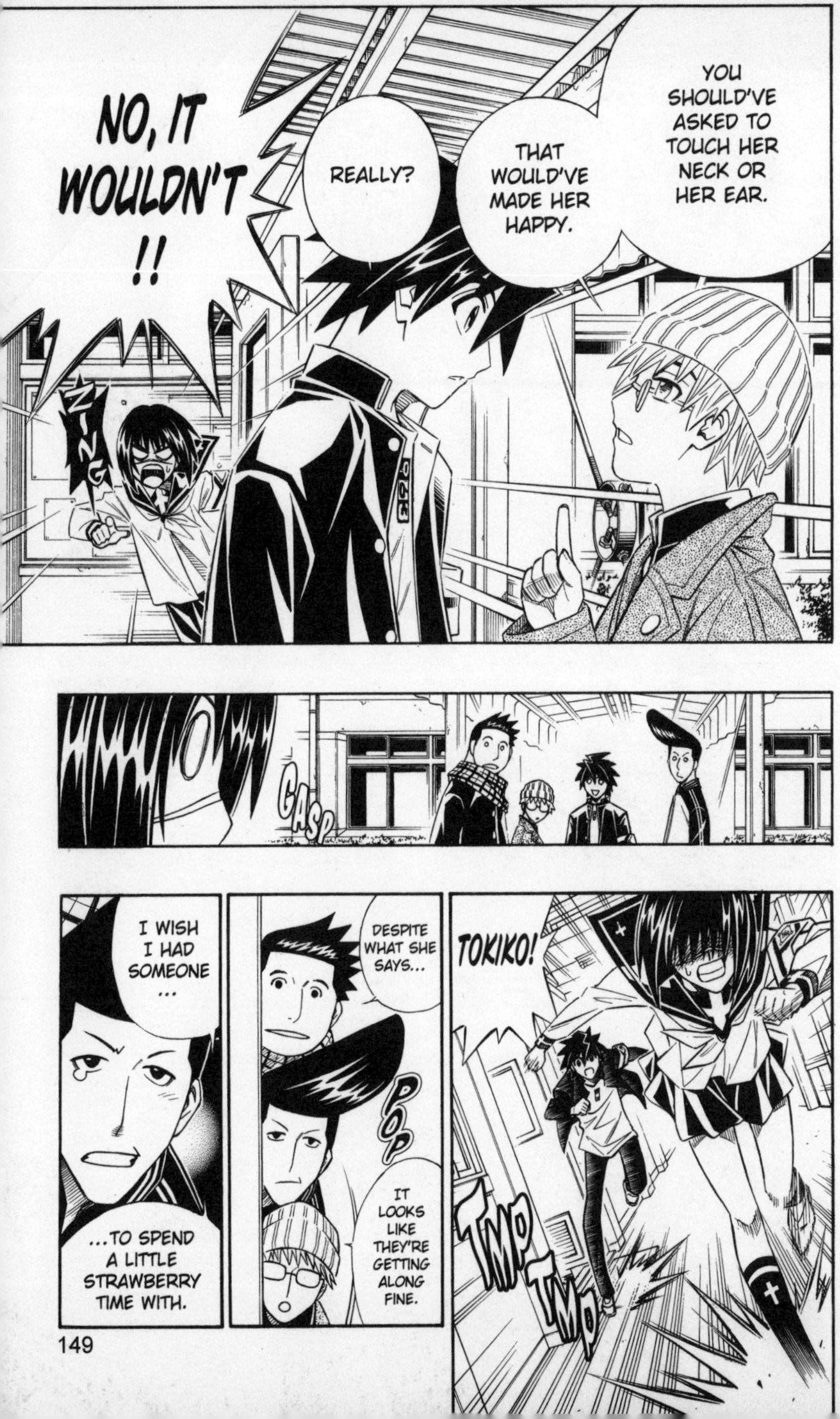
YOU SHOULD'VE ASKED TO TOUCH HER NECK OR HER EAR.
THAT WOULD'VE MADE HER HAPPY.
REALLY?
NO, IT WOULDN'T !!
ZING
GASP
TOKIKO!
TMP TMP
DESPITE WHAT SHE SAYS...
POP
IT LOOKS LIKE THEY'RE GETTING ALONG FINE.
I WISH I HAD SOMEONE ...
...TO SPEND A LITTLE STRAWBERRY TIME WITH.

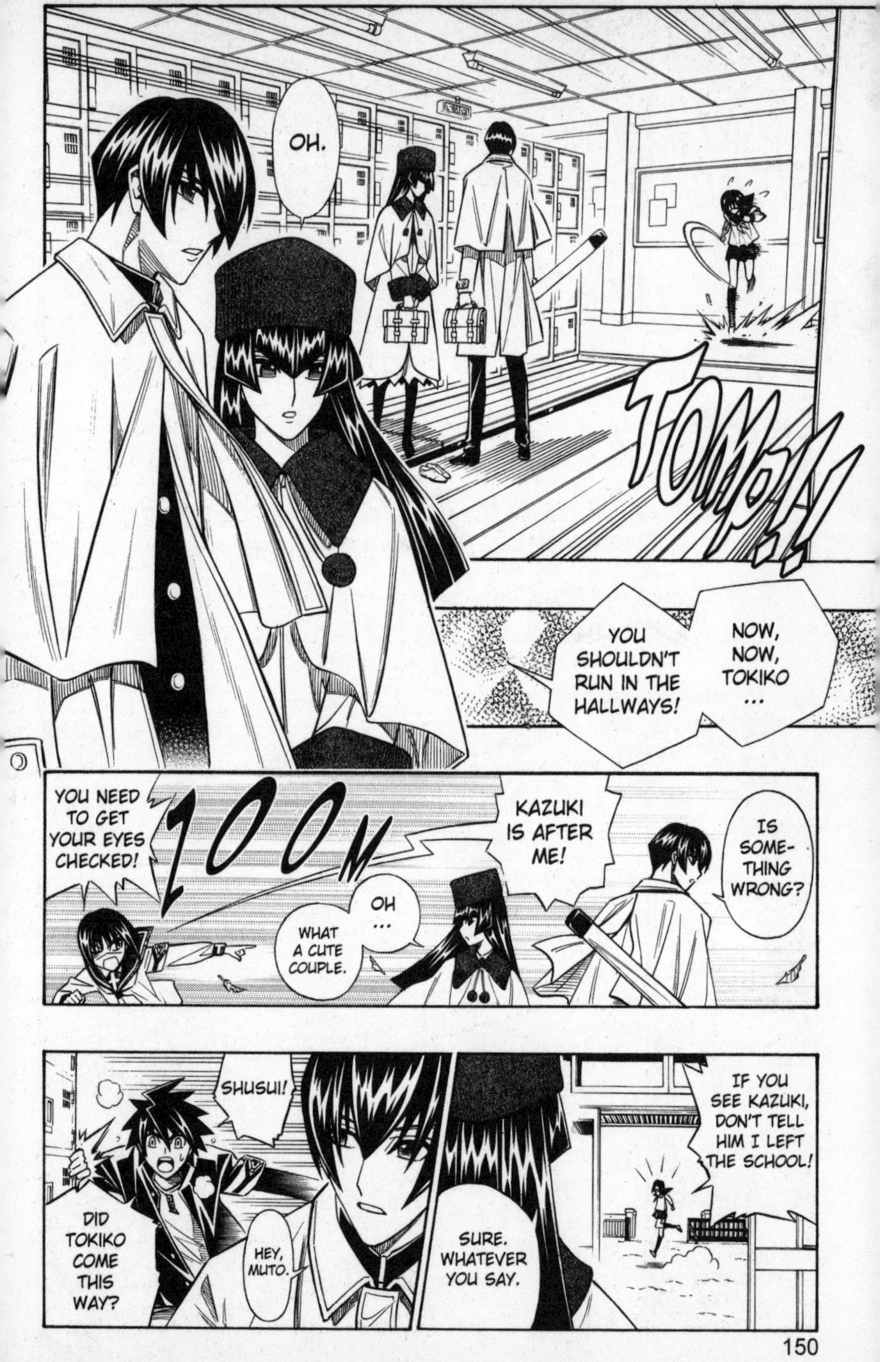
TOMP!!
OH.
NOW, NOW, TOKIKO ...
YOU SHOULDN'T RUN IN THE HALLWAYS!
IS SOMETHING WRONG?
KAZUKI IS AFTER ME!
OH ...
WHAT A CUTE COUPLE.
ZOOM
YOU NEED TO GET YOUR EYES CHECKED!
IF YOU SEE KAZUKI, DON'T TELL HIM I LEFT THE SCHOOL!
SURE. WHATEVER YOU SAY.
SHUSUI!
HEY, MUTO.
DID TOKIKO COME THIS WAY?

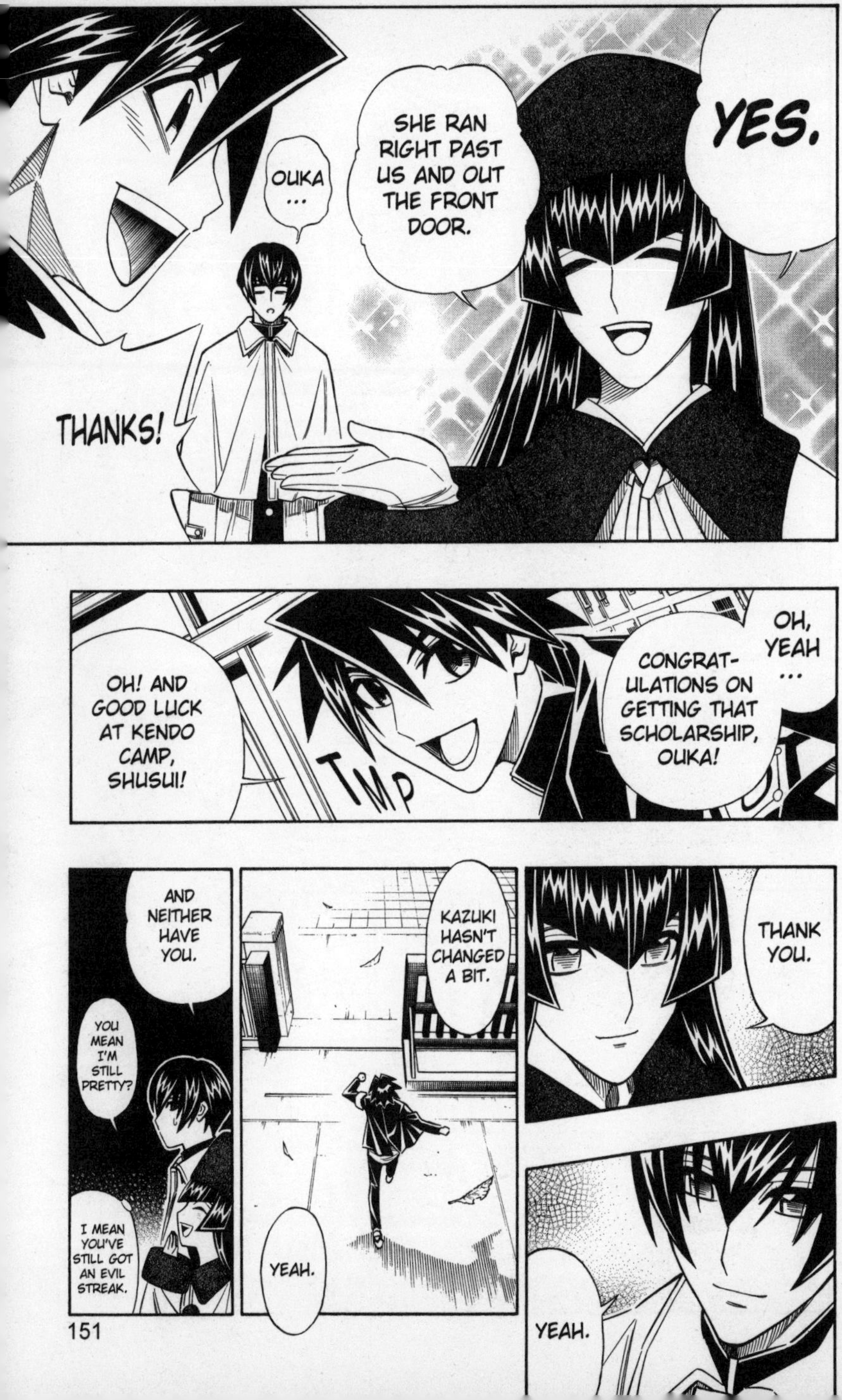
YES.
SHE RAN RIGHT PAST US AND OUT THE FRONT DOOR.
OUKA ...
THANKS!
OH, YEAH ...
CONGRAT-ULATIONS ON GETTING THAT SCHOLARSHIP, OUKA!
TMP
OH! AND GOOD LUCK AT KENDO CAMP, SHUSUI!
THANK YOU.
YEAH.
KAZUKI HASN'T CHANGED A BIT.
YEAH.
AND NEITHER HAVE YOU.
YOU MEAN I'M STILL PRETTY?
I MEAN YOU'VE STILL GOT AN EVIL STREAK.

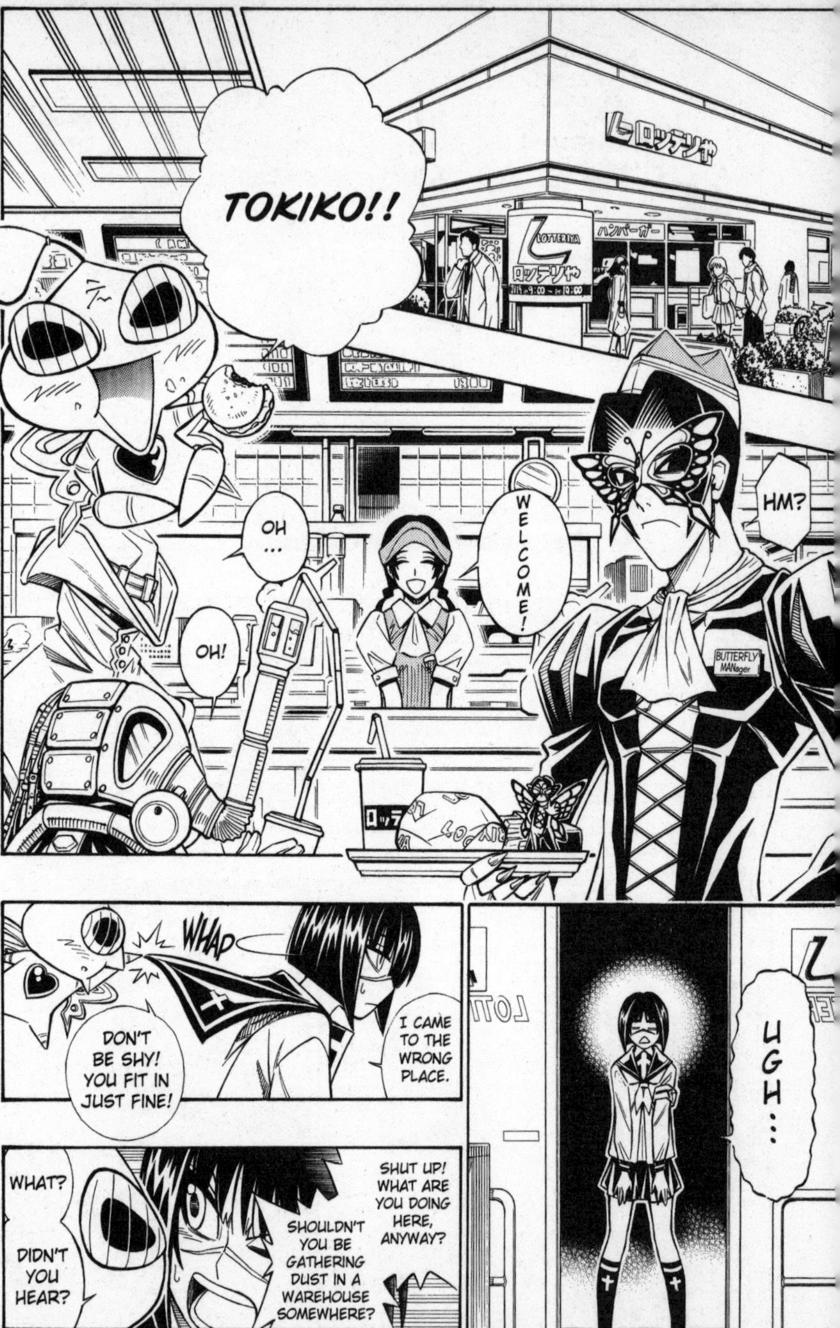

ロッテリヤ
TOKIKO!!
LOTTERIYA ロッテリヤ
ハンバーガー
HM?
WELCOME!
BUTTERFLY MANager
OH...
OH!
UGH...
I CAME TO THE WRONG PLACE.
WHAP
DON'T BE SHY! YOU FIT IN JUST FINE!
SHUT UP! WHAT ARE YOU DOING HERE, ANYWAY?
SHOULDN'T YOU BE GATHERING DUST IN A WAREHOUSE SOMEWHERE?
WHAT?
DIDN'T YOU HEAR?

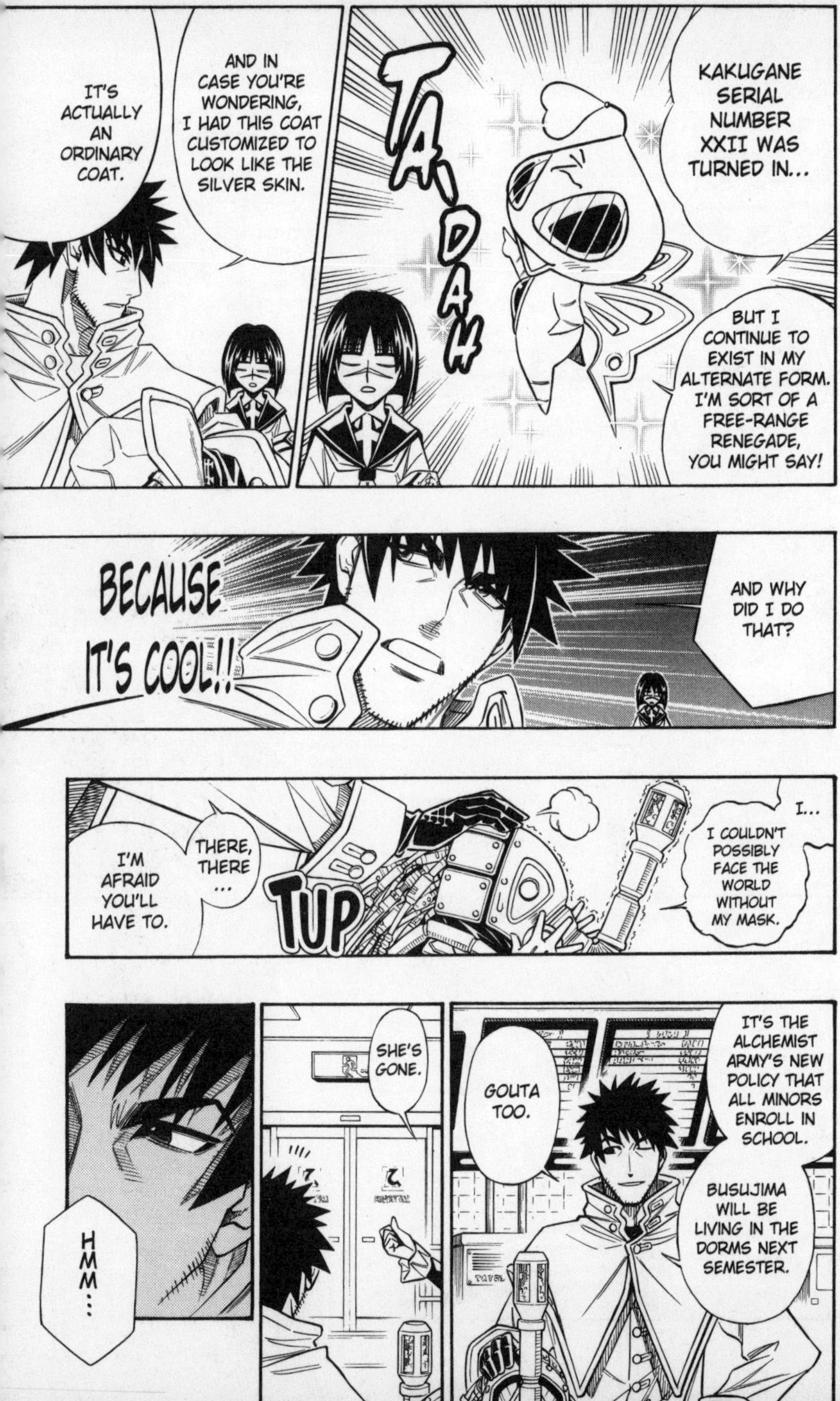
KAKUGANE SERIAL NUMBER XXII WAS TURNED IN...
TA-DAH
BUT I CONTINUE TO EXIST IN MY ALTERNATE FORM. I'M SORT OF A FREE-RANGE RENEGADE, YOU MIGHT SAY!
AND IN CASE YOU'RE WONDERING, I HAD THIS COAT CUSTOMIZED TO LOOK LIKE THE SILVER SKIN.
IT'S ACTUALLY AN ORDINARY COAT.
AND WHY DID I DO THAT?
BECAUSE IT'S COOL!!
I...
I COULDN'T POSSIBLY FACE THE WORLD WITHOUT MY MASK.
TUP
THERE, THERE...
I'M AFRAID YOU'LL HAVE TO.
IT'S THE ALCHEMIST ARMY'S NEW POLICY THAT ALL MINORS ENROLL IN SCHOOL.
BUSUJIMA WILL BE LIVING IN THE DORMS NEXT SEMESTER.
GOUTA TOO.
SHE'S GONE.
HMM...

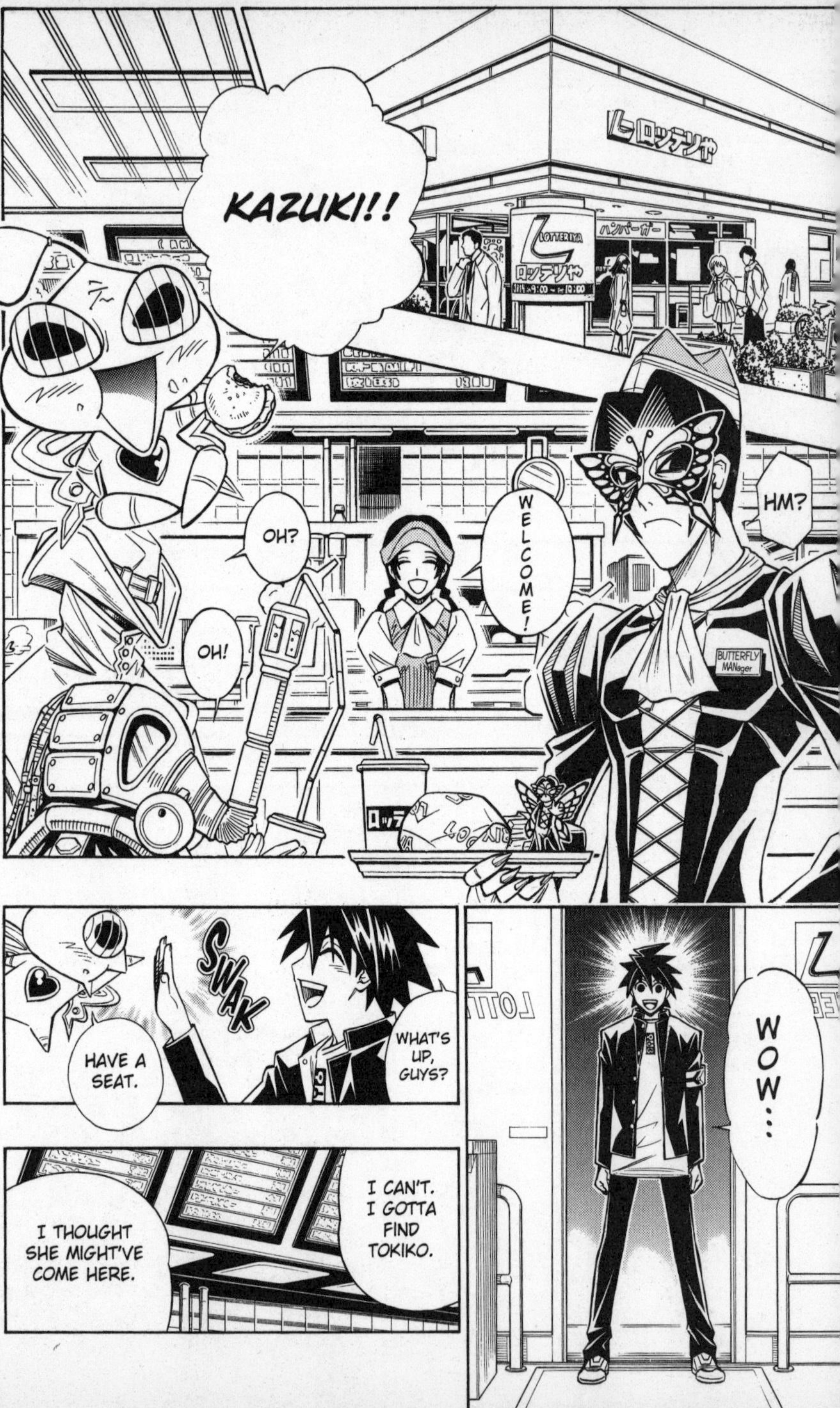
LOTTERIYA
WELCOME!
HM?
BUTTERFLY MANager
OH?
OH!
KAZUKI!!
WOW...
WHAT'S UP, GUYS?
SWAK
HAVE A SEAT.
I CAN'T. I GOTTA FIND TOKIKO.
I THOUGHT SHE MIGHT'VE COME HERE.

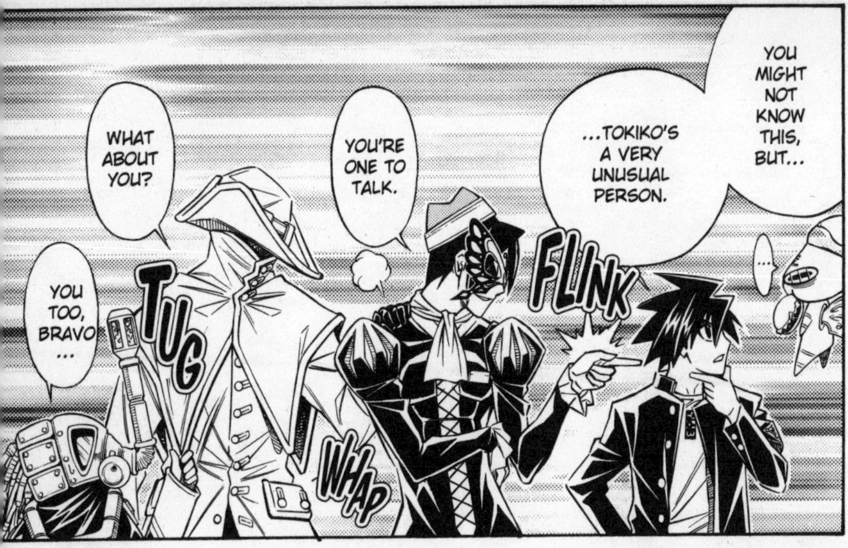
YOU MIGHT NOT KNOW THIS, BUT...
...TOKIKO'S A VERY UNUSUAL PERSON.
...
FLINK
YOU'RE ONE TO TALK.
WHAP
WHAT ABOUT YOU?
TUG
YOU TOO, BRAVO...

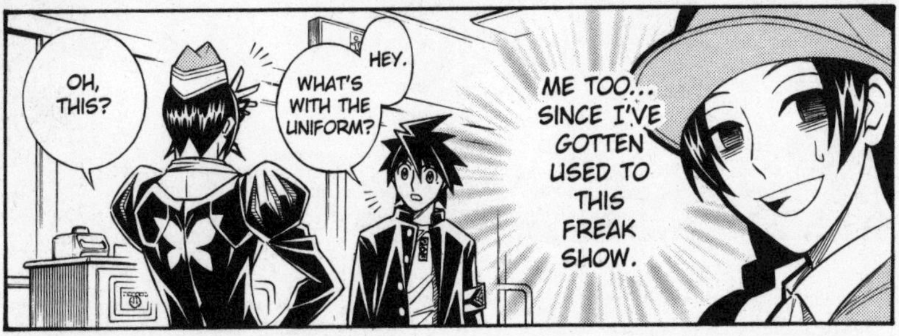
ME TOO... SINCE I'VE GOTTEN USED TO THIS FREAK SHOW.
HEY.
WHAT'S WITH THE UNIFORM?
OH, THIS?

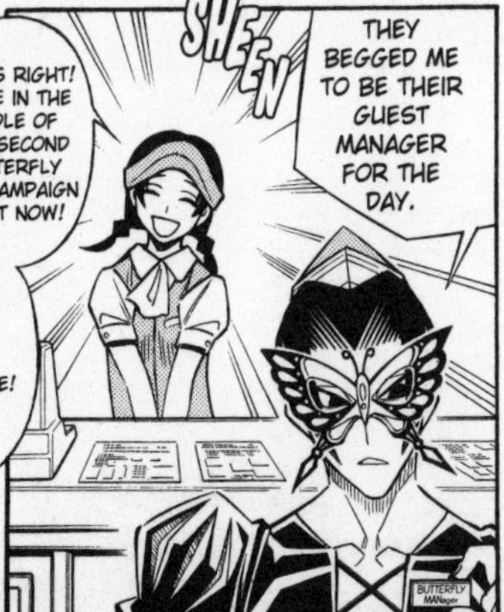
SHEEN
THEY BEGGED ME TO BE THEIR GUEST MANAGER FOR THE DAY.
THAT'S RIGHT! WE'RE IN THE MIDDLE OF OUR SECOND BUTTERFLY MAN CAMPAIGN RIGHT NOW!
THANK YOU FOR YOUR PATRONAGE!
BUTTERFLY MANager

○ **Butterfly Man Campaign Series 2 Figures**

- ○ Butterfly Man Papillon, version 2
- ○ Rival: Hypocrite Boy
- ○ Monster: Gut-Splatter Girl

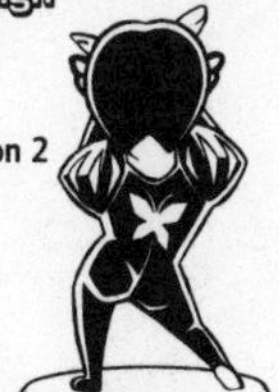

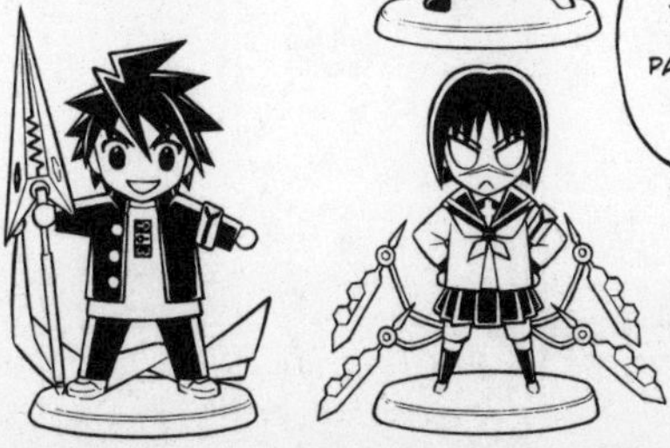

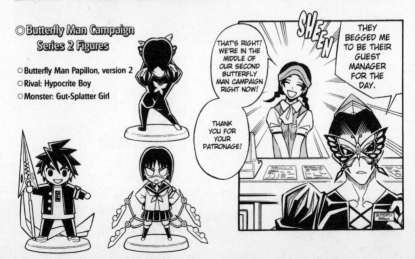

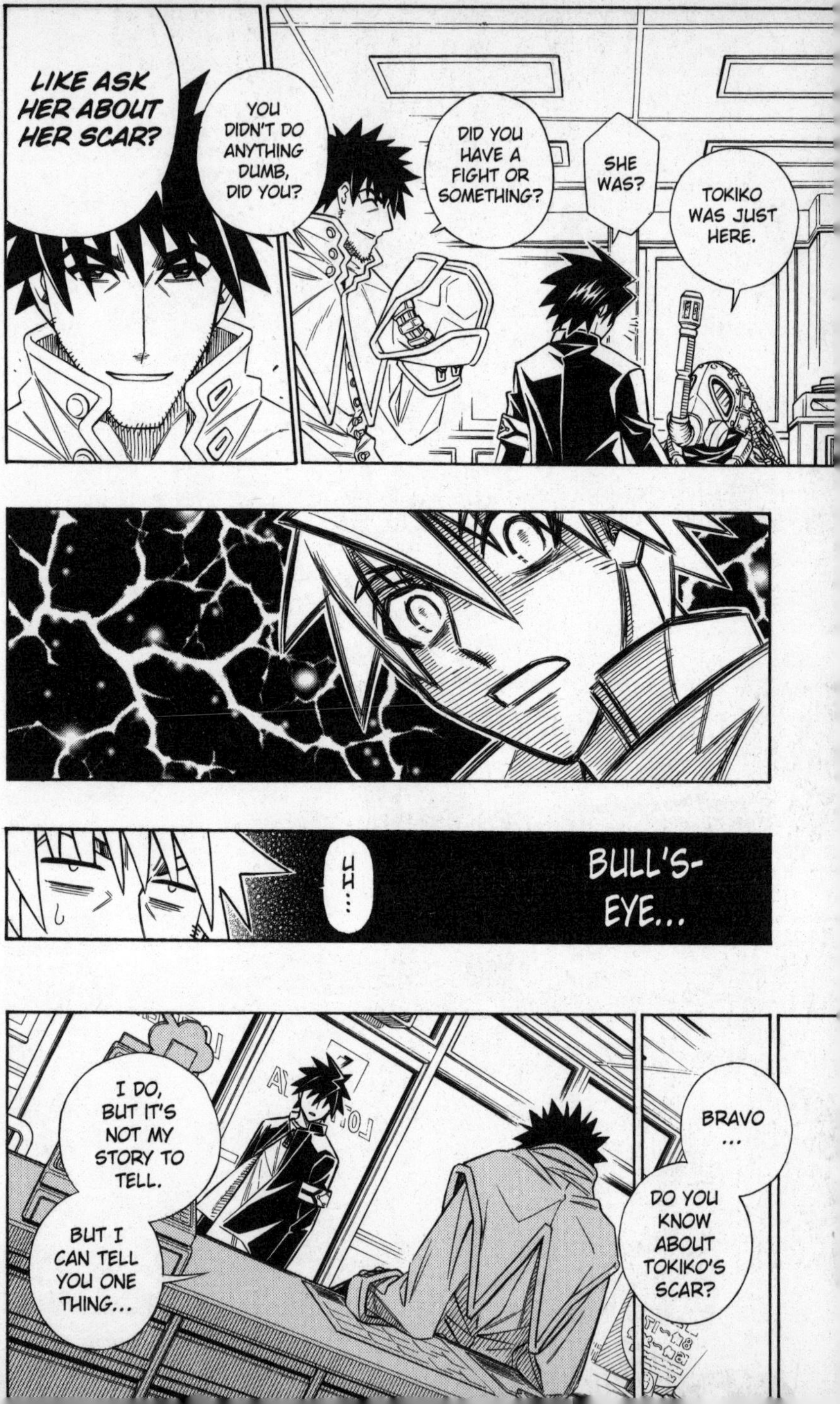
TOKIKO WAS JUST HERE.
SHE WAS?
DID YOU HAVE A FIGHT OR SOMETHING?
YOU DIDN'T DO ANYTHING DUMB, DID YOU?
LIKE ASK HER ABOUT HER SCAR?
BULL'S-EYE...
UH...
BRAVO...
DO YOU KNOW ABOUT TOKIKO'S SCAR?
I DO, BUT IT'S NOT MY STORY TO TELL.
BUT I CAN TELL YOU ONE THING...

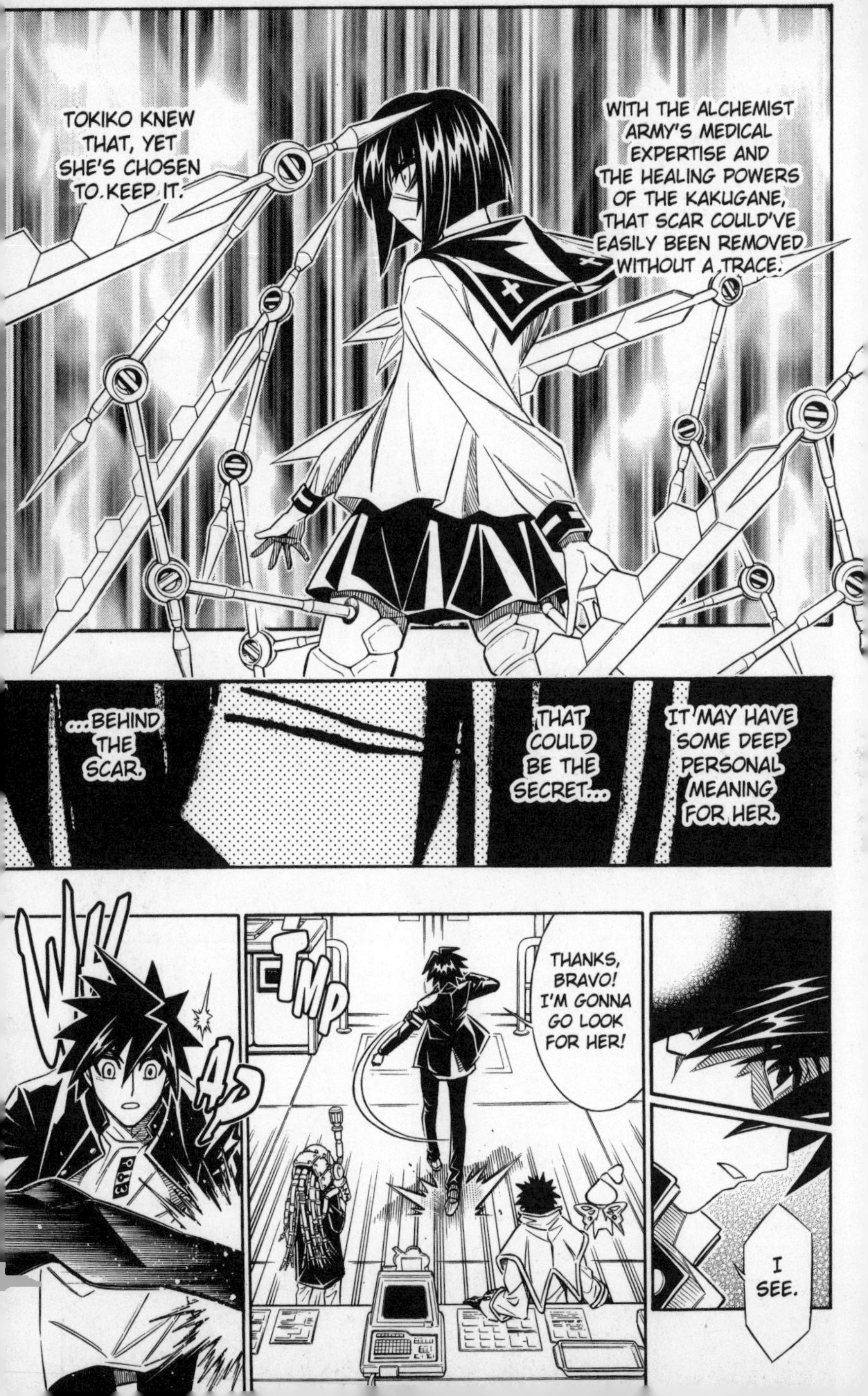
WITH THE ALCHEMIST ARMY'S MEDICAL EXPERTISE AND THE HEALING POWERS OF THE KAKUGANE, THAT SCAR COULD'VE EASILY BEEN REMOVED WITHOUT A TRACE.
TOKIKO KNEW THAT, YET SHE'S CHOSEN TO KEEP IT.
IT MAY HAVE SOME DEEP PERSONAL MEANING FOR HER.
THAT COULD BE THE SECRET...
...BEHIND THE SCAR.
I SEE.
THANKS, BRAVO! I'M GONNA GO LOOK FOR HER!
TMP

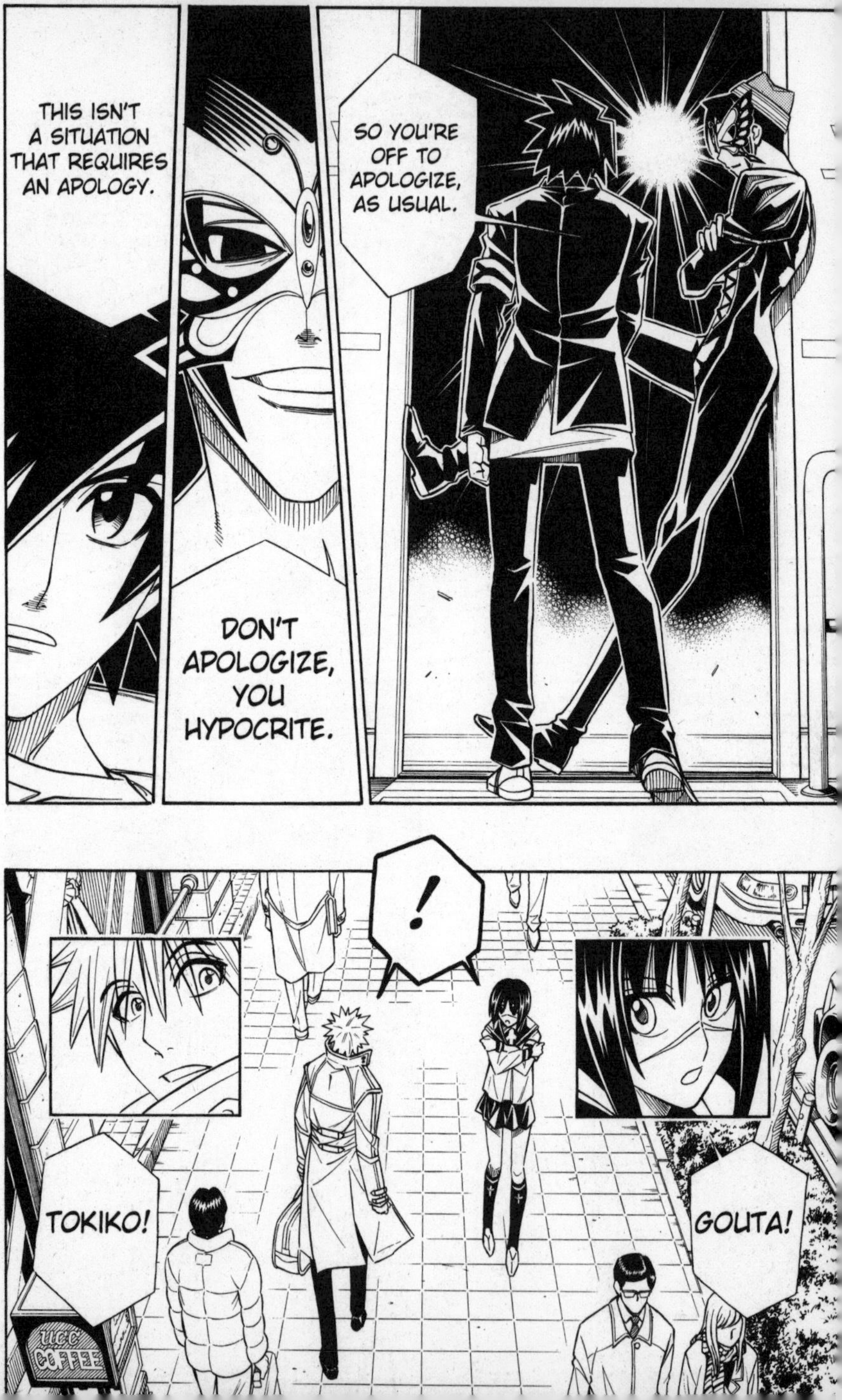
SO YOU'RE OFF TO APOLOGIZE, AS USUAL.
DON'T APOLOGIZE, YOU HYPOCRITE.
THIS ISN'T A SITUATION THAT REQUIRES AN APOLOGY.
!
GOUTA!
TOKIKO!
UCC COFFEE

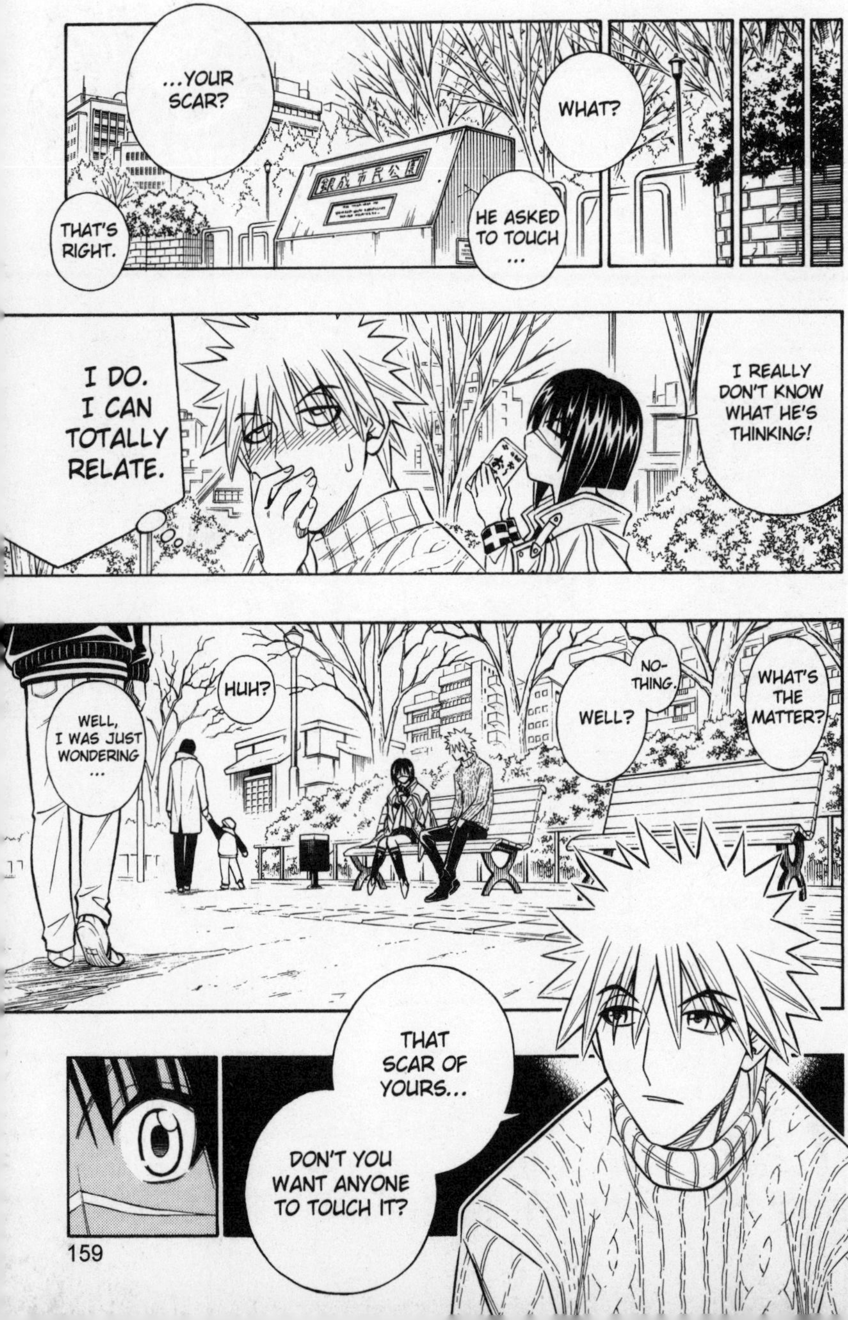
WHAT?
HE ASKED TO TOUCH ...
...YOUR SCAR?
THAT'S RIGHT.
I REALLY DON'T KNOW WHAT HE'S THINKING!
I DO. I CAN TOTALLY RELATE.
WHAT'S THE MATTER?
NO-THING.
WELL?
HUH?
WELL, I WAS JUST WONDERING ...
THAT SCAR OF YOURS...
DON'T YOU WANT ANYONE TO TOUCH IT?

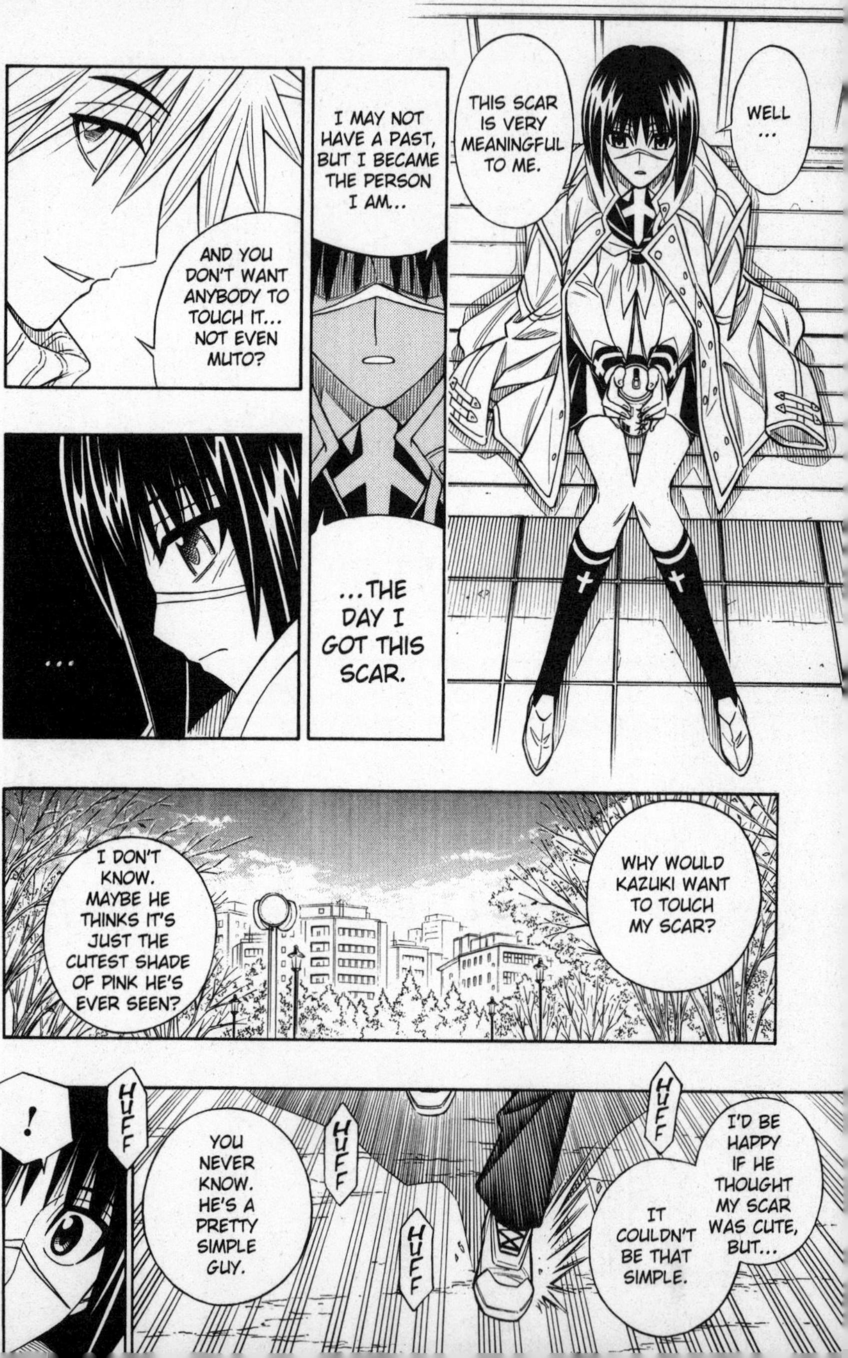
WELL...
THIS SCAR IS VERY MEANINGFUL TO ME.
I MAY NOT HAVE A PAST, BUT I BECAME THE PERSON I AM...
...THE DAY I GOT THIS SCAR.
AND YOU DON'T WANT ANYBODY TO TOUCH IT... NOT EVEN MUTO?
...
WHY WOULD KAZUKI WANT TO TOUCH MY SCAR?
I DON'T KNOW. MAYBE HE THINKS IT'S JUST THE CUTEST SHADE OF PINK HE'S EVER SEEN?
I'D BE HAPPY IF HE THOUGHT MY SCAR WAS CUTE, BUT...
IT COULDN'T BE THAT SIMPLE.
HUFF
HUFF
HUFF
YOU NEVER KNOW. HE'S A PRETTY SIMPLE GUY.
HUFF
!

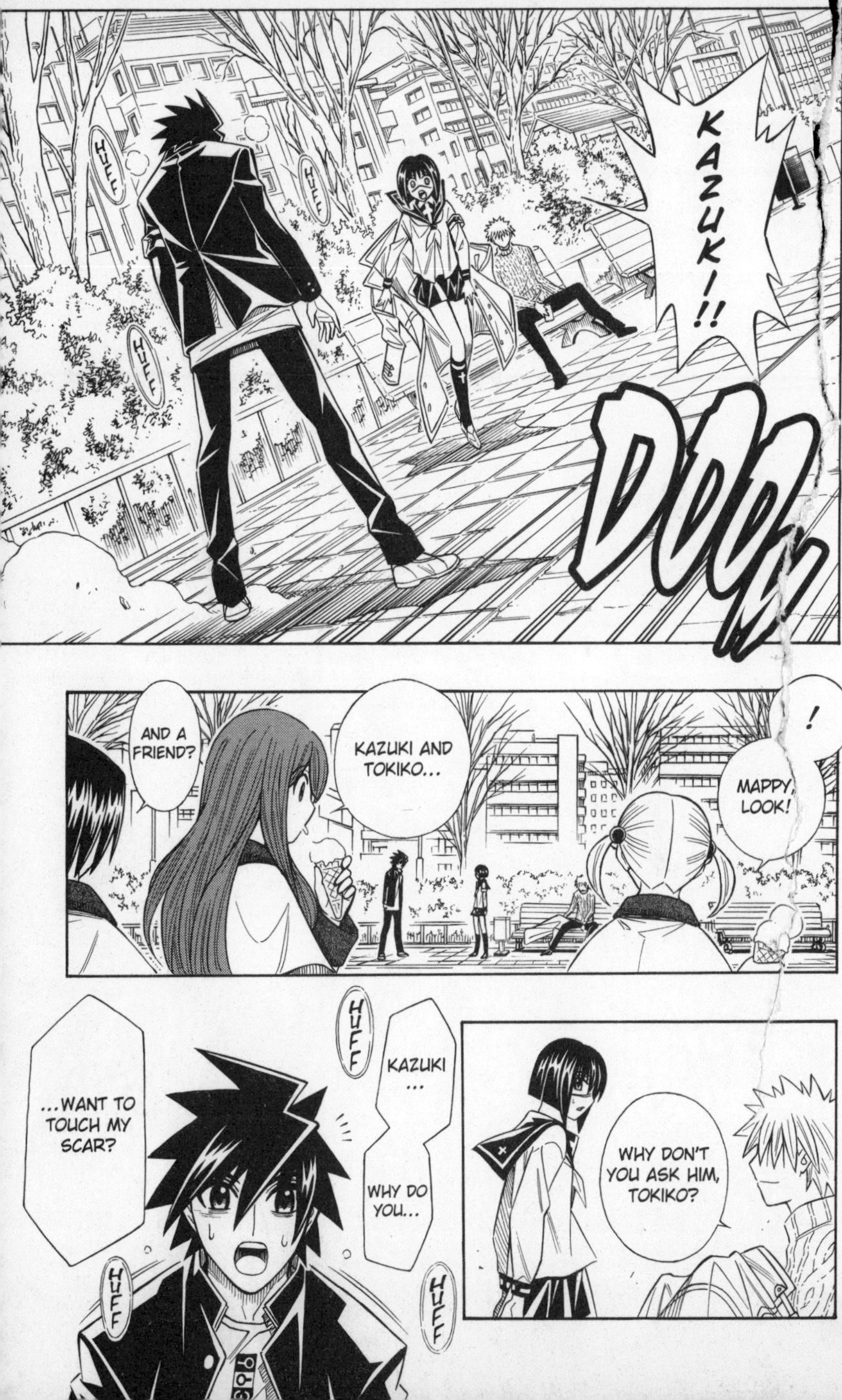
KAZUKI!!
DOZ
HUFF
HUFF
HUFF
!
MAPPY, LOOK!
KAZUKI AND TOKIKO...
AND A FRIEND?
WHY DON'T YOU ASK HIM, TOKIKO?
HUFF
KAZUKI ...
WHY DO YOU...
...WANT TO TOUCH MY SCAR?
HUFF
HUFF

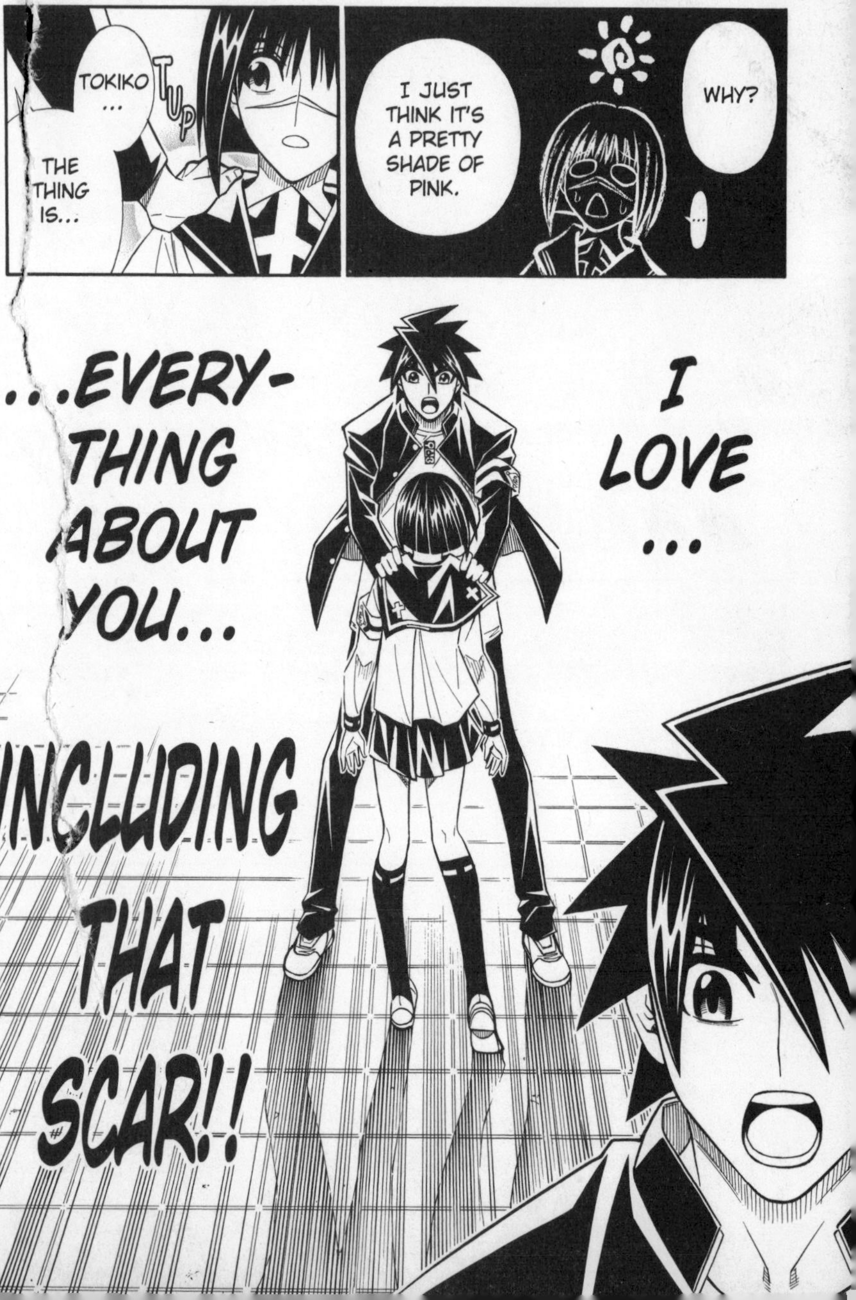
WHY?
...
I JUST THINK IT'S A PRETTY SHADE OF PINK.
TOKIKO ...
TUP
THE THING IS...
I LOVE ...
...EVERY-THING ABOUT YOU...
INCLUDING THAT SCAR!!

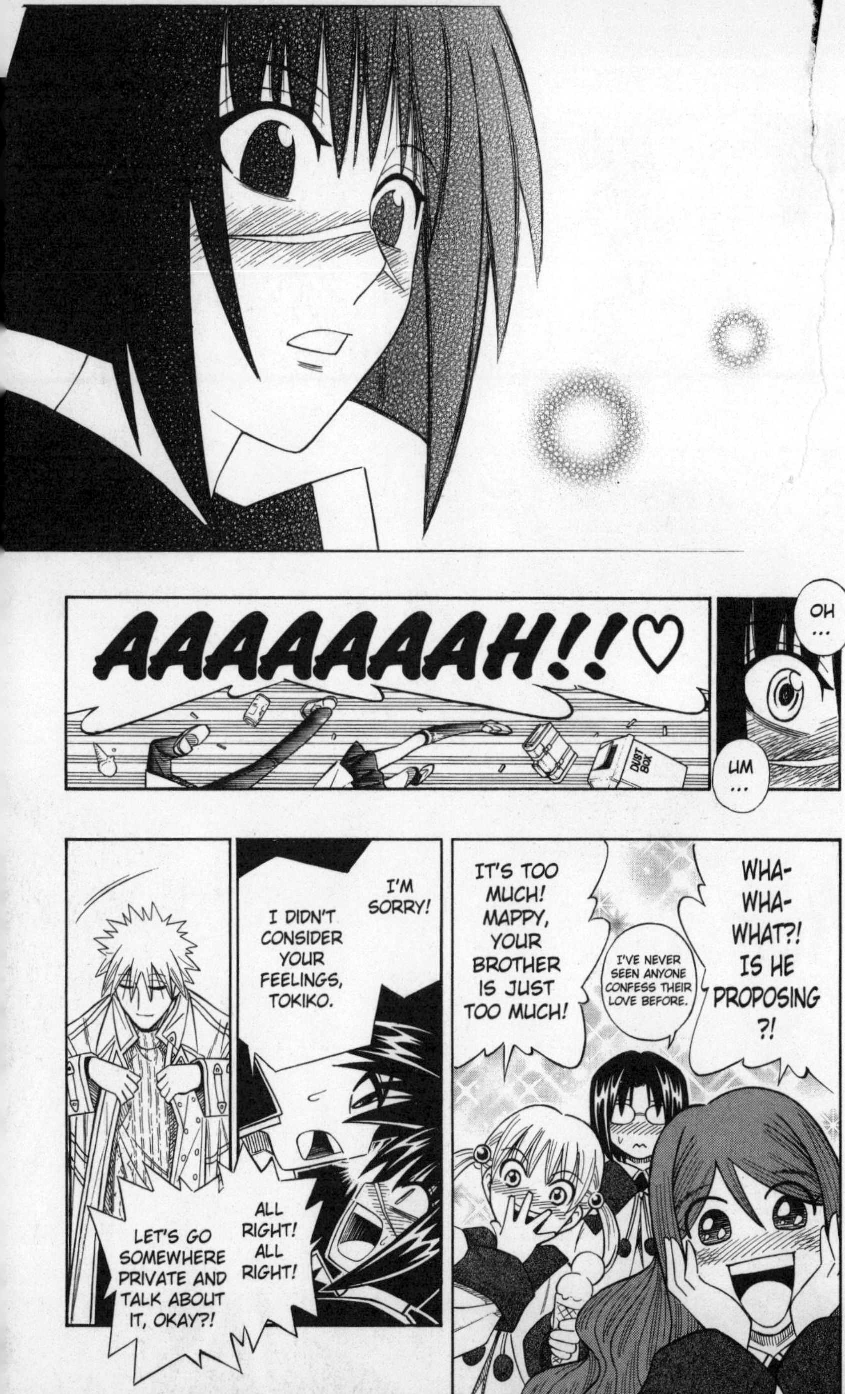
OH ...
UM ...
AAAAAAAAH!!♡
WHA-WHA-WHAT?! IS HE PROPOSING?!
IT'S TOO MUCH! MAPPY, YOUR BROTHER IS JUST TOO MUCH!
I'VE NEVER SEEN ANYONE CONFESS THEIR LOVE BEFORE.
I'M SORRY!
I DIDN'T CONSIDER YOUR FEELINGS, TOKIKO.
ALL RIGHT! ALL RIGHT!
LET'S GO SOMEWHERE PRIVATE AND TALK ABOUT IT, OKAY?!
DUST BOX

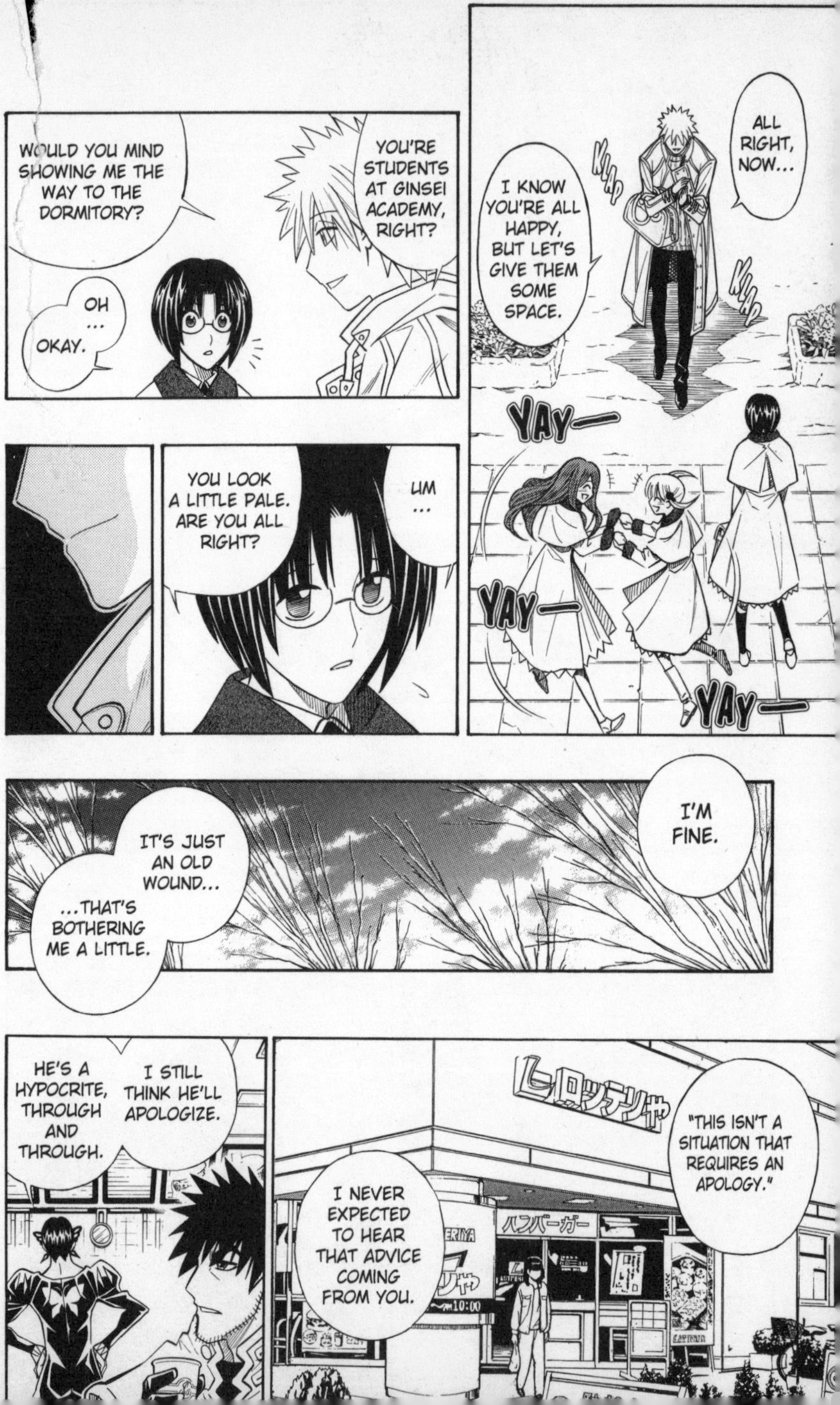
ALL RIGHT, NOW...
KLAP
I KNOW YOU'RE ALL HAPPY, BUT LET'S GIVE THEM SOME SPACE.
KLAP
YAY—
YAY—
YAY—
YOU'RE STUDENTS AT GINSEI ACADEMY, RIGHT?
WOULD YOU MIND SHOWING ME THE WAY TO THE DORMITORY?
OH ... OKAY.
UM ...
YOU LOOK A LITTLE PALE. ARE YOU ALL RIGHT?
I'M FINE.
IT'S JUST AN OLD WOUND...
...THAT'S BOTHERING ME A LITTLE.
"THIS ISN'T A SITUATION THAT REQUIRES AN APOLOGY."
I NEVER EXPECTED TO HEAR THAT ADVICE COMING FROM YOU.
ハンバーガー
I STILL THINK HE'LL APOLOGIZE.
HE'S A HYPOCRITE, THROUGH AND THROUGH.

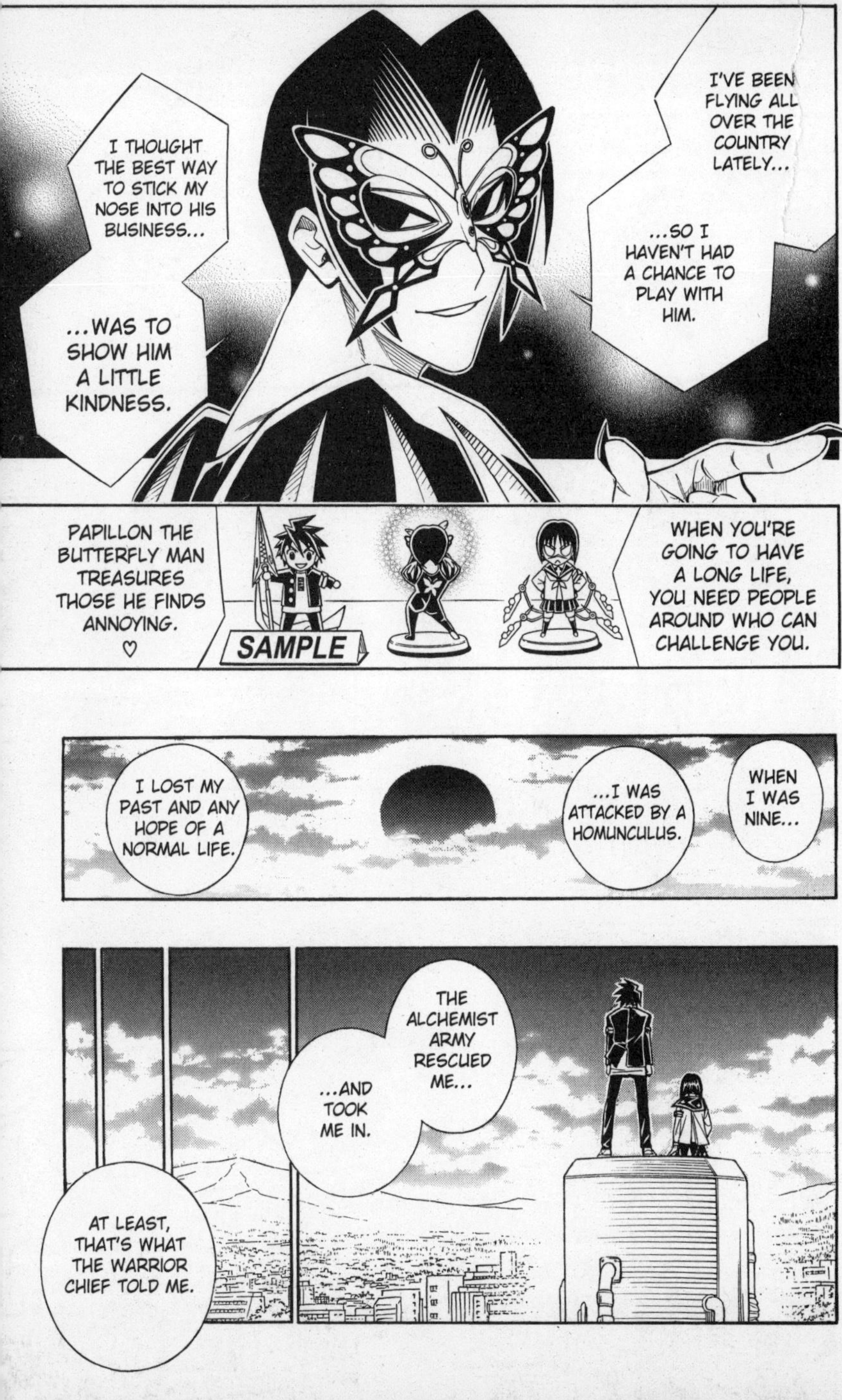
I'VE BEEN FLYING ALL OVER THE COUNTRY LATELY...
...SO I HAVEN'T HAD A CHANCE TO PLAY WITH HIM.
I THOUGHT THE BEST WAY TO STICK MY NOSE INTO HIS BUSINESS...
...WAS TO SHOW HIM A LITTLE KINDNESS.
WHEN YOU'RE GOING TO HAVE A LONG LIFE, YOU NEED PEOPLE AROUND WHO CAN CHALLENGE YOU.
SAMPLE
PAPILLON THE BUTTERFLY MAN TREASURES THOSE HE FINDS ANNOYING. ♡
WHEN I WAS NINE...
...I WAS ATTACKED BY A HOMUNCULUS.
I LOST MY PAST AND ANY HOPE OF A NORMAL LIFE.
THE ALCHEMIST ARMY RESCUED ME...
...AND TOOK ME IN.
AT LEAST, THAT'S WHAT THE WARRIOR CHIEF TOLD ME.

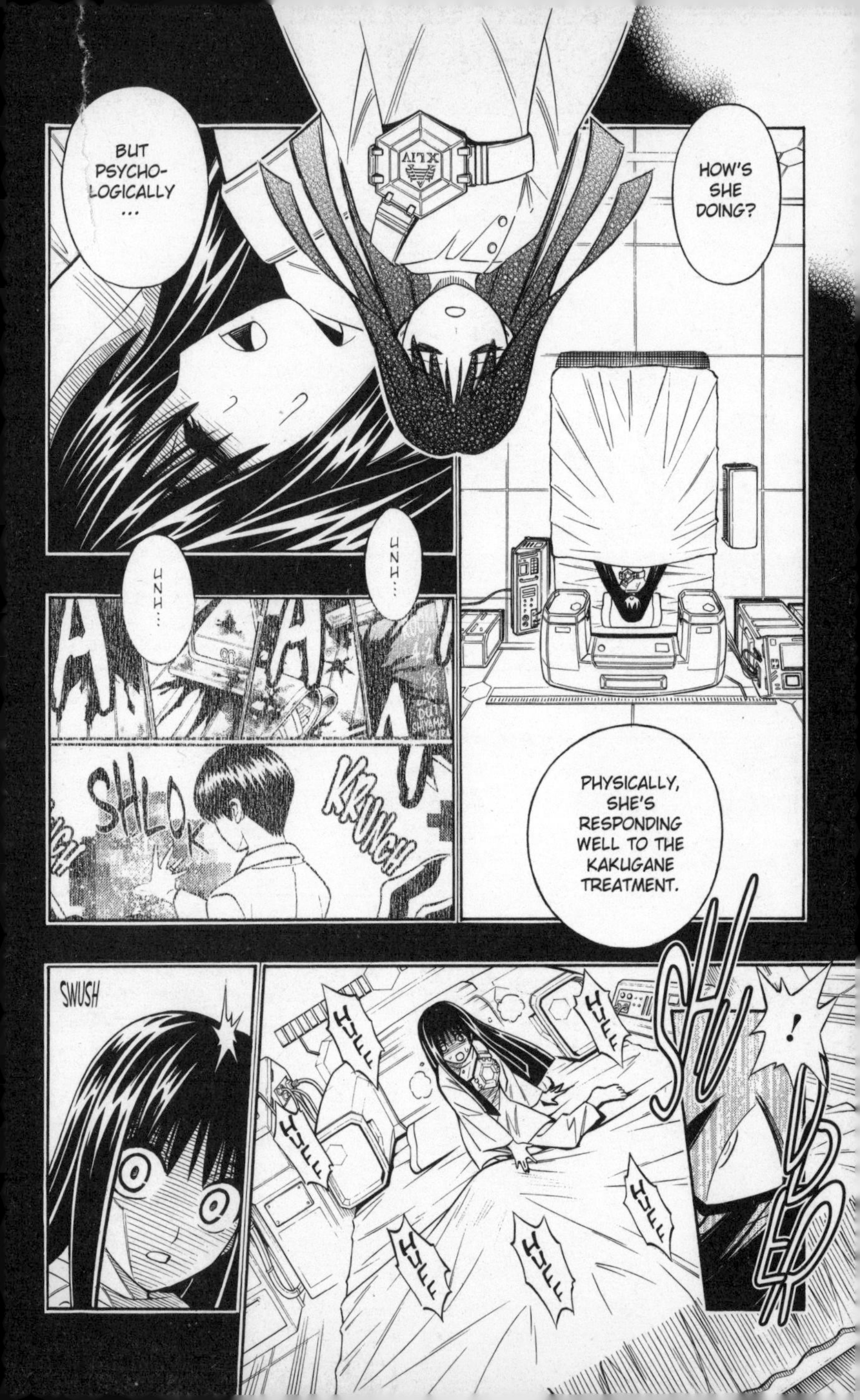
HOW'S SHE DOING?
PHYSICALLY, SHE'S RESPONDING WELL TO THE KAKUGANE TREATMENT.
BUT PSYCHO-LOGICALLY ...
UNH...
UNH...
KRUNCH
SHLOK
!
HUFF
HUFF
HUFF
HUFF
HUFF
HUFF
SWUSH

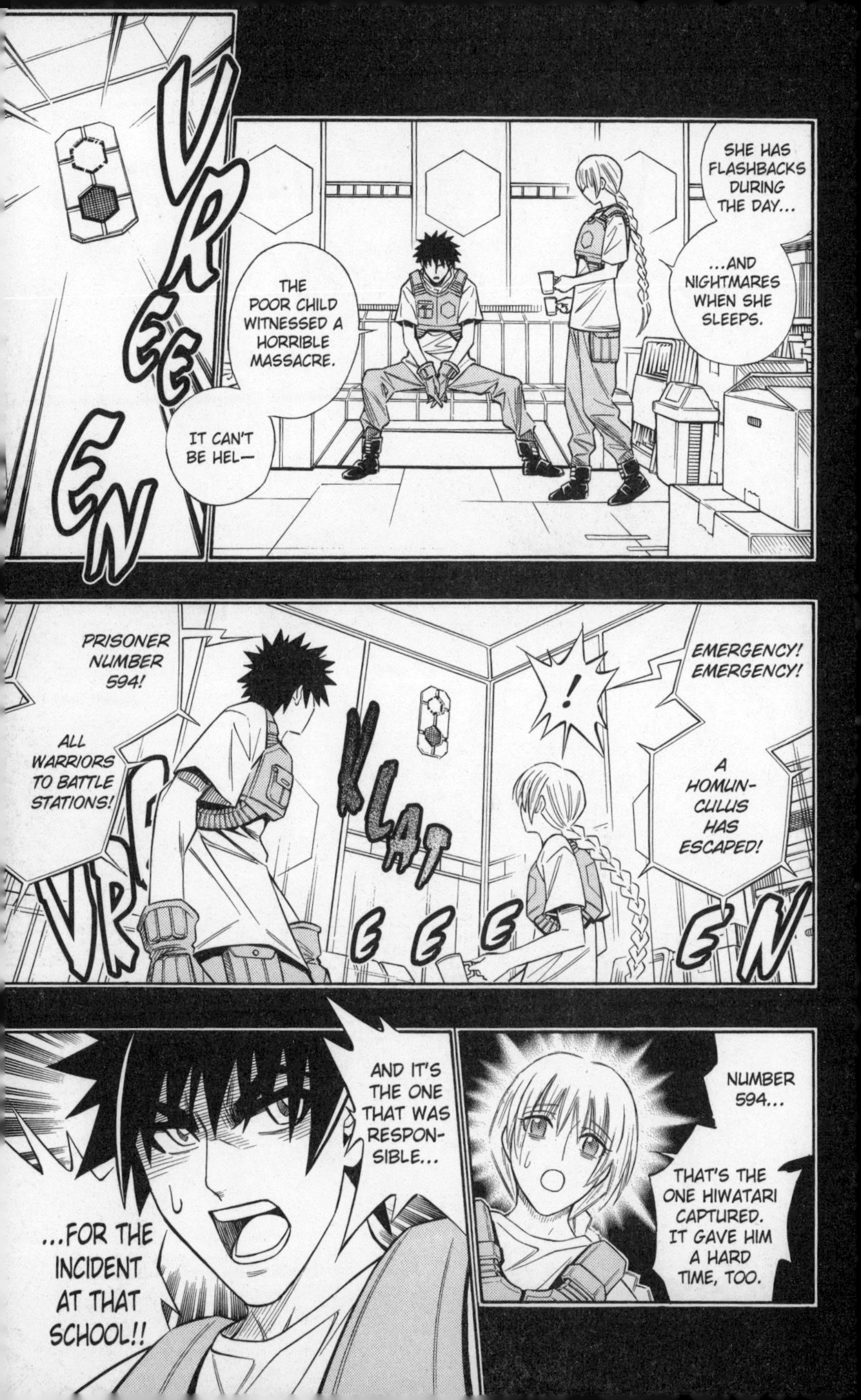
SHE HAS FLASHBACKS DURING THE DAY...
...AND NIGHTMARES WHEN SHE SLEEPS.
THE POOR CHILD WITNESSED A HORRIBLE MASSACRE.
IT CAN'T BE HEL—
VREEEN
EMERGENCY! EMERGENCY!
!
A HOMUN-CULUS HAS ESCAPED!
KLAT
PRISONER NUMBER 594!
ALL WARRIORS TO BATTLE STATIONS!
VREEEEEN
NUMBER 594...
THAT'S THE ONE HIWATARI CAPTURED. IT GAVE HIM A HARD TIME, TOO.
AND IT'S THE ONE THAT WAS RESPON-SIBLE...
...FOR THE INCIDENT AT THAT SCHOOL!!

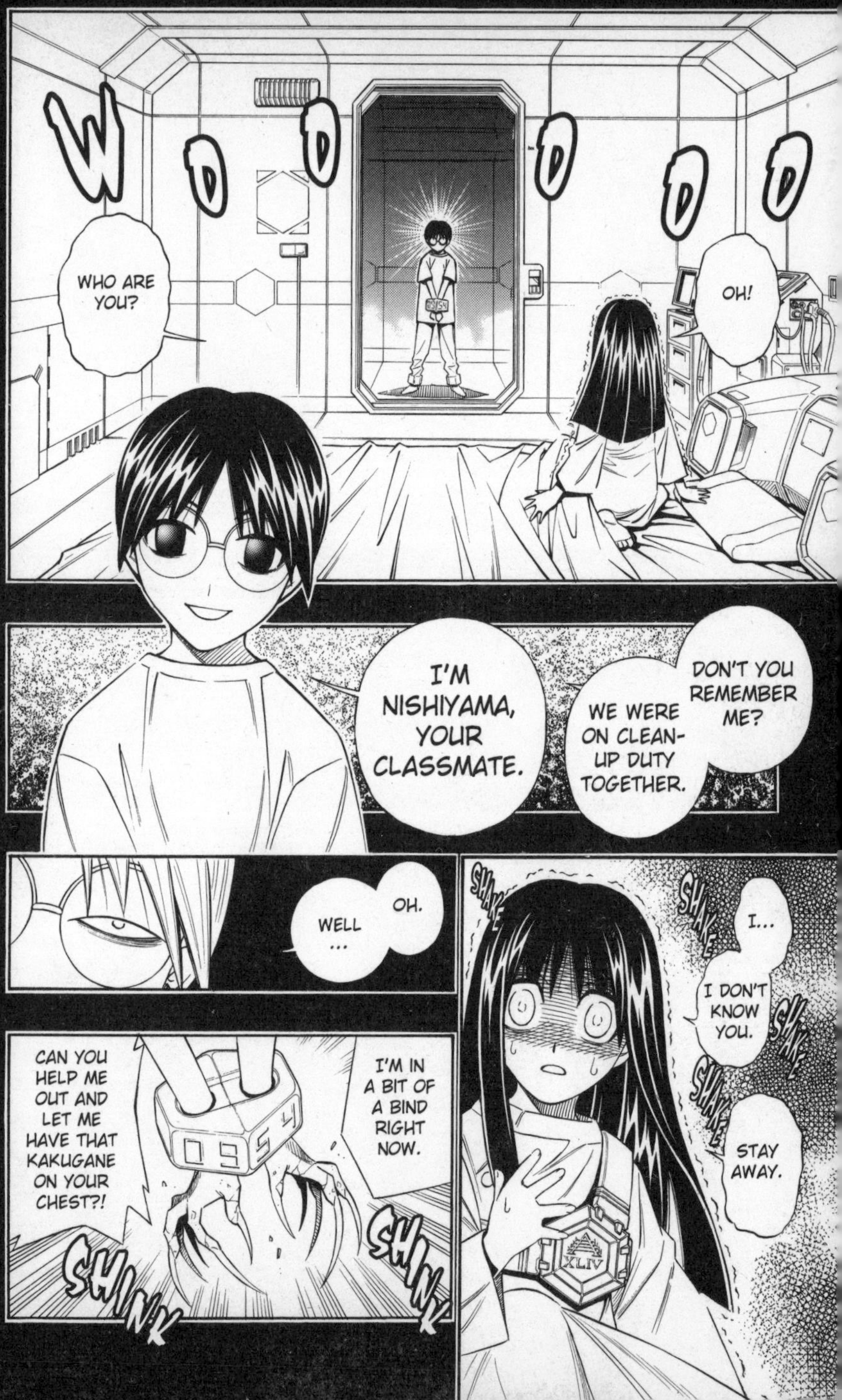
WDDDDDD
OH!
WHO ARE YOU?
DON'T YOU REMEMBER ME?
WE WERE ON CLEAN-UP DUTY TOGETHER.
I'M NISHIYAMA, YOUR CLASSMATE.
SHAKE
SHAKE
I...
I DON'T KNOW YOU.
SHAKE
SHAKE
STAY AWAY.
XLIV
OH.
WELL...
I'M IN A BIT OF A BIND RIGHT NOW.
CAN YOU HELP ME OUT AND LET ME HAVE THAT KAKUGANE ON YOUR CHEST?!
SHINK
SHINK

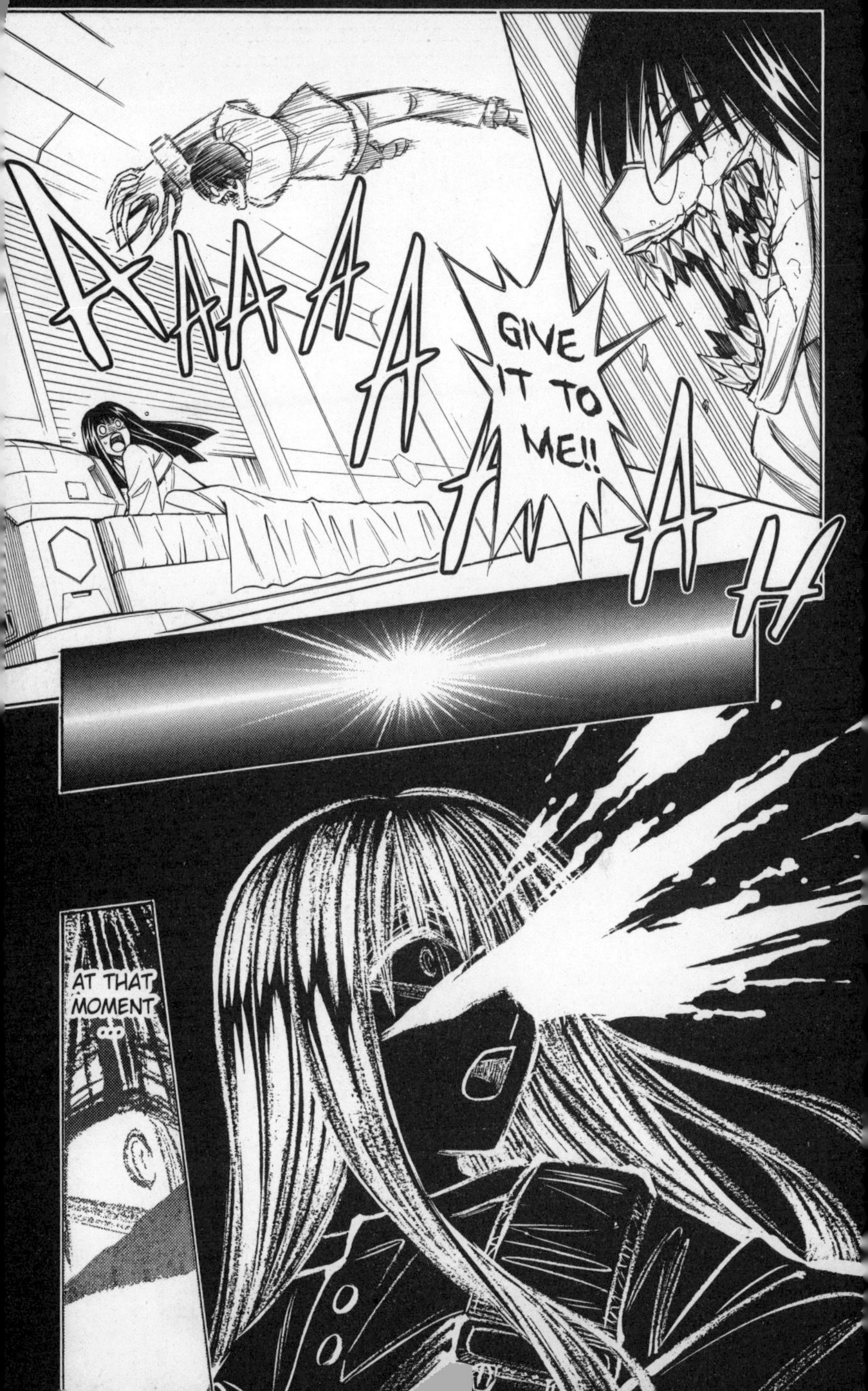
AAAAAAAAH
GIVE IT TO ME!!
AT THAT MOMENT...

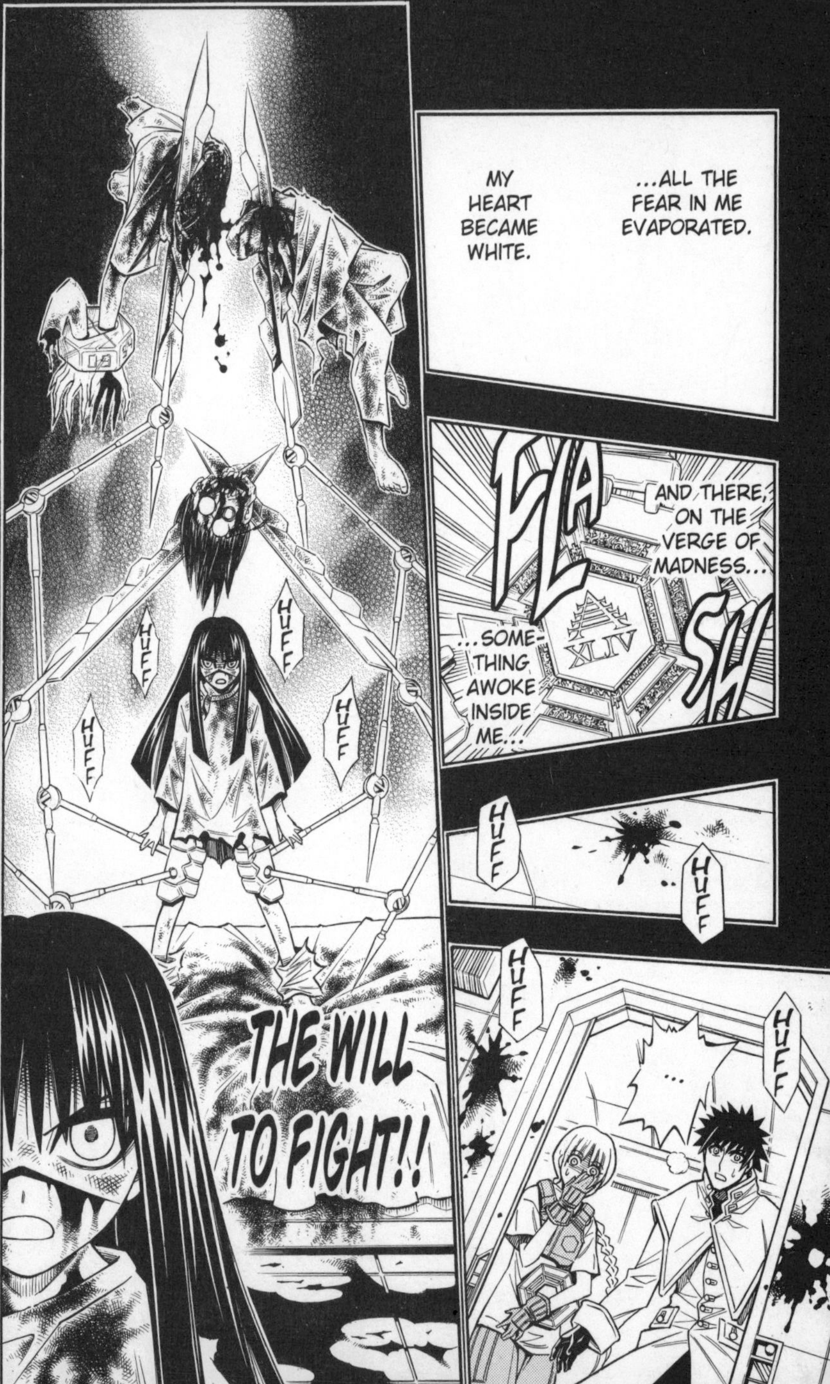
...ALL THE FEAR IN ME EVAPORATED.
MY HEART BECAME WHITE.
FLA
AND THERE, ON THE VERGE OF MADNESS...
XLIV
SH
...SOME-THING AWOKE INSIDE ME...
HUFF
HUFF
HUFF
HUFF
...
HUFF
HUFF
HUFF
HUFF
THE WILL TO FIGHT!!

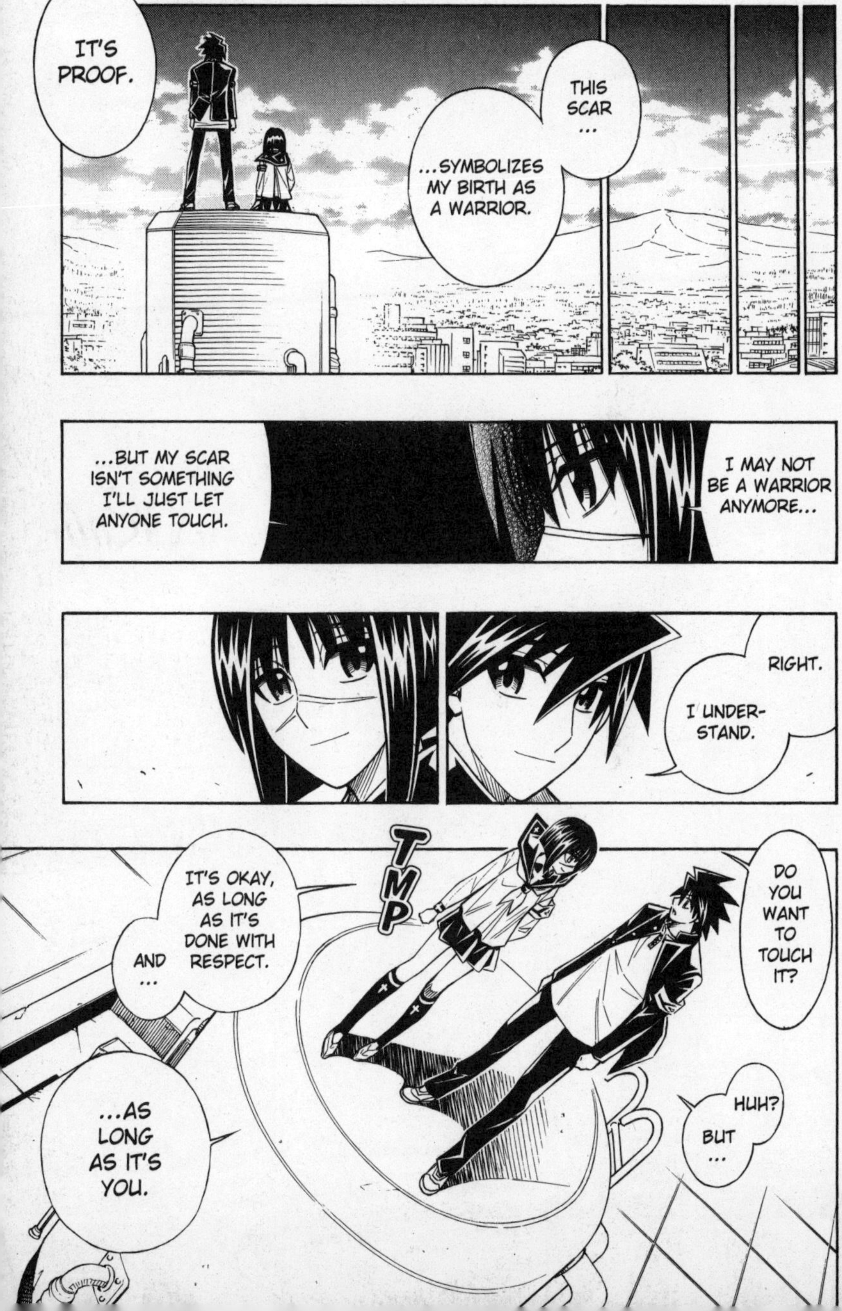
THIS SCAR ...
...SYMBOLIZES MY BIRTH AS A WARRIOR.
IT'S PROOF.
I MAY NOT BE A WARRIOR ANYMORE...
...BUT MY SCAR ISN'T SOMETHING I'LL JUST LET ANYONE TOUCH.
RIGHT.
I UNDER-STAND.
DO YOU WANT TO TOUCH IT?
TMP
IT'S OKAY, AS LONG AS IT'S DONE WITH RESPECT.
AND ...
HUH?
BUT ...
...AS LONG AS IT'S YOU.

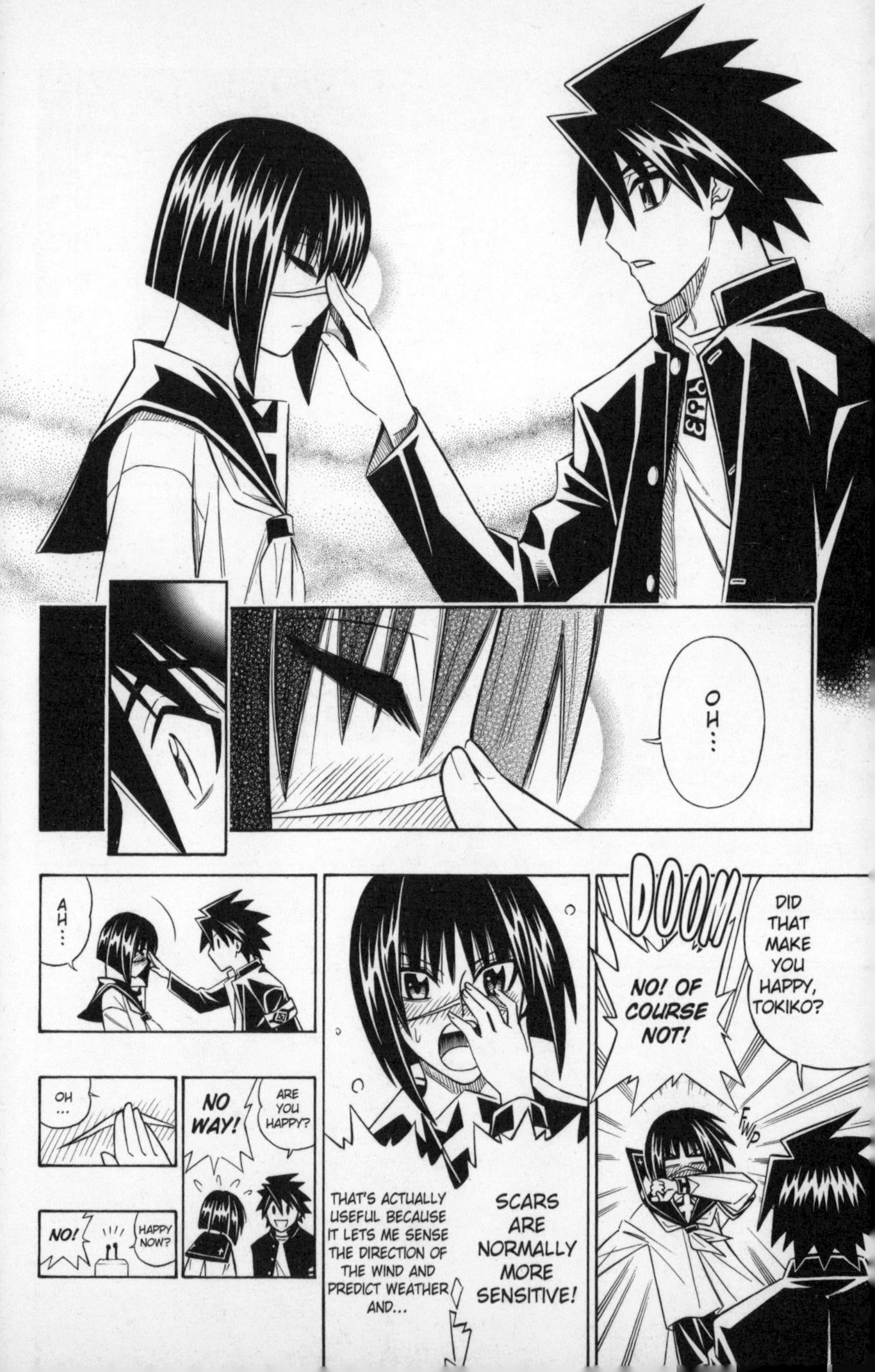
OH...
DID THAT MAKE YOU HAPPY, TOKIKO?
DOOM
NO! OF COURSE NOT!
FWIP
SCARS ARE NORMALLY MORE SENSITIVE!
THAT'S ACTUALLY USEFUL BECAUSE IT LETS ME SENSE THE DIRECTION OF THE WIND AND PREDICT WEATHER AND...
AH...
ARE YOU HAPPY?
NO WAY!
OH...
HAPPY NOW?
NO!

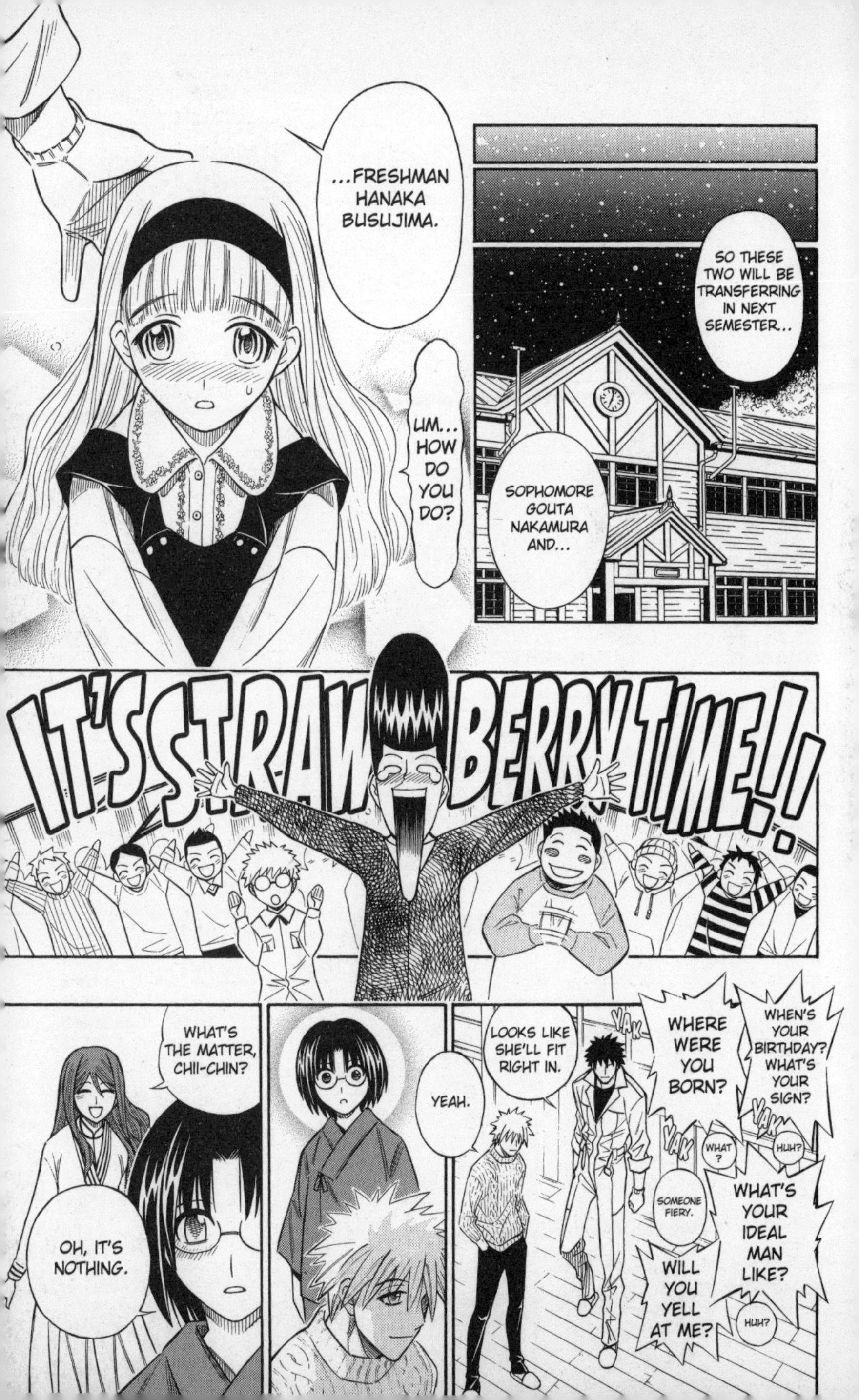
SO THESE TWO WILL BE TRANSFERRING IN NEXT SEMESTER...
SOPHOMORE GOUTA NAKAMURA AND...
...FRESHMAN HANAKA BUSUJIMA.
UM... HOW DO YOU DO?
IT'S STRAWBERRY TIME!!
WHEN'S YOUR BIRTHDAY? WHAT'S YOUR SIGN?
WHERE WERE YOU BORN?
YAK
YAK
YAK
LOOKS LIKE SHE'LL FIT RIGHT IN.
HUH?
WHAT?
WHAT'S YOUR IDEAL MAN LIKE?
SOMEONE FIERY.
WILL YOU YELL AT ME?
HUH?
YEAH.
WHAT'S THE MATTER, CHII-CHIN?
OH, IT'S NOTHING.

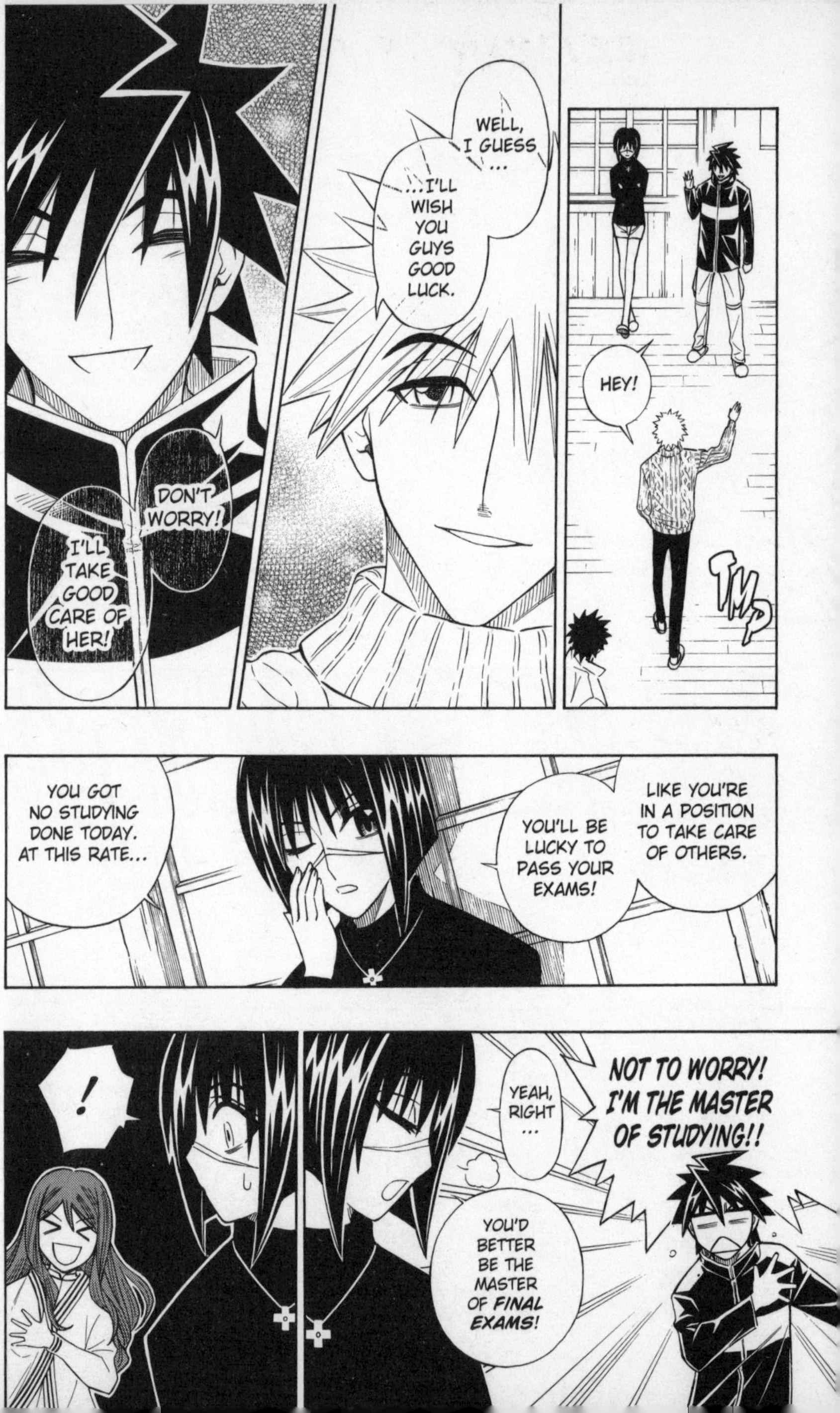
HEY!
TMP
WELL, I GUESS...
...I'LL WISH YOU GUYS GOOD LUCK.
DON'T WORRY!
I'LL TAKE GOOD CARE OF HER!
LIKE YOU'RE IN A POSITION TO TAKE CARE OF OTHERS.
YOU'LL BE LUCKY TO PASS YOUR EXAMS!
YOU GOT NO STUDYING DONE TODAY. AT THIS RATE...
NOT TO WORRY! I'M THE MASTER OF STUDYING!!
YEAH, RIGHT...
YOU'D BETTER BE THE MASTER OF *FINAL EXAMS!*
!

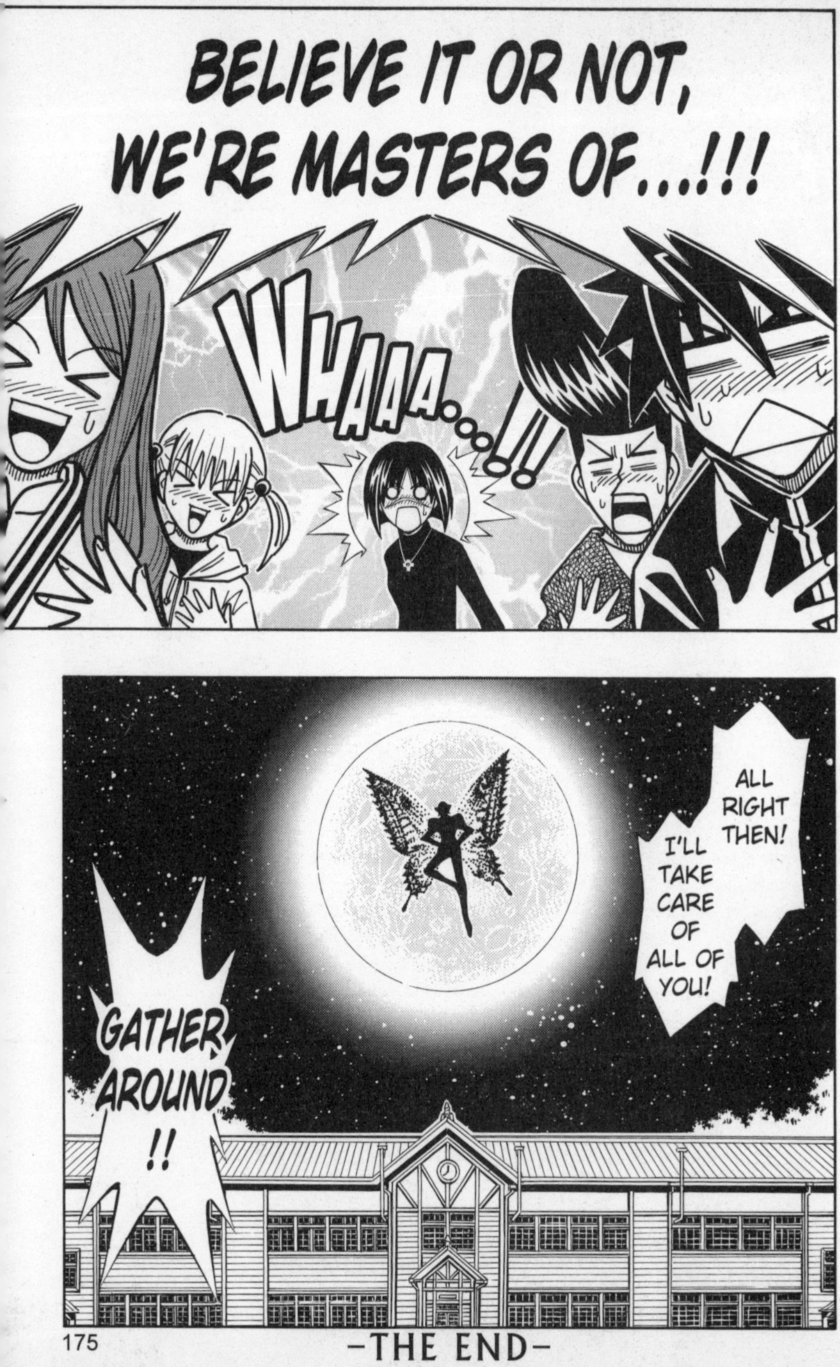
BELIEVE IT OR NOT, WE'RE MASTERS OF...!!!
WHAAAA...!!
ALL RIGHT THEN!
I'LL TAKE CARE OF ALL OF YOU!
GATHER AROUND!!

-THE END-

Buso Renkin: Period

· Like it or not, this is the last chapter.

· It was difficult to fit everything I wanted into 65 pages. The original idea of Victoria and Moonface leading a revolution on the Moon had to be scrapped. I concentrated on Kazuki, Tokiko and Papillon. By playing with the timeline and incorporating flashbacks, I tried to show what happened to Tokiko between "Final" and "Period" as best I could. Unfortunately, it may have been hard for some readers to follow.

· The wedding dress and tuxedo that Tokiko and Kazuki are wearing on the title page started out as normal school uniforms, but just as I was about to start inking, the idea came to me. So then we scrambled to find pictures of wedding dresses and tuxedos. It was hard to get the veil just right, but I was pleased with the results. As I was drawing it, I thought, "Tokiko, what are you doing? You're supposed to be the Battle Girl!" But I think maybe the idea came from Tokiko herself.

· Shosei does his part to account for the millennia of history behind alchemy. It was done rather simply, but the content was deep. I think this course of action was the only proper one for him.

· The "taste of mother" scene would never have made it into the weekly magazine even with the censoring.

· I managed to bring back the original homunculi that Chouno created. Well, actually, they were clones of the originals, but I wanted to give them one last shot. I put a lot of work into those early characters. They have distinctive looks, so I'm glad I did this.

· The opening shot is of Ouka, Shusui, Gouta and Tokiko. During the production of this section, I was visited by a famous American comic book artist who wanted to see what a Japanese manga studio was like. I used the pages of "Period" as my samples and when I showed him the opening page he said, "Very nice!" Maybe it was professional courtesy or just flattery, but I was so happy I felt like I could die right then. Blagh! (sound of spitting up blood and falling)

· Tokiko vs. Papillon. As with so many scenes in *Buso Renkin*, I had a hard time depicting this battle. It's one of the things I still need to work on.

· Tears drip from Tokiko's eyes as a light suddenly shines from the Moon. I couldn't think of any other way to show the beginning of Kazuki's return.

· The Hermes Drive, Aerial Operator and other Buso Renkin I hadn't featured make appearances as the Buster Baron takes off into space. Since it was the last chapter, I figured anything goes.

· Happy moments flash by like a slideshow, then the scene switches to Tokiko's look of despair and the smiles vanish from the faces of his friends. Kazuki decides he has to return, no matter what.

· The final battle between Kazuki and Victor ends. All the scenes I had planned for this battle had to be cut, but I got what I needed to get across through the dialogue.

· "I'm going to protect everybody, but who will protect me?" The truth is, when I was finishing the last volume, I'd already decided that Victor would be the one who returned Kazuki to Earth. But when Kaoru Kurosaki gave me that line to work with, I realized it should be the people back on Earth who saved Kazuki. So, after much debate, it was decided that Kazuki would be saved in space between the moon and the Earth.

· I didn't think the reunion in space would look very visually appealing with Kazuki in his Victor form and Tokiko covered by the Silver Skin, so I drew them as they normally look. Kurosaki suggested that since I was going to do that, I should make them tastefully nude. I said I wasn't ready to depict one of my heroines in that manner, and even if I were, I'd wait till I got better at drawing nudes.

· Gouta falls out of love. When you get over your first true love, you grow up a lot. Don't cry, Gouta! You're on your way to becoming a man!

· The second half of the story centers on Kazuki and Papillon. I reworked the pages from when they were published in the magazine to make the story flow better. The sumi-e (ink and wash painting) battle action was similar to that at the end of volume 2. I'm very interested in that style of art right now. I love black and white especially; I'm not into color as much.

· Victor and Victoria are reunited and the homunculi all go to the moon. Actually, I thought this was a bit drastic, but I knew I couldn't end the story without some kind of resolution with the homunculi. Their food from now on will be the base materials of the cloning process made into meat pies. Moonface is jumping around merrily, Hanabusa's eyes have turned into hearts, Kawazui is in tears—it looks like the moon's going to be a fun place. Victoria will probably be their leader and Victor will ride on her coattails...probably.

· Kazuki and Gouta finally shake hands. There are a lot of different kinds of friendships, but a comrade-in-arms is the best kind of all.

· When Papillon first appeared in volume 2, I decided he was going to become an urban legend—nobody has seen him, but everybody knows someone who has. He started out as a scary, man-eating boogieman and evolved into a more sympathetic character that people really like. As with Tokiko and her wedding dress, Papillon must've transmitted this ending to me telepathically. The last line says it all.

· The final shot is of Kazuki and Tokiko returning to their normal lives. In the beginning, Tokiko leads Kazuki into a world of battle, and in the end Kazuki leads Tokiko back to normal life. This is the ending I had in mind from the beginning of the series.

· The shot of Kazuki and Tokiko on the first page was redone for the graphic novel version. In the magazine, it was just a close-up of the two of them, but I wanted them to look like they were charging boldly into the future.

· It felt like a long series, but it also felt really short. But now the story is over. Thank you very much for all your support. But little did I realize...

Buso Renkin: Afterward

· What? There aren't enough pages to make a graphic novel?! So I created another 31-page story. The first thing that came to mind was something to do with Tokiko's past, only that would've excluded the rest of the cast, and it would've probably been really depressing. Well, I didn't want *Buso Renkin* to end on a downer, so I decided to do a romantic comedy instead.

· Tokiko pokes Kazuki in the eyes and he just takes it. They've become that annoying couple you always see.

· The chase is on. Kazuki's friends haven't changed, but Ouka and Shusui have a more normal relationship. But the fact that Shusui commented on his sister's evil streak was a surprise even to me.

· Welcome to the freak show burger shop. I thought it would be sad if Gozen wasn't around, so I made him be a renegade who survived the confiscation of the kakugane by the Alchemist Army. Bravo has taken a permanent position at the dormitory and—though it wasn't shown—he, Hiwatari, and Chitose have become close friends once more. Also, the girl behind the counter has gotten used to all these "interesting" people.

· The burger shop is having its second Butterfly Man figure series promotion with Papillon's support. But Kazuki and Tokiko weren't even consulted before their images were used! No respect for likeness rights!

· The story takes a more serious turn with the reunion of Gouta and Tokiko. Gouta understands how Kazuki feels since they both have strong feelings for Tokiko. Tokiko is wearing Gouta's coat in the park, which shows how much he's grown.

· Kazuki's line about loving everything about Tokiko is one that I had in mind for a long time. I never managed to fit it in before this, but I was given one more chance and I took it.

· Papillon has become the "Butterfly Man," but he's still something of an egomaniac. It's Papillon's nature to do whatever he wants just because it's fun. Despite what he may think, Kazuki and Tokiko are his friends for life.

· Kazuki finds out that Tokiko could've had her scar removed. When I created her, I hadn't really figured out how she got that scar; it was just the mark of a warrior. By the end of the series, I had a pretty good idea how it happened, but I was only able to offer an abridged version of the incident. To those who expected more, I apologize.

· The homunculus Nishiyama who briefly showed up in volume 3 was created off the cuff. In fact, when my assistant came and asked me what name to put on the blackboard for this character, I said, "Why don't you write your name on there?"

· Kazuki finally touches Tokiko's scar. Is Kazuki some kind of sadist? You can decide for yourself whether Tokiko enjoyed it or not.

· Busujima's face is finally revealed. Forced to deal with the face behind the mask, I decided to make her pretty, but I wasn't sure I could pull it off. I'd avoided it up till then, but, prodded by Kurosaki, I attempted it for just one panel.

· Of the three girls from the dormitory, Chii-chin was the first to notice Gouta's growth as a man.

- With high hopes for their new life at school, the story comes to a close with a bit of comedy. And of course Papillon had to make a final appearance.
- At last the manga version of *Buso Renkin* is truly finished. Thank you again for all your support.

Embalming–Corpse and Bride–

- It's been seven or eight years since I last did a stand-alone short story.
- After *Buso Renkin* ended in the weeklies, I was asked to do an original story for a new magazine that was starting up. Part of me wanted to concentrate on the production of "Final" and "Period," but I had this Frankenstein idea, so I decided to do it.
- When I was first developing *Buso Renkin*, I thought about the story of Frankenstein because it has a link to alchemy.
- The term "embalming" in Japanese means a procedure for protecting a dead body from decay. This includes repairing bodies that have been damaged in accidents and making them presentable for viewing. It's an important art that allows people to say goodbye to their departed loved ones. The title came from the image I had of Marigold's peaceful death, but upon reflection, it really wasn't a good fit. If this short story ever spawns a series, I think I'll change the title.
- I tried to give the cover the feel of an American comic book. This was fairly easy because I didn't have to use a lot of tones. I think I'll experiment with this style more in the future.
- 1.21 gigawatts. It's an homage to one of my favorite movies, *Back to the Future*, in which a lightning bolt generates this amount of power. I found out later that I'd written the word wrong in Japanese, but I liked the way it sounded so I didn't correct it for the graphic novel.
- Frankenstein is actually the name of a fictional genius who reanimated a dead body and not the name of the monster itself. But let's just say that in my world, "Victor Frankenstein" is the genius, and "Frankenstein" is an artificial human.
- Lord Corpse's factory headquarters incorporates 19th-century building design. The architecture of the Victorian age was wonderful, but if this story becomes a series, I want to take that style and "pollute" it with images of factories and industrial structures.
- One of the most problematic parts of this story was the fact that the heroine has no legs. The reaction of the fans was mixed. Those who started reading my work with *Rurouni Kenshin* liked it, but those who started with *Buso Renkin* did not.

· Here we have a Frankenstein who gets paid in female body parts because he wants to assemble a bride for himself. He isn't driven by a sense of morality or by malice. It took me a while to come up with a reason that I could live with for John Doe to do what he does.

· For Marigold's nightmare flashback, I wanted something that would come across as really evil, but this was harder than I thought. Maybe it was lacking something.

· Anger, hatred, and suffering all culminate in Marigold's scream. That's proof of her humanity.

· Having John Doe destroy an enemy while holding Marigold was a page-saving measure, but it was surprisingly popular with the fans.

· The battle scenes had more of a boy's manga feel than I really wanted. I'd like to draw some really violent battles worthy of Frankenstein's monster.

· I think John Doe's special attack, the Blood Thrust, should have been fancier.

· Little Rosé was going to be a "Needle Master," but once I started drawing, I realized she was more of a "Thread Master."

· The scene where John Doe chills his hand and allows the beautiful bride to die in peace was an idea I'd had from the moment I decided to do this story. It was also the reason I came up with the subtitle, "Corpse and Bride."

· With many mysteries still unsolved, the story ends. I wanted to leave the reader wondering and wanting more. I hope I achieved that.

· I came up with a legend that I really liked: "Every time lightning strikes, a Frankenstein is being born."

· I did this story as a possible pilot for a new series. But, as usual, I ran out of pages. My dentist's assistant told me, "You crammed too much into it." Actually, I wanted to put even more into it, but if this ever becomes a series, I now know what I have to do to improve it. For that reason alone, it was worth doing.

· This is the first story I ever did that wasn't definitely for boys. The heroine dies and the characters have flaws, which may have surprised some of my readers. For that, I apologize. But this is still a Nobuhiro Watsuki manga. A happy ending may not be possible, but I'll keep trying for better endings as I continue to draw manga.

=Character File=

○ John Doe

· Frankenstein, as I envision him. He's a man looking for a mate. I suppose he's partially a reincarnated form of Makoto Shishio from *Rurouni Kenshin*. He uses his destructive powers to achieve his own ends! He's a character that embodies opposites—good and evil, clean and dirty, right and wrong, and life and death. And he's really fun to draw.

· He's kind of like a big, dangerous hipster. I considered red jackets, black jackets, sunglasses, round glasses, spiky hair, long back hair, a big gun, two guns, and other elements borrowed from characters I can't name, and finally came up with the scarred character you see. I'm very pleased with him. His charm comes from his right eye that has no pupil.

○ Little Rosé

· In some ways, she is John Doe's bride. She moves the story along and her true purpose is unknown. Her concept was "multifaceted." I have ideas about her real identity, but she was overshadowed in this story by Marigold.

· Her design concept is the "mousey student council girl." Her short hair caused some readers to mistake her for a boy, which was kind of disappointing. I put her in a kimono because I wanted her to look a bit shapeless, but it didn't work as well as I'd hoped it would. I think I'll change her design a little if I get the chance.

○ Marigold

· A little rich girl with no legs. Her concept was, "Speak your mind!" I wanted her to have a real hatred of Lord Corpse and a hunger for revenge, so I cut off both her legs. Did I go too far? Her ending wasn't exactly happy, but I don't think it was a bad ending for her.

· Her design concept was "Gothic Lolita." After a lot of research and numerous trial versions, I finally came up with her design. I think maybe I could've made her look a bit more grown up. Some people told me that her panting and flushed face made her seem a bit erotic, but I think I'll put that back on the people who see her that way.

○ Lord Corpse

· A cruel necrophile. His concept was "a 19th-century count," or at least it was supposed to be. But due to lack of pages, I had to cut his back-story. I really need to work harder on my antagonists.

· His design concept is the "parlor trick magician." The kanji character for "death" on his hat was just a thematic reminder I used when I was roughing him in. I handed it off to my assistants for clean up and was surprised to see it come back as is. But it made him seem mysterious, so I kept it.

○ Zapper

· Muscle-bound executioner. His concept was "look at all my muscles." Since his only purpose was combat, I didn't work on his personality at all.

· The design concept is "look at all my muscles" too. He has the upper body of a Viking and the lower body of a Greek god. The sword he carries is of Aztec design. He's a patchwork of cultures.

○ The Butler

· This character is pretty straightforward. His concept is "pointing out the other characters' flaws." If I'd had more pages, I would've explained why he was interested in Frankensteins.

· His design concept is the "false gentleman." I whipped it out in three minutes.

Afterword

Thank you for reading through to the end. It seems like various action figures and drama CDs have started to come out, but the *Buso Renkin* manga has come to an end.

I thought to myself that this might be my last boys' manga series, so over the last year and a half I tried to do everything I ever wanted to do in that genre. At times I thought I would burn out and blow away in the wind, but I got through it and find myself very pleased with the work I did.

This was a very challenging and eventful series in many ways. Though I thought I was good at drawing battles, they were often harder than I expected and caused me a lot of suffering. I struggled with the comedic elements. The Buso Renkin and homunculi drifted away from my original ideas. I caught four severe colds that laid me up for many days one winter.

The fourth time I was so sick I actually missed a deadline and the manga didn't come out that week (which was a first for me as a manga artist). I was so weak and exhausted that I wet the bed for the first time in 30 years. Then there was the trip I took with my fellow manga artists despite our busy schedules. And when I found out the series had been cancelled, I ran away to a hot springs in Hakone for a night because I didn't want see anyone. And finally, after much pleading, I was allowed to finish the series.

I am extremely fond of the main characters I created for *Buso Renkin*. I really had a good time playing with Kazuki and Tokiko, but the characters from "Embalming" and the new characters always forming in my head all cry out to be played with, so I have to keep moving forward. And in order to do that, I'll have to start pleading again.

Surprisingly, the process of creating manga just gets more interesting the longer I work in this industry.

March 2006
At my new workplace
Nobuhiro Watsuki

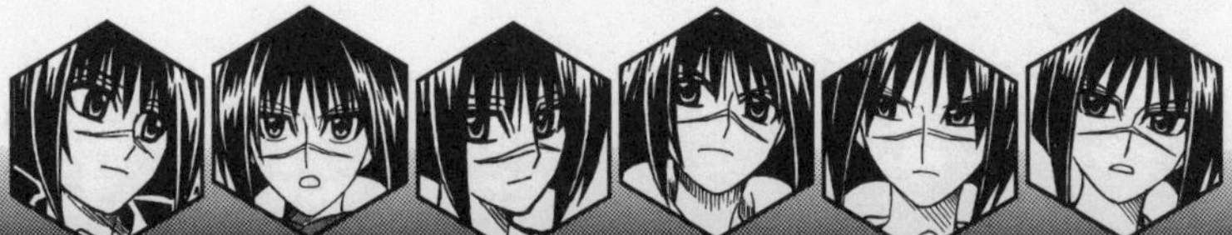

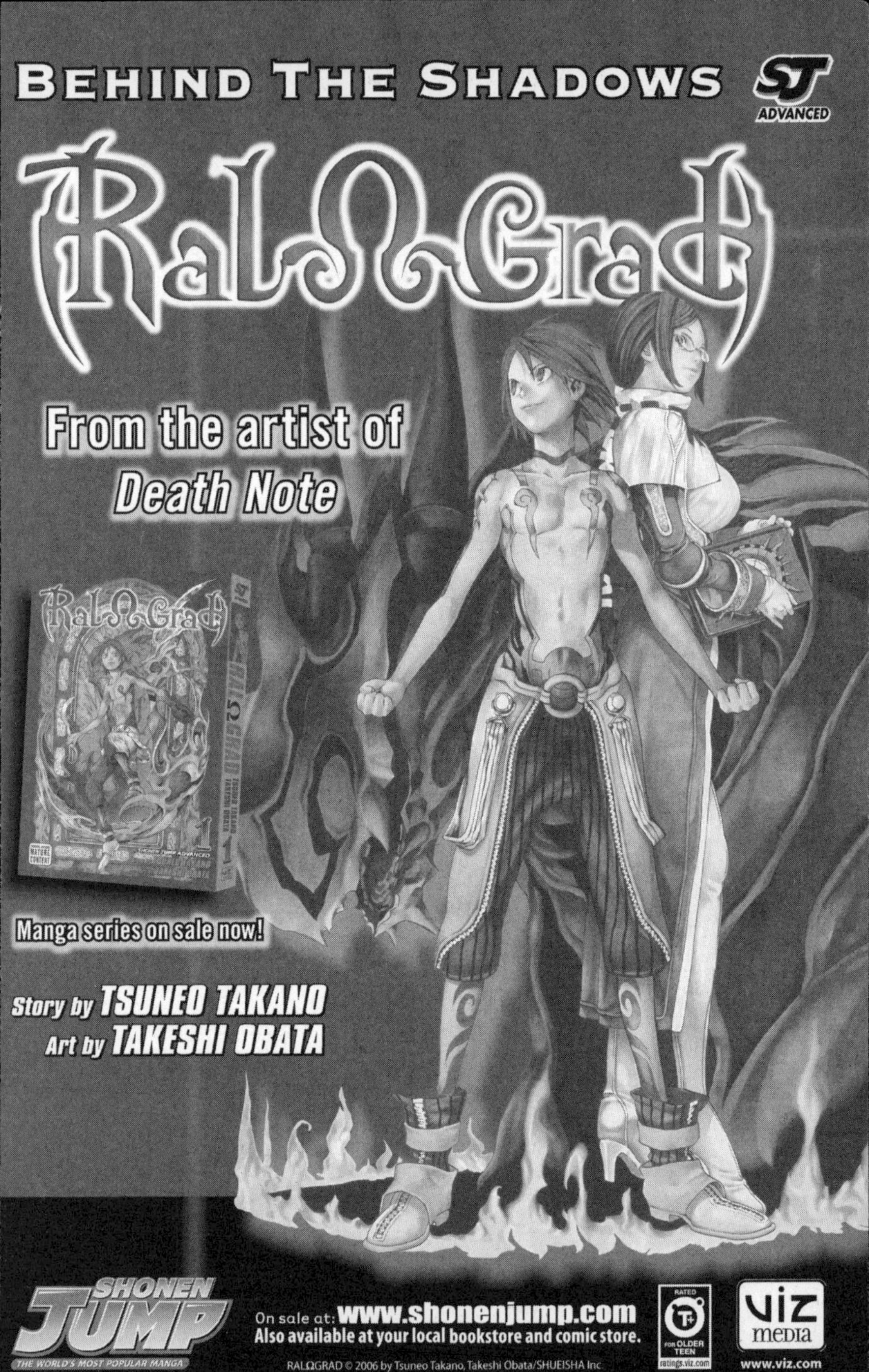
BEHIND THE SHADOWS
SJ ADVANCED
RalΩGrad
From the artist of
Death Note
Manga series on sale now!
Story by TSUNEO TAKANO
Art by TAKESHI OBATA
SHONEN JUMP
THE WORLD'S MOST POPULAR MANGA
On sale at: www.shonenjump.com
Also available at your local bookstore and comic store.
RATED T+ FOR OLDER TEEN
ratings.viz.com
viz media
www.viz.com
RALΩGRAD © 2006 by Tsuneo Takano, Takeshi Obata/SHUEISHA Inc.

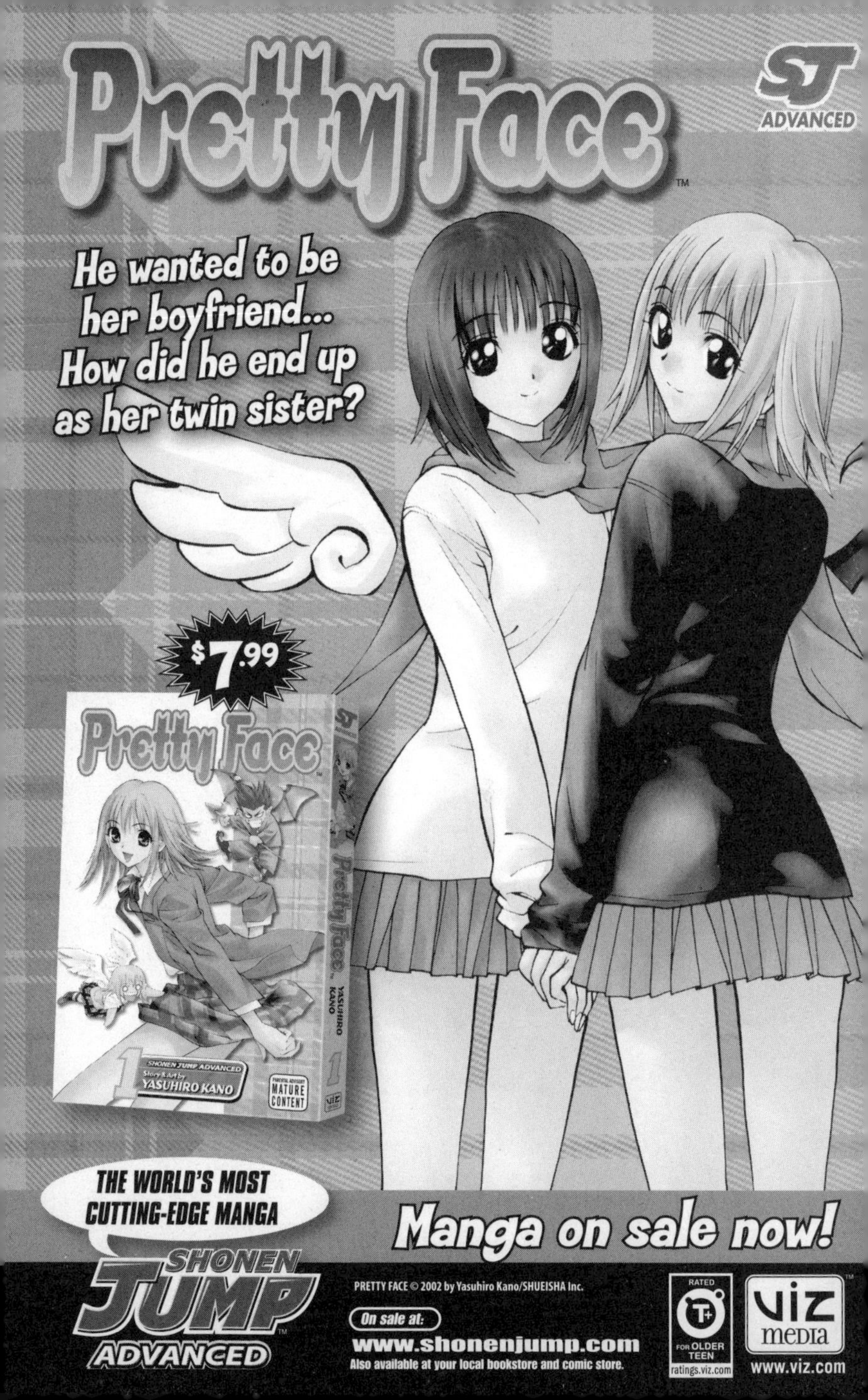
Pretty Face™
SJ ADVANCED
He wanted to be her boyfriend... How did he end up as her twin sister?
$7.99
Pretty Face
SHONEN JUMP ADVANCED
Story & Art by YASUHIRO KANO
PARENTAL ADVISORY MATURE CONTENT
THE WORLD'S MOST CUTTING-EDGE MANGA
Manga on sale now!
SHONEN JUMP ADVANCED
PRETTY FACE © 2002 by Yasuhiro Kano/SHUEISHA Inc.
On sale at:
www.shonenjump.com
Also available at your local bookstore and comic store.
RATED T+ FOR OLDER TEEN
ratings.viz.com
VIZ media
www.viz.com

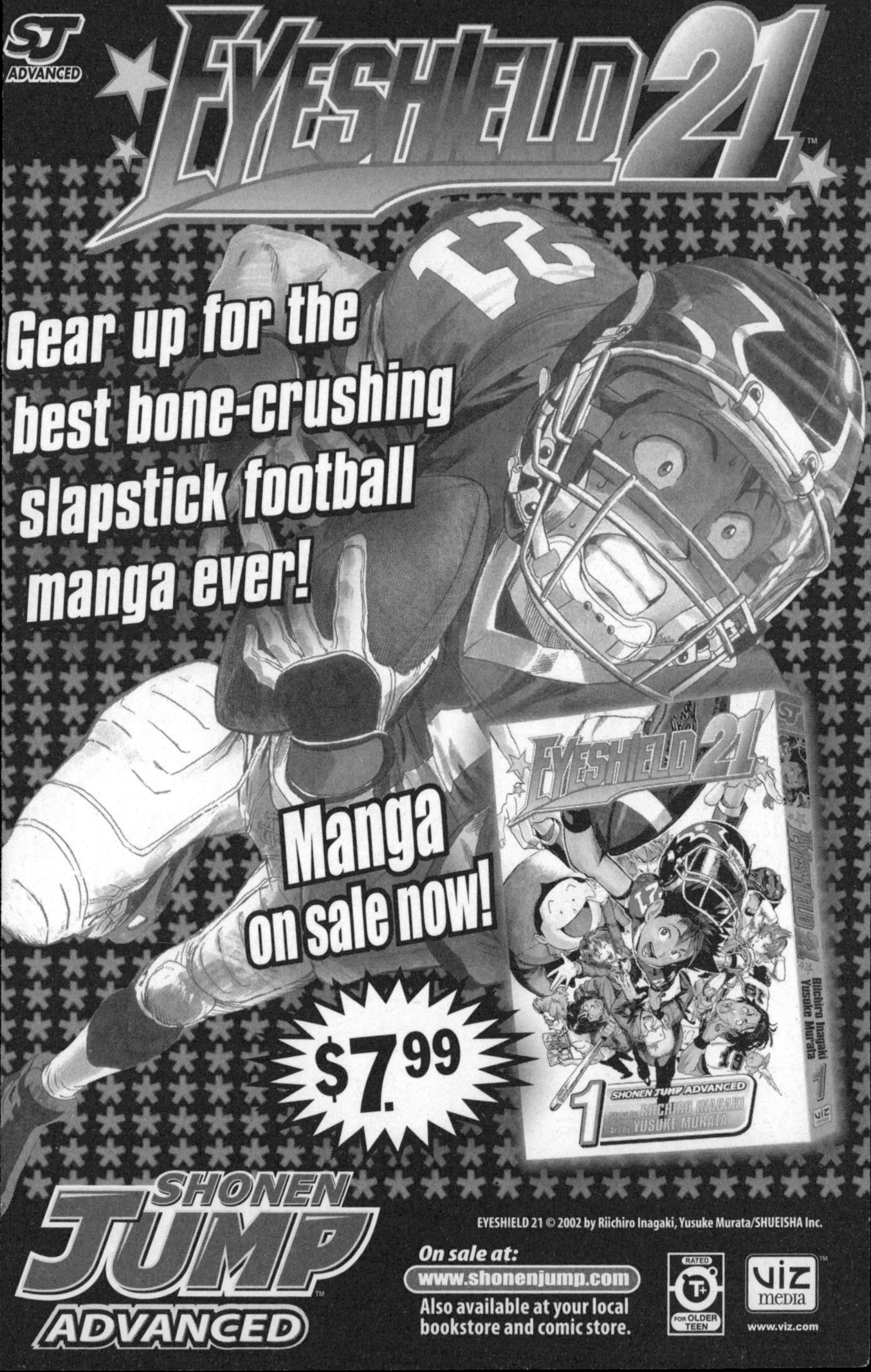
SJ ADVANCED
EYESHIELD 21
Gear up for the best bone-crushing slapstick football manga ever!
Manga on sale now!
$7.99
SHONEN JUMP ADVANCED
EYESHIELD 21 © 2002 by Riichiro Inagaki, Yusuke Murata/SHUEISHA Inc.
On sale at:
www.shonenjump.com
Also available at your local bookstore and comic store.
RATED T+ FOR OLDER TEEN
viz media
www.viz.com

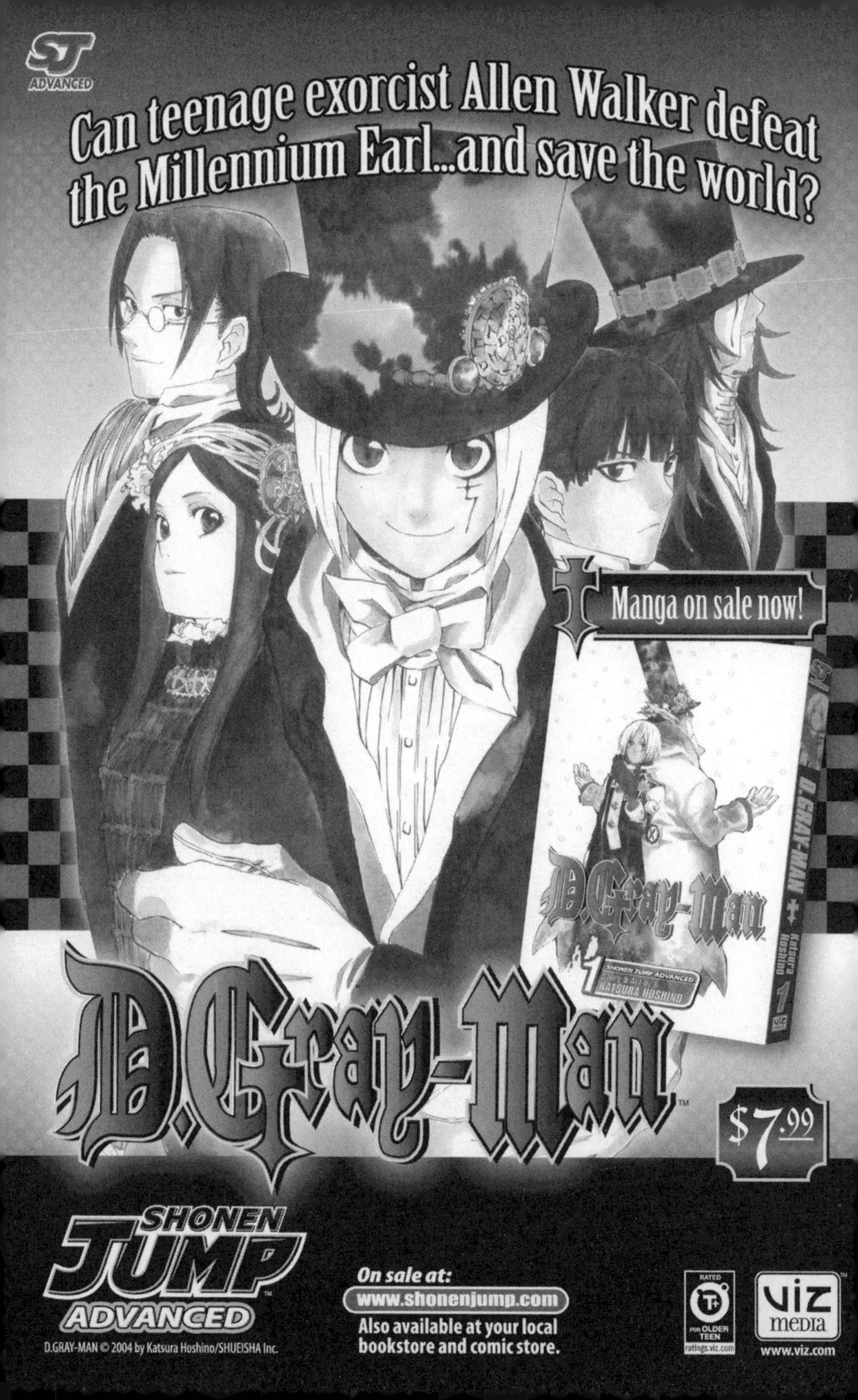
SJ ADVANCED
Can teenage exorcist Allen Walker defeat the Millennium Earl...and save the world?
Manga on sale now!
D.Gray-man™
$7.99
SHONEN JUMP ADVANCED
On sale at:
www.shonenjump.com
Also available at your local bookstore and comic store.
RATED T+ FOR OLDER TEEN
ratings.viz.com
viz media
www.viz.com
D.GRAY-MAN © 2004 by Katsura Hoshino/SHUEISHA Inc.

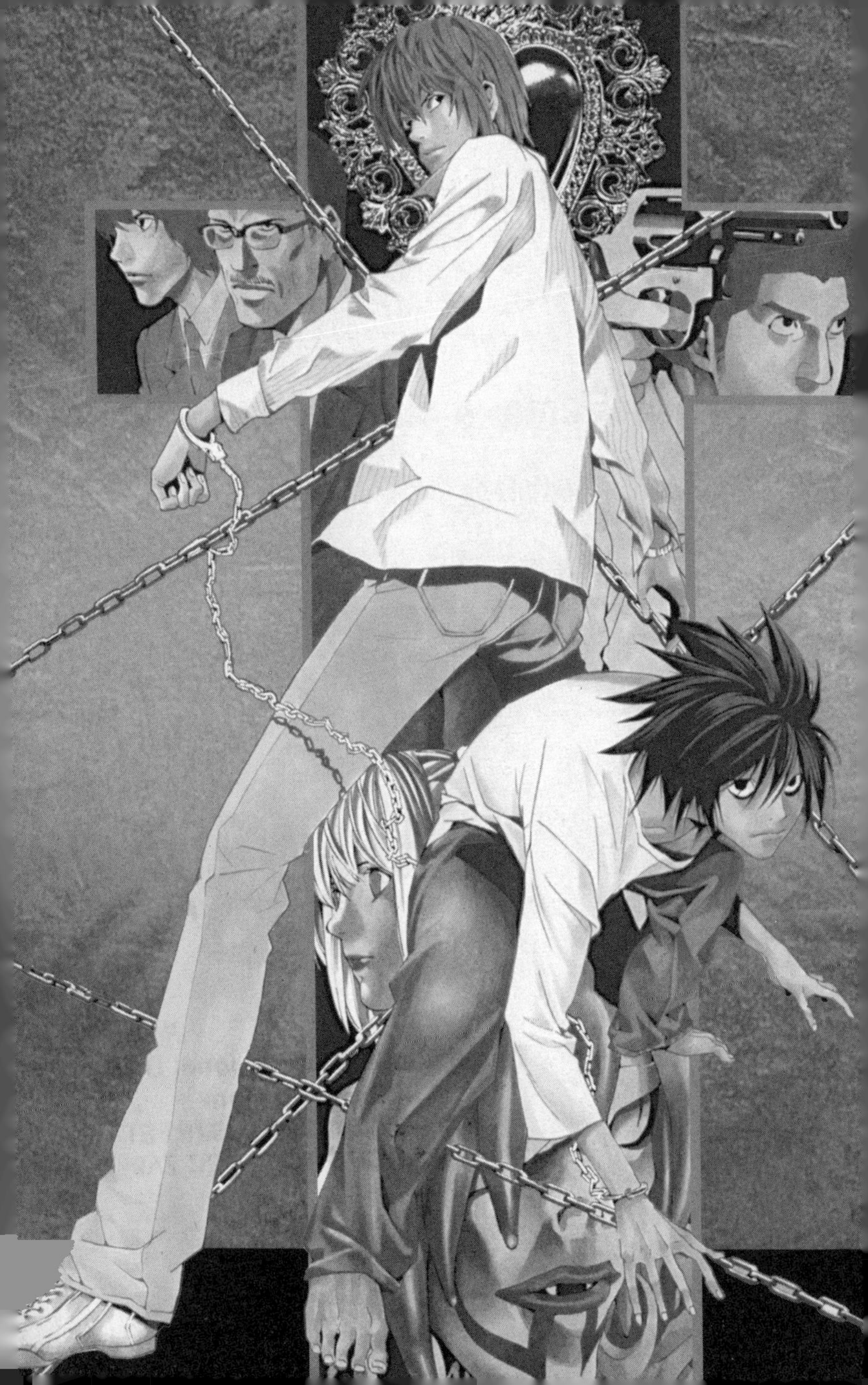

Save 50% OFF the cover price!

over pages issue!

JUMP

THE WORLD'S MOST POPULAR MANGA

Each issue of SHONEN JUMP contains the coolest manga available in the U.S., anime news, and info on video & card games, toys AND more!

☑ **YES!** Please enter my one-year subscription (12 HUGE issues) to **SHONEN JUMP** at the LOW SUBSCRIPTION RATE of **$29.95!**

NAME

ADDRESS

CITY   STATE   ZIP

E-MAIL ADDRESS   P7GNC1

☐ MY CHECK IS ENCLOSED (PAYABLE TO SHONEN JUMP)   ☐ BILL ME LATER

CREDIT CARD: ☐ VISA ☐ MASTERCARD

ACCOUNT #   EXP DATE

SIGNATURE

CLIP AND MAIL TO → SHONEN JUMP
Subscriptions Service Dept.
P.O. Box 515
Mount Morris, IL 61054-0515

Make checks payable to: **SHONEN JUMP**. Canada price for 12 issues: $41.95 USD, including GST, HST and QST. US/CAN orders only. Allow 6-8 weeks for delivery.

BLEACH © 2001 by Tite Kubo/SHUEISHA Inc. NARUTO © 1999 by Masashi Kishimoto/SHUEISHA Inc.
ONE PIECE © 1997 by Eiichiro Oda/SHUEISHA Inc.

RATED T FOR TEEN
ratings.viz.com